WordPerfect® 6.0 for Windows®

Made Easy

Covers Version 6.0a

Katie Layman
Gavilan College, Gilroy, California

and

LaVaughn Hart
Chabot College, Hayward, California

PRENTICE HALL
Englewood Cliffs, New Jersey 07632

Library of Congress Cataloging-in-Publication Data

Layman, Katie.
WordPerfect 6.0 for Windows made easy / Katie Layman and LaVaughn Hart.
p. cm.
Includes index.
ISBN 0-13-142986-8
1. WordPerfect for Windows (Computer file) 2. Word processing. I. Hart, LaVaughn.
Z52.5.W655L39 1994 94-12097
652.5'536--dc20 CIP

Acquisition editor: *Carolyn Henderson*
Editorial/production supervision: *Tally Morgan, WordCrafters Editorial Services, Inc.*
Cover design: *Maureen Eide*
Buyer: *Paul Smolinski*
Editorial assistant: *Jane Avery*

Printed in the United States of America

10 9 8 7 6 5 4 3 2 1

ISBN 0-13-142986-8

Prentice-Hall International (UK) Limited, *London*
Prentice-Hall of Australia Pty. Limited, *Sydney*
Prentice-Hall of Canada Inc., *Toronto*
Prentice-Hall Hispanoamericana, S.A., *Mexico*
Prentice-Hall of India Private Limited, *New Delhi*
Prentice-Hall of Japan, Inc., *Tokyo*
Simon & Schuster Asia Pte. Ltd., *Singapore*
Editora Prentice-Hall do Brasil, Ltda., *Rio de Janeiro*

CONTENTS

Appendices

Introduction

The purpose of this textbook is to provide students with simple step-by-step instructions to quickly master WordPerfect 6.0 for Windows. Numerous hands-on activities and easy-to-follow instruction lists within the text's chapters allow students to learn by doing. All of these carefully guided walk-throughs are accompanied by thorough, precise explanations of each WordPerfect feature being introduced, making ***WordPerfect 6.0® for Windows® Made Easy*** appropriate for use in individualized instruction programs as well as for use in traditional classrooms.

By focusing on the *tasks* students need to perform with the help from WordPerfect (rather than how WordPerfect "works"), ***WordPerfect 6.0 for Windows Made Easy*** aids instructors in their efforts to help students acquire the work-ready skills needed to succeed in today's job market. But the book's commitment to students' acquisition of these skills does not stop here.

As students work through the text's activities, they are introduced to the proper format for various business documents (e.g., memorandums, letters, reports, résumés, and newsletters). What's more, all of the text's activities are based on authentic, real-world documents—"just what students will encounter in everyday life on the job," according to one reviewer. And because students can never have too much training in or reinforcement of their basic English and grammar skills, each chapter includes an *Enriching Language Arts Skills* section and activity.

Finally, the end-of-chapter and end-of-part sections—*The Next Step* and *Checking Your Step* sections, respectively—are designed to fulfill the compentencies and basic skill requirements that have been identified by the Secretary's Commission on Achieving Necessary Skills (SCANS), U. S. Department of Labor. *The Next Step* and *Checking Your Step* activities reinforce students' reading, writing, thinking, and decision-making skills. SCANS icons are placed within the text so that instructors and students can quickly identify the activities that build SCANS competencies.

Content Highlights

Above all else, ***WordPerfect 6.0 for Windows Made Easy*** is committed to providing students with the work-ready skills they need to excel. The book's pedagogical system and the features described in the following section have been carefully crafted to achieve this end. Some of the key components of this performance-based system are as follows:

The chapter opening *Features Covered* sections identify the WordPerfect features introduced in the chapter and provide students with a clear road map of precisely what is to come.

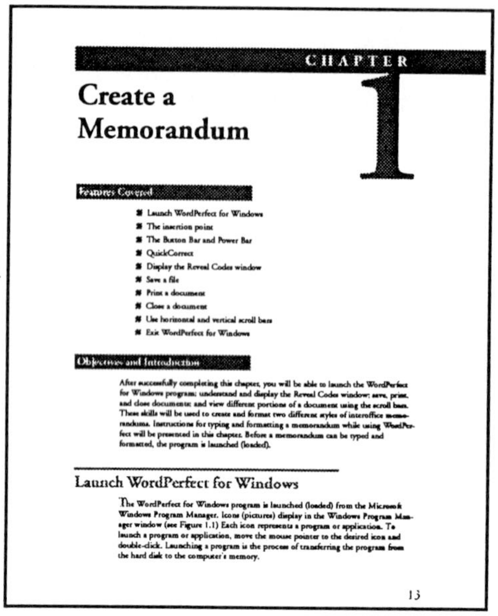
CHAPTER 1

Create a Memorandum

Features Covered

- Launch WordPerfect for Windows
- The insertion point
- The Button Bar and Power Bar
- QuickCorrect
- Display the Reveal Codes window
- Save a file
- Print a document
- Close a document
- Use horizontal and vertical scroll bars
- Exit WordPerfect for Windows

Objectives and Introduction

After successfully completing this chapter, you will be able to launch the WordPerfect for Windows program; understand and display the Reveal Codes window; save, print, and close documents; and view different portions of a document using the scroll bars. These skills will be used to create and format two different styles of interoffice memoranda. Instructions for typing and formatting a memorandum while using WordPerfect will be presented in this chapter. Before a memorandum can be typed and formatted, the program is launched (loaded).

Launch WordPerfect for Windows

The WordPerfect for Windows program is launched (loaded) from the Microsoft Windows Program Manager. Icons (pictures) display in the Windows Program Manager window (see Figure 1.1) Each icon represents a program or application. To launch a program or application, move the mouse pointer to the desired icon and double-click. Launching a program is the process of transferring the program from the hard disk to the computer's memory.

13

Objectives and Introduction preview chapter material in terms of the actual tasks students will perform as they work through the chapter and provide a narrative overview of the chapter material.

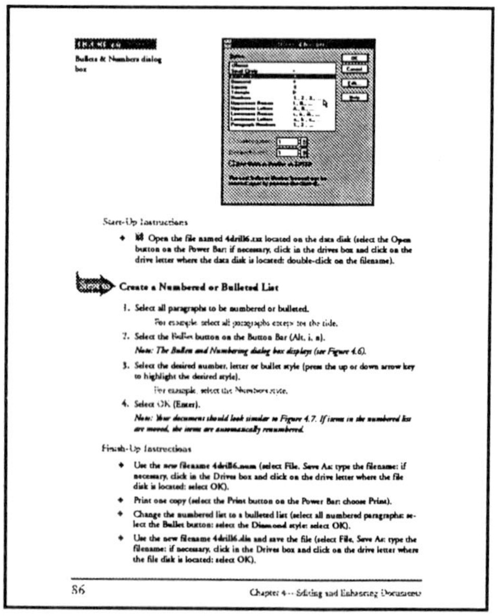
Bullets & Numbers dialog box

Start-Up Instructions

- Open the file named 4drill6.txt located on the data disk (select the Open button on the Power Bar; if necessary, click in the drives box and click on the drive letter where the data disk is located; double-click on the filename).

Create a Numbered or Bulleted List

1. Select all paragraphs to be numbered or bulleted.
2. Select the Bullets button on the Button Bar (Alt, i, n).
   Note: The Bullets and Numbering dialog box displays (see Figure 4.6).
3. Select the desired number, letter or bullet style (press the up or down arrow key to highlight the desired style).
4. Select OK (Enter).

Finish-Up Instructions

- Print one copy (select the Print button on the Power Bar; choose Print).

86 Chapter 4—Editing and Enhancing Documents

Numerous screen captures clarify concepts and instructions for students as they proceed through each chapter.

Careful step-by-step instruction lists are provided in the body of the chapter and are accompanied by a *Steps to* icon in the margin to make them easy for students to find when referring back to the text later.

In addition to the step-by-step instruction lists, activity-specific *Start-Up Instructions* and *Finish-Up Instructions* are clearly identified and provide information necessary to the completion of in-chapter activities. These, coupled with the *Steps to* icon, give students the best of both worlds—detailed, enumerated step-by-step tutorials now and easy-to-locate generic instruction lists later, when the text needs to function as a reference manual.

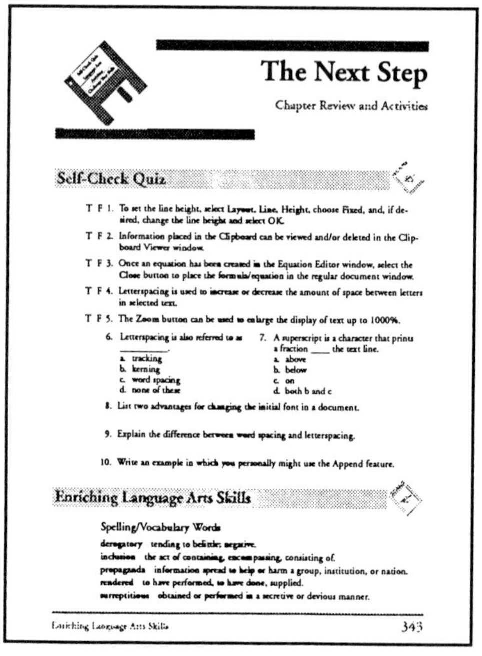
The Next Step

Chapter Review and Activities

Self-Check Quiz

T F 1. To set the line height, select Layout, Line, Height, choose Fixed, and, if desired, change the line height and select OK.

T F 2. Information placed in the Clipboard can be viewed and/or deleted in the Clipboard Viewer window.

T F 3. Once an equation has been created in the Equation Editor window, select the Close button to place the formula/equation in the regular document window.

T F 4. Letterspacing is used to increase or decrease the amount of space between letters in selected text.

T F 5. The Zoom button can be used to enlarge the display of text up to 1000%.

6. Letterspacing is also referred to as ______.
   a. tracking
   b. kerning
   c. word spacing
   d. none of these

7. A superscript is a character that prints a fraction ____ the text line.
   a. above
   b. below
   c. on
   d. both b and c

8. List two advantages for changing the initial font in a document.

9. Explain the difference between word spacing and letterspacing.

10. Write an example in which you personally might use the Append feature.

Enriching Language Arts Skills

Spelling/Vocabulary Words

derogatory tending to belittle; negative.
inclusion the act of containing, encompassing, consisting of.
propaganda information spread to help or harm a group, institution, or nation.
rendered to have performed, to have done, supplied.
surreptitious obtained or performed in a secretive or devious manner.

Enriching Language Arts Skills 343

Each end-of-chapter *Self-Check Quiz* includes true/false, multiple choice, and short answer questions, enabling students to check their understanding of key chapter concepts and procedures. (Answers are provided at the back of the book.)

A unique *Enriching Language Arts Skills* section at the end of each chapter reinforces students' spelling and grammar skills—skills the student is called on to use in the chapter's final hands-on activity.

Many guided, hands-on *Activities* at the close of each chapter let students practice—in a structured, unintimidating environment—what they've learned in the chapter.

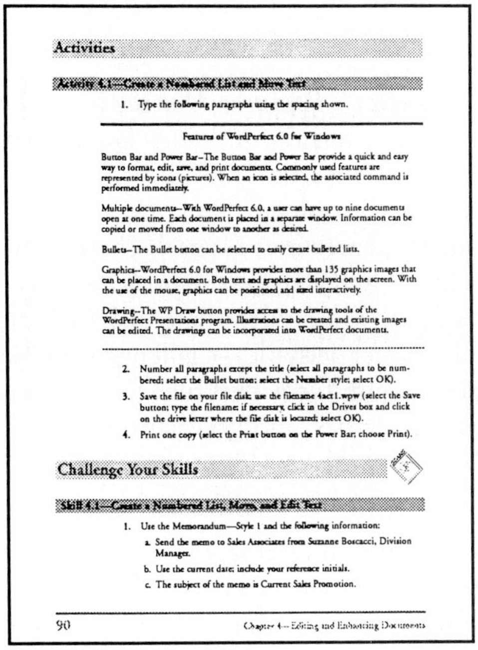

Activities

Activity 4.1—Create a Numbered List and Move Text

1. Type the following paragraphs using the spacing shown.

Features of WordPerfect 6.0 for Windows

Button Bar and Power Bar–The Button Bar and Power Bar provide a quick and easy way to format, edit, save, and print documents. Commonly used features are represented by icons (pictures). When an icon is selected, the associated command is performed immediately.

Multiple documents–With WordPerfect 6.0, a user can have up to nine documents open at one time. Each document is placed in a separate window. Information can be copied or moved from one window to another as desired.

Bullets–The Bullet button can be selected to easily create bulleted lists.

Graphics–WordPerfect 6.0 for Windows provides more than 135 graphics images that can be placed in a document. Both text and graphics are displayed on the screen. With the use of the mouse, graphics can be positioned and sized interactively.

Drawing–The WP Draw button provides access to the drawing tools of the WordPerfect Presentations program. Illustrations can be created and existing images can be edited. The drawings can be incorporated into WordPerfect documents.

2. Number all paragraphs except the title (select all paragraphs to be numbered; select the Bullet button; select the Number style; select OK).
3. Save the file on your file disk; use the filename 4act1.wpw (select the Save button; type the filename; if necessary, click in the Drives box and click on the drive letter where the file disk is located; select OK).
4. Print one copy (select the Print button on the Power Bar; choose Print).

Challenge Your Skills

Skill 4.1—Create a Numbered List, Move, and Edit Text

1. Use the Memorandum—Style 1 and the following information:
   a. Send the memo to Sales Associates from Suzanne Boscacci, Division Manager.
   b. Use the current date; include your reference initials.
   c. The subject of the memo is Current Sales Promotion.

90 Chapter 4—Editing and Enhancing Documents

Independent *Challenge Your Skills* activities at the close of each chapter give students ample practice to apply what they have learned without the help of guided instructions.

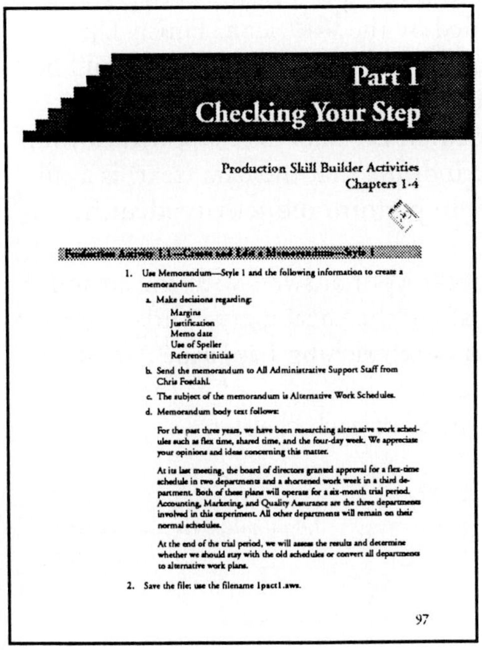

Part 1
Checking Your Step

Production Skill Builder Activities
Chapters 1-4

Production Activity 1.1—Create and Edit a Memorandum—Style 1

1. Use Memorandum—Style 1 and the following information to create a memorandum.
   a. Make decisions regarding:
      Margins
      Justification
      Memo date
      Use of Speller
      Reference initials
   b. Send the memorandum to All Administrative Support Staff from Chris Foedahl.
   c. The subject of the memorandum is Alternative Work Schedules.
   d. Memorandum body text follows:

      For the past three years, we have been researching alternative work schedules such as flex time, shared time, and the four-day week. We appreciate your opinions and ideas concerning this matter.

      At its last meeting, the board of directors granted approval for a flex-time schedule in two departments and a shortened work week in a third department. Both of these plans will operate for a six-month trial period. Accounting, Marketing, and Quality Assurance are the three departments involved in this experiment. All other departments will remain on their normal schedules.

      At the end of the trial period, we will assess the results and determine whether we should stay with the old schedules or convert all departments to alternative work plans.
2. Save the file; use the filename 1pact1.aws.

97

End-of-part *Checking Your Step* production skill-builder activities allow students to stretch their mastery of the program and to develop their decision-making and critical-thinking skills. The production skill-builder activities can be used for testing, hands-on projects, or as brief office simulation exercises.

An excellent reference source is the *QuickClicks* booklet provided with each copy of the text. The *QuickClicks* booklet lists all the WordPerfect features presented and includes page references should the student want to go back to a chapter for additional information.

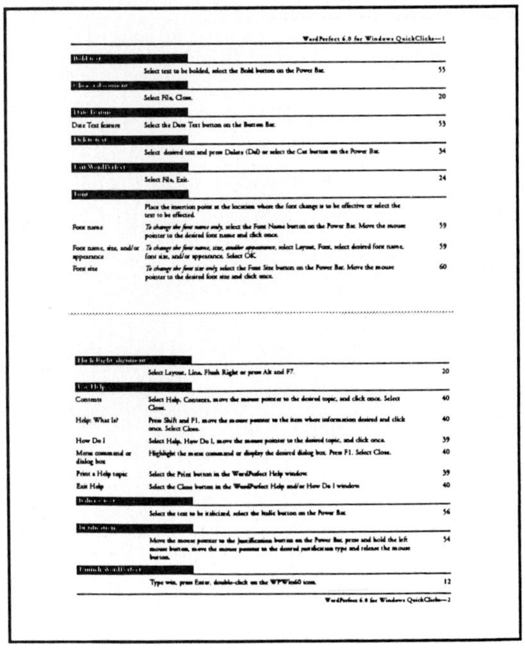

Instructor Support Materials

A comprehensive ***Instructor's Resource Manual*** is available which contains solutions for the end-of-chapter short-answer questions and *all* practice activities, end-of-chapter activities, challenge activities, and skill-builder production activities. The manual includes a chapter overview, student objectives, lecture notes, teaching suggestions, and one or more additional activities for each chapter. Also provided are production and theory tests. Included with the ***Instructor's Resource Manual*** are a student data disk and instructor's disks. The student data disk includes unformatted files for practice activities, end-of-chapter activities, challenge activities, and production activities. The instructor's disks contain formatted files for the practice activities, end-of-chapter activities, challenge activities, and production and theory tests.

To the Student

Every chapter is divided into several sections with each section explaining a different WordPerfect feature. An overview of each feature is provided followed by Start-Up Instructions which present information or actions to be taken in order to prepare you for a hands-on practice activity. Following the Start-Up Instructions are numbered step-by-step instructions which guide you through each action necessary to perform the feature being learned. These are identified by the Steps to icon. Finish-Up Instructions follow each set of step-by-step instructions and indicate what should be performed in order to complete the practice activity.

The text for many chapter activities is provided on the data disk supplied to your instructor. You will see this icon in the text to indicate that the data (text) is available on disk. This saved text is necessary in order to perform the activity identified by the disk icon.

Answer the Self-Check Quiz questions and check your answers with the answer key provided at the back of the book. If desired, study the vocabulary words, punctuation, capitalization, or typing rule provided in the Enriching Language Arts section. Many of these vocabulary words and punctuation rules are used in the last activity of the Challenge Your Skills section at the end of each chapter.

ACKNOWLEDGMENTS

A sincere thank you to our editor, Carolyn Henderson, for her avid support and constant attention to our business *and* personal needs. Using your superb editorial skills, you guided us through every detail needed to improve our book(s). Thank you! Your open-door policy to "call if you need me" is appreciated more than we can express. We prize your ideas, energy, and enthusiasm that you give to us and our projects!

Thank you, Jeanette Hart, for your meticulous keystroke testing of the *WordPerfect 6.0 for Windows* manuscript. Your questions and suggestions were extremely useful in creating correct instructions for the hands-on activities and for assisting with the explanation of features. Many thanks too, for writing a comprehensive ***Instructor's Resource Manual*** and for creating the student and instructor disks. And thank you again for developing excellent teacher and student resources.

A huge thank you to the sales representatives and support staff at Prentice Hall, Inc. who have contributed and continue to contribute outstanding support for the success of the ***Made Easy*** series.

To Debbie Emry, our marketing manager, we extend our gratefulness to you for the countless hours you have spent creating advertisements, handling phone calls, organizing travel appointments, and processing sales requests. Thank you!

A special salute to Jane Avery for assisting with our many phone calls, swiftly processing contract agreements, and promptly responding to our numerous requests. Your expert clerical skills and amiable service are highly praised and very much appreciated.

Tally Morgan at WordCrafters, thank you again for applying your expert production skills to our many and varied needs. We value your *thoroughness* and appreciate your meeting our tight schedule! We treasure your continued support of our projects.

Debbie Merrill at Maine Proofreading service, you are the best! We appreciate your superb copyediting skills and your quick turn-around time. Your queries and comments assisted us in making many improvements to our manuscript.

We are most grateful to our reviewers, who shared pertinent suggestions for the organization of material and specific ideas for improving the book. Your confirmation(s) of the activities, step-by-step procedures, and text content were appreciated. Thank you, Quinthia Foster, Microcomputer Technology Institute; Dianne Pannell, Harrisburg Area Community College; Kaye Peterson, Yavapai College; and Deborah Wareing, Scottsdale Community College.

To the participants at the Focus Group in Boston, Massachusetts, we extend our biggest thank you for sharing your teaching ideas and specific suggestions for enhancing the appearance and content of the book. Thank you, Susan McGowan, Caroleann Bready-Lyons, and Marilyn Sherry of Massasoit Community College; Eileen Zisk of the Community College of Rhode Island–Lincoln; Mary Belluardo and Jack Szeredy of Quinsigamond Community College; Barbara Cotoia and Roberta Neuschatz of Mt. Wachusett Community College; and Hannah Darling of the Computer Learning Center, Somerville, Massachusetts.

What Is a Microcomputer System?

A *microcomputer system* is a small computer system designed to provide methods for creating, processing, storing, and printing data. A small computer system normally includes the computer, keyboard, mouse, monitor, printer, and software programs. Many microcomputer systems today, however, include internal fax modems, sound boards, CD ROM players, and stereo speakers, and are referred to as *multimedia* systems.

The microcomputer system consists of two basic elements: hardware and software. The physical components of the microcomputer system are called hardware; the programs that instruct the computer to perform functions are called software.

Hardware

The microcomputer hardware includes the monitor (TV-like screen), keyboard, mouse, computer unit, disk drives, and printer. The hardware can be seen, felt, and touched. The IBM PC and compatible computers enclose the disk drive(s) with the computer. The monitor, keyboard, mouse, and printer are attached to the computer via cables (see Figure I.1). The computer unit and the attached hardware make up a microcomputer system.

The computer unit holds the electronic circuitry where the main memory and central processing unit (CPU) reside. The CPU processes and controls information by storing data, performing operations, and transferring information from one location to another. The CPU is often referred to as the "brains" of the computer.

Software

Software programs are lists of instructions that tell the computer what to do. The master program is the disk operating system (DOS). DOS directs the basic operation of the microcomputer system and carries out procedures within application programs. Application programs are more advanced software designed to perform specific tasks. Common applications are word processing, spreadsheet, database, communications, graphics, drawing, and desktop publishing programs.

DOS and application programs are stored on master disks. A copy of DOS and an application program can be transferred to the computer's memory when the computer is turned on. Transferring a copy of a program to the computer's memory is called "loading the program." The disk is being "read" when a copy of a program or other information is transferred from the disk into the computer's memory.

FIGURE I.1

The PC hardware

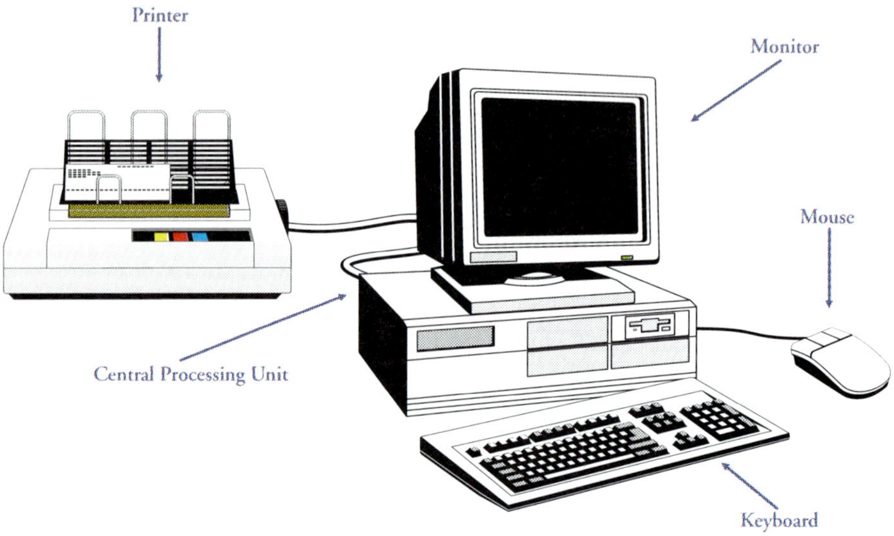

System Requirements and Recommendations for WordPerfect for Windows 6.0 and 6.0a

Minimum System Requirements*	Recommended System Requirements
386 IBM PC or compatible	386 (or higher) IBM PC or compatible
6M RAM	8M (or more) RAM
32M hard disk space, Version 6.0; 28M hard disk space, Version 6.0a	30–32M hard disk space free
Windows 3.1 running in enhanced mode	Windows 3.1 running in enhanced mode
VGA graphics adapter and monitor	SVGA graphics adapter and monitor
Mouse or other pointer device	Mouse or other pointer device

*WordPerfect features may not perform in an acceptable way when using the minimum system requirements.

What Are Disks?

Disks are storage devices. Information that is processed and used by a computer must be stored on either a hard or floppy disk. Because the computer's memory is temporary, all programs and data are erased when the computer is turned off. Therefore, disks are used to store programs and data.

The rigid hard disk usually resides inside the computer and is not removed by the user. Programs are normally stored on a hard disk. However, removable hard disks, contained in plastic cartridges, are also available. A floppy disk, contained in a plastic

FIGURE I.2

Hard disk and floppy disks

cartridge or paper jacket, is flexible and can be handled by the user. Floppy disks are generally used to store data or files. The most commonly used disk sizes are 5.25" and 3.5" (see Figure I.2).

Information that has been created is saved on either a floppy disk or a hard disk. A floppy disk is referred to as a *file disk* or *data disk.* If information, such as a letter, memorandum, or statistical data, is not saved on a disk, the information will be lost from the computer's temporary memory when the computer is turned off. When a copy of the information is transferred from the computer's memory to a disk, the process is called *saving.* Saving information to a disk is also called "writing" to a disk.

Care for Floppy Disks

Floppy disks should be labeled using a felt-tip pen. Store disks in a dry, protected location. Avoid dust, smoke, bending, and extreme temperatures. (Keep disks out of the sun and away from beverage containers!) Any magnet or magnetized object can damage the data on a disk; therefore, avoid using a paper clip on a disk, especially a paper clip that has been stored in a holder with a magnetized ring at the top.

Formatting a Floppy Disk

Before information can be saved on a disk, the disk must be formatted (prepared) with electronic instructions to partition the disk into storage areas, to create a directory, to check for disk defects, etc.

The formatting process is usually performed only once. If a disk is formatted a second time, all information previously saved on the disk is erased.

Steps to **Format a File Disk Using Windows' File Manager**

1. If necessary, turn on the computer and load Windows.

2. Double-click on the **File Manager** icon usually located in the Window's Main group.
3. Select **Disk, Format Disk.**
4. Select the down arrow button in the Disk In option box; select the disk drive letter where the disk to be formatted is located (e.g., select Drive A: or Drive B:).
5. Generally, the Capacity option box displays the appropriate disk capacity. If necessary, however, select the down arrow button in the Capacity option box and select the correct disk capacity.
6. Select **OK.**

   Note: *The message, "Formatting will erase ALL data from your disk...," displays.*
7. Select **Yes.**

   Note: *A "Formatting disk" message displays with various messages indicating the formatting progress.*
8. When the Format Complete dialog box displays, select **Yes** or **No** to indicate whether you want to format another disk (e.g., select **No**).
9. Select **File, Exit.**

What Is DOS?

DOS is the disk operating system for IBM PC and compatible microcomputers. DOS is a collection of related programs that controls and manages the computer's operations. DOS is necessary to handle the temporary storage and processing of information and to direct the orderly transfer or sharing of information between the computer unit and the disk, monitor, keyboard, printer, etc. In order for the computer to operate, the DOS programs must be accessible when the computer is turned on. Generally, DOS programs are stored on the hard disk.

What is Windows?

Windows is a program that works in conjunction with DOS to enable a user to perform computer tasks more easily. Windows provides a structure within which many programs can operate. Windows programs have a common way of accomplishing tasks. For example, the procedure for saving a file is the same when working with most Windows programs. In addition, data can be easily transferred from one Windows program to another. For example, a graph created in a Windows spreadsheet program can be easily transferred to a Windows word processing program.

The Windows program allows the user to complete tasks such as launching (loading) programs, copying files, formatting disks, and deleting files. When performing traditional DOS tasks such as copying files, formatting a disk, etc., using a mouse and the Window's drop down menus is usually much easier than remembering and typing DOS commands.

When Windows is loaded, the Program Manager window displays on the screen (see Figure 1.1 on page 12). The Windows program is often referred to as a graphical user interface because icons (pictures) display on the screen to represent each program. The user can launch a program simply by placing the mouse pointer on the program icon and pressing the left mouse button twice rapidly. This is called double-clicking (see page 6).

Windows allows multiple programs to run at the same time. Each program is placed in a separate *window.* The windows for each application program share common elements. For example, the Title bar, Menu bar, scroll bars, and control boxes are elements common to each application program. These common elements provide a standard method for accomplishing tasks. For example, the File, Print option is used in any Windows application to print a document. As more and more application programs are written to operate in Windows, the more common the elements will become to simplify the learning of additional Windows programs.

Windows programs are also compatible with each other (i.e., the information in each program can be transferred and shared easily between programs). For example, a spreadsheet file can be transferred to a WordPerfect document window. A *link* is established between the spreadsheet and WordPerfect files so that any changes made in the spreadsheet file are automatically changed in the linked file.

What are Directories and Paths?

A *directory* is a named location on a disk where a group of files is stored. A directory is used to keep files organized in separate areas on the disk under different directory names. Application programs such as word processing, spreadsheet, and database programs are usually stored on the computer's hard disk. The files for each application program can be kept together in one directory location. For example, all the WordPerfect program files are stored in a directory named *wpwin60.*

Other directories can be created and grouped together in the *wpwin60* directory. Any directories created in the *wpwin60* directory are called subdirectories. For example, if the subdirectory named *memos* was created, *memos* would be a subdirectory of the *wpwin60* directory.

A path is a route from a disk drive letter (root directory) to the location of a file or subdirectory. For example, the path for a file named *mem3* that is located in the subdirectory named *memos* that is in the *wpwin60* directory is: *c:\wpwin60\memos\mem3.* When using WordPerfect 6.0 for Windows, the various directories and subdirectories can be chosen in the Directories boxes that are available in the Open and Save As dialog boxes.

Filenames

Every file to be saved is assigned a filename. Filenames can contain one to eight characters and, if desired, a filename extension of one to three characters. The filename extension is separated from the first 1–8 characters by a period. For example, *morris.ltr* or *martin.ltr* are valid filenames. However, *morganstern.ltr* is not a valid filename because there are more than eight characters before the filename extension.

Any letter (a to z) or number (0–9) and most symbols can be used in a filename. A filename cannot contain spaces, commas, backslashes, asterisks, or a second period.

A filename should represent the information and/or person's name contained in the file. For example, a letter written to Gerry Anderson concerning a tax assessment could be assigned the name *g-andsn.tax* or *anderson.ltr.*

What Is WordPerfect 6.0 for Windows?

The WordPerfect word processing program is one of the most popular programs in the world. WordPerfect 6.0 for Windows is the most current version of WordPerfect for the Windows environment. In addition to the WordPerfect 6.0 for Windows program, a WordPerfect 6.0 for DOS program is available. WordPerfect 6.0 for DOS and WordPerfect 6.0 for Windows contain many common elements such as a Menu bar, Button Bar, Ribbon, Ruler, and dialog boxes which enable the user to perform editing, saving, text formatting, etc. more quickly and efficiently.

The Mouse (Pointer Device)

There are various types of pointer devices. The mouse pointer device and the track-ball are presently the most popular. The mouse is a hand-held device used to move an arrow or rectangular symbol (pointer symbol) on the screen. The mouse pointer is moved over the screen area until the pointer symbol touches the item or items to be selected. The left button on the mouse device is pressed to initiate the desired action, such as selecting options, sizing windows, formatting text, or creating objects.

Generally, the mouse is held between the thumb and little or ring finger. The index finger or middle finger is used to press the mouse buttons. To maintain consistent control of the mouse, hold the mouse motionless when pressing the mouse buttons.

When the mouse is moved over a flat surface, the pointer symbol moves in the same direction on the screen. When the mouse reaches the edge of the flat surface, hold the mouse firmly, lift, and relocate. Also, alternating between a short rubbing stroke and lifting the mouse slightly using wrist movement can be very helpful when the mouse reaches the flat surface edge.

The track-ball pointer device is stationary; the "ball" is moved by a finger or the palm of the hand. The track-ball can be built into the keyboard, or it can be connected to the computer via a cable.

The pointer symbol changes shape depending on the location on the screen where the pointer is positioned. For example, the pointer symbol changes to a two-headed arrow when sizing graphic boxes or windows and to a four-headed arrow when moving graphic boxes or windows (see chapters 13 and 16). The mouse pointer shapes are shown in Figure I.3.

Different techniques are used to initiate an action with the pointer device. The following list shows the basic actions:

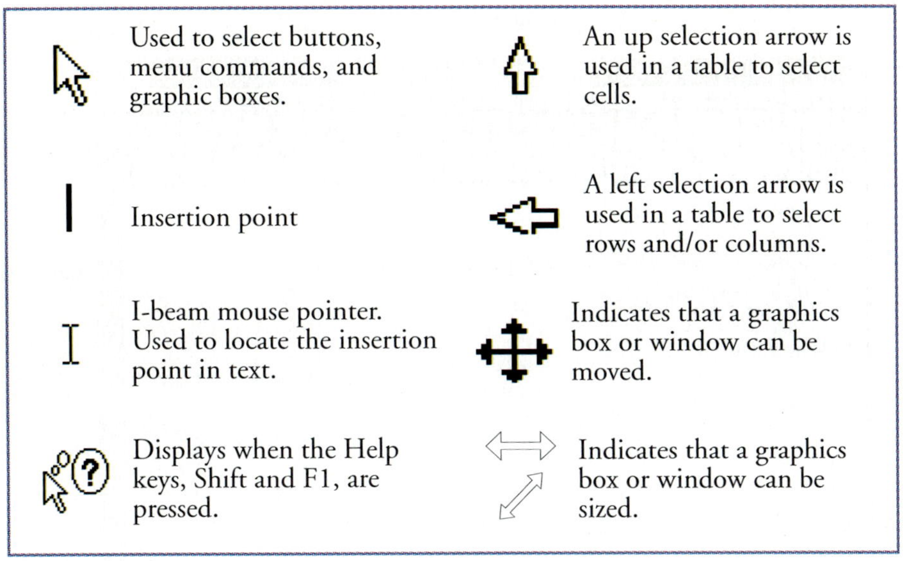

FIGURE I.3

Mouse pointer shapes

Click	Press the left button once and release.
Double-click	Press the left button twice rapidly.
Drag	Press and hold down the left button while moving the mouse or trackball.
Point	Move the pointer to a specific position on the screen.

The WordPerfect Document Window

The WordPerfect document window displays after the program is launched (loaded). The window is displayed in full size (maximized). (See Chapter 16 for changing the window size.) Each part of the window is shown in Figure I.4.

The Title bar displays at the top of the window and contains the application name and document title. The Control box displays on the left side of the Title bar and when selected provides keyboard users the capability to size, move, close, or switch to another program. The Minimize and Restore buttons are displayed on the right side of the title bar and are used to change the size of the application window. When the *Minimize* button is selected, the application is reduced to a small icon and the Program Manager or another application window is displayed. To return the program to the screen, double-click on the WPWIN 6.0 icon. If the WPWIN 6.0 icon cannot be seen on the screen, press **Ctrl** and **Esc** to display the Task List and double-click on WordPerfect. (See Chapter 16 for additional information on managing document windows.)

The Menu bar displays directly below the Title bar. Each menu in the Menu bar contains commands that are used to instruct WordPerfect to perform specific functions. To view the menu commands, click to select the Menu. The menu "drops down" and a list of the menu commands displays with the first item highlighted. When a menu command is highlighted, a brief description of that command displays at the top of the screen.

Each drop-down menu has a list of additional menu commands that are accessed easily by pointing and clicking the mouse or by pressing a designated letter from the

FIGURE I.4

WordPerfect 6.0 for Windows document window

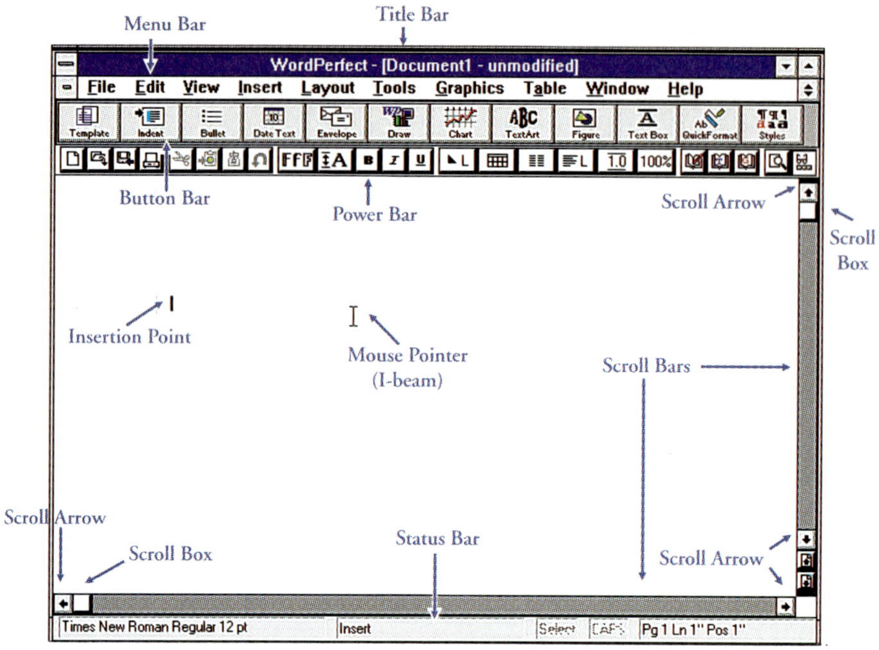

keyboard. The first item listed in a drop-down menu is highlighted. An underline displays beneath one letter in each menu command that can be typed to select the desired option. Listed beside some of the commands are keystrokes that can be used to activate a command. For example, in the File menu F3 displays next to the Save As command and Ctrl + S displays next to the Save command. Some menu commands are followed by three periods (**Save As...**) or a right arrow to indicate that, if selected, a dialog box or list of additional commands will display.

A *Button Bar* or *Power Bar* can be displayed and used to quickly activate frequently used functions. Once a button is selected, a dialog box displays or the function is performed immediately. (The Button Bar contains text and pictures whereas the Power Bar contains only pictures.)

The Button Bar and Power Bar are defaulted (preset) to display on the screen. By selecting the **View** menu, however, the user can choose to display only the Button Bar or the Power Bar. A checkmark beside the bar name in the **View** menu indicates that the bar is displayed. If desired, the Button Bar and/or Power Bar can be removed from the screen in order to see more of a document on the screen. The Button Bar and/or Power Bar can be chosen to display when the program is launched.

The Power Bar is used to quickly format text such as fonts, point sizes, columns, and justification. The Power Bar contains other buttons that are used to create tables, set decimal tab alignment and/or cut and paste text.

A Ruler contains a measurement scale that shows the placement of tabs, column margins, and left and right margins. The Ruler is used to change tabs and margin settings without accessing a menu.

Dialog Boxes

Dialog boxes provide additional WordPerfect commands. The dialog boxes display after menu commands or Button Bar buttons are selected. For example, when the **Print** button or the **File**, **Print** comand is selected, the Print dialog box displays (see Figure I.5).

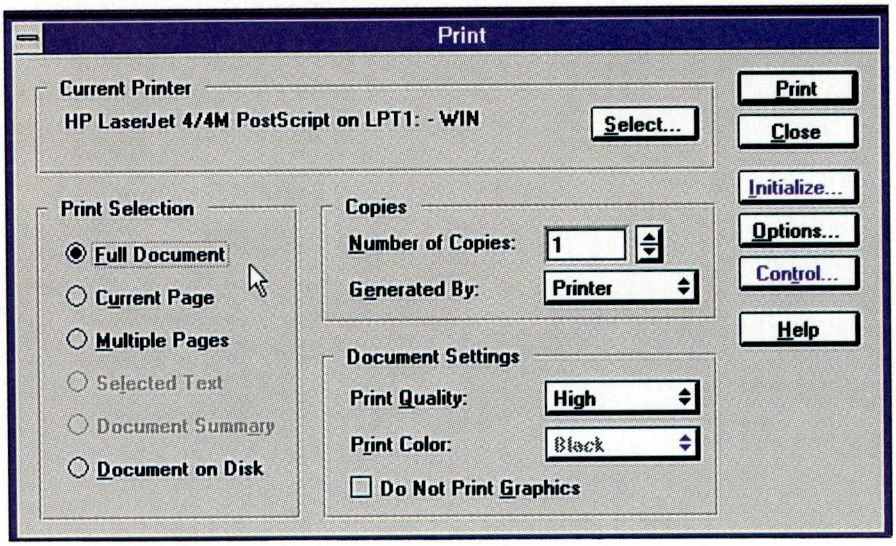

FIGURE I.5

Print dialog box

In a dialog box, instructions are supplied to the program by selecting from a list of options and/or by typing information. Often a dialog box contains commands followed by three periods (...). When these commands are selected, a second dialog box with additional options displays. The second dialog box allows the user to provide more specific information on how the chosen command is to be accomplished.

Part 1
The Beginning Step

Create and Edit Business Documents

Chapters 1-4

- Launch WordPerfect
- The Button Bar and Power Bar
- Center text
- Reveal Codes
- Scroll bars
- Print a document
- Save a document
- Close a document
- Exit WordPerfect
- Open a document
- Select text
- Delete and insert text
- Undo and Undelete
- View a document
- Use the Help feature
- Use the automatic date feature
- Change justification
- Bold, underline, and italic text attributes
- Change margins
- Font changes
- Speller
- Page Zoom Full view
- Move and copy text
- Find and replace text
- Indent and double-indent
- Numbered and bulleted lists
- Print selected text

CHAPTER 1

Create a Memorandum

Features Covered

- Launch WordPerfect for Windows
- The insertion point
- The Button Bar and Power Bar
- QuickCorrect
- Display the Reveal Codes window
- Save a file
- Print a document
- Close a document
- Use horizontal and vertical scroll bars
- Exit WordPerfect for Windows

Objectives and Introduction

After successfully completing this chapter, you will be able to launch the WordPerfect for Windows program; understand and display the Reveal Codes window; save, print, and close documents; and view different portions of a document using the scroll bars. These skills will be used to create and format two different styles of interoffice memorandums. Instructions for typing and formatting a memorandum while using WordPerfect will be presented in this chapter. Before a memorandum can be typed and formatted, the program is launched (loaded).

Launch WordPerfect for Windows

The WordPerfect for Windows program is launched (loaded) from the Microsoft Windows Program Manager. Icons (pictures) display in the Windows Program Manager window (see Figure 1.1) Each icon represents a program or application. To launch a program or application, move the mouse pointer to the desired icon and double-click. Launching a program is the process of transferring the program from the hard disk to the computer's memory.

FIGURE 1.1

Sample of the Windows Program Manager screen. (Icons may be arranged differently on each computer screen, because icons can easily be rearranged in the Program Manager.)

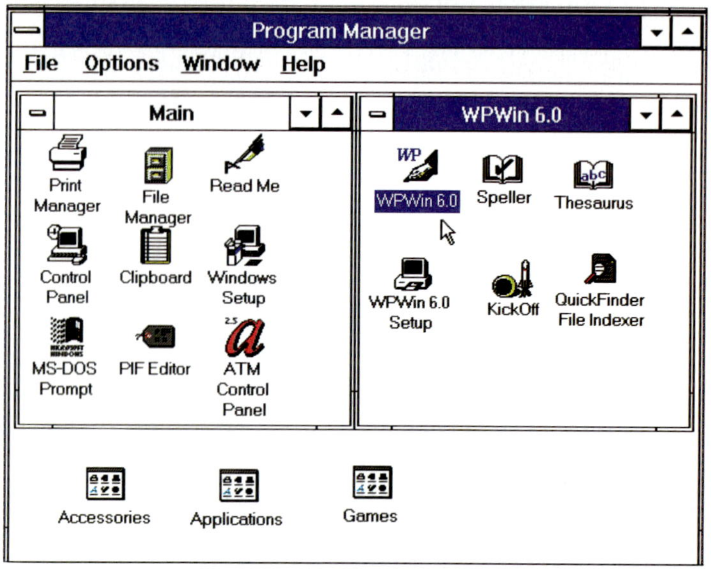

When the WordPerfect for Windows program is launched, the WordPerfect document window displays with a Title bar, Menu bar, Button Bar, and Power Bar at the top of the screen and a Status bar at the bottom of the screen (see Figure 1.2).

Note: *The first set of instructions in each step-by-step instruction in this textbook uses the mouse/trackball device. Place the mouse pointer on the option desired; press the left mouse button (click once) to select. The instructions for using the keyboard keys immediately follow the instructions for using the mouse and are indicated in braces { }, e.g., {Alt, f, c* **or** *Ctrl and F4}.*

Start-Up Instructions

- The computer and monitor should be turned on and the Windows Program Manager displayed on the screen. If necessary, see your instructor and write down the steps needed to display the Program Manager on your screen.

  ____

  ____

- Place a formatted file disk in drive A or B.

Steps to Launch (Load) the WordPerfect for Windows Program

1. Move the mouse pointer to the WPWin6.0 icon; quickly press the left mouse button twice (double-click).

   Note: *An hourglass displays on the screen to indicate that the program is being launched. Keys pressed while the hourglass is present are ignored by the program. The copyright screen displays briefly, then the WordPerfect document window displays (see Figure 1.2).*

   If a different method is used to launch (load) WordPerfect for Windows on your computer, see your instructor or instructional assistant and write the steps needed on the following lines.

   ____

   ____

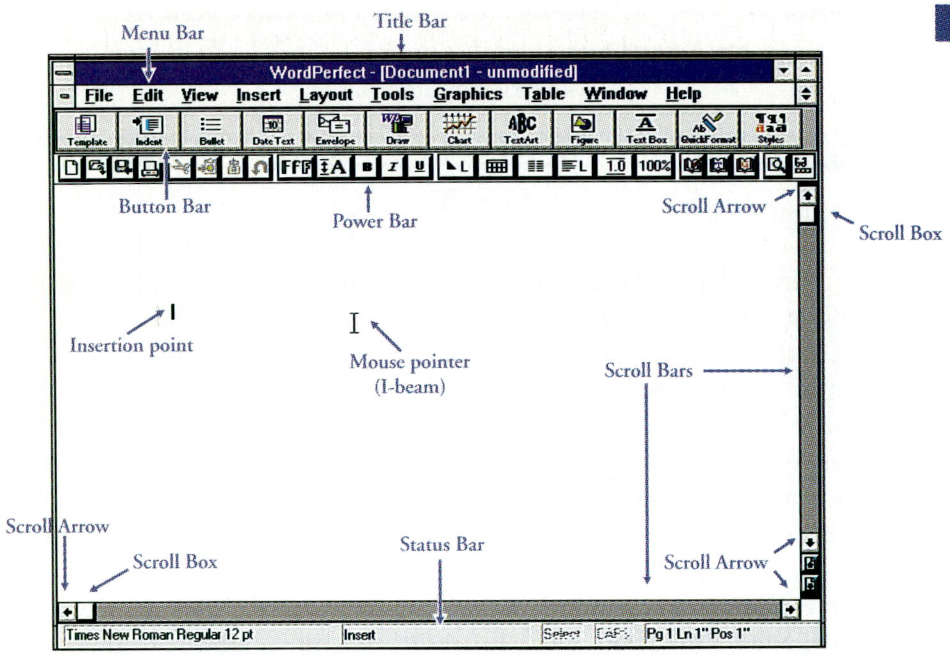

FIGURE 1.2

WordPerfect 6.0 for Windows document window

Insertion Point

The traditional cursor has been separated into two parts—an insertion point and a mouse pointer. The insertion point indicates the location where the next action takes place and displays as a bold, blinking vertical line. The insertion point will move to characters and lines that have been typed. However, the insertion point will not move into blank space unless the **Enter** key or **Spacebar** is pressed. As the **Enter** key or **Spacebar** is pressed or text is typed, the insertion point moves. See also Steps to Move the Insertion Point Quickly, page 25.

The second part of the traditional cursor is the mouse pointer. The mouse pointer symbol moves around the screen as the mouse is moved on the desktop. The shape of the mouse pointer changes depending on the location of the mouse pointer on the screen. For example, the mouse pointer is an I-beam when located in the text area, but usually changes to an arrow when the mouse pointer is out of the text area. See the Introduction, Figure I.3, for a list of the various mouse pointer shapes.

The mouse device can be used to move the insertion point by placing the pointer at the desired location and pressing (clicking) the left mouse button once. When *Num Lock* is turned off, the direction (arrow) keys on the 10-key numeric keypad can be used to move the insertion point up, down, left, or right one character or line at a time. On many keyboards, a duplicate set of arrow keys is provided on separate keys.

The Button Bar and Power Bar

WordPerfect provides an easy way to access frequently used commands via the *Button Bar* and *Power Bar* (see Figure 1.3). The Button Bar and Power Bar are two rows of buttons that display below the Menu bar. A mouse must be used to select a button on the Button Bar and Power Bar. When the mouse pointer is placed on a button on the Button Bar or Power Bar, the name of the button and a brief description of the purpose of the button displays in the Title bar.

FIGURE 1.3

The Button Bar and Power Bar

WordPerfect Button Bar

Power Bar

The WordPerfect Button Bar is the preset (default) Button Bar and is usually displayed because it contains options for working more quickly with commonly-used WordPerfect features. Other Button Bars can be accessed by moving the mouse pointer to any button in the Button Bar and clicking the *right* mouse button once to display a list of available Button Bars. For example, the Graphics Button Bar could be selected when working with graphic images.

If the Button Bar is not displayed on the screen, select **View**, **Button Bar**. If a Button Bar is displayed, selecting **View**, **Button Bar** will remove the Button Bar from the screen.

The Power Bar option buttons represent other commonly used features such as New Document, Open, Save, Print, Font Face, Justification, and Columns. If the Power Bar is not displayed on the screen, select **View**, **Power Bar**. If the Power Bar is displayed, selecting **View**, **Power Bar** will remove the Power Bar from the screen.

In addition to the Button Bar and Power Bar, a Ruler Bar and feature-specific Feature Bars can be displayed on the screen. The use of the Ruler Bar and Feature Bars will be discussed in later chapters.

QuickCorrect

The QuickCorrect feature automatically corrects common typing and spelling errors. For example, if the characters "teh" are typed followed by a space, WordPerfect will automatically display the correct word "the." Also, if two uppercase letters are typed followed by other lowercase letters and a space, WordPerfect will change the second uppercase letter to a lowercase letter. Customizing the QuickCorrect feature is covered in Appendix A.

Formatting

Formatting is the process of determining the placement and arrangement of a document when it is printed on a page. The arrangement of a document includes the amount of blank space in the left, right, top, and bottom margins. Formatting also includes alignment, underline/bold text, capitalization, and the number of vertical and horizontal spaces used between words and lines.

The purpose of formatting is to arrange text in a manner that is attractive and easy to read. This textbook includes information on formatting memorandums, letters, tables, reports, mailing labels, newsletters, reports, etc.

In this chapter, formatting using different justification options will be introduced to create memorandum styles. The Center and Flush Right alignment options will be discussed as well as the format for the main text of a memorandum called *body text.* The justification options and body text format will be used throughout this book.

Wordwrap

One automatic formatting feature of word processing programs is wordwrap. As you type text, the **Enter** key is pressed only at the end of a paragraph or short line. When text reaches the right margin, the insertion point automatically returns to the beginning of the next line. This automatic return feature is called *wordwrap.*

When wordwrap is used, a hidden code, *SRt* (soft return), is inserted at the end of each line. The hidden code can be viewed by using the Reveal Codes features (see the section on Reveal Codes beginning on page 18). Wordwrap automatically formats the document paragraph to adjust to the left and right margins. If words are inserted or deleted from the paragraph, text automatically readjusts to the margins.

Memorandum—Style 1

There are many acceptable formats for memorandums. In a traditional memorandum, a heading, such as *Memorandum, Memo,* or *Interoffice Correspondence,* is typed or preprinted at the top of the page. The memorandum heading is followed by the recipient's name, author's name, date, and subject. The words, *To:, From:, Date:,* and *Subject:* usually precede the recipient's name, author's name, the date and subject and are called "lead words." The lead words can be typed in the memorandum or preprinted.

The main text of the memorandum (body text) is typed using wordwrap within each paragraph to automatically begin new lines. The **Enter** key is pressed twice after each paragraph. Each paragraph begins at the left margin. After the final paragraph, the **Enter** key is pressed twice followed by the initials of the person typing the memorandum.

Start-Up Instructions

- Use the following information to begin creating the memorandum shown in Figure 1.4.

Steps to Use Center Alignment (Horizontal Centering)

1. The insertion point should be located on the left side of the screen.
2. Select **Layout, Line, Center** {Alt, L, L, c *or* Shift and F7}.

   Note: *The insertion point moves to the middle of the document window.*
3. Type the word(s) to be centered.

   For example, type **Memorandum.**
4. Press **Enter** once.

   Note: *The word(s) are now horizontally centered on the screen and a hidden center code is placed in the document. (See Reveal Codes on page 19.) The insertion point is now located at the left margin one line below the heading.*

FIGURE 1.4

Memorandum—Style 1

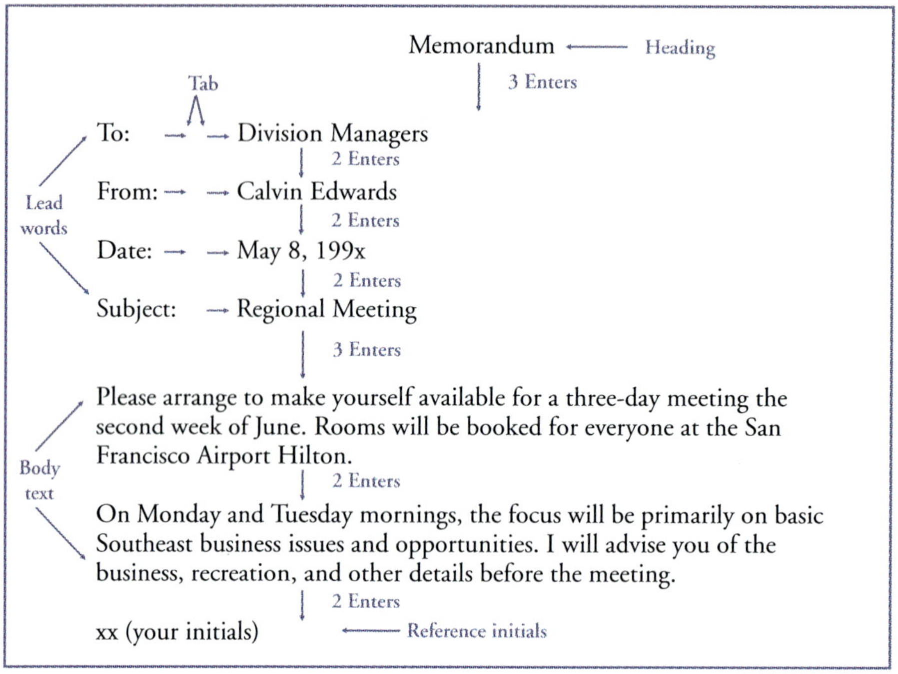

Start-Up Instructions

- Press the **Enter** key two more times to create two blank lines after the heading.
- Backspace to correct errors made while typing. For now, ignore any errors noticed after the memorandum is typed.
- Use wordwrap when typing the body text paragraphs.

  Note: *The paragraph lines may not end with the same words as shown in Figure 1.4.*

Steps to Create a Memorandum

1. Press the Tab key once or twice after the lead words as shown in Figure 1.4.

   Note: *The **Tab** key is pressed once or twice after the lead words in order to align the heading information. Visually check that the information following the lead words is aligned.*
2. Press the Enter key three times after the subject line and two times after each paragraph, including the last paragraph.
3. With the insertion point at the left margin, begin typing the text of the first paragraph. When the insertion point reaches the right margin, continue typing. Wordwrap will automatically return the insertion point to the left margin.
4. Press Enter twice after the last paragraph, then type your initials in lowercase letters.

Reveal Codes

When formatting options such as Center alignment are selected, WordPerfect places *hidden* codes in the document. To view these codes on the screen, the Reveal Codes feature is used. When Reveal Codes is activated, the screen is divided into two sections. The regular document window with the typed document displays at the top of the screen. The document text and formatting (hidden) codes display at the bottom of the

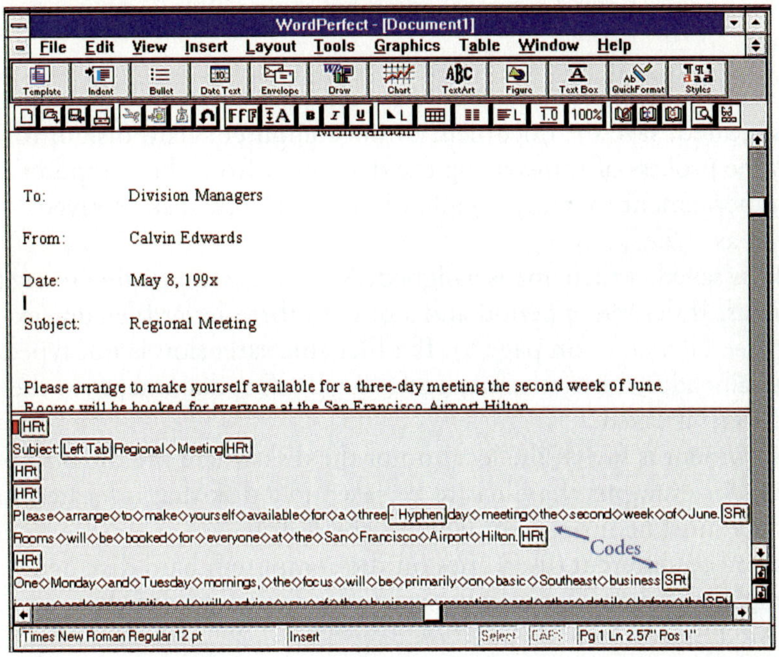

FIGURE 1.5

Reveal Codes window

screen. This section is known as the Reveal Codes window. The first code displayed in the Reveal Codes window is *Open Style: InitialStyle* (explained in Chapter 15).

The Reveal Codes window is routinely used to identify codes. The exact position of the insertion point is indicated by a red or shaded block. The movement of the red or shaded block in the Reveal Codes window corresponds to the movement of the insertion point in the document window.

A diamond (◊) is placed in the Reveal Codes window when the **Spacebar** is pressed. Two of the most frequently inserted codes are *SRt* and *HRt.* A soft return, *SRt,* occurs automatically each time wordwrap returns the insertion point to the left margin. A hard return, *HRt,* occurs each time the **Enter** key is pressed.

Start-Up Instructions

- Press and hold the **Ctrl** key and tap the **Home** key once to move the insertion point to the top of the document.

Steps to Turn on Reveal Codes

1. Select View, Reveal Codes {Alt, v, c *or* Alt and F3}.

   Note: *The screen is divided into two sections: the document window at the top and the Reveal Codes window at the bottom (see Figure 1.5). Notice that the insertion point in the document window and the red or shaded block in the Reveal Codes window are located at the exact same position in the document. Press the down arrow key repeatedly to move simultaneously the insertion point in the document and the red or shaded block in the Reveal Codes window.*

Steps to Turn Off Reveal Codes

1. When the Reveal Codes window is displayed on the screen, selecting View, Reveal Codes removes the Reveal Codes window {Alt, v, c *or* Alt and F3}.

Save a File

After a document is created, save the document to the computer's hard disk or to a floppy disk. Saving is the process of transferring the document from the computer's temporary memory to permanent memory on a hard disk or floppy disk. A saved document is referred to as a *file.*

When a document is saved, a filename is assigned. A filename can be one to eight characters with no spaces. If desired, a period and a one- to three-letter filename extension can be added (see Filenames on page 5). If a filename extension is not typed, WordPerfect automatically adds the extension *.wpd* (WordPerfect document) to the filename when a document is saved.

Before a named document is saved, the location of the disk where the file is to be saved must be selected. For example, if a file is to be saved to a disk that is located in the A drive, WordPerfect must be instructed to access the A drive.

Files can also be saved to different directories on the computer's hard disk or floppy disks. For example, a memo file could be saved to a directory named c:\memos (see What Are Directories and Paths? on page 5.)

Once a document has been saved, the filename and location display in the Title bar (as long as the mouse pointer is below the Power Bar). If a saved document is changed, selecting the **Save** button on the Power Bar or choosing **File**, **Save** will save the edited file immediately using the filename displayed in the Title bar. To save the edited file with a new filename, see Steps to Use Save As to Rename a File on page 38.

Start-Up Instructions

- A file disk should be placed in the A or B disk drive.

Steps to Save a New File

1. Select the Save button  on the Power Bar {Alt, f, s *or* Ctrl and s}.

   Note: *The Save As dialog box displays. The current drive and directory display below the words "Save As" at the top center of the dialog box, e.g., a:\ or c:\wpwin60\wpdocs. The insertion point is located in the Filename box.*

2. In the Filename box, type a filename with eight characters or less (no spaces).

   For example, type **1drill1**. (Do not type the period.)

   Note: *Check the accuracy of the filename before continuing. If necessary, use the Backspace key to erase an incorrect filename and type the corrected filename.*

To Select a Different Drive

3. Move the mouse pointer to the box below the word "Drives" and click the left mouse button once {Alt and v, press the down arrow key}.

   Note: *A list of available drives displays.*

4. Move the mouse pointer to the desired drive letter and click once {press the up or down arrow key to highlight the desired drive letter, press Enter}.

   For example, move the mouse pointer to the drive letter containing your file disk, i.e., a: or b:, and click once.

Note: The newly selected drive displays below the words "Save As" at the top center of the dialog box.

To Complete the Save Process

5. Select OK {press Enter}.

   Note: *The document is saved on the file disk that is located in the selected disk drive. If the mouse pointer is located below the Power Bar, the document name is displayed in the Title bar of the WordPerfect document window, e.g., a:\1drill1.wpd–unmodified. The three letter extension .wpd is added automatically to the filename when the file is saved.*

   Note: *If the message displays, "File: a:\1drill1.wpd already exists. Do you want to replace it?," select **Yes** to replace, select **No** to return to the Save As dialog box and type a new filename, or select **Cancel** to return to the WordPerfect document window without saving the document.*

Steps to Select a Different Directory

Note: *The following steps are provided for your information.*

1. In the Directories box, click on the root directory symbol, e.g., c:\.

   Note: *A list of available directories displays in the Directories box.*

2. Move the mouse pointer to the desired directory name and click once.

   Note: *A list of available subdirectories displays in the Directories box.*

Print a Document

A document can be printed by using the **File, Print** command or by selecting the **Print** button on the Power Bar. After **Print** is selected in the Print dialog box, the entire document will be printed. Individual pages or sections of a document can be printed if desired. Additional information concerning printing is discussed in Chapters 5 and 10.

Start-Up Instructions

- The printer should be turned on. If you are sharing a printer, check that the switch box or local area network printer is selected for your printer.
- The document to be printed should be displayed in the document window.

Steps to Print a Document

1. Select the Print button on the Power Bar {Alt, f, p *or* F5}.
2. Select Print to print the document {press Enter}.

Close a Document

Once a document has been typed, saved, and printed, the document is usually cleared from the document window before a new document is begun. However, more than one document window can be displayed on the screen at one time. (See Chapter 16, The Windows in WordPerfect.) Closing a document is often referred to as *clearing a document* from the screen. After a document is closed, a blank WordPerfect document window displays and a new document can be typed or an existing document can be opened. If more than one document has been opened, you may need to close another document window or select **File**, **New** to obtain a clear document window.

Steps to Close a Document

1. Select File, Close {press Alt, f, c *or* Ctrl and F4}. The document will be removed from the document screen.

   Note: *If a message displays, "Save changes to...?", select* **No** *{press n} to close without saving changes. Repeat Step 1 if more than one window is open.*

Memorandum—Style 2

Memorandum—Style 2 illustrates a second acceptable memo format. The lead words and body text format are the same as Memorandum—Style 1. However, the heading "Interoffice Correspondence" is used, and the lead words are arranged on only two lines. See Figure 1.6.

In Memorandum—Style 2, the date and subject are typed at the right margin. The Flush Right alignment feature is used to move the insertion point to the right margin. As text is typed, the insertion point moves back towards the left margin. The final character in the line is located at the right margin. When **Enter** is pressed, the insertion point returns to the left margin.

When using Memorandum—Style 1 or Style 2, the lead word "To:" is followed by the recipient's name or a name that identifies a group of individuals, e.g., sales representatives, district managers, etc. Also, a distribution list can be typed after the body text, identifying the individuals who are part of the group. If copies of the memo are to be sent to other individuals, the notation "c:" is typed below the distribution list and followed by a list of people to whom copies are to be sent.

Start-Up Instructions

- Use the following steps to type the memorandum shown in Figure 1.6.
- Use Center alignment (**Shift** and **F7**) before typing the memorandum heading, **Interoffice Correspondence**. Press the **Enter** key three times.
- Type the lead word **To:** and press the **Tab** key once. Type **Sales Representatives**.

FIGURE 1.6

Memorandum—Style 2

Interoffice Correspondence ← Heading

3 Enters

Lead words

To: Sales Representatives Date: March 4, 199x

2 Enters

From: Nancy Owens Subject: Flash Tennis Shoes

3 Enters

Body text

During our next quarter, the new Flash Tennis Shoes will be introduced. Each sales representative in the Oregon Division is to sell 35 units.

2 Enters

Because of the unique design, this product should become our most popular shoe. A special sales exhibit is being developed for displays in area stores. Good luck and good selling!

2 Enters

xx (your initials) ← Reference initials

2 Enters

Distribution:

2 Enters

G. Martin
P. Turner
R. Morrison

Steps to Use Flush Right Alignment

1. Select **Layout, Line, Flush Right** {Alt and F7}.

   Note: The insertion point moves to the right margin. As text is typed, the insertion point remains at the right margin and the text moves back towards the left margin.

2. Type the desired text.

   For example, type the lead word **Date** followed by a colon, two spaces, and the current date. Press the **Enter** key twice.

Finish-Up Instructions

- Continue to type the memorandum with the spacing indicated in Figure 1.6.
- Save the memorandum on your file disk; use the filename **1drill2**—Chapter 1, drill 2. (Select the **Save** button on the Power Bar; type the filename in the Filename box; if necessary, click in the Drives box and click on the drive letter where the file disk is located; select **OK**.)
- Print one copy (select the **Print** button on the Power Bar; choose **Print**).

Scrolling Horizontally and Vertically

Scrolling is the process of moving text quickly up, down, left, or right in order to view parts of the document not displayed in the document window. A vertical scroll bar displays at the right of the screen and a horizontal scroll bar displays at the bottom of the screen. Each scroll bar contains a scroll box and scroll arrows (controlled by the mouse) that can be used to view various parts of a document. To scroll quickly from page to page in a multiple-page document, the Previous Page and Next

FIGURE 1.7

WordPerfect for Windows document window with scroll bars

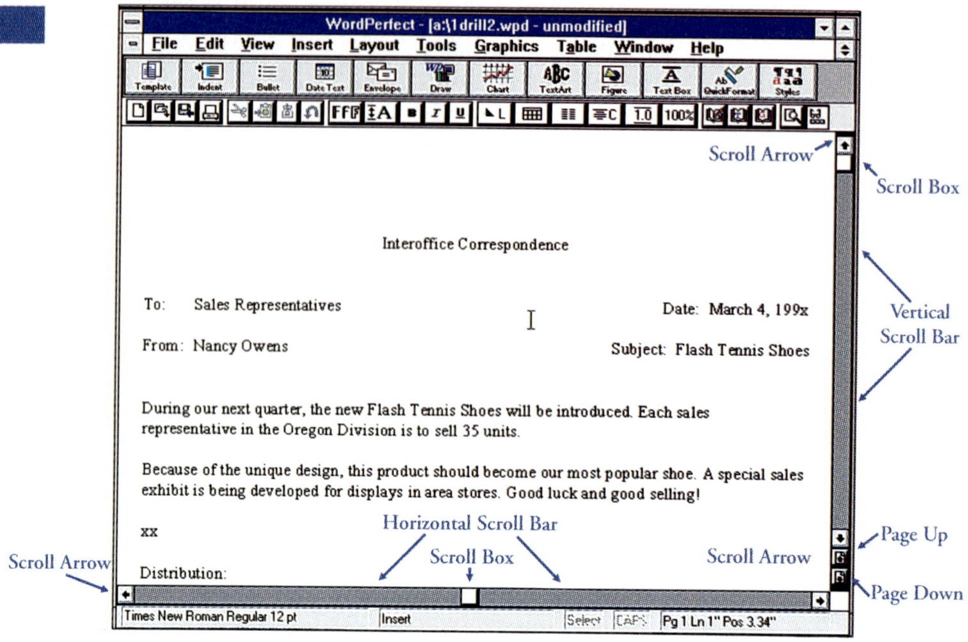

Page buttons located at the bottom of the vertical scroll bar can be used. See Figure 1.7.

Start-Up Instructions

- With the file named **1drill2.wpd** displayed in the document window, use the following steps to practice vertical and horizontal scrolling.
- Press and hold the **Ctrl** key and tap the **Home** key once to move the insertion point to the top of the document.

Steps to Use the Mouse for Vertical or Horizontal Scrolling

1. Place the mouse pointer on the scroll box in the vertical scroll bar on the right side of the document window; press and hold the left mouse button, then drag the scroll box up or down to scroll. Release the mouse button.

   For example, move the mouse pointer to the vertical scroll box; press and hold the left mouse button while dragging the box down; release the mouse button.

   Note: *The text on the screen scrolls. However, the insertion point does not change location in the text. To change the location of the insertion point, see the Steps to Move the Insertion Point Quickly on page 25.*

2. Place the mouse pointer on the up scroll arrow located at the top of the vertical scroll bar or the down scroll arrow located at the bottom of the vertical scroll bar and click the left mouse button once to scroll the text down or up a single line.

   For example, place the mouse pointer on the down scroll arrow located at the bottom of the scroll bar and click once or twice.

   Note: *Holding down the left mouse button while pointing to the up or down scroll arrows will cause the text to move continuously up or down.*

3. Place the mouse pointer on the scroll box in the horizontal scroll bar at the bottom of the document window; press and hold the left mouse button and drag the scroll box to the left or right. Release the mouse button.

   For example, move the mouse pointer to the scroll box in the horizontal scroll bar; press and hold the left mouse button while dragging the box to the right. Release the mouse button.

Move the Insertion Point

To relocate the insertion point to various parts of the document, use the arrow keys or move the mouse pointer and click on the desired location. For example, the mouse can be used to relocate the insertion point to any position in the document by pointing on the desired position and clicking once. The up, down, left, and right arrow keys as well as the **Page Up** (PgUp), **Page Down** (PgDn), **Home**, and **End** keys can also be used to relocate the insertion point.

Steps to Move the Insertion Point Quickly

Using the Mouse

1. Move the mouse pointer to any location in the document and click. The insertion point moves to that location.

   Note: If the desired location is not visible in the document window, scroll the text to display the desired location. (See Steps to Use the Mouse for Vertical or Horizontal Scrolling on page 24.)

Using the Keyboard

1. To move the insertion point to the left side of a line, press the **Home** key.
2. To move the insertion point to the right side (end) of a line, press the **End** key.
3. To move the insertion point to the beginning of the document, press and hold the **Ctrl** key and tap the **Home** key once.

   *Note: Press **Ctrl** and **Home**, **Ctrl** and **Home** to move the insertion point to the right of the "Open Style: InitialStyle" code and in front of any other codes that could be at the top of the document.*

4. To move the insertion point to the last character in the document, press and hold the **Ctrl** key and tap the **End** key once.
5. To move the insertion point to the top of the document window, press the **Page Up** key once.
6. To move the insertion point to the bottom of the document window, press the **Page Down** key once.
7. To move the insertion point to the left one word, press the **Ctrl** and **left arrow** keys.
8. To move the insertion point to the right one word, press the **Ctrl** and **right arrow** keys.

9. To move the insertion point to the top of the previous page, press the Alt key and then press the Page Up key once.

10. To move the insertion point to the top of the next page, press the Alt key and then press the Page Down key once.

11. To move the insertion point to a different page, press Ctrl and g (Go To), type the page number desired, press Enter.

Exit WordPerfect

After completing your work, the WordPerfect for Windows program is exited and the Windows Program Manager screen displays. If desired, Windows can be closed and the cursor returned to the system prompt, e.g., C:\. Remember to always save your files before exiting the WordPerfect program.

Steps to Exit WordPerfect

Note: If necessary, save your file before exiting the WordPerfect program using the Steps to Save a New File on page 20.

1. Select File, Exit {Alt, f, x *or* Alt and F4}.

   Note: If a message displays, "Do you want to save changes to...?", select ***Yes*** *to save changes or select* ***No*** *to abandon changes.*

The Next Step

Chapter Review and Activities

Self-Check Quiz

T F 1. Launching is the process of transferring the WordPerfect program from a hard disk to the computer's memory.

T F 2. Formatting is the process of determining the placement and arrangement of a document when it is printed on a page.

T F 3. To center a line of text, select **Layout, Line, Center.**

T F 4. To print all the text in a file, select **File, Print, Close.**

T F 5. A document can be saved only to a floppy disk.

6. The Reveal Codes window displays
   a. hidden codes.
   b. in the document window at all times.
   c. by selecting **View, Page.**

7. The Button Bar
   a. is referred to as the Power Bar.
   b. can be removed from the screen by selecting View, **Button Bar.**
   c. can be accessed by using keystrokes.

8. Press the **Enter** key to
   a. begin a new paragraph.
   b. end a short line.
   c. both a and b.

9. What is the difference between the insertion point and the mouse pointer?

10. List the two steps to use Flush Right alignment.

Enriching Language Arts Skills

SCANS

Each chapter contains vocabulary/spelling words and basic rules for punctuation, capitalization, or grammar. The last *Challenge Your Skills* activity in each chapter is identified by the ➜ symbol and has mistakes in spelling, punctuation, capitalization, and/or grammar that are to be corrected. These activities should be proofread and corrected to produce a document that is grammatically accurate and ready for distribution.

Spelling/Vocabulary Words

acquisition the act of purchasing or obtaining an item.

spiraling increasing upward or downward in a circular motion.

enormous huge, big.

liquidation to close a business in order to receive cash for the assets.

Introductory Adverbs and Phrases

A comma often follows an introductory adverb or phrase, because the word or phrase provides a transition from the previous sentence. Some common introductory adverbs/phrases are: *however, for example, also, consequently, in other words.*

Examples:

A decision was made yesterday to postpone the approval of the budget. Consequently, the purchase order for the new desks will be delayed.

The post office requested that we use the new extended zip code. In other words, use the current 5-digit zip code followed by the new 4-digit extension.

Activities

Activity 1.1—Create a Memorandum—Style 1

1. If necessary, launch (load) the WordPerfect program (see page 14).
2. If errors are made while typing, use the **Backspace** key to delete. For this chapter, ignore any errors noticed *after* the memo is typed.
3. Use Memorandum—Style 1 (see page 17) and type the following memorandum.

Memorandum

To: Al Lindsay

From: Virginia Ashlan

Date: (Use current date)

Subject: Action Plan Version 5.0

The newest version of the Action Plan program is currently available.

An information bulletin is being sent to all consultants informing them that the instructional materials are now available at all our regional offices. Old versions of Action Plan diskettes and manual contents can be destroyed. The binders can be reused with the new material, and the diskettes can be recycled.

xx (your initials)

---

4. Save the file on your file disk; use the filename **1act1** (Chapter 1, activity 1). (Select the **Save** button on the Power Bar; type the filename; if necessary, click in the Drives box and click on the drive letter where the file disk is located; select **OK**.)
5. Print one copy (select the **Print** button on the Power Bar; choose **Print**).
6. Close the document to clear the document window (select **File**, **Close**).

Activity 1.2—Create a Memorandum—Style 1

1. If necessary, launch (load) the WordPerfect program (see page 14).
2. If errors are made while typing, use the **Backspace** key to delete. For this chapter, ignore any errors noticed *after* the memo is typed.
3. Use Memorandum—Style 1(refer to page 17) and type the following memorandum.

Memorandum

To: All Sales Agents

From: Peter Roth, Division Manager

Date: (Use current date)

Subject: Application Procedures for Multiple Contracts

The purpose of this memorandum is to clarify the procedure for processing exchanges when more than one contract is involved.

The correct procedure is to list each company name along with the policy number for each policy that will be relinquished for the purpose of exchange.

At policy delivery, the policyowner will sign both of the contract forms. Return the forms and policies to the Policy Change Department. If you have questions, please feel free to contact us in Marketing Services.

xx (your initials)

4. Save the file on your file disk; use the filename **1act2** (Chapter 1, activity 2). (Select the **Save** button on the Power Bar; type the filename; if necessary, click in the Drives box and click on the drive letter where the file disk is located; select **OK**.)
5. Print one copy (select the **Print** button on the Power Bar; choose **Print**).
6. Close the document to clear the document window (select **File**, **Close**).

Activity 1.3—Create a Memorandum—Style 2

1. If necessary, launch (load) the WordPerfect program (see page 14).
2. If errors are made while typing, use the **Backspace** key to delete. For this chapter, ignore any errors noticed *after* the memo is typed.
3. Use Memorandum—Style 2 (refer to page 23) and type the following memorandum.

Interoffice Correspondence

To: See Distribution Below	Date: (Use current date)
From: Gene Hunter	Subject: Reimbursement Rates

All offices have been provided with the new fuel reimbursement rates that should be placed into effect immediately. Each office will photocopy a set of the rates and forward the rate sheets to all area representatives.

You will notice that an additional amount for the seasonal adjustment has been added to each rate. If gasoline prices decline this fall, revised rates will be published to reflect any changes at that time.

xx (your initials)

Distribution:

S. Bentley
L. Jardine
W. Moyer

4. Save the file on your file disk; use the filename **1act3** (Chapter 1, activity 3). (Select the **Save** button on the Power Bar; type the filename; if necessary, click in the Drives box and click on the drive letter where the file disk is located; select **OK**.)
5. Print one copy (select the **Print** button on the Power Bar, choose **Print**).
6. Close the document to clear the document window (select **File**, **Close**).

Challenge Your Skills

The *Challenge Your Skills* section at the end of each chapter contains a group of activities that reinforce understanding of the chapter's concepts. The activities require decision-making skills. The *Challenge Your Skills* activities should be completed only after completing appropriate chapter drills and activities.

Skill 1.1—Create a Memorandum—Style 1

1. If necessary, launch the WordPerfect program.
2. If errors are made while typing, use the **Backspace** key to delete. For this chapter, ignore any errors noticed *after* the memo is typed.
3. Use Memorandum—Style 1 and the following information.

a. Send the memorandum to the MIS Staff from Veronica Pearson. The subject of the memorandum is Network Access Problems.

b. Use the current date; include your reference initials.

The network has caused loss of productivity in recent weeks. Explanations of known problems are summarized below.

The recent Broadway virus that attacked the entire network caused a productivity loss of two days. MIS took effective action in returning us to operation quickly.

On Monday and Tuesday the network could not be accessed from the IBM PS/2. An unreliable connection was found between the network and the PS/2. Printing could not be accomplished from the Compaq AT. The printer cable had been disconnected from the switch box.

Angelo's computer receives a high number of "Error on Network Server ONEA Abort, Retry?" messages. Jayne Gurry has been notified. This is a recoverable error.

Thanks to all MIS users for your interest in resolving network problems rapidly.

---

4. Save the file on your file disk; use the filename **1skill1** (Chapter 1, skill 1).
5. Print one copy and close the document to clear the document window.

Skill 1.2—Create a Memorandum—Style 2

1. If necessary, launch the WordPerfect program.
2. If errors are made while typing, use the **Backspace** key to delete. For this chapter, ignore any errors noticed *after* the memo is typed.
3. Use Memorandum—Style 2 and the following information.

   a. Send the memorandum to USL Agents from Joyce Bixler. The subject of the memorandum is Purchase of Policies.

   b. Use the current date; include your reference initials.

   c. The memo is to be distributed to the following persons: Russell Crimmins, Catherine Goldfarb, Marilyn Scutro, and Edith Zehr.

United Security Life will soon acquire the life and annuity policies of Hampton Insurance Company. Hampton Insurance Company (HIC) is a small-stock life insurer that has experienced financial difficulty and is being liquidated.

As a part of the liquidation process, USL has agreed to purchase HIC's life and annuity policies. This will ensure that all the life and most of the annuity policies continue without loss to the policyholders.

We think that the acquisition of HIC will help us control our unit expenses, which is certainly in everyone's best interest. If you have any questions regarding the acquisition, please contact my assistant, Lois Schloneger.

4. Save the file on your file disk; use the filename **1skill2** (Chapter 1, skill 2).
5. Print one copy and close the document to clear the document window.

Skill 1.3—Create a Memorandum—Style 2; Language Arts

1. If necessary, launch the WordPerfect program.
2. If errors are made while typing, use the **Backspace** key to delete. For this chapter, ignore any typing errors noticed *after* the memo is typed.
3. Use Memorandum—Style 2 and the following information.
   a. Send the memorandum to GLI Representatives from I. Arigone, Field Manager. The subject of the memo is Blood Test Limit.
   b. Use the current date; include your reference initials.
   c. The memo is to be distributed to the following persons: T. Deyo; B. Hurwicz; R. Juarez; E. Tang; L. Tolleson; and M. Warrick.
   d. While typing, correct two spelling errors and one punctuation error.

This is a reminder that effective with new business written next month, Global Life Insurance's new blood test rules call for a blood test at $100,000. GLI participated in a recent study involving a large number of the better known insurance companies and a solid majority are requiring blood tests for any policies amounting to $100,000 or greater. Our research combined with the spireling increase in medical costs, makes this adjustment necessary.

We need your full cooperation involving applications for amounts between $95,000 to $99,999, which occur on persons opposed to a blood test. Most people who object to obtaining a blood test are not trying to hide a prior condition. Unfortunately, there is a small segment of people who already know they have a pre-existing condition, and we cannot discern which type of person is objecting. Consequently you are to arrange a blood test on those individuals whose policy amounts barely slide in under the actual rule limits.

It is widely believed that many companies will eventually be forced to increase premiums in order to avoid the consequence of liquidtion. It is our hope that by seeking your cooperation on the above measures, GLI can forestall or avoid sterner remedies later.

---

4. Save the file on your file disk; use the filename **1skill3** (Chapter 1, skill 3).
5. Print one copy.
6. If you have completed your work, exit WordPerfect (select **File**, **Exit**).

CHAPTER 2

Edit a Memorandum

Features Covered

- Open a document
- Select text
- Delete text
- Insert text
- Replace text using the Typeover mode
- Save and rename a document file
- Undo and Undelete
- View a document
- Use the Help feature

Objectives and Introduction

After successfully completing this chapter, you will be able to open a previously created document; delete, insert and replace text; and save a document with a new filename. You will also be able to use the Viewer and Help features. Once a memorandum has been created, the author can make revisions to the document. Revisions can include information to be deleted, inserted, or replaced.

Open a Document

Before a file is edited, the saved document is opened and displayed in the document window. Opening a document is the process of transferring a document file from a disk to the computer's memory. When a file is opened, the document displays in a new document window. As many as nine files can be opened (in memory) at the same time (see Chapters 9 and 16). To open a file, select the **Open** button on the Power Bar, choose the desired drive/directory, and double-click on the filename.

The last four files that have been opened are listed at the bottom of the File menu. To open one of the four listed files, move the mouse pointer to the filename and click once. If WordPerfect cannot locate the selected file, a message displays ". . . File not found."

FIGURE 2.1

Open File dialog box

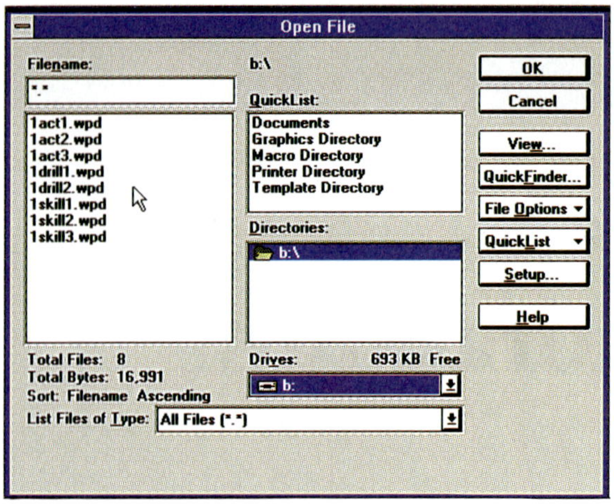

Steps to Open a File

1. Select the Open button  on the Power Bar {Alt, f, o *or* Ctrl and o}.

   Note: The Open File dialog box displays (see Figure 2.1).

2. *To display the files stored on a different drive,* move the mouse pointer to the Drives box and and click once. Move the mouse pointer to the desired drive letter and click once {Alt and v, press the down arrow key, press the up or down arrow key to highlight desired drive letter, press Enter}.

3. Move the mouse pointer to the desired filename and double-click {Alt and n, press the Tab key once, press the down arrow key to highlight the desired filename, press Enter}.

   For example, double-click on the file named **1drill1.wpd**.

   Note: Wait a moment and the selected file displays in the document window.

Delete and Insert Text

Text can be deleted by using the Backspace key or the Delete (Del) key. When the Backspace key is pressed, the character or space to the left of the insertion point is erased. When the Delete key is pressed, the character or space to the right of the insertion point is erased. Text deleted by using the Backspace or Delete keys can be returned to the screen by using the Edit, Undo or Edit, Undelete commands (see Undo Erased Text, page 38.

Selected text can be erased and replaced without using either the Delete or Backspace key. The text to be deleted is selected. When the first character of the new text is typed, the selected text is deleted.

Text can be selected and deleted. A character, word, sentence, line, paragraph, or entire document can be selected and deleted. After text is selected and the Delete or Backspace key is pressed, the deleted text is placed in the Clipboard. The Clipboard is temporary memory that holds the deleted text. When additional text is selected and deleted, the original text held in the Clipboard is erased and replaced with the last deleted text.

Text is inserted by placing the insertion point at the location where the new characters are to be typed and typing the characters. As the inserted text is typed, the characters to the right of the insertion point move over and provide space for the new text.

Steps to Select Text

Using the Mouse

a. *Drag method:* To select any quantity of text, move the mouse pointer (I-beam) to the beginning of the text to be selected; press and hold the left mouse button while dragging the mouse to highlight the desired text. Release the mouse button.

b. *Shift and Click method:* To select any quantity of text, move the mouse pointer (I-beam) to the left of the first character to be selected and click the left mouse button once. Move the mouse pointer (I-beam) to the right of the last character to be selected. Press and hold the **Shift** key and click the left mouse button once. Release the **Shift** key.

c. *To select a word,* move the mouse pointer to any character in the desired word and double-click.

d. *To select a sentence,* move the mouse pointer to any word in the desired sentence and triple-click, or move the mouse pointer into the left margin next to the desired sentence and click once.

e. *To select a paragraph,* move the mouse pointer to any location within the paragraph and click four times, or move the mouse pointer into the left margin beside the desired paragraph and double-click.

Using the Edit, Select Command

a. To select a sentence, place the insertion point in the desired sentence and choose **Edit, Select, Sentence** {Alt, e, e, s}.

b. To select a paragraph, place the insertion point in the desired paragraph and choose **Edit, Select, Paragraph** {Alt, e, e, a}.

c. To select a page, place the insertion point anywhere in the desired page and choose **Edit, Select, Page** {Alt, e, e, p}.

d. To select the entire document, choose **Edit, Select, All** {Alt, e, e, L}.

Using Keystrokes

1. Place the insertion point to the left of the character at the beginning of the text to be selected.

2. Press **F8**.

   Note: *The word **Select** displays in bold in the Status bar.*

3. Use any of the following keystrokes.

   a. To select one character to the right or left, press the **right arrow** or **left arrow** key.

b. To select one line up or down, press the **up** or **down arrow** key.

c. To select to the end of the line, press the **End** key.

d. To select to the beginning of the line, press the **Home** key.

e. To select to the beginning of the document, press the **Ctrl** and **Home** keys.

f. To select to the end of the document, press the **Ctrl** and **End** keys.

g. To select to the top of the screen, press **Page Up** (PgUp).

h. To select to the bottom of the screen, press **Page Down** (PgDn).

i. To select one word to the right or left, press **Ctrl** and the **left** or **right arrow** key.

j. To select one paragraph up or down, press **Ctrl** and the **up** or **down arrow** key.

Steps to Turn Off Select

1. To turn off select and remove the highlight from text, click once {F8}.

Steps to Delete Text

1. Once the desired text has been selected, press the **Delete** (Del) key.

Shortcuts for Deleting Text Without Selecting Text

a. To delete an entire word, position the insertion point to the left of any character in the word to be deleted and press **Ctrl** and **Backspace**.

Steps to Delete an Enter/Blank Line or Tab Code

1. Turn on Reveal Codes (Alt and F3).
2. Move the insertion point to left of the *HRt* or *Left Tab* code.
3. Press the **Delete** key.
4. Turn off Reveal Codes (Alt and F3).

Steps to Insert Text or Spaces

1. Place the insertion point to the left of the character or space that will follow the inserted text or space.
2. Type the text or space to be inserted.

   Note: *If text is erased as new text is typed, press the Insert (Ins) key once to turn off the Typeover mode. See also the Replace Text Using the Typeover Mode section which follows.*

Replace Text Using the Typeover Mode

When text is replaced using the Typeover mode, the original character(s) are deleted and new characters are substituted. For example, if the insertion point is located to the left of the character "b" in the word "band" and the character "s" is typed, the "b" is deleted and the character "s" displays on the screen, changing the word to "sand." Replacing text using the Typeover mode is accomplished by first pressing the **Insert** (Ins) key, then typing the new character(s). When the Insert key is pressed, the word *Typeover* displays in the Status bar. When the **Insert** key is pressed again, the word *Insert* displays in the Status bar.

Steps to Replace Text

1. Place the insertion point to the left of the first character of the text to be replaced.
2. Press the **Insert** (Ins) key.

   Note: The word "Typeover" displays in the Status bar.
3. Type the new character(s).
4. When you have finished replacing the text, press **Insert** again to turn Typeover off.

   *Note: If desired, select **Edit, Undo** to restore the replaced text.*

Start-Up Instructions

- The file named **1drill1.wpd** typed in Chapter 1 (Figure 1.4) should be opened and displayed in the document window. (If necessary, select the **Open** button on the Power Bar; if necessary, click in the Drives box and click on the drive letter where the file disk is located; double-click on the desired filename.)
- Review the steps to select and/or delete text and the steps to replace text using the Typeover mode.
- Make the changes shown in Figure 2.2.
- Continue with the Steps to Use Save As to Rename a File.

Save and Rename a File

Once a document (file) has been edited, the changed file can be saved using a new filename. Using a different filename keeps a copy of the original file and saves the changed file under a new filename. If the changed file is saved with the original filename, the original file is erased and replaced by the corrected file.

Start-Up Instructions

- The file named **1drill1.wpd** should be displayed in the document window.

FIGURE 2.2

Changes for Memorandum—Style 1

Memorandum

To: Division Managers

From: Calvin Edwards, Regional Manager

Date: May 8, 199x

Subject: Western Regional Meeting

Please arrange to make yourself available for a three-day meeting the second week of June. Rooms will be booked for everyone at the San Francisco Airport Hilton for three days and two nights.

On ~~Monday~~ Tuesday and ~~Tuesday~~ Wednesday mornings, the focus will be primarily on basic South~~east~~west business issues and opportunities. I will advise you of the business, recreation, and other details before the meeting. On Thursday we will join with Jan Hasimi's group to discuss the new marketing promotion.

¶ Casual attire will be appropriate for Tuesday and Wednesday. Thursday's attire will be announced pending the determination of the meeting location.

xx

Steps to Use Save As to Rename a File

1. With the document displayed in the document window, select File, Save As button {Alt, f, a *or* F3}.
2. Type the new filename. (If necessary, select the drive where the file disk is located by clicking the Drives box and clicking on the desired drive letter).

   For example, type **a:2drill1r**. (Do not type the period.)
3. Select OK {press Enter}.

Finish-Up Instructions

- Print one copy (select the **Print** button on the Power Bar; choose **Print**).
- If additional changes are made to the document, select the **Save** button on the Power Bar to save but to not rename the document. If no changes are made to the document after printing, clear the screen (select **File**, **Close**).

Undo Erased Text

Text that has been selected and deleted with the Delete or Backspace keys can be reinserted (or put back) into the document. When text is reinserted, the deleted text is retrieved to the screen. Reinserting text is referred to as "undo" or "undelete."

> The Association rules have been updated. The updated rules will be placed in your mailboxes over the weekend. The revised rules are easy to read and comprehend.

FIGURE 2.3
Practice paragraph to use for Undoing and Undeleting erased text

There are two methods for reinserting text: Undo and Undelete. When the **Undo** command is selected, the deleted text is restored to the original location. If **Undelete** is selected, the text will be restored at the location of the insertion point.

The **Undo** command must be selected immediately before another action is attempted. Text that has been reinserted using Undo can be deleted again by selecting the **Undo** command a second time.

Start-Up Instructions

- Type the paragraph shown in Figure 2.3.
- Select and delete the first sentence.

Steps to Undo Deleted Text

1. After the text has been selected and deleted, select the Undo button on the Power Bar {Alt, e, u *or* Ctrl and z}.

   Note: The text returns to the screen and displays in its original location.

Start-Up Instructions

- The paragraph typed previously from Figure 2.3 should be displaying in the document window.
- Select the second sentence including the space following; press **Delete**.

Steps to Undelete Deleted Text

1. After text has been selected and deleted, move the insertion point to the location where the deleted text is to be restored.

   For example, move the insertion point to the left of the first character in the first sentence.

2. Select Edit, Undelete {Alt, e, n *or* Ctrl and Shift and z}.

   Note: The deleted text displays highlighted in the document window where the insertion point is located.

3. Select Restore {Enter}.

   *Note: To stop the undelete process, select **Cancel** {Esc}.*

Finish-Up Instructions

- Close the document without saving (select **File**, **Close**).

The Viewer

The contents of a file can be displayed in the Viewer window before a file is opened by selecting the **View** button in the Open File or Save As dialog box. By displaying a document in the Viewer window, you can quickly scan the document's contents to determine whether or not you want to open the file. The Viewer window may not display all of the document's formatting.

Steps to Use the Viewer to View a Document

1. Select the **Open** button on the Power Bar {Alt, f, o *or* Ctrl and o}.
2. If necessary, select a different drive by clicking in the Drives box and then clicking on the desired drive letter.

   For example, check that the drive where your file disk is located displays at the top center of the dialog box. If necessary, select the a: or b: drive.
3. Move the mouse pointer to the desired filename and click once {press the Tab key once, press the up or down arrow key to highlight the desired filename}.

   For example, move the mouse pointer to the file named **1drill1.wpd** and click once.
4. Select the **View** button in the Open File dialog box.

   Note: *The Viewer window displays the text for the selected file. The displayed text cannot be edited in the Viewer window. Also note that formatting, such as centering, does not display in the Viewer.*
5. To view another file, move the mouse pointer to another filename and click once {press the up or down arrow key to highlight the desired filename}.

   For example, move the mouse pointer to the file named **2drill1r.wpd** and click once.
6. Select **OK** to open the file displayed in the Viewer window {Enter} or select **Cancel** to close the Open File dialog box without opening a file {Esc}.

   For example, select **OK** to open the file named **2drill1r.wpd**.

Finish-Up Instructions

- Close the document (select **File**, **Close**).

Using Help

WordPerfect has an online Help feature that provides detailed information about program topics and specific instructions for performing commands. The Help feature can be accessed at any time through the Help menu or from any dialog box or menu.

The Help feature can be accessed in several ways. One method is to select the **Help** menu and choose the **How Do I** option. A list of of topics displays (see Figure 2.4). The

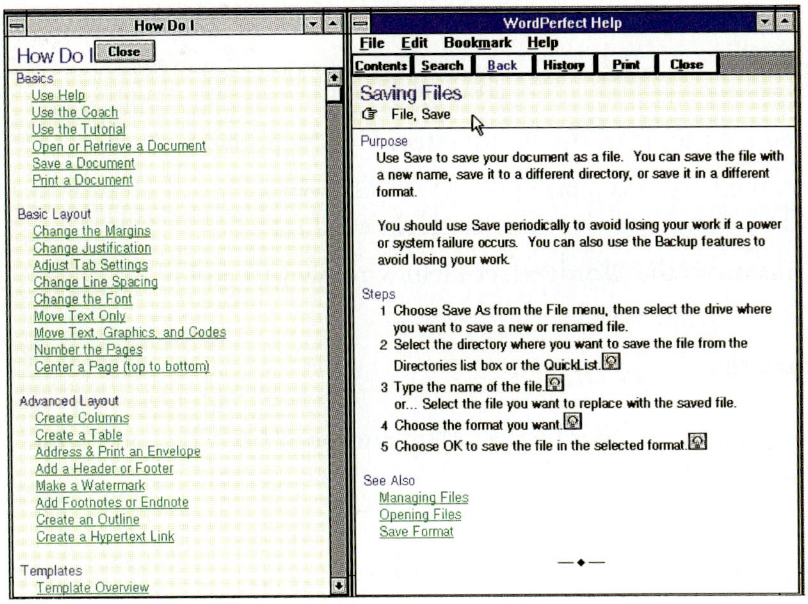

FIGURE 2.4

How Do I and WordPerfect Help windows

desired topic is selected in order to display the WordPerfect Help information for the chosen topic. A list of topics can also be displayed by selecting **Help**, **Contents**.

When a topic is selected, additional information can be viewed by selecting "jump terms," "pop-up terms," or a "lightbulb hint" icon. Words that display with an underline are referred to as *jump terms*. When a jump term is selected, a new WordPerfect Help window displays with information on a related topic. Words that display with a dotted underline are referred to as *pop-up terms*. When a pop-up term is selected, additional information displays on the screen. The *lightbulb hint* icon can be selected to obtain information on how to use a feature. To remove pop-up or lightbulb hint information from the screen, click the mouse button once.

Another method of accessing the Help feature is to select a menu command or display a dialog box and press **F1**. Help information displays for the menu command or for each option shown in the dialog box. To display help information about buttons on the Button Bar or Power Bar or other areas of the document window, the Help: What Is? feature is accessed by pressing the **Shift** and **F1** keys, moving the mouse pointer to the item, and clicking the mouse button once.

WordPerfect also provides a Coach option that walks you through the steps necessary to complete a task. With the Coach option, WordPerfect will prompt each step and if desired, hints can be viewed to assist you in completing a task. A tutorial covering basic WordPerfect features such as creating, saving, and printing files can be accessed by selecting the **Help**, **Tutorial** option.

Steps to Access Help Using the How Do I Command

1. Select the **Help** menu {Alt, h}.
2. Select **How Do I** {h}.
3. Move the mouse pointer to the desired topic and click once {press the Tab key repeatedly until the desired topic is highlighted, press Enter}.

   For example, select **Save a Document.**

   Note: The WordPerfect Help window containing information on the selected topic displays (see Figure 2.4). Continue with Steps to Print a Help Topic.

Steps to Print a Help Topic

1. Display the desired help topic in the WordPerfect Help window.

   For example, the Directory Dialog Box (Save As) help topic should be displaying in the WordPerfect Help window.

2. Select the **Print** button in the WordPerfect Help window {Alt and p}.

Steps to Exit the Help Feature

1. Select the **Close** button in the WordPerfect Help and/or in the How Do I windows {Al and L *or* Alt and F4}.

Steps to Access Help Using the Contents Command

1. Select **Help, Contents** {Alt, h, c}.
2. Move the mouse pointer to the desired topic and click once {press the Tab key repeatedly to highlight the desired topic, press Enter}.

   For example, select **Keystrokes**.

3. Select **Close** to exit the WordPerfect Help window {Alt and L *or* Alt and F4}.

Steps to Access the Help Feature for a Menu Command or Dialog Box

1. Highlight the menu command desired or display the desired dialog box.

   For example, select the Open button on the Power Bar {Alt, f, o}.

   Note: The Open File dialog box displays on the screen.

2. Press **F1**.

   Note: The WordPerfect Help window explaining the Open command displays. Additional information can be obtained by selecting words that have a dotted underline or by selecting a lightbulb hint icon. Also, in some WordPerfect Help windows, a list of related topics displays at the bottom of the help information. The additional help information can be accessed by selecting words that are underlined.

3. Select **Close** {Alt and L *or* Alt and F4}.

   Note: The dialog box for the option selected displays again on the screen.

4. If desired, complete any actions necessary using the options in the dialog box or select **Cancel** {Esc} to return to the WordPerfect document window.

Steps to Access the Help: What Is? Feature

1. Press the **Shift** and **F1** keys.

   Note: A question mark is added to the mouse pointer.

2. Move the mouse pointer to the item where information is desired and click once.

For example, move the mouse pointer to the **Undo** button on the Power Bar and click once.

Note: *A WordPerfect Help window displays containing information on the Undo feature.*

3. Select **Close** to exit the WordPerfect Help window {Alt and L *or* Alt and F4}.

The Next Step

Chapter Review and Activities

Self-Check Quiz

T F 1. Once text has been selected and deleted, it is not possible to undo the deleted text.

T F 2. A file can be opened by selecting the **Open** button on the Power Bar, clicking in the Drives box and selecting the drive letter where the file disk is located, and then double-clicking on the desired filename.

T F 3. Place the insertion point to the left of a character and press the **Delete** key once to delete the character.

T F 4. The **Backspace** key is used to delete characters to the left of the insertion point.

T F 5. When text is replaced, the original characters are deleted and new characters are substituted.

6. Typeover is turned on and off by pressing the _______ key.
   a. **Home**
   b. **Up arrow**
   c. **F1**
   d. **Insert**

7. Before a document can be viewed in the Viewer window, the _____ button is selected.
   a. **Save**
   b. **Open**
   c. **Close**

8. The Help feature can be used by
   a. selecting **Help, Contents.**
   b. pressing **F1.**
   c. selecting **Help, How Do I.**
   d. all of the above.

9. State the difference between the Undo and Undelete features.

10. List the steps to save and rename a file.

Enriching Language Arts Skills

SCANS

Spelling/Vocabulary Words

commendable being of high quality; approved of.
nominated suggested appointment to some position.
negotiations the process of reaching an agreement.

Introductory (Dependent) Clauses

A comma should follow a dependent clause. (A dependent clause has both a subject and verb but cannot stand alone as a sentence.) An introductory dependent clause often begins with *if, in, when, since,* or *as.*

Example:

As you prepare your expense report, remember to use the updated gasoline rate schedule.

Activities

Activity 2.1—Open a File and Edit a Memorandum

1. If necessary, launch the WordPerfect program.
2. Open the file named **1act1.wpd** that was typed in Chapter 1, page 28. (Select the **Open** button on the Power Bar; if necessary, click in the Drives box and click on the drive letter where the file disk is located; double-click on the desired filename.)
3. Make the revisions shown.

Memorandum

To: Al Lindsay

From: Virginia ~~Ashlan~~ Paragon, CSS Director

Date: (Use current date)

Subject: Action Plan Version 5.0

The newest version of the Action Plan (Version 6.1) program is currently available.

An information bulletin is being sent to all consultants informing them that the instructional materials are now available at all our regional offices or from CSS. Old versions of

Action Plan diskettes and manual contents can be destroyed. The binders can be reused with the new material, and the diskettes can be recycled. If you have binders, please either send them to CSS or let us know the number of binders you have and we will send you the newest contents.
¶ To install Action Plan on a PC, insert Disk 1 in drive A and type A:APINSTAL at the DOS prompt.

xx

---

4. Proofread and correct any errors.
5. Use the *new* filename **2act1r** (Chapter 2, activity 1, revised) and save the revised file. (Select **File**, **Save As**; type the new filename; if necessary, click in the Drives box; select **OK**.)
6. Print one copy (select the **Print** button on the Power Bar; choose **Print**).
7. Close the document to clear the document window (select **File**, **Close**).

Activity 2.2—View and Open a File; Edit a Memorandum

1. If necessary, launch the WordPerfect program.
2. View the files on your file disk and find the memorandum from Gene Hunter that was typed in Chapter 1, pages 29–30. Open the memorandum. (Select the **Open** button on the Power Bar; if necessary, click in the Drives box and click on the drive letter where your file disk is located; click on the first filename; select **View**; if necessary, select the next filename; select **OK** to open the file.)
3. Make the revisions shown.

Interoffice Correspondence

To:	See Distribution Below	Date: (Use current date)
From:	G. ~~Gene~~ Hunter and B. Wills	Subject: Reimbursement Rates

All offices have been provided with the new fuel reimbursement rates that should be placed into effect immediately. We are requesting that Each division office will photocopy a set of the rates and forward the rate sheets to all area representatives.
¶ Also, the sales offices have been provided with the rates for all area offices under their authority. Please forward the ~~You will notice that an additional amount for the seasonal adjustment has been added to each rate.~~ rate sheets to your area operations manager.

If gasoline prices decline this fall, revised rates will be published to reflect any changes at that time.

xx (your initials)

Distribution:

S. Bentley
L. Jardine
W. Moyer
Penny McManus
Ed Salas

---

4. Proofread and correct any errors.
5. Use the *new* filename **2act2r** (Chapter 2, activity 2, revised) and save the revised file. (Select **File**, **Save As**; type the new filename; if necessary, click in the Drives box and click on the drive letter where the file disk is located; select **OK**.)
6. Print one copy (select the **Print** button on the Power Bar; choose **Print**).
7. Close the document to clear the document window (select **File**, **Close**).

Activity 2.3—Create and Edit a Memorandum

1. If necessary, launch the WordPerfect program.
2. Type the following memorandum. Use Memorandum—Style 1 (see Chapter 1, Figure 1.4).

Memorandum

To: See Distribution Below

From: D. P. Crenshaw

Date: (Use current date)

Subject: Employee Changes

Tim will end full-time employment with DPA at the end of the month. He will, however, continue working with us part-time.

Li Jean will be promoted to take over Tim's duties effective immediately.

On behalf of DPA, I want publicly to wish Tim the best of luck in his new life. By next month, we should all see one of his creations, HOW TO SURVIVE NETWORKS, in bookstores.

xx (your initials)

Distribution:

Bing Chiou
Isabel Fan
Mike Martinez
Darrell Russo

---

3. Save the file as **2act3** (Chapter 2, activity 3). (Select the **Save** button on the Power Bar; type the filename; if necessary, click in the Drives box and click on the drive letter where the file disk is located; select **OK**.)

4. Make the revisions shown.

Memorandum

To: See Distribution Below

From: ~~D.~~ Denise P. Crenshaw, Human Resources Director

Date: (Use current date)

Subject: Employee Changes

Tim will end full-time employment with DPA ~~at the end of the month~~. He will, however, continue working with us part-time.

Li Jean will be promoted to take over Tim's duties effective immediately. If you have training or graphic needs, please direct your request to Li Jean.

On behalf of DPA, I want publicly to wish Tim the best of luck in his new life. By next month, we should all see one of his creations, HOW TO SURVIVE NETWORKS, in bookstores .

¶ Tim's work at DPA contributed to our professional-looking courses and slides and to more knowledgeable coworkers on WordPerfect for Windows and PageMaker.

xx

Distribution:

Bing Chiou
Isabel Fan
Mike Martinez
Darrell Russo

---

5. Proofread and correct any errors.
6. Use the *new* filename **2act3r** (Chapter 2, activity 3, revised) and save the revised file. (Select **File, Save As**; type the new filename; if necessary, click in the Drives box and click on the drive letter where the file disk is located; select **OK.**)
7. Print one copy (select the **Print** button on the Power Bar, choose **Print**).
8. Close the document to clear the document window (select **File, Close**).

Challenge Your Skills

Skill 2.1—Create and Edit a Memorandum

1. If necessary, launch the WordPerfect program.
2. Use Memorandum—Style 1 (see Chapter 1, Figure 1.4) and the following information.
   a. Send the memorandum to All Jacobson Transport Drivers from T. D. Van Wetter. The subject of the memorandum is Vehicle Inspection.
   b. Use the current date; include your reference initials.

When delivering vehicles, it is important to inspect each vehicle thoroughly. The following are items to assist you with delivery inspections.

The floor mats will be coded. Codes are located in the trunk on a sticker, under the mat, or on the trunk lid. The codes begin with a "B." For example, B-36, B-37, etc.

Remember to submit the inspection checklists to your immediate supervisor. If you have any questions, please contact me by the end of next week at 555-6880.

---

3. Save the file; use the filename **2skill1** (Chapter 2, skill 1).
4. Use the following information to edit the memorandum:
   a. Change the T. in the From line to Theresa and add her title, Manager.
   b. Delete the last sentence in the second paragraph that begins "For example, . . ."
   c. Insert the following new paragraph between the last two paragraphs:
      The vans have fog lights. Check the fog light switch that is located on the left side of the dashboard.
   d. Change the phone number in the last paragraph to (408) 555-6999.
5. Proofread and correct any errors.
6. Use the *new* filename **2skill1r** (Chapter 2, skill 1, revised) and save the file.
7. Print one copy of the memo.

8. Close the document.

Skill 2.2—Create and Edit a Memorandum

1. If necessary, launch the WordPerfect program.
2. Use Memorandum—Style 2 (see Chapter 1, Figure 1.6) and the following information.
    a. Send the memorandum to Manuel Espinosa from J. C. Kornhaus. The subject of the memorandum is PLD Briefing.
    b. Use the current date; include your reference initials.

Thank you for your help in preparing the materials for the Jefferson County Board of Supervisors last week.

As a result of your work, our laboratory team was able to provide a well documented presentation that responded to our critics and answered the questions posed by the Supervisors. We hope to have results of the briefing before the next board meeting.

In the future, if I can be of any assistance to you, please contact me at (314) 555-6767.

---

3. Save the file; use the filename **2skill2** (Chapter 2, skill 2).
4. Use the following information to edit the memorandum:
    a. Change the subject of the memo to Preliminary Lab Data Briefing.
    b. In the first paragraph insert the words PLD Briefing before the word materials.
    c. Insert the following paragraph between the last two paragraphs:
    I deeply appreciate the extra effort you put forth to meet the many deadlines required in putting together this briefing package.
    d. Two returns after your reference initials, use the following format to indicate that a copy of the memo will be sent to another person.
    c: Jaimi Callegari, Lab Director
5. Proofread and correct any errors.
6. Use the *new* filename **2skill2r** (Chapter 2, skill 2, revised) and save the file.
7. Print one copy of the memo.
8. Close the document.

Skill 2.3—Create and Edit a Memorandum; Language Arts

1. If necessary, launch the WordPerfect program.
2. Use Memorandum—Style 2 (Chapter 1, Figure 1.6) and the following information.

a. Send the memorandum to Local 70 Shop Stewards from Jane Avery. The subject of the memo is Contract Negotiations.

b. Use the current date; include your reference initials.

c. The memo is to be distributed to the following persons (alphabetize by last name): Tamis, D.; Kerdasha, P.; Metzger, A.; DuBoce, R.; Pham, N.; Giovanette, M.; and Taslim, E.

d. Correct three spelling words and two punctuation errors. Remember to check for the spelling words and grammar rules discussed in both Chapters 1 and 2.

Negotations on a new contract are set to begin next month. In order to avoid any pitfalls we need to have a well-prepared bargaining team. Last year's bargaining team did a comendable job and worked hard to negotiate a strong, well-written contract.

A new bargaining team will be selected by secret ballot at the membership meeting next week. A list of members who have been nomminated to serve on the bargaining team is available at the Union Hall.

Also a form requesting ideas on the contract issues to be negotiated can be picked up at the Union Hall. Some of the areas open for negotiation are: wages, eligibility for retirement benefits, medical benefits, conference reimbursements, and working conditions.

---

3. Save the file; use the filename **2skill3** (Chapter 2, skill 3).

4. Use the following information to edit the memorandum:

   a. Delete the second sentence of the first paragraph.

   b. Insert the following sentence at the end of the second paragraph:

      If desired, members can drop by and pick up the list before the meeting.

   c. Insert the following new paragraph after the last paragraph:

      Please remind union members at your location of the upcoming membership meeting. If a union member cannot be present, contact George Nazzaro for proxy forms. Let me know if I can be of further assistance.

5. Proofread and correct any errors.

6. Use the *new* filename **2skill3r** (Chapter 2, skill 3, revised) and save the file.

7. Print one copy and close the document.

8. If you have completed your work, exit WordPerfect (select **File**, **Exit**).

CHAPTER 3

Create Business Letters

Features Covered

- Use the automatic date feature
- Change justification
- Use bold, underline, and italic text attributes
- Change margins
- Change fonts
- Use Speller
- Use Page Zoom Full view

Objectives and Introduction

After successfully completing this chapter, you will be able to use the automatic date feature, change justification, use text attributes such as bold, italic, and underline, and change margins to create business letters. Convenient WordPerfect features such as fonts, Speller, and Page Zoom Full view are often used in preparing business letters.

Business Letters

A letter is formal written communication used to convey information from one business to another or from one individual to another. Business letters are one of the most important types of written communications.

Traditionally, letters have followed one of two styles: a modified block or block style. With the development of word processing machines and programs, the block style has become the most frequently used letter style. With the block style, all lines of the letter begin at the left margin (see Figure 3.1).

Another style of letter that is now being used is the AMS (Administrative Management Society) letter simplified style. The AMS simplified style omits the salutation and complimentary closing. A subject line and the typewritten signature are

FIGURE 3.1

Traditional style letter

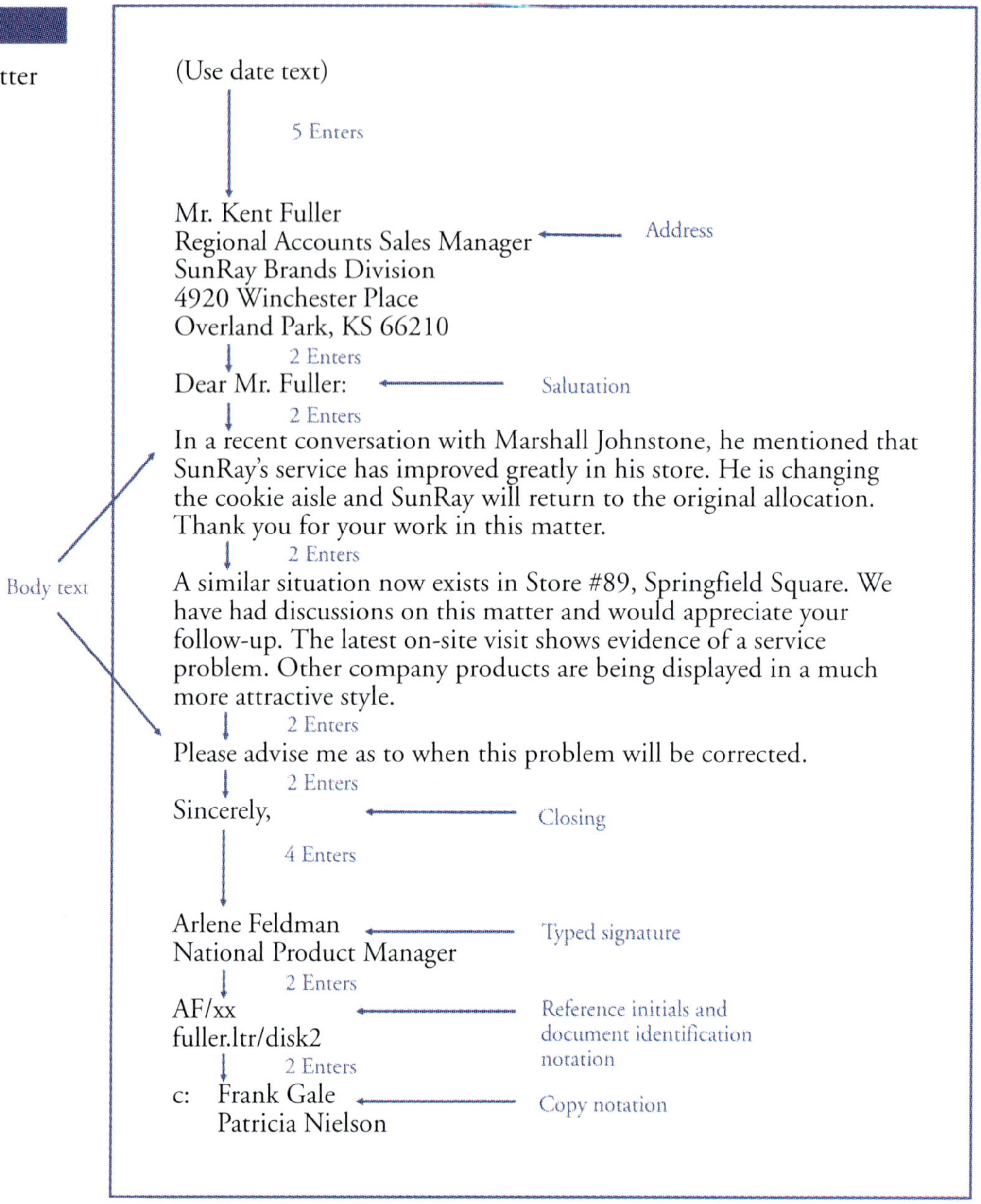
(Use date text)

Mr. Kent Fuller
Regional Accounts Sales Manager
SunRay Brands Division
4920 Winchester Place
Overland Park, KS 66210

Dear Mr. Fuller:

In a recent conversation with Marshall Johnstone, he mentioned that SunRay's service has improved greatly in his store. He is changing the cookie aisle and SunRay will return to the original allocation. Thank you for your work in this matter.

A similar situation now exists in Store #89, Springfield Square. We have had discussions on this matter and would appreciate your follow-up. The latest on-site visit shows evidence of a service problem. Other company products are being displayed in a much more attractive style.

Please advise me as to when this problem will be corrected.

Sincerely,

Arlene Feldman
National Product Manager

AF/xx
fuller.ltr/disk2

c: Frank Gale
Patricia Nielson

typed in uppercase letters. Like the traditional block style, all lines of the letter begin at the left margin (blocked). See Figure 3.2.

At the bottom of a letter the following information may be included:

- ☐ The author's initials in capital letters and the typist's initials in lowercase letters, e.g., AF/xx (the x's indicate where you type your initials).
- ☐ A document identification notation showing the filename and location of the document, e.g., fuller.ltr/disk2.
- ☐ If a photocopy of the letter is to be sent to another person(s), a copy notation is typed. Generally a photocopy is indicated by a lowercase "**c**" followed by a colon (c:). Press the **Tab** key once and type the name; press **Enter**.

  Note: *Always press the* ***Tab*** *key before each listed name; otherwise the names may not align when fonts are changed.*

FIGURE 3.2

AMS simplified style letter

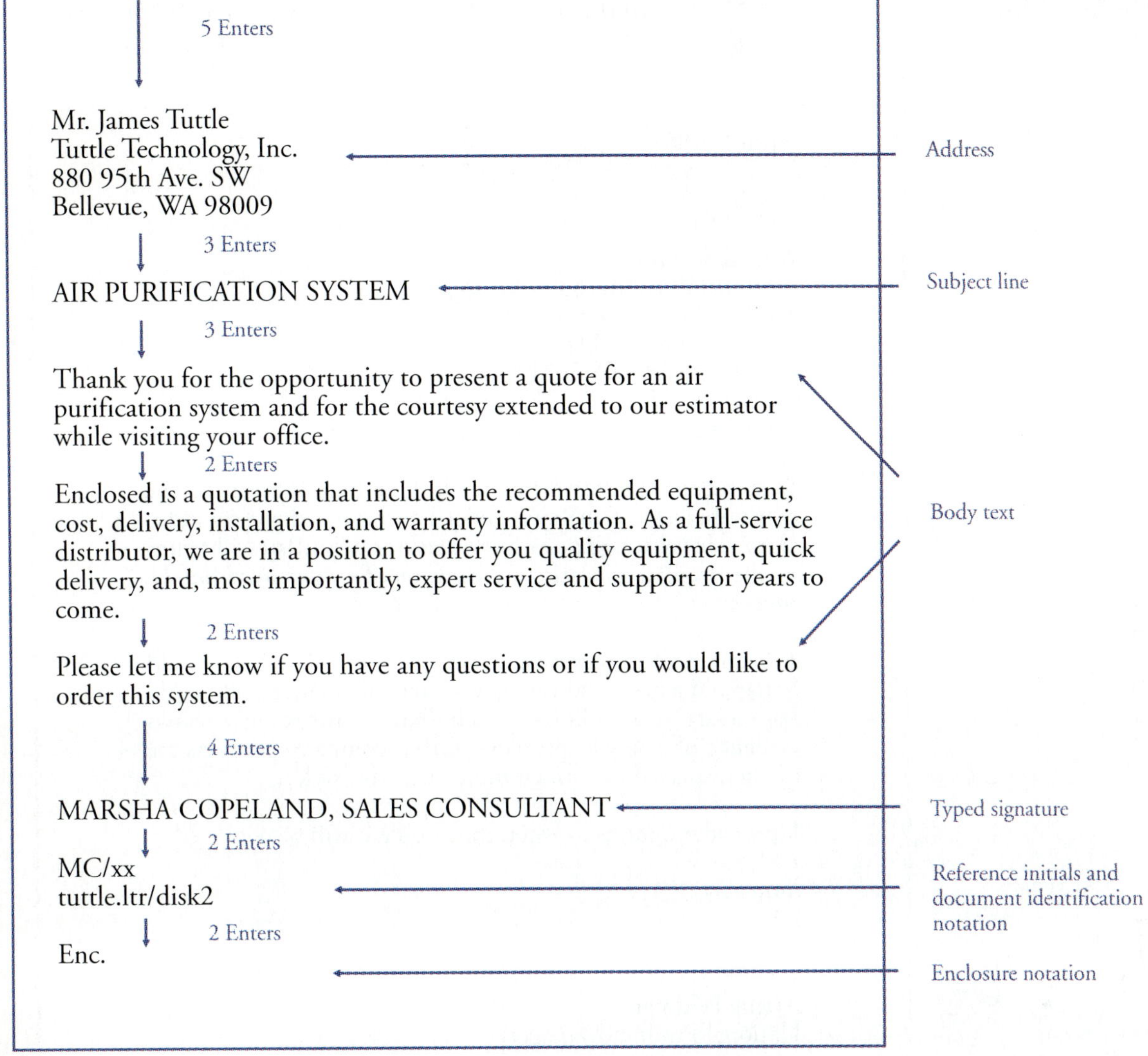
February 3, 199x

5 Enters

Mr. James Tuttle
Tuttle Technology, Inc.
880 95th Ave. SW
Bellevue, WA 98009

3 Enters

AIR PURIFICATION SYSTEM

3 Enters

Thank you for the opportunity to present a quote for an air purification system and for the courtesy extended to our estimator while visiting your office.

2 Enters

Enclosed is a quotation that includes the recommended equipment, cost, delivery, installation, and warranty information. As a full-service distributor, we are in a position to offer you quality equipment, quick delivery, and, most importantly, expert service and support for years to come.

2 Enters

Please let me know if you have any questions or if you would like to order this system.

4 Enters

MARSHA COPELAND, SALES CONSULTANT

2 Enters

MC/xx
tuttle.ltr/disk2

2 Enters

Enc.

☐ If the letter contains a statement that an item(s) is being enclosed, type an enclosure notation two **Enters** below the document identification notation or two **Enters** below a copy notation, e.g., type **Enc.**

After a business letter has been typed, formatted, reviewed, and proofread, a final copy is printed. A final letter is customarily printed on letterhead stationery. The letterhead information usually includes the company name, address, phone number, and fax number. Typically, the letterhead information is preprinted on company stationery. Today, however, many individuals who use word processing and desktop publishing programs create their own letterheads. In Chapter 13, a letterhead will be created. A letter printed on company letterhead in final form will look similar to Figure 3.3.

FIGURE 3.3

Traditional style letter printed on letterhead

SunRay Industries
580 Deharo Street, San Francisco, CA 94107
(415) 555-8303 FAX (415) 555-8318

April 2, 199x

Mr. Kent Fuller
Regional Accounts Sales Manager
SunRay Brands Division
4920 Winchester Place
Overland Park, KS 66210

Dear Mr. Fuller:

In a recent conversation with Marshall Johnstone, he mentioned that **SunRay's** service has improved greatly in his store. He is changing the cookie aisle and **SunRay** will return to the original allocation. ***Thank you for your work in this matter.***

A similar situation now exists in Store #89, Springfield Square. We have had discussions on this matter and would appreciate your follow-up. The latest on-site visit shows evidence of a service problem. Other company products are being displayed in a much more attractive style.

Please advise me as to when this problem will be corrected.

Sincerely,

Arlene Feldman
National Product Manager

AF/xx
fuller.ltr/disk2

c: Frank Gale
Patricia Nielson

Automatic Date Feature

WordPerfect provides two methods for automatically inserting the current date into a document: **Date Text** and **Date Code**. In order for the date to be inserted by WordPerfect, the current date must be stored in the computer's memory.

When **Insert, Date, Date Text** is selected, the current date is placed in the document by WordPerfect. If the document is opened on a different day, the date will not change unless edited manually. The current date can also be inserted into a document by selecting the **Date Text** button on the Button Bar.

When **Insert**, **Date**, **Date Code** is selected, a special code is inserted by WordPerfect. If the document is opened on a later date, the date is automatically changed to the current date.

Different formats for the current date can be inserted by selecting **Insert**, **Date**, **Date Format** and choosing a desired date format option in the Date Format dialog box. For example, the day can be printed followed by the month and year (2 May 1994).

Start-Up Instructions

- An empty document window should be displayed on the screen.

Steps to Use the Date Text Feature

1. Select the Date Text button on the Button Bar {Alt, i, d, t *or* Ctrl and d}.

   Note: *The current date is inserted at the location of the insertion point. If necessary, the date can be changed by the user.*

Finish-Up Instructions

- Type the traditional block style letter shown in Figure 3.1 on page 52 using the spacing shown. Use wordwrap to type the body text paragraphs of the letter.
- After typing the letter, use the filename **3drill1** and save the file (select the **Save** button on the Power Bar; type the filename; if necessary, click in the Drives box and click on the drive letter where the file disk is located; select **OK**).

Justification

The term *justification* in WordPerfect is used to describe the alignment of text in relation to the left and right margins. The five different types of justification are Left, Right, Center, Full, and All. (See Figure 3.4.) With Left justification, text is aligned at the left margin and is not aligned at the right margin (ragged right). Left justification is the default setting for WordPerfect 6.0. Right justification is the opposite of Left justification, i.e., text is aligned at the right margin and not at the left margin (ragged left). Center justification aligns text so that an equal amount of blank space displays left and right of the centered text. Full justification adjusts lines to begin and end exactly at the left and right margins. The All option is used to evenly space letters of a title or heading between the left and right margins.

When justification is changed, a code is inserted at the beginning of the paragraph where the insertion point is located. The selected justification remains in effect from that location forward in the document or until a different justification is chosen.

In addition to the Right justification type, WordPerfect provides a Flush Right alignment feature for aligning text at the right margin. The Flush Right alignment feature is used to right align a single line or a portion of a line. However, in WordPerfect, the Right justification type is used to right align multiple lines.

The Center alignment (see Chapter 1) and the Center justification are the two types of horizontal centering provided by WordPerfect. When the Center alignment command is used before text is typed, the line is centered and the insertion point returns to the left margin after the Enter key is pressed. The code displayed in Reveal

FIGURE 3.4

The five types of justification

This is an example of Left justification. The text is aligned at the left margin.	This is an example of Right justification. The text is aligned at the right margin.	This is an example of Center justification. An equal amount of blank space displays on the left and right of the centered text.
This is an example of Full justification. Text begins and ends exactly at the left and right margin, except for the last line of the paragraph.	The All justification option is used to evenly space letters between the left and right margins including short lines. This is used for titles and headings, e.g., W o r d P e r f e c t .	

Codes for Center alignment is *Hd Center on Marg.* However, if a group of lines is selected (and no codes or text follow) and the Center alignment command is used, the insertion point remains in the center of the document window.

When the Center justification command is used before text is typed, the line(s) is centered and after the Enter key is pressed the insertion point remains in the center of the document screen. However, if text is selected, only the blocked lines are centered. The expanded code *Just:Center* displays in Reveal Codes.

With Full justification, additional spaces are placed between words in order to align the text at both the left and right margins. The extra spaces between words may make the text difficult to read and may be visually unattractive. Therefore, Left justification is used for most business correspondence and Full justification may be used for documents such as books.

The All option places additional space between words and between letters in words and is useful when creating a heading for a newsletter (see Chapter 13). Also, the All justification option fully justifies the last line in a paragraph.

Start-Up Instructions

- The file named **3drill1.wpd** should be displayed in the document window.

Steps to Change Justification

1. The insertion point should be located where the justification is to be changed.

   For example, place the insertion point at the beginning of the document (**Ctrl** and **Home**).

2. Move the mouse pointer to the **Justification** button on the Power Bar. Press and hold the left mouse button {Alt, L, L, j}.

   Note: A drop-down list of justification choices displays.

3. Move the mouse pointer to highlight the desired justification type.

   For example, highlight **Full** {f}.

4. Release the mouse button.

Finish-Up Instructions

- Use the *new* filename **3drill1.ful** and save the file on your file disk (select **File, Save As**; type the filename; if necessary, click in the Drives box and click on the drive letter where the file disk is located; select **OK**).
- Print one copy (select the **Print** button on the Power Bar; choose **Print**).

Text Attributes

Emphasis can be added to text by using text attributes such as bold, underline, and italic. Text attributes can be set in the Font dialog box by selecting the desired attribute(s) in the Appearance box. In addition, text attributes can be set by using the **Bold**, **Underline**, and **Italic** options on the Power Bar. More than one text attribute can be applied to the same text characters, e.g., **bold and underline**.

The bold text attribute prints words darker on the page as compared to other printed words. Text to be printed in bold will be displayed darker than the other characters on the screen. When bold is selected, WordPerfect inserts a bold code on each side of the text. Display Reveal Codes to view the bold codes.

Words are underlined in printed text to show emphasis. Once the text to be underlined is selected and the underline feature is used, the text displays underlined in the document window. Traditionally, underlining was used in the place of italic because many typewriters were unable to create italic text. Since most printers now support italic, the trend is to replace underline with italic or bold to add emphasis.

The italic text attribute prints text somewhat slanted to the right. However, there are some dot matrix printers that do not print italicized text. Once the text to be italicized is selected and the italic attribute is applied, the text displays slightly slanted on the screen.

Start-Up Instructions

- The file named **3drill1.ful** should be displayed in the document window.

Steps to Bold Text

1. Select the text to be printed in bold (see Chapter 2, page 35 for information on selecting text).

   For example, select **SunRay's** in the first sentence of the letter.

2. Select the **Bold** button on the Power Bar {Ctrl and b}.

Steps to Underline Text

1. Select the text to be underlined (see Chapter 2, page 35 for information on selecting text).

   For example, select **Store #89, Springfield Square** in the first sentence of the second paragraph.

2. Select the **Underline** button on the Power Bar {Ctrl and u}.

Steps to Italicize Text

1. Select the text to be italicized (see Chapter 2, page 35) for information on selecting text).

   For example, select the final sentence of the first paragraph.

2. Select the Italic button [I] on the Power Bar {Ctrl and i}.

Finish-Up Instructions

- Select the word SunRay in the second sentence of the first paragraph and bold the text.
- Select the final sentence in the first paragraph and bold the text. This sentence will be both bold and italic.
- Use the *new* filename **3drill1.txt** and save the file on your file disk (select **File, Save As**; type the new filename; if necessary, click in the Drives box and click on the drive letter where the file disk is located; select **OK**).

  Note: *The following Steps to Remove Bold, Underline, or Italic Text Attributes are for your information.*

Steps to Remove Bold, Underline, or Italic Text Attributes

1. Select the desired text.
2. Select the Bold, Underline, or Italic buttons on the Power Bar {Ctrl and b, Ctrl and u, *or* Ctrl and i}.

Change Margins

Generally, WordPerfect's default (preset) margins are used to print a final letter. If a letter is unusually short or long, however, it may be desirable to change the document's margins. Margins can be changed in the Margins dialog box or by using the Ruler Bar (see Chapter 7, page 158).

The top and bottom margins are preset to 1 inch. Using a standard size 8½ x 11-inch paper and a combined top and bottom margin of 2 inches, 9 inches remain for typed lines on a page. Depending on the information preprinted in a letterhead, the top margin can vary between 2 and 2½ inches. The bottom margin on an average length letter generally remains unchanged. The left and right document margins are preset for 1 inch. With these settings, 6.5 inches are available across the page.

When the margins are changed, codes display in the Reveal Codes window for each changed margin, for example, *Lft Mar, Rgt Mar, Top Mar.* When a margin code is highlighted in Reveal Codes, the code is expanded to show the margin measurement, e.g., *Lft Mar:1.5".*

Once the margins have been changed, the new margins remain effective from that location forward in the document or until different margins are selected. Therefore, if the margins are to be effective for the entire document, the insertion point should be located at the beginning of the document before the margins are changed.

The margins can be changed in the document at any time, i.e., before or after the document is typed. Changing the margins is best accomplished after the document is completed, because a decision can more easily be made as to whether margins should be changed depending on the length of the document. After typing a document, estimate the desired placement of the document. A letter should be printed on the page with the space around the edges of the letter evenly balanced.

The number of words in the letter body text and the depth of the letterhead are used to make decisions regarding margin changes. The following are some suggested margin settings for letters:

	Top Margin	Left and Right Margins
Short letter (under 100 words*)	2.5"	2.0"
Average letter (100–200 words)	2.0"	1.5"
Long letter (over 200 words)	1.75"	1.0"

*See Document Information in Chapter 9.

Before printing the final letter, preview the entire document on the screen by selecting the **Page Zoom Full** button on the Power Bar (see Page Zoom View later in this chapter).

Start-Up Instructions

- The file named **3drill1.txt** should be displayed in the document window, or type the letter shown in Figure 3.1.
- The insertion point must be located at the top of the document.

Steps to Change Margins

1. Place the insertion point at the location in the document where the margin change is to take effect.

   For example, locate the insertion point at the top of the document (**Ctrl** and **Home**).

2. Select **Layout, Margins** {Alt, L, m *or* Ctrl and F8}.

   Note: *The Margins dialog box displays.*

3. *To change the left margin,* move the mouse pointer to the box located beside the word **Left**; double-click to highlight the measurement and type the desired margin in inches {Alt and L, type desired margin, press Enter}.

   For example, type **1.5**. (Do not type the last period.)

   Note: *With the margin amount displayed in the measurement box highlighted, the new amount is typed, automatically replacing the existing figure(s). If the insertion point displays in the measurement amount box and the amount is not highlighted, the original amount must be deleted and the new amount typed. Typing the final zero and the quotation mark is not necessary.*

FIGURE 3.5

Margins dialog box

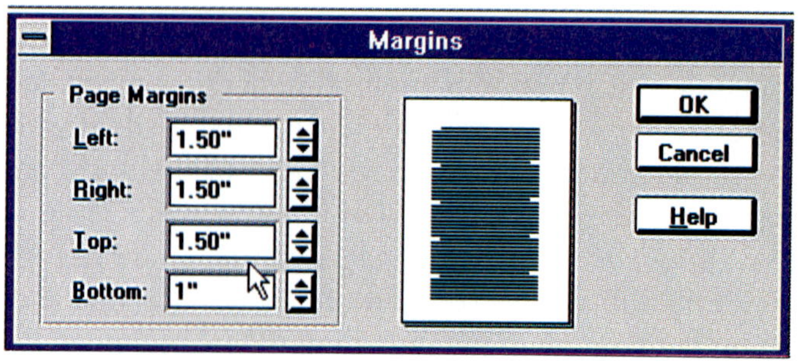

To change the right margin, move the mouse pointer to the box located beside the word **Right**, double-click to highlight the measurement, and type the desired margin in inches {Alt and r, type desired margin, press Enter}.

For example, type **1.5**. (Do not type the last period.)

To change the top margin, move the mouse pointer to the box located beside the word **Top**, double-click to highlight the measurement, and type the desired margin in inches {Alt and t, type desired margin, press Enter}. (See Figure 3.5.)

For example, type **1.5**. (Do not type the last period.)

To change the bottom margin, move the mouse pointer to the box located beside the word **Bottom**, double-click to highlight the measurement, and type the desired margin in inches {Alt and b, type desired margin, press Enter}.

For example, check that the default margin of 1" displays.

4. Select **OK** to accept the new margin settings {press Enter twice}.

Finish-Up Instructions

- Use the *new* filename **3drill1.mar** and save the file on your file disk (select **File**, **Save As**; type the filename; if necessary, click in the Drives box and click on the drive letter where the file disk is located; select **OK**).
- Print one copy (select the **Print** button on the Power Bar; choose **Print**).

Font Changes

By using a variety of typefaces (fonts) and sizes, the appearance of letters, reports, résumés, or other business documents can be enhanced. A typeface is a specific design of type (shape), such as Arial or Times New Roman. A font includes all the letters, numbers, symbols, and punctuation marks for a given typeface in one size and style. For example, Arial 14-point bold is one font and Times New Roman 10-point italic is another font.

Each printer has one or more built-in fonts. Many built-in fonts, such as Courier, are monospaced and fixed-pitch (i.e., each character is allocated the same amount of horizontal space).

WordPerfect provides additional fonts that can be used with any printer that can print graphics (if necessary, see your instructor). The fonts provided by WordPerfect, such as Arrus BT and Humanst521 Lt BT, are proportional and scalable (i.e., the horizontal space allocated for each character varies based on the width of the character and the characters can be printed in almost any size).

These scalable/proportional fonts are measured in points. There are approximately 72 points in an inch. A 24-point character is approximately one-quarter of an inch tall. A ruler at the back of this book shows the letter "E" in various point sizes and can be used to assist you in determining appropriate point sizes to use in different documents. Generally, a 10- to 12-point font is used for the text of business letters, memorandums, and reports.

Traditionally when using a typewriter with monospaced fonts, the Spacebar was pressed twice after a final punctuation mark. When using proportional spaced fonts, the Spacebar is pressed only once after a final punctuation mark, because a single space is sufficient to visually separate sentences.

Font characteristics such as font name, font size, and appearance (bold, underline, italics) can be changed by selecting the **Font** option on the Layout menu. In addition, the font can be changed by selecting the **Font Face** button on the Power Bar; the font size can be changed by selecting the **Font Size** button on the Power Bar; and the appearance of text can be changed by selecting the **Bold**, **Underline**, or **Italic** buttons on the Power Bar. When the **Font Face** button is selected, the last four fonts used are displayed at the top of the Font Face list.

The font change is effective from the location of the insertion point forward in the document or until another font is selected. However, if text is selected and the font is changed, the new font will be in effect for the selected text only. Font codes can be viewed in the Reveal Codes window.

Start-Up Instructions

- The file named **3drill1.mar** should be displayed in the document window.

Steps to Change Font Name, Size, and/or Appearance

Note: Changing fonts is most effectively accomplished using a mouse. Therefore, keystrokes have not been included with the following steps.

1. Place the insertion point at the location where the font change is to begin or select the text to be affected.

   For example, place the insertion point at the top of the document.

2. Move the mouse pointer to the Font Face button FFF on the Power Bar and click once.

   Note: A list of available fonts displays.

3. Move the mouse pointer to the desired font name and click once.

   For example, select **Arrus BT** or **make a decision of your own**.

   Note: The text has been changed to display the new font. Use Reveal Codes (Alt and F3) to view the font code.

To Change the Font Size and Appearance for Selected Text Only

4. Select the text for which the font is to be changed.

   For example, select the document notation (**fuller.ltr/disk2**).

5. Select **Layout, Font.**

   Note: The Font dialog box displays containing font names, font sizes, and text appearance.

6. Move the mouse pointer to the desired font size and click once.

   For example, select **10** in the Size box or **make a decision of your own**.

7. Move the mouse pointer to the desired text attribute in the Appearance box and click once.

   For example, select **Italic**.

   Note: WordPerfect displays a sample of the chosen font name, size, and appearance in the Resulting Font box located below the font list. The displayed sample is only an approximate size and style.

8. Select **OK** {press Enter}.

To Change Font Size Only

9. Move the insertion pointer to the location where the new font size is to take effect or select the text to be affected.

   For example, move the insertion point to the left of the **c** in the copy notation.

10. Move the mouse pointer to the **Font Size** button on the Power Bar and click once.

11. Move the mouse pointer to the desired size and click once.

    For example, select **10**.

Finish-Up Instructions

- A final letter printed on letterhead is shown in Figure 3.3.
- Use the *new* filename **3drill1.fon** and save the file on your file disk (select **File, Save As**; type the new filename; if necessary, click in the Drives box and click on the drive where the file disk is located; select **OK**).
- Print one copy (select the **Print** button on the Power Bar; select **Print**).
- Close the document (select **File, Close**).

The Speller

The Speller is a WordPerfect feature that checks the spelling of each word and identifies duplicate words and irregular capitalization in a document. When a word is found that is not in one of WordPerfect's dictionaries, a list of words similar to the unrecognized word is displayed on the screen. If the correctly spelled word is displayed in the list of words, it can be selected. If the correctly spelled word is not displayed in the list, the word can be added to one of the WordPerfect dictionaries.

WordPerfect has two types of dictionaries: a main dictionary and supplemental dictionaries. The main dictionary is used to check the spelling of words for all documents. Supplemental dictionaries are created by individual users of WordPerfect and contain terms that an individual uses frequently. For example, a medical secretary might create a supplemental dictionary that contains medical terms. An unlimited number of supplemental dictionaries can be created.

If an entire document is to be checked for spelling accuracy, the insertion point can be located anywhere in the document. If only part of the document or a single word is to be checked, the desired portion of the document or the individual word is selected.

If the same word is typed twice, the Speller will identify the duplicated word. The duplicated word can be removed by selecting **Replace**. To leave both occurrences of the duplicated word, **Skip Once** is selected.

The Speller will also identify words that contain irregular capitalization, such as tHe or THe. When a word with irregular capitalization is identified, the Speller suggests that the word be changed to all uppercase letters, all lowercase letters, or initial capital, e.g., THE, the, or The.

Not all errors in a document are discovered by the spelling command. For example, words easily misspelled or mistyped, such as there/their, form/from, she/he, are not identified as incorrect words. Therefore, once the document is checked for spelling, it should also be carefully proofread for accurate meaning.

Start-Up Instructions

Note: The icon indicates that the data (text) is available on disk. The data disk is supplied to your instructor.

- Open the file named **3drill2.wpd** which is located on the data disk (select the **Open** button on the Power Bar; if necessary, click in the Drives box and click on the drive where the data disk is located; double-click on the filename).
- Use the following steps and spell-check the file named **3drill2.wpd**. After using the Speller, be sure to proofread the document.

Steps to Use the Speller

1. Select the Speller button on the Power Bar {Alt, t, s *or* Ctrl and F1}.

   Note: The Speller dialog box displays. The name of the document to be reviewed displays in the Title bar of the dialog box.

2. Select Start to begin the spell check {press Enter}.

   *Note: The first unrecognized word is highlighted in the document and displays to the right of the words "Not found" in the Speller dialog box (see Figure 3.6). WordPerfect displays the word that most closely matches the spelling of the unrecognized word in the **Replace With** box and the word is highlighted at the top of the list of suggested words.*

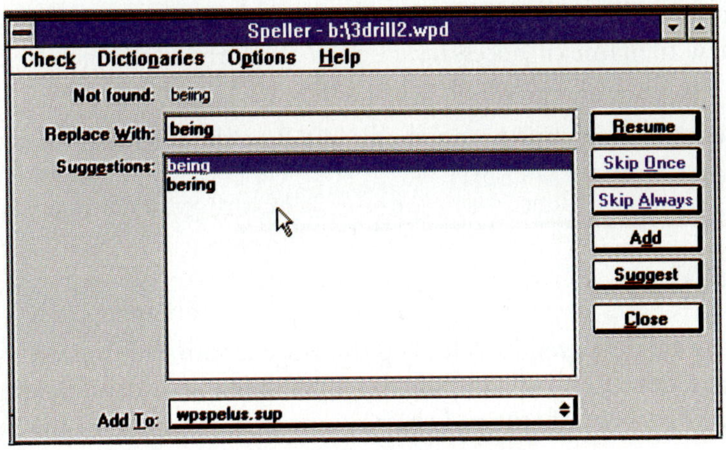

FIGURE 3.6
Speller dialog box

3. *To accept the highlighted word,* select **Replace** {Alt and r}. If desired, another word in the list of suggestions can be highlighted.

For example, select **Replace** to accept the suggested word "being."

If the correctly spelled word is shown in the list of suggestions, select the suggested word and select **Replace** {press the down arrow key to highlight the word, r}. The identified word is corrected on the screen and the spell check continues.

4. *To delete one occurrence of a duplicated word,* select **Replace** {Alt and r}.

For example, select **Replace** to delete one occurrence of the word "of."

To retain both occurrences of a duplicated word, select **Skip Once** {Alt and o}.

5. T*o correct irregular capitalization,* select the desired suggestion and choose **Replace** {Alt and r}.

For example, "and" should display in the Replace With box. Select **Replace.**

6. If the correct spelling of a word is not on the list, other options can be selected.

   a. Select **Skip Once** to skip the current instance of the word {Alt and o}.

   For example, select **Skip Once** to skip the reference initial "PJM" and continue with the spell check. Select **Skip Once** to skip the document name and file location.

   b. Select **Skip Always** to ignore the word throughout the remainder of the document {Alt and a}.

   c. Select **Add** to add the word to a WordPerfect supplemental dictionary {Alt and d}. The word will be added to the default supplemental dictionary. *To choose a different supplemental dictionary,* choose **Add to** and select the desired dictionary {Alt and t}.

   d. Click in the Replace With box and type the correct word in the document. Select **Replace** {Alt and w, type the correction, Enter}.

   Note: *To discontinue the Speller before completion, select* ***Close*** *{Alt and c}.*

7. When the entire document has been checked, the message "Spell-check completed. Close Speller?" displays. Select **Yes** {press Enter}.

Finish-Up Instructions

- Use the *new* filename **3drill2.spe** and save the file on your file disk (select **File, Save As**; type the new filename; if necessary, click in the Drives box and click on the drive where the file disk is located; select **OK**).
- Print one copy (select the **Print** button on the Power Bar; choose **Print**).

Page Zoom Full View

A full document page can be displayed by selecting the **Page Zoom Full** button on the Power Bar. Using Page Zoom Full view to display a document assists in making decisions concerning the alignment of text and the amount of blank space in the mar-

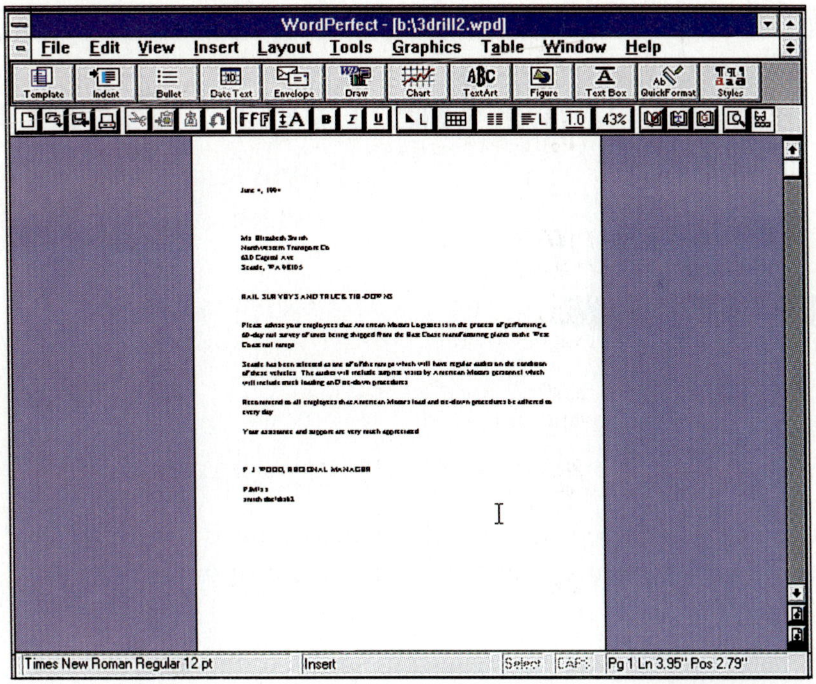

FIGURE 3.7

Page Zoom Full view

gins. When the Page Zoom Full button is selected a second time, the view returns to the original view size. Other zoom views can be selected by choosing the **Zoom** button on the Power Bar and choosing the desired view (see Steps to Use Zoom Feature, Chapter 14, page 337).

Start-Up Instructions

- A mouse must be used to complete the following steps.
- The file named **3drill2.spe** should be displayed in the document window.

Steps to Use Page Zoom Full View

1. Select the Page Zoom Full button on the Power Bar.

   Note: The entire document page displays on the screen. (see Figure 3.7).

2. To exit Page Zoom Full view, select the **Page Zoom Full** button again.

Start-Up Instructions

- Optional. Type the AMS simplified style letter shown in Figure 3.2. Use the Speller to review the document for spelling errors. After using the Speller, be sure to proofread the document. Use the filename **3drill3** and save the file.
- Print one copy (select the **Print** button on the Power Bar; choose **Print**).
- Close the document (select **File**, **Close**).

The Next Step

Chapter Review and Activities

Self-Check Quiz

T F 1. Once a font change is made for selected text, the changed font is effective from the location of the insertion point forward in the document or until another font is selected.

T F 2. When using the Speller, you can correct a word that is not found in any of the WordPerfect dictionaries.

T F 3. The document identification notation is typed above the reference initials.

T F 4. In the traditional letter style, the **Enter** key is pressed four times after typing the last paragraph.

5. The ______ button is selected to view an entire page in the document window.
   a. **Open**
   b. **Page Zoom Full**
   c. **Print**

6. WordPerfect's default margins are
   a. 1" top and bottom; 1.25" left and right.
   b. 1" left and right; 1.25" top and bottom.
   c. 1" left, right, top and bottom.

7. The current date can be placed in a document by selecting the ______
   a. **Date Text** button on the Power Bar.
   b. **Date Code** button on the Button Bar.
   c. **Date Text** button on the Button Bar.

8. List the top, left, and right margins that are suggested for an average letter (100–200 words).

9. List the five different types of justification.

10. Explain the difference between Right justification and the Flush Right alignment feature.

Enriching Language Arts Skills

Spelling/Vocabulary Words

telecommunications electronic transfer of information between two locations.

tailored made to fit a specific need.

existence having presence; being; having life.

description a verbal or written explanation.

Appositives

Appositives are words that immediately follow a noun and further identify the noun but usually are not necessary to the meaning of the sentence. Appositives are set off by commas.

Example:

Ester Tam, a copyeditor for eight years, will be our new senior editor.

Activities

Activity 3.1—Create a Traditional Style Letter; Use the Bold Text Attribute

1. Type the following letter using the traditional style letter (see Figure 3.1 on page 52).

(Use date text)

Hugh and Mary Ellis
752 Cherry Rd.
Newport News, VA 23602

Dear Mr. and Mrs. Ellis:

During the last six months, you have visited Horizon Estates on the Chesapeake Bay. You have experienced the panoramic views and the quiet country setting. And you have seen the large, family-oriented floor plans.

Now we have some exciting news! Horizon Estates is releasing seven new homes for sale. We invite you to revisit our sales office to choose from the home sites now available.

The moment you have been waiting for is NOW! It is time to own your own home at Horizon Estates.

Cordially,

Angela H. Santos
Sales Manager

AHS/xx
ellis.ltr/d1

---

2. Bold each occurrence of the words "Horizon Estates" (select the text; select the **Bold** button on the Power Bar).
3. Save the file on your file disk; use the filename **3act1** (Chapter 3, activity 1). (Select the **Save** button on the Power Bar; type the filename; if necessary, click in the Drives box and click on the drive letter where the file disk is located; select **OK**.)
4. Print one copy (select the **Print** button on the Power Bar; choose **Print**).
5. Close the document (select **File**, **Close**).

Activity 3.2—Create a Traditional Style Letter; Use Full Justification; Change Margins and Font

1. Type the following letter using the traditional style letter (see Figure 3.1 on page 52).

(Use date text)

Ms. Marcy Flores
Manager, Systems and Processing
Turtle Markets
850 W. Natanes Rd.
Phoenix, AZ 85017-4168

Dear Marcy:

Thank you for taking the time to speak with me yesterday. Please find enclosed a copy of our 8.1 Migration Seminar brochure.

As we discussed, Syncon Business Consulting will be holding Migration Seminars at the end of next month. I highly recommend that one of your team members plan to attend the Los Angeles seminar.

If SBC can be of any other service to Turtle Markets, please do not hesitate to give us a call.

Regards,

Louis Noble
Operations Manager

LN/xx
flores.ltr/d2

c: M. T. Silverman

Enc.

---

2. Change the left, right, and top margins to 1.5" (place the insertion point at the beginning of the document; select **Layout**, **Margins**; type the desired margins; select **OK**).
3. Change to **Full** justification (move the mouse pointer to the **Justification** button on the Power Bar; press and hold the mouse button; move the mouse pointer to **Full**; release the mouse button).
4. Change the font to **BernhardtMod BT** or make a choice of your own (with the insertion point located at the top of the document, select the **Font Face** button on the Power Bar; move the mouse pointer to **BernhardtMod BT**; click once).
5. Save the file on your file disk; use the filename **3act2** (Chapter 3, activity 2). (Select the **Save** button on the Power Bar; type the filename; if necessary, click in the Drives box and click on the drive letter where the file disk is located; select **OK**.)
6. Print one copy (select the **Print** button on the Power Bar; choose **Print**).
7. Close the document (select **File**, **Close**).

Activity 3.3—Create an AMS Simplified Style Letter; Use Bold and Italic; Change Margins and Font Size; Use Speller and Page Zoom Full View

1. Type the following letter using the AMS simplified style letter (see Figure 3.2 on page 53). Use the bold and italic text attributes as shown.

(Use date text)

Mr. Dennis Eaton
2295 Miranda Place
Alamo, CA 94507

SPRING MEMBERSHIP PROMOTION

As you are well aware, in the past year *Diablo Fitness Center* has made a great deal of progress in managing, rebuilding, and improving its facility and equipment.

With our spring membership promotion, you will receive **FREE** a beautiful, deluxe bathrobe and three months added to your present membership, compliments of *Diablo Fitness Center.* All you have to do is introduce two new members to the club during the next two months.

We are looking forward to your participation in this program!

MARIZE LOCKE, PRESIDENT

ML/xx
eaton.ltr/disk3

---

2. Change the left and right margins to **2"** and the top margin to **1.75"** (place the insertion point at the beginning of the document; select **Layout, Margins**; type the desired margins; select **OK**).
3. Select the words "SPRING MEMBERSHIP PROMOTION" and change the font size to **14** point (select the **Font Size** button on the Power Bar; move the mouse pointer to **14;** click once).
4. Use the Speller to find and correct misspelled words. (Select the **Speller** button on the Power Bar; select **Start**. When the spell check is complete, select **Yes** to close the Speller.)
5. Use the Page Zoom Full view to display the entire document in the document window (select the **Page Zoom Full** button on the Power Bar; select the **Page Zoom Full** button again to return to normal view).
6. Save the file on your file disk; use the filename **3act3** (Chapter 3, activity 3). (Select the **Save** button on the Button Bar; type the filename; if necessary, click in the Drives box and click on the drive letter where the file disk is located; select **OK**.)
7. Print one copy (select the **Print** button on the Power Bar; choose **Print**).

8. Close the document (select **File**, **Close**).

Challenge Your Skills

Skill 3.1—Create and Edit a Traditional Style Letter

1. Use the traditional style letter and the following information.
   a. Use the current date.
   b. Send the letter to Mrs. Consuelo Sundheimer, 80 Patriot Place, Apt. #5, Downers Grove, IL 60515.
   c. Use Dear Mrs. Sundheimer for the salutation.
   d. Use an appropriate complimentary closing.
   e. The letter is from Debby Reiter, M.D.
   f. Include your reference initials and document identification notation.
   g. Make decisions regarding:
      Justification
      Margins
      Fonts
      Use of bold, italic, and underline text attributes
   h. The letter body text follows:

      At the end of the month, I will be leaving the Lincoln Medical Group in order to enter private practice in Des Plaines, Illinois.

      Our records indicate that you or a member of your family has been seen by me during the past year. Hopefully, you will not be inconvenienced by a change in physicians. I would like to assist you with the transition to a new health care provider.

      Your health is important to me, and Lincoln Medical is committed to assuring you continuity of care. My entire staff and I will be available to assist you with this transition. Please call if you have any questions or concerns.

2. Save the file on your file disk; use the filename **3skill1** and print one copy.
3. Use the following information to change the letter:
   a. Insert the following paragraph between the middle and last paragraphs:

      If you have specific concerns regarding a medical condition or are undergoing prenatal care, please give me a call directly at (708) 555-8900. Otherwise, you may call Celeste Renshaw or Bertha Lenhardt at (708) 555-6303 and they will be happy to help you select another physician.

4. Use the Speller to find and correct any misspelled words; also proofread carefully for accurate meaning.

5. Save the file on your file disk; use the filename **3skill1r** (Chapter 3, skill 1, revised).

6. Print one copy and close the document.

Skill 3.2—Create and Edit an AMS Simplified Style Letter

1. Use the AMS simplified style letter and the following information.

   a. Use the current date.

   b. Send the letter to Mrs. Sabrina Alvares, 77 Hazelwood Ln., Menomonee Falls, WI 53051.

   c. The subject of the letter is TAX PLANNING.

   d. The letter is from Tami Nguyen, C.P.A.

   e. Include your reference initials, document identification notation, and enclosure notation.

   f. Make decisions regarding:

      Justification
      Margins
      Fonts
      Use of bold, italic, and underline text attributes

   g. The letter body text follows:

      Enclosed is your new tax organizer. Although it may seem like you just finished last year's taxes, it is not too early to begin thinking about the preparation of this year's taxes.

      As for new law changes, the new 31 percent bracket kicks in, as well as the new "haircut" for itemized deductions. Remember that for federal tax purposes, capital gains are still taxed at 28 percent.

      As you thumb through your tax organizer, you will see that it contains the prior year's figures. Knowing your information from the prior year will help you to verify the accuracy and completeness of the current year information. Please include cost and purchase date of all assets sold.

      If you feel that your tax situation merits an appointment or that you need to discuss any matters with me, please call Bob to schedule an appointment.

2. Save the file on your file disk; use the filename **3skill2**.

3. Use the following information to change the letter:

   a. Insert the following paragraph above the last paragraph.

      Forward your estimated tax partnership papers to me as soon as possible. We do not need to delay the filing of your partnership taxes while you gather your individual information.

4. Use the Speller to find and correct any misspelled words; also proofread carefully for accurate meaning.

5. Save the file on your file disk; use the filename **3skill2r** (Chapter 3, skill 2, revised).

6. Print one copy and close the document.

Skill 3.3—Create and Edit a Traditional Style Letter; Language Arts

1. Use the traditional style letter and the following information.

   a. Use the current date.

   b. Send the letter to Mr. Clinton Nomura, Engineering Productivity Division, 18023 Shawsheen St., Andover, MA 01810-1086.

   c. The letter is from Josephine Reyes, Membership Chairperson.

   d. Include your reference initials, document identification, and enclosure notation.

   e. Make decisions regarding:

      Appropriate salutation
      Justification
      Margins
      Fonts
      Use of bold, italic, and underline text attributes

   f. Correct three spelling and two punctuation errors.

   g. The letter body text follows:

   The enclosed brochure is provided to inform you of the existence of a professional organization taylored to meet the specific needs of telecommuncation professionals.

   The NORAM Telecommunications Association is more than 15 years old and has more than 600 members. There are members from all 50 states and Canada.

   The membership brochure will provide you with a describtion of our programs and information on next month's conference. Our conference will be held in Chicago, Illinois. Hurry now to register and take advantage of the early registration reduced fee.

   If you have any questions feel free to contact me or my assistant Billie Detweiler, at (215) 555-8303. Thank you for taking time to consider becoming a member of the NORAM Telecommunications Association.

2. Use the Speller to find and correct any misspelled words; also proofread carefully for accurate meaning.

3. Save the file on your file disk; use the filename **3skill3**.

4. Print one copy.

5. If you have completed your work, exit WordPerfect (select **File**, **Exit**).

CHAPTER 4

Editing and Enhancing Documents

Features Covered

- Move text
- Copy text
- Find text
- Replace text
- Indent text
- Double indent text
- Numbered and bulleted text
- Print selected text

Objectives and Introduction

After successfully completing this chapter, you will be able to rearrange text using the Move and Copy features, search for specified text, and replace text automatically. You will also be able to create enumerated list and bulleted lists using the Bullets feature as well as indent paragraphs from the left margin and from both the left and right margins.

Move Text

Moving text is the process of relocating text. For example, a paragraph in the middle of a letter can be moved to the end of the letter. Paragraphs, sentences, or lines can be moved. Generally, once text has been typed, retyping should be unnecessary.

The text to be moved must first be selected. Once the text is selected, WordPerfect provides several methods for moving the text. Two methods for moving text are described in the Steps to Move Text Using the Cut and Paste Commands on page 76 and in the Steps to Move Text Using the Drag and Drop Text Feature on page 76. The Undelete feature covered in Chapter 2, page 39, can also be used to move text.

Start-Up Instructions

- Open the file named **4drill1.cut** located on the data disk (select the **Open** button on the Power Bar; if necessary, click in the Drives box and click on the drive letter where the data disk is located; double-click on the filename).

Steps to Move Text Using the Cut and Paste Commands

1. Select the desired text.

   For example, move the mouse pointer into the left margin beside the second paragraph and double-click to select the paragraph and the following blank line {Alt, e, e, a}.

2. Select the Cut button on the Power Bar {Alt, e, t *or* Ctrl and x}.

   Note: The text is deleted (cut) from the original location and placed in the Clipboard. The Clipboard is temporary memory that holds deleted or copied text.

3. Place the insertion point to the left of the first character or space that will follow the moved text.

   For example, move the insertion point to the left of the first character in the first paragraph.

4. Select the Paste button on the Power Bar to insert the text at the new location {Alt, e, p *or* Ctrl and v}.

   Note: The second paragraph is now the first paragraph. A copy of the moved text remains in the Clipboard (temporary memory) until replaced by other cut or copied text or until Windows is exited.

Finish-Up Instructions

- Use the *new* filename **4drill1.cap** and save the file on your file disk (select **File, Save As**; type the filename; if necessary, click in the Drives box and click on the drive letter where the file disk is located; select **OK**).
- Print one copy (select the **Print** button on the Power Bar; choose **Print**).
- Close the document (select **File, Close**).

Start-Up Instructions

- Open the file named **4drill1.cut** located on the data disk (select the **Open** button on the Power Bar; if necessary, click in the Drives box and click on the drive letter where the data disk is located; double-click on the filename).

Steps to Move Text Using the Drag and Drop Text Feature

Note: A mouse must be used to drag and drop text.

1. Select the desired text.

   For example, move the mouse pointer into the left margin beside the second paragraph and double-click to select the paragraph and the following blank line {Alt, e, e, a}.

2. Move the mouse pointer into the selected (highlighted) text.

3. Press and hold the left mouse button while dragging the mouse pointer and insertion point to the new location.

   For example, while holding the mouse button, drag the mouse pointer and insertion point to the left of the first character of the first paragraph.

   Note: A small square and an outline of a square display at the bottom of the mouse pointer.

4. Release the mouse button.

   Note: The paragraph is moved to the new location.

5. Click the left mouse button once to deselect the text.

Finish-Up Instructions

- Use the *new* filename **4drill1.dad** and save the file on your file disk (select **File, Save As**; type the filename; if necessary, click in the Drives box and click on the drive letter where the file disk is located; select **OK**).
- Print one copy (select the **Print** button on the Power Bar, choose **Print**).
- Close the document (select **File, Close**).

Copy Text

Copying text is the process of duplicating text. For example, a document, sentence, name, or paragraph may need to appear again on the page, in another part of the current document, or in a different document. Text can be copied from the original location and repeated in a second location. The text to be copied must first be selected. Once the text has been selected, WordPerfect provides several methods for copying text. Two methods for copying text are described in the following Steps to Copy Text Using the Copy and Paste Commands and in the Steps to Copy Text Using the Drag and Drop Text Feature.

Start-Up Instructions

- Open the file named **1drill2.wpd** typed in Chapter 1, page 23 (select the **Open** button on the Power Bar; if necessary, click in the Drives box and click on the drive letter where the file disk is located; double-click on the filename).
- The following steps will be used to make a copy of all the memorandum text in the file named **1drill2.wpd**. Both copies will appear on the same page.

Steps to Copy Text Using the Copy and Paste Commands

1. Select the text to be copied.

   For example, select the existing text by choosing **Edit, Select, Page** {Alt, e, e, p}.

2. Select the **Copy** button on the Power Bar {Alt, e, c *or* Ctrl and c}.

Note: A copy of the selected text is placed in the Clipboard (temporary memory). The Clipboard is temporary memory that holds deleted or copied text.

3. Place the insertion point to the left of the first character or space that will follow the copied text.

   For example, move the insertion point to the right of the last name in the distribution list and press the **Enter** key three times.

4. Select the **Paste** button on the Power Bar to insert the copied text into the document {Alt, e, p *or* Ctrl and v}.

   Note: When the copied text is inserted, the insertion point is located at the end of the copied text. Use the arrow keys to move up through the document to see the copied text. The copied text remains in the original location and is displayed in the new location. A copy of the copied (or deleted) text also remains in temporary memory until replaced by other copied (or deleted) text or until Windows is exited.

Finish-Up Instructions

- Use the *new* filename **4drill2.dup** and save the file on your file disk (select **File**, **Save As**; type the filename; if necessary, click in the Drives box and click on the drive letter where the file disk is located; select **OK**).
- Print one copy (select the **Print** button on the Power Bar; choose **Print**).
- Close the document (select **File**, **Close**).

Start-Up Instructions

- Open the file named **1drill2.wpd** typed in Chapter 1, page 23 (select the **Open** button on the Power Bar; if necessary, click in the Drives box and click on the drive letter where the file disk is located; double-click on the filename).
- With the insertion point at the top of the document, press the **Enter** key once. Move the insertion point to the bottom of the document (**Ctrl** and **End**) and press **Enter** twice.
- The following steps will be used to make a copy of all the memorandum text. Both copies will appear on the same page.

Steps to Copy Text Using the Drag and Drop Text Feature

Note: A mouse must be used to drag and drop text.

1. Select the desired text.

   For example, select the existing text by choosing **Edit, Select, Page**.

2. Move the mouse pointer into the selected (highlighted) text.
3. Press and hold the left mouse button while dragging the mouse pointer and insertion point to the new location.

   For example, while holding the mouse button, drag the mouse pointer and insertion point to the second blank line below the last name in the distribution list.

Note: A small square and an outline of a square display at the bottom of the mouse pointer.

4. Press and hold the **Ctrl** key while releasing the mouse button.
5. Click the left mouse button once to deselect the text.

   Note: The copied memo displays in the original location and the new location. Press the up arrow key to view the copied memo and the original memo.

Finish-Up Instructions

- Use the *new* filename **4drill2.d2** and save the file on your file disk (select **File, Save As**; type the filename; if necessary, click in the Drives box and click on the drive letter where the file disk is located; select **OK**).
- Print one copy (select the **Print** button on the Power Bar; choose **Print**).
- Close the document (select **File, Close**).

Find Text

The Find command is used to locate a word or group of words in a document. The Find command can also be used to locate codes, such as margins and justification (see Chapter 10 for additional information on finding codes.) When the Find command is accessed, the Find Text dialog box displays. Menu options in the Find Text dialog box are used to give WordPerfect more information on how to perform the search. See Figure 4.2 for information on each menu option.

Start-Up Instructions

- Open the file named **4drill3.txt** located on the data disk (select the **Open** button on the Power Bar; if necessary, click in the Drives box and click on the drive letter where the data disk is located; double-click on the filename).

Steps to Find Text

1. Select Edit, Find {Alt, e, f *or* F2}.

   Note: The Find Text dialog box is displayed. The insertion point is located in the Find box (see Figure 4.1).

2. Type the word or words to be found in the Find box.

   For example, type **LFS** in the Find box.

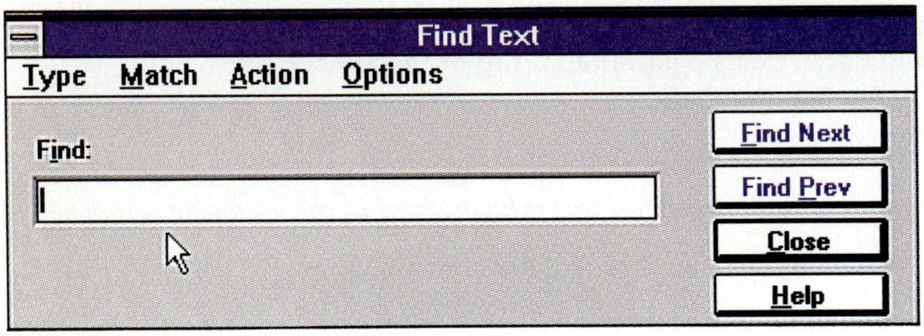

FIGURE 4.1

Find Text dialog box

FIGURE 4.2

Find Text dialog box menu options

Type:	
Text	Tells WordPerfect to locate specific text.
Specific Code	Displays a list of codes, such as margins and justification, that WordPerfect can locate.
Match:	
Whole Word	Select the Whole Word option to locate the next occurrence of matching text that is a word by itself.
Case	Select the Case option to instruct WordPerfect to locate words that exactly match the case of the text typed in the Find box.
Font	Select the Font option to tell WordPerfect to locate text in a particular font name, size, and/or attribute.
Codes	Select Codes to display an extensive list of codes that can be located by WordPerfect.
Action:	
Select Match	Use Select Match to tell WordPerfect to highlight the specific text in the document window when a match is located.
Position Before	Select Position Before to place the insertion point to the left of the first character when a match is located.
Position After	Select Position After to place the insertion point to the right of the last character when a match is located.
Extend Selection	Use Extend Selection to select text from the location of the insertion point to the location of the next occurrence of the text to be found.
Options:	
Begin Find at Top of Document	Instructs WordPerfect to start the search beginning at the top of the document.
Wrap at Beg./End of Document	Instructs WordPerfect to begin the search at the location of the insertion point. When the end of the document is reached, the search continues at the beginning of the document and continues until the insertion point is reached.
Limit Find Within Selection	Instructs WordPerfect to limit the search to the selected text.
Include Headers, Footers, etc.	Instructs WordPerfect to search for specified text in headers, footers, footnotes, graphic boxes, etc.

3. Select each menu in the Find Text dialog box and check that the desired options are selected.

   For example, select **Type** and check that **Text** is selected (a check-mark displays beside a selected option) {Alt and t}. Select **Match** and check that **Whole Word** is selected {Alt and m}. Select **Action** and check that **Select Match** is selected {Alt and a}. Select **Options** and check that **Begin Find at Top of Document** is selected {Alt and o}.

4. Select **Find Next** {Alt and f}.

   Note: *The first occurrence of the specified text is highlighted in the document window.*

5. The text can be edited and the Find procedure continued.

a. Edit by deleting, inserting, or replacing.

For example, move the mouse pointer to the highlighted text in the document window and click once. Type **LaGrande Federal Savings** {Alt and c; Ctrl and Backspace; type the text and press the Spacebar once}.

b. To continue to search for the next occurrence of the same text, select **Find Next** in the Find Text dialog box {F2, Enter}.

For example, continue the Find process and change all occurrences of **LFS** to **LaGrande Federal Savings**.

Note: *When the message "Not Found" displays, no additional occurrences of the specified text can be located.*

6. Select **OK** {Enter}.
7. Select **Close** {Alt and c}.

Finish-Up Instructions

- When the entire text has been searched, use the *new* filename **4drill3.fin** and save the file on your file disk (select **File**, **Save As**; type the filename; if necessary, click in the Drives box and click on the drive letter where the file disk is located; select **OK**).
- Print one copy (select the **Print** button on the Power Bar; choose **Print**).
- Close the document (select **File**, **Close**).

Replace Text Automatically

Replacing text automatically is the process of locating and deleting specific text or codes and inserting new text or codes. The document is searched for a specific word/code or group of words/codes. Each occurrence of the specified text can be replaced automatically with new text. When the Replace command is accessed, the Find and Replace Text dialog box displays. Menu options in the Find and Replace Text dialog box are used to give WordPerfect more information on the text to be replaced. The Type, Match, and Options menus contain the same options that are available in the Find Text dialog box (see Figure 4.2 for information on these menu options). In addition, the Option menu contains an option that is not available in the Find Text dialog box, Limit Number of Changes. Two additional menus are available in the Find and Replace Text dialog box: Direction and Replace (see Figure 4.3 for an explanation of the Find and Replace menu options).

Start-Up Instructions

- Open the file named **4drill3.txt** located on the data disk (select the **Open** button on the Power Bar; if necessary, click in the Drives box and click on the drive letter where the data disk is located; double-click on the filename).

FIGURE 4.3

Find and Replace Text dialog box menu options. (See Figure 4.2 for Type, Match, and Options menu options.)

Options:	
Limit Number of Changes	Specify the number of times the designated text should be replaced. (See Figure 4.2 for explanation of other Option menu items.)
Replace:	*Note: This menu is available only when the insertion point is located in the Replace With box.*
Case	Select the Case option to instruct WordPerfect to replace text exactly as the text is shown in the Replace With box.
Font	Select the Font option to specify the font name, size, and/or attribute for the text shown in the Replace With box.
Codes	Select Codes to display an extensive list of codes that can be inserted in the Replace With box.
Direction:	
Forward	Instructs WordPerfect to find and replace the specified text from the insertion point to the end of the document.
Backward	Instructs WordPerfect to find and replace the specified text from the insertion point to the beginning of the document.

Steps to Replace Text Automatically

1. Select **Edit, Replace** {Alt, e, r *or* Ctrl and F2}.

   Note: The Find and Replace Text dialog box is displayed at the bottom of the screen. The insertion point is located in the Find box (see Figure 4.4).

2. In the Find box, type the text to be replaced.

   For example, type **LFS** in the Find box.

3. Select the **Type, Match, Direction,** and **Options** menu in the Find and Replace Text dialog box and check that desired options are selected.

   For example, select **Type** and check that **Text** is selected (a checkmark displays beside a selected option) {Alt and t}. Select **Match** and check that **Whole Word** is selected {Alt and m}. Select **Direction** and check that **Forward** is selected {Alt and d}. Select **Options** and check that **Begin Find at Top of Document** is selected {Alt and o}.

4. Click in the **Replace With** box {Tab}.

5. Type the new text in the Replace With box.

   For example, type **Landmark Financial Services.** (Do not type the period.)

FIGURE 4.4

Find and Replace Text dialog box

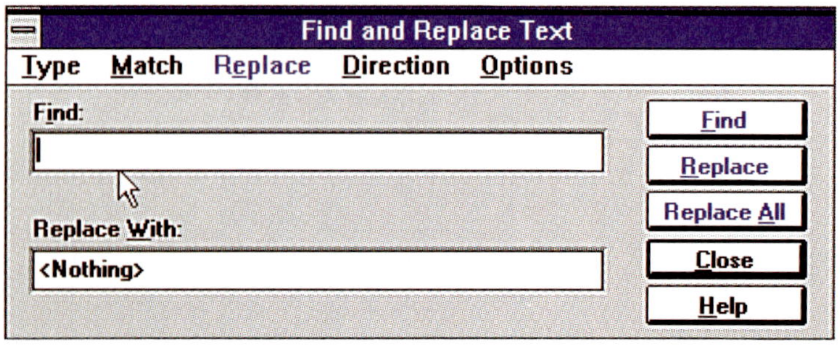

6. If desired, select the Replace menu and use the options to provide additional information about the replacement text.

   For example, change the font for the replacement text to bold by selecting **Replace, Font, Font Style, Bold, OK** {Alt and e, f; Alt and y; press the down arrow key to display Bold; Enter}.

7. Select Replace All {Alt and a}.

   Note: WordPerfect instantly changes the specified text.

8. When all occurrences of the specified text are replaced, text in the Find box of the Find and Replace dialog box is highlighted. Select **Close** {Alt and c}.

Finish-Up Instructions

- Use the *new* filename **4drill3.rep** and save the file on your file disk (select **File, Save As**; type the filename; if necessary, click in the Drives box and click on the drive letter where the file disk is located; select **OK**).
- Print one copy (select the **Print** button on the Power Bar; choose **Print**).
- Close the document (select **File, Close**).

Undo Replaced Text

Since WordPerfect replaces all occurrences of specified text rapidly, it may be necessary to undo the replaced text if word(s) are found that should not have been changed. To undo the replaced text, select **Edit, Undo** {Alt and e, u} before performing any other actions.

Create Text Using the Bullet, Indent, and Double Indent Features

Text can be indented to improve readability and enhance the document's appearance. If the Indent feature is used, all lines of a paragraph are indented from the left margin until the **Enter** key is pressed. The first time the **Indent** button is selected, the insertion point or text moves to the first preset tab and all text is indented at that position. If the **Indent** button is selected a second time the insertion point or text moves to the second preset tab which is used to indent the text.

Both sides of a paragraph or line can be indented using the Double Indent feature. Often a paragraph is double-indented in a letter to show emphasis (see Figure 4.6).

Numbers, letters, or bullets (special characters placed at the left of a paragraph) can be inserted to provide extra emphasis or to improve readability. The desired number, letter, or bullet style is chosen from a list of available styles displayed in the Bullets & Numbers dialog box. Various number styles are available such as 1., 2., 3., or I., II., III. Uppercase and lowercase letter styles are also available, i.e., A., B., C., or a., b., c. Some of the bullet styles available are small or large circles (• or ●), and a diamond (♦).

Numbers, letters, or bullets can be inserted as text is typed or after the text has been typed. If numbers, letters, or bullets are to be inserted as text is typed, the **New Bullet or Number on ENTER** option is selected in the Bullets & Numbers dialog box. If numbers, letters, or bullets are to be inserted after the text is typed, the text is selected before the **Bullet** button is selected.

Start-Up Instructions

- Open the file named **4drill4.obj** located on the data disk (select the **Open** button on the Power Bar; if necessary, click in the drives box and click on the drive letter where the data disk is located; double-click on the filename).

Steps to Create Paragraphs Using the Indent Feature

1. With the paragraph(s) to be indented displayed in the document window, place the insertion point to the left of the first character of the paragraph to be indented.

   For example, place the insertion point to the left of the **R** in the paragraph that begins Results-Oriented.

2. Select the Indent button on the Button Bar {Alt, L, a, i or F7}.

   Note: All lines of the paragraph are indented.

Finish-Up Instructions

- Repeat steps 1 and 2 and indent the last three paragraphs of the document.
- Use the new filename **4drill4.den** and save the file (select **File**, **Save As**; type the filename; if necessary, click in the Drives box and click on the drive letter where your file disk is located; select **OK**).
- Print one copy (select the **Print** button on the Power Bar; choose **Print**).
- Close the document (select **File**, **Close**).

Start-Up Instructions

- In a clear document window, type the salutation and the first paragraph of the letter shown in Figure 4.5. Press **Enter** twice after the first paragraph.

Steps to Create Paragraphs Using the Double Indent Feature

1. Select Layout, Paragraph, Double Indent to turn on the Double Indent feature {Alt, L, a, d *or* Ctrl and Shift and F7}.

2. Type the paragraph to be indented from both the left and right margins. Press **Enter** twice at the end of the paragraph.

   For example, type: **If you were to die as a result of an accident, the All-in-One Plan would cancel your mortgage debt and leave your family secure in a mortgage-free home.**

   Note: When the ***Enter*** *key is pressed, the insertion point returns to the left margin and the Double Indent feature is turned off.*

Dear Mortgage Customer:

Recently we wrote to you about a unique plan of insurance that would provide flexible protection for your family.

> If you were to die as a result of an accident, the All-in-One Plan would cancel your mortgage debt and leave your family secure in a mortgage-free home.

This insurance plan would also provide your family with an important financial cushion when they would need it most. After the plan pays off the mortgage balance, any remaining benefit goes to the beneficiary of your choice.

> You simply cannot be turned down, regardless of your health or occupation. No medical exam or answers to health questions are required.

Take action today. Send for your application form by filling out the enclosed, postage-paid card.

Sincerely,

Jean Silverburg
Vice President

JS/xx

FIGURE 4.5

Paragraphs indented using the Double Indent feature

Finish-Up Instructions

- Use the Steps to Create Paragraphs Using the Double Indent Feature and complete the document shown in Figure 4.5.
- Save the file on your file disk; use the filename **4drill5.all** (select the **Save** button; type the filename; if necessary, click in the Drives box and click on the drive letter where the file disk is located; select **OK**).
- Print one copy (select the **Print** button on the Power Bar, choose **Print**).
- Close the document (select **File, Close**).

Start-Up Instructions

- Open the file named **4drill6.txt** located on the data disk (select the **Open** button on the Power Bar; if necessary, click in the drives box and click on the drive letter where the data disk is located; double-click on the filename).

Steps to Create a Numbered or Bulleted List

1. Select all paragraphs to be numbered or bulleted.

   For example, select all paragraphs except for the title.

2. Select the **Bullet** button on the Button Bar (Alt, i, n}.

   ***Note:** The Bullets and Numbers dialog box displays (see Figure 4.6).*

FIGURE 4.6

Bullets & Numbers dialog box

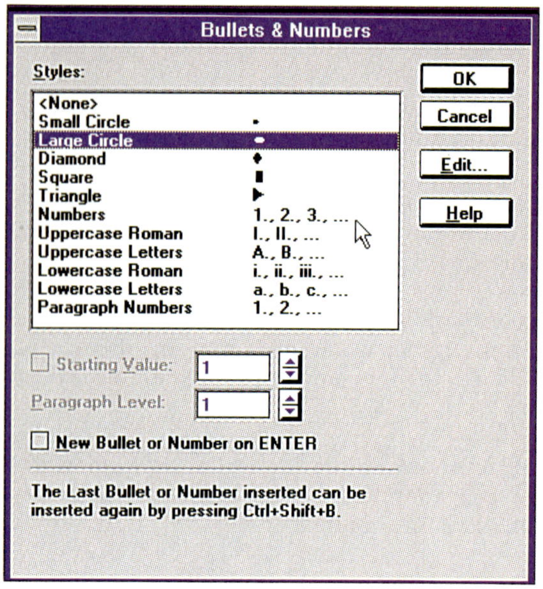

3. Select the desired number, letter or bullet style {press the up or down arrow key to highlight the desired style}.

   For example, select the **Numbers** style.

4. Select OK {Enter}.

   Note: *Your document should look similar to Figure 4.7. If items in the numbered list are moved, the items are automatically renumbered.*

Finish-Up Instructions

- Use the *new* filename **4drill6.num** (select **File**, **Save As**; type the filename; if necessary, click in the Drives box and click on the drive letter where the file disk is located; select **OK**).
- Print one copy (select the **Print** button on the Power Bar; choose **Print**).
- Change the numbered list to a bulleted list (select all numbered paragraphs; select the **Bullet** button; select the **Diamond** style; select **OK**).

FIGURE 4.7

Numbered paragraphs

Applicant Requirements--Air Conditioning Mechanic

1. Any combination equivalent to completion of high school and three years of increasingly responsible experience in the operation, repair, and maintenance of heating, ventilation, and cooling systems.

2. Hold a valid driver's license authorizing operation of motor vehicles.

3. Successful compliance with job-related medical standards as determined by a medical examination conducted by a company-approved physician.

4. Proof of U.S. citizenship or proof of legal authorization to work in the United States.

- Use the *new* filename **4drill6.dia** and save the file (select **File**, **Save As**; type the filename; if necessary, click in the Drives box and click on the drive letter where the file disk is located; select **OK**).
- Print one copy (select the **Print** button on the Power Bar; choose **Print**).
- Close the document (select **File**, **Close**).

Print Selected Text

Once a document has been typed, just a portion of the text can be printed if desired. The text to be printed is selected. The **Print** button is chosen. The selected text prints at the location on the page where the text would have printed had the entire document been printed. For example, if the selected text is located in the middle of the page, the text will print in the middle of the page.

Start-Up Instructions

- Open the file named **4drill6.num** located on your file disk (select the **Open** button on the Power Bar; if necessary, click in the Drives box and click on the drive letter where the file disk is located; double-click on the filename).

Steps to Print Selected Text

1. Select the text to be printed.

   For example, select the entire third paragraph.

2. Select the **Print** button on the Power Bar {Alt and f, p *or* F5}.

   Note: *When the Print dialog box displays, a black dot appears to the left of the Selected Text option in the Print Selection box.*

3. Select **Print** to print the selected text {Enter}.

Finish-Up Instructions

- Close the document (select **File**, **Close**).

The Next Step

Chapter Review and Activities

Self-Check Quiz

T F 1. The Find command is used to locate a word or group of words in a document.

T F 2. Moving text is the process of duplicating text.

T F 3. Before text can be copied or moved, the text is selected.

T F 4. To begin the Replace function, select **Edit**, **Replace**.

T F 5. A single paragraph cannot be selected and printed.

6. Bullet characters can be inserted to the left of selected paragraphs by choosing
   a. the **Bullet** button on the Button Bar.
   b. the **Bullet** button on the Power Bar.
   c. **Edit**, **Bullets and Numbering**.

7. When using the drag and drop method to move text,
   a. the text must be selected.
   b. a mouse must be used.
   c. keystrokes can be used.
   d. both a and b.

8. When the **Indent** button is selected
   a. the text is indented from both the left and right margins.
   b. a bullet character is inserted at the left of the selected paragraphs.
   c. all lines of a paragraph are indented from the left margin until the Enter key is pressed.

9. Which option in the Find and Replace Text dialog box should be selected in order to instruct WordPerfect to find only the whole word(s) typed in the Find box?

10. What is the difference between the Indent feature and the Double Indent feature?

Enriching Language Arts Skills

SCANS

Spelling/Vocabulary Words

dues fees paid by members to an organization at regular intervals.
affiliation act of belonging or being connected to a specific group.
outweigh to be of more importance or value.
distinguished worthy of notice; excellent; outstanding.

Compound Adjectives and Coordinating Conjunctions

Hyphenate two words that precede and describe a noun and function as a single adjective.

Example:

The designer sent a well-defined sample of the proposed meeting area.

A comma is placed before a coordinating conjunction (e.g., *and, or, because*) that joins two independent clauses (i.e., clauses that are complete sentences). No comma is placed before a coordinating conjunction if *one* or both clauses are dependent.

Example:

We will respond promptly to the questionnaire, ***because*** *our company would like to maintain a good working relationship with our clients.* (Two independent clauses.)

We mailed 400 surveys yesterday ***and*** *expect to obtain a 3 percent response by the end of May.* (One independent and one dependent clause.)

Activities

Activity 4.1—Create a Numbered List and Move Text

1. Type the following paragraphs using the spacing shown.

Features of WordPerfect 6.0 for Windows

Button Bar and Power Bar--The Button Bar and Power Bar provide a quick and easy way to format, edit, save, and print documents. Commonly used features are represented by icons (pictures). When an icon is selected, the associated command is performed immediately.

Multiple documents--With WordPerfect 6.0, a user can have up to nine documents open at one time. Each document is placed in a separate window. Information can be copied or moved from one window to another as desired.

Bullets--The Bullet button can be selected to easily create bulleted lists.

Graphics--WordPerfect 6.0 for Windows provides more than 135 graphics images that can be placed in a document. Both text and graphics are displayed on the screen. With the use of the mouse, graphics can be positioned and sized interactively.

Drawing--The WP Draw button provides access to the drawing tools of the WordPerfect Presentations program. Illustrations can be created and existing images can be edited. The drawings can be incorporated into WordPerfect documents.

---

2. Number all paragraphs except the title (select all paragraphs to be numbered; select the **Bullet** button; select the **Number** style; select **OK**).
3. Save the file on your file disk; use the filename **4act1.wpw** (select the **Save** button; type the filename; if necessary, click in the Drives box and click on the drive letter where the file disk is located; select **OK**).
4. Print one copy (select the **Print** button on the Power Bar; choose **Print**).
5. Move the items as shown.

Features of WordPerfect 6.0 for Windows

1. Button Bar and Power Bar--The Button Bar and Power Bar provide a quick and easy way to format, edit, save, and print documents. Commonly used features are represented by icons (pictures). When an icon is selected, the associated command is performed immediately.
2. Multiple documents--With WordPerfect 6.0, a user can have up to nine documents open at one time. Each document is placed in a separate window. Information can be copied or moved from one window to another as desired.
3. Bullets--The Bullet button can be selected to easily create bulleted lists.
4. Graphics--WordPerfect 6.0 for Windows provides more than 135 graphics images that can be placed in a document. Both text and graphics are displayed on the screen. With the use of the mouse, graphics can be positioned and sized interactively.
5. Drawing--The WP Draw button provides access to the drawing tools of the WordPerfect Presentations program. Illustrations can be created and existing images can be edited. The drawings can be incorporated into WordPerfect documents.

---

6. Save the file on your file disk; use the filename **4act1.rev** (select **File**, **Save As**; type the filename; if necessary, click in the Drives box and click on the drive letter where the file disk is located; select **OK**).
7. Print one copy (select the **Print** button on the Power Bar; choose **Print**).
8. Close the document (select **File**, **Close**).

Activity 4.2—Create a Bulleted List and Replace Text Automatically

1. Use the traditional style and type the following letter.

(Use current date)

Mr. Austin Estes
55 Johnston Rd., #8
Albany, NY 12203

Dear Mr. Estes:

Enclosed is a copy of the GTA Constant Traveler newsletter highlighting our expanded world of service and membership benefits.

Our latest expansion opens new corners of the globe to you for mileage building and award opportunities. Wherever you fly on GTA, you will earn our minimum of 1,500 miles per flight segment. No airline offers more.

In addition to our expanded service, the newsletter highlights:

New fares for GTA business-class fliers.

Triple mileage for selected GTA intercontinental routes.

Special "GTA Partners Program" holiday promotion.

To increase your flexibility when traveling within North America, GTA has introduced upgrade awards for our business fliers. Also, members may continue to purchase a GTA First Class seat at reduced rates any time before departure through our paid upgrade program.

We at GTA thank you for flying with us and look forward to serving your air travel needs.

Sincerely,

Anna R. Ingram
Senior Vice President

ARI/xx
estes.ltr/disk4

Enc.

2. Select the three sentences that followed the third paragraph which begin "In addition to our expanded. . ." and create a bulleted list (select the **Bullet** button; select the **Small Circle** style; select **OK**).

3. Save the file on your file disk; use the filename **4act2.mae** (select the **Save** button; type the filename; if necessary, click in the Drives box and click on the drive letter where the file disk is located; select **OK**).
4. Print one copy (select the **Print** button on the Power Bar; choose **Print**).
5. Replace all occurrences of GTA with Global Trans Airline (select **Edit**, **Replace**; type **GTA** in the Find box; type **Global Trans Airline** in the Replace With box; select **Replace All**).
6. Save the file on your file disk; use the filename **4act2.rep** (select **File**, **Save As**; type the filename; if necessary, click in the Drives box and click on the drive letter where the file disk is located; select **OK**).
7. Print one copy (select the **Print** button on the Power Bar; choose **Print**).
8. Close the document (select **File**, **Close**).

Activity 4.3—Copy, Edit, and Print Selected Text

1. Open the file named **4drill6.num** or type the document shown on page 86 (Figure 4.7).
2. Change the numbered list to a bulleted list (select the numbered items, select the **Bullet** button on the Button Bar, move the mouse pointer to the **Diamond** bullet and click, select **OK**). Click once to deselect the list.
3. Add three **Enters** at the bottom of the document.
4. Select the entire document.
5. Copy the entire document by selecting **Edit**, **Copy**.
6. Move the insertion point to the blank line at the bottom of the document and select **Edit**, **Paste** to insert a copy of the document.
7. Make the changes shown to the pasted copy. (Do not change the line spacing.)

Applicant Requirements-~~Air Conditioning Mechanic~~ Maintenance Supervisor

1. Any combination equivalent to completion of high school and ~~three~~ five years of increasingly responsible experience in the operation ~~, repair, and maintenance of heating, ventilation, and cooling systems.~~ of janitorial services, as well as supervising a staff of ten or more persons.

2. Hold a valid California state driver's license authorizing operation of motor vehicles.

3. Successful compliance with job-related medical standards as determined by a medical examination conducted by a company-approved physician.

4. Proof of U.S. citizenship or proof of legal authorization to work in the United States.

---

8. Save the file on your file disk; use the filename **4act3.app** (select **File, Save As**; type the filename; if necessary, click in the Drives box and click on the drive letter where the file disk is located; select **OK**).

9. Select the edited copy and print one copy of the selected text (select the **Print** button on the Power Bar; choose **Print**).

10. Close the document (select **File, Close**).

Activity 4.4—Create Paragraphs Using the Double Indent Feature

1. Use the traditional block style and type the following letter. Use the Double Indent feature to indent the second and third paragraphs from both the left and right margins (select **Layout, Paragraph, Double Indent**).

(Use current date)

Mr. Phil Emerson
P. O. Box 7526
London, KY 40741-9945

Dear Mr. Emerson:

We have great news for you! Your application for a ValueCard account has been preliminarily approved. However, before we can send you your new card, we need your assistance in verifying all income.

> Please send us a copy of your last two paycheck stubs issued within the last thirty (30) days. If you have listed other income, please provide verification.

> If we receive the requested information within thirty (30) days, we will be able to complete your evaluation.

We certainly hope to hear from you so that we can complete our approval process and you can begin to enjoy the many advantages that a ValueCard has to offer.

Sincerely,

Carol Shaw
Credit Card Director

CS/xx
emerson.ltr/d2

---

2. Save the file on your file disk; use the filename **4act4.pem** (select the **Save** button; type the filename; if necessary, click in the Drives box and click on the drive letter where the file disk is located; select **OK**).

3. Print one copy (select the **Print** button on the Power Bar; choose **Print**).

4. Close the document (select **File**, **Close**).

Challenge Your Skills

Skill 4.1—Create a Numbered List, Move, and Edit Text

1. Use the Memorandum—Style 1 and the following information:

   a. Send the memo to Sales Associates from Suzanne Boscacci, Division Manager.

   b. Use the current date; include your reference initials.

   c. The subject of the memo is Current Sales Promotion.

   d. Send copies to J. Matarazzo and G. Higgins.

   e. The unformatted memorandum body text follows:

   Enclosed are photographs to assist in building your current sales promotion displays.

   Please note the following:

   Wingits have been discontinued and Chocwiz quantities reduced in order to incorporate Ultimate Almonds and expand on the successful Cheesecake Minis. Chocwiz should be placed next to snack crackers for a common price point. Ultimate Almonds should be placed in the space previously occupied by Chocwiz.

   Order quantities will be communicated through the central ordering office and will be processed automatically. Sales associates will not key in any orders.

   Orders reflect only the quantities necessary to build displays. Make plans to order refill quantities when necessary.

   Stores will require extra service calls during this promotion. Let your stores know when you will be visiting their sites.

   Announcement to the stores of this promotion has already been distributed. Orders will now be processed electronically. The new electronic order processing will ensure accurate and timely delivery of products.

   Remember--proper point of sale, displays, and shelf!

2. Select and number the third, fourth, fifth, and sixth paragraphs.

3. Move items 3 and 4 above item number 2.

4. Delete the last paragraph and insert the following two paragraphs:

Advise stores now of their upcoming shipment and make plans to build displays. Stores resisting this promotion should be advised to call Leonard Koenig or Laura Gonzales (department buyers) at 555-3422.

LET'S SELL SOME PRODUCTS!

5. Save the file on your file disk; use the filename **4skill1.sas**.
6. Print one copy and close the document.

Skill 4.2—Copy and Edit Text

1. Create the following form using the format and spacing shown.

   Hint: *Press* ***Enter*** *twice after all lines of text, except press* ***Enter*** *three times after typing the store number and after typing the last line of the form. Use Flush Right justification to align items at the right margin.*

SALES INVENTORY SUMMARY

SALES ASSOCIATE: JACQUELINE VILLEGAS

STORE #: 286

Item Name	Amount Purchased
Cheesecake Minis	12 gross
Chocwiz	10 gross
Ultimate Almonds	20 gross

---

2. Copy the form below the original form. Change the data in the copied form as follows:

   Sales Associate: David Novak
   Store #: 235
   Cheesecake Minis: 10 gross
   Chocwiz: 5 gross
   Ultimate Almonds: 22 gross

3. Copy the original form again and place below the second form. Change the data in the copied form as follows:

   Sales Associate: Monie Lucero
   Store #: 182
   Cheesecake Minis: 15 gross
   Chocwiz: 8 gross
   Ultimate Almonds: 18 gross

4. Save the file on your file disk; use the filename **4skill2.sum.**
5. Print one copy and close the document.

Skill 4.3—Replace Text Automatically; Language Arts

1. Use the Memorandum—Style 1 and the following information:
   a. Change both the left and right margins to 1.25" and the top margin to 1.5".
   b. Send the memo to Consolidated Life Insurance Field Force from Juan Valdivia, Vice President.
   c. Use the current date; include your reference initials.
   d. The subject of the memo is IUA Membership.
   e. Correct three spelling and four punctuation errors.

To qualify for the National Quality, National Sales Achievement, Health Insurance, or the Million Dollar Roundtable Awards, your IUA membership dues must be current.

If you are a recent member of the Consolidated Life Insurance field force and were previously a member of IUA under another company's name, please write a letter to IUA National Headquarters and ask that your afilliation be changed to Consolidated Life Insurance.

Your IUA membership is important because of the awards or honors it can bring you personally. Additionally IUA has a long and distinguished history in representing professional agents in the Life, Health, and Financial Services industry. The benefits far outweight the membership dues. IUA provides information for agents to learn from each other and share sales ideas, and it serves as a platform for defending your interests in relation to state and federal legislation.

In order to help us fight legislative efforts to control the insurance industry we need your help by renewing or beginning your membership with IUA.

Consolidated Life Insurance takes great pride in the number of agents who are members of the IUA and the dissinguished service rendered by members of our field force. We here at Consolidated Life Insurance appreciate your services and applaud you for a well done job. If you are not a member of IUA please give this serious consideration.

---

2. Automatically replace all occurrences of IUA with Insurance Underwriters Association.
3. Automatically replace all occurrences of Consolidated Life Insurance with CLI.
4. Save the file on your file disk; use the filename **4skill3.iua**.
5. Print one copy.
6. If you have completed your work, exit WordPerfect (select **File**, **Exit**).

Part 1
Checking Your Step

Production Skill Builder Activities
Chapters 1-4

Production Activity 1.1—Create and Edit a Memorandum—Style 1

1. Use Memorandum—Style 1 and the following information to create a memorandum.

   a. Make decisions regarding:

      Margins
      Justification
      Memo date
      Use of Speller
      Reference initials

   b. Send the memorandum to All Administrative Support Staff from Chris Fosdahl.

   c. The subject of the memorandum is Alternative Work Schedules.

   d. Memorandum body text follows:

      For the past three years, we have been researching alternative work schedules such as flex time, shared time, and the four-day week. We appreciate your opinions and ideas concerning this matter.

      At its last meeting, the board of directors granted approval for a flex-time schedule in two departments and a shortened work week in a third department. Both of these plans will operate for a six-month trial period. Accounting, Marketing, and Quality Assurance are the three departments involved in this experiment. All other departments will remain on their normal schedules.

      At the end of the trial period, we will assess the results and determine whether we should stay with the old schedules or convert all departments to alternative work plans.

2. Save the file; use the filename **1pact1.aws**.

3. Revise the memorandum as shown:

For the past three years, we have been researching alternative work schedules such as flex time, shared time, and ~~the~~ a four-day week. ~~We appreciate~~ your opinions and ideas ~~concerning this matter~~ have been very much appreciated.

At its last meeting, the board of directors granted approval for a flex-time schedule in ~~two~~ three departments and a shortened work week in a ~~third~~ fourth department. ~~Both~~ All of these plans will operate for a ~~six~~ four-month trial period. Accounting, Marketing, Personnel, and Quality Assurance are the ~~three~~ four departments involved in this experiment. All other departments will remain on their normal schedules.

¶ Personnel in the affected departments should discuss their new work schedules with their respective managers. A survey will be sent out to all employees to obtain each individual's opinion concerning the new work schedules.

At the end of the trial period, ~~we will assess~~ the results will be assessed and a decision will be made to determine whether we should stay with the old schedules or convert all departments to alternative work plans.

---

4. Use the *new* filename **1pact1.rev** and save the file.
5. Print one copy and close the document.

Production Activity 1.2—Create a Numbered List and Copy Text

1. Type the following information and use center and bold as shown.
2. Press **Enter** three times after the last item.
3. Center and bold as shown.

Golden Plan Realty Marketing Strategy

Enter the information about your home in the MLS computer.

Inform all GPR sales representatives about your home.

Develop a list of features and benefits of your home to be given to company sales agents and area brokers.

Develop a list of items to give your home more **curb appeal**.

Contact twenty homeowners in the surrounding area and ask if they know anyone who would like to purchase your home.

Hold **open houses** as needed.
Prepare and distribute **advertising** for your home.

---

4. Press the Enter key three times after the last paragraph.
5. Select all paragraphs except the title and create a numbered list using the Bullet button.
6. Select a font of your choice with a point size of 12 to 14 for the entire document.
7. Save the file; use the filename **1pact2.gpr**.
8. Print one copy.
9. Select and copy the entire document and place the copied text below the original copy.

   Note: Three Enters should follow the last item. Both the copy and the original will be on the same page. It may be necessary to center and bold the title of the copied list.
10. Save the file again using the same filename, **1pact2.gpr**.
11. Print one copy.
12. Close the document.

Production Activity 1.3—Create a Numbered List, Move, and Replace Text

1. Use Memorandum—Style 1 and the following information to create a memorandum.

   a. Make decisions regarding:

      Margins
      Justification
      Fonts
      Memo date
      Reference initials
      Indention

   b. Send the memorandum to Kirsten R. Muller, Regional Vice President.

   c. The memorandum is from P. W. Cooper, Sales Manager.

   d. The subject of the memorandum is Promotion of Jeanine Castello.

   e. Memorandum body text follows:

   As part of the Sales Compensation Program, the company will be setting up new job titles for all secretarial and clerical employees. The new job titles will be: Division Administrative Assistant, Division Secretary, and Sales Clerk.

Under the previous system, I am budgeted for three (3) clerical support people, but have utilized two (2) clerical people (Meagan O'Hara and Jeanine Castello).

I would like to recommend that J. M. Castello be upgraded from a Division Secretary, Grade 5, to a Division Administrative Assistant, Grade 7. The following are my reasons for requesting this promotion:

J. M. Castello has been a Division Secretary for over two and one-half (2.5) years. In addition, she has provided secretarial support for the District Account Managers.

J. M. Castello filled in for Meagan O'Hara when Meagan was on maternity leave. J. M. Castello displayed her ability to perform the duties of a Division Administrative Assistant during that time.

When our new facility is ready for our account managers to occupy, J. M. Castello will be the secretary for three (3) sales managers and five (5) account managers. She will also have a part-time clerk reporting to her.

J. M. Castello has proven her skills by preparing the current sales manual and annual budget, as well as handling telephones and greeting visitors.

Your consideration of J. M. Castello's promotion is very much appreciated.

2. Select the fourth, fifth, sixth, and seventh paragraphs and create a numbered list using the Bullet button.
3. Move item number four above item number two.
4. Replace J. M. with Jeanine.
5. Save the file; use the filename **1pact3.pro**.
6. Print one copy.
7. Close the document.

Production Activity 1.4—Edit, Move, and Use Speller and Bullets

1. Open the file named **1pact4.wpd** located on the data disk.
2. Change the font to **Arrus BT** or make a choice of your own.
3. Revise the text as shown.

Steps to Attract a Mentor

ital

Learn how to listen. Never interrupt others before they have completed their comments. Listen sixty percent of the time. You will learn much from what others have to say.

Develop a presentation that demonstrates your personal pride. Walk straight, keep your head up, shake hands firmly, and establish eye contact whenever you are in a conversation.

¶ Accept the outcome of any situation as a *result* -- not a failure. Examine any situation with the thought of improvement.

Be persistent and flexible. People who persist develop excellence in their fields faster than those who settle for second best.

Set realistic goals. Set short-term goals (6 months) as well as long-term goals (5 years).

4. Use the Bullet button to insert a bullet character to the left of each paragraph. Use your choice for the bullet style.
5. Use the Speller to find and correct any misspelled words; also proofread carefully for accurate meaning.
6. Use the *new* filename **1pact4.sam** and save the file on your file disk.
7. Print one copy.
8. Close the document.

Production Activity 1.5—Create and Edit an AMS Simplified Style Letter; Language Arts Skills

1. Use the AMS simplified style letter and the following information to create a letter.
   a. Make decisions regarding:
      Margins
      Justification
      Fonts
      Subject line
      Text attributes (bold, underline, italic)
      Use of Speller
      Reference initials
      Documentation identification
      Enclosure notation
   b. Correct three spelling and two punctuation errors.
   c. The letter should be sent to Leland and Nelly Kroff, 2403 Mill Glenn Court, Atlanta, GA 30338.
   d. The letter is from Shane Treakle, Vice President.
   e. The letter body text follows:

   You have undoubtedly read and heard a lot recently about the problems of the nation's financial institutions, including some insurance companies. Therefore we are pleased to send you a copy of last year's annual report for Global Consolidated Life Insurance (GCL).

We have just experienced one of the most comendable years in the company's 93-year history. We had a record net income of $30 million on total revenues of almost $890 million. We actually held operating expenses below the previous year's level, and the company reached a new milestone last month--$5 billion in assets.

More than 95 percent of the company's assets are invested in bonds, short-term debt instruments, and first mortgage loans. At year end, not a single bond issue was in payment default, and not a single mortgage was in foreclosure.

When you need additional insurance or seek a high return on an individual anuity, we hope you will contact your GCL agent. Our company has been in existance for more than 90 years, and you can count on GCL being there when you need us.

2. Save the file; use the filename **1pact5.gcl**.
3. Use the following information to revise the letter.
   a. In the second paragraph change the word "company's" to GCL's and delete the word "the."
   b. Change the net income to $32.5 million and total revenues to $900 million.
   c. Delete the last sentence of the third paragraph and insert the following sentences:

      Based on the company's financial condition and operating performance, GCL continues to earn a superior rating. We have had a top rating recommendation since 1955.

   d. Insert the following paragraph above the third paragraph:

      Of course, the financial strength of the company really rests on the quality of our invested assets, and we believe that our invested assets are first-rate.

4. Use the *new* filename **1pact5.glo** and save the file again.
5. Print one copy and close the document.

Part 2
A Step Further

Work with Special Features

Chapters 5-8

- Create a table
- Join cells
- Change column widths
- Insert columns and rows
- Convert tabbed text to a table
- Set row height and fill (shade) cells
- Center a table horizontally and vertically
- Change the table borders and lines
- Set and customize the number type
- Align figures at the decimal point
- Move and delete a row or column
- Change table row margins
- Copy and delete a table
- Calculate column/row totals
- Copy a formula
- Omit table lines and borders
- Use single and double underlines
- Convert case
- Use a hard space
- Insert special characters
- Set tabs
- Change margins using the Ruler Bar
- Create newspaper style columns
- Place a border line between columns
- Change column definition
- Insert a column break
- Use hyphenation
- Create parallel columns
- Convert text in parallel columns to a table

CHAPTER 5

Create a Table

Features Covered

- Create a table
- Insert a row
- Join cells
- Change justification for multiple cells
- Insert a column
- Set row height
- Change column widths
- Set and customize the number type
- Align figures at the decimal point
- Center a table horizontally and vertically
- Convert tabbed text to a table
- Change table borders and lines
- Fill (shade) cells

Chapter Objectives and Introduction

After successfully completing this chapter, you will be able to create a table, increase and decrease column widths, insert columns and rows, join table cells, and align figures at the decimal point. In addition, you will be able to change row height, center a table horizontally and vertically, use the Tables Button Bar, and create a table using existing text. Traditionally, a table has been created by calculating the location of column tabs so that when the table is printed it will be centered horizontally on the page. Tables in this book will be created using the Table feature, which will determine the column widths automatically and display lines around each column and row.

The Table feature is used to organize information into columns and rows without using tab settings. A sample table containing information is shown in Figure 5.1. Table information can include either text or numbers or both.

FIGURE 5.1

Sample table

Software Requirements	
WordPerfect 6.0 for Windows	**Microsoft Word 6.0 for Windows**
386 or higher	286/386 or higher
6–8 Mb of RAM	4 Mb of RAM
Mouse or track ball device	Mouse or track ball device
28 Mb hard disk space	6–24 Mb hard disk space
Windows 3.1	Windows 3.1
DOS 3.1 or higher	DOS 3.1 or higher
VGA graphics adapter	Graphics adapter

Create a Table

A table can be easily created using the **Table Quick Create** button on the Power Bar. Also, text typed in columns can be converted to a table using the Convert Tabular Text feature. Once the number of table columns and rows are specified, lines for the columns and rows display in the document window. The table lines are set by default to print but can be omitted if desired (see Chapter 6, page 143).

The table lines form columns and rows. The columns are identified by letters A, B, C, etc., and the rows are numbered 1, 2, 3, etc. The intersection of each column and row is called a cell. Each cell is identified by an address. When the insertion point is located in the third column (column C) and row 2, the cell address is C2. The cell address displays in the bottom middle of the Status bar. When the mouse pointer is moved to a cell, the cell address also displays in the left side of the Title bar.

When the insertion point is located in a table cell, the Tables Button Bar displays (see Figure 5.4). If the insertion point is moved outside the table cells, the WordPerfect Button Bar automatically displays.

Text typed in each table cell wraps around in the cell. If the **Enter** key is pressed in a cell, the cell automatically increases in height. If text within a cell is to be indented, press the **Ctrl** and **Tab** keys to activate the tab or press the **F7** key.

The **Tab** key, **Shift** and **Tab** keys, or the arrow keys are used to move the insertion point from cell to cell. After text is typed in one cell, the **Tab** key or an arrow key is used to move the insertion point to the next cell. To return to the previous cell, press **Shift** and **Tab**.

Steps to Create a Table

1. Move the mouse pointer to the Table Quick Create button on the Power Bar. Press and hold the mouse button {Alt, a, c, *or* F12}.

   Note: A miniature grid displays at the location of the Table Quick Create button (see Figure 5.2).

2. Continue to press and hold the mouse button while dragging to highlight the desired number of columns and rows. Release the mouse button {type the number of columns, press Tab, type the number of rows, press Enter}.

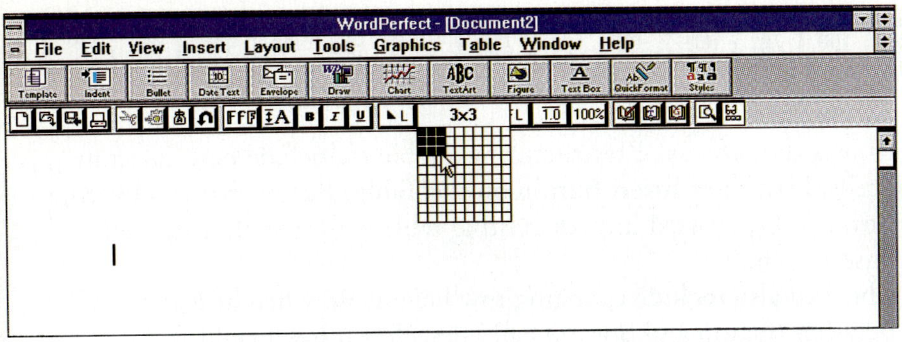

FIGURE 5.2

Miniature table grid

For example, drag to highlight a 3 x 3 table; release the mouse button.

Note: The empty columns and rows for the table and the Tables Button Bar display in the document window.

Finish-Up Instructions

- To type the unformatted information in each cell, press the **Tab** key or the arrow keys to move from cell to cell and row to row. Type the unformatted information shown in Figure 5.3.

  *Note: If the **Enter** key is mistakenly pressed while typing information into a table cell, press the **Backspace** key to delete the unwanted return. If the **Tab** key is pressed after the last cell entry, check that the insertion point is in a cell in the row to be deleted, then select the **Delete Tbl** button on the Tables Button Bar, check that "1" displays in the Rows option, and select **OK**.*
- Use the filename **5drill1.tbl** and save the file (select the **Save** button; type the filename; if necessary, click in the Drives box and click on the drive letter where the file disk is located; select **OK**).
- Optional. Print one unformatted copy.

Format and Modify a Table

Formatting a table is the process of completing such tasks as aligning figures at the decimal point, centering text in the cell, increasing or decreasing the column widths, and centering the table horizontally on the page. The primary goals of formatting a table are to present a pleasing appearance and to make reading easier. To produce a table that is formatted for an appealing appearance, *visually* adjust the width and height of cells and the alignment of text within the cells. (If desired, the ruler provided in the back of this book can be used to assist in estimating column width.)

The Tables Button Bar automatically displays when the insertion point is located in a table cell (see Figure 5.4). The Tables Button Bar contains many buttons that assist in the formatting and modification of tables.

Emma Croft	Western	155575.25
Tan Nguyen	Central	155295.95
Lloyd Guevara	Southern	155333.75

FIGURE 5.3

Unformatted table

FIGURE 5.4

Tables Button Bar

Modifying a table is the process of restructuring a table to include new columns or rows or to join cells. If the **Tbl Insert** button on the Tables Button Bar is selected, a new column or row can be inserted into an existing table before or after the cell that contains the insertion point.

Modifying a table can also include changing row height. Row height is the amount of space between the top and bottom cell lines. When row height is increased, the cell text will be placed at the top of the cell and the additional space will be added between the text and the bottom cell line. Two row height options are available: Auto and Fixed. Auto is the default row height setting.

With the Auto setting selected, WordPerfect will increase or decrease the row height to accommodate any amount and size of text typed in the cells. The height for the row will be adjusted to the maximum height needed for any cell in the row. When the Fixed setting is selected, an exact amount of space can be specified for each row. When text is added or deleted, the row height will not adjust automatically. If necessary, a new Fixed row height amount can be entered.

Two or more cells in a row can be joined in order to provide space for information that relates to more than one cell or column. Also, some or all of the cells in the column can be joined.

Table numbers can be formatted by selecting from a list of standard formats, such as Currency and Commas. When the Currency format is selected, WordPerfect automatically inserts a dollar sign in front of the table numbers and inserts commas to separate thousands within the table numbers ($12,652.00).

With the Commas format, the table numbers are formatted with commas to separate thousands (12,652.00). The default number of digits after the decimal for both the Currency format and Commas format is two. The number of digits after the decimal can be changed. For example, to eliminate the decimal point and zeros in the number 12,652.00, the number of digits after the decimal can be changed to zero.

WordPerfect provides QuickMenus for easy access to menu items related to a specific feature. The right mouse button is pressed to obtain a QuickMenu. For example, if several cells are selected and the right mouse button is pressed, the QuickMenu displays with various options such as Copy, Insert, Join Cells, etc.

Start-Up Instructions

- The file named **5drill1.tbl** should be displayed in the document window.

Steps to Insert a Table Row

1. Place the insertion point in the row that will be located before or after the inserted row.

   For example, place the insertion point in any cell in the first row.

2. Select the Tbl Insert on the Tables Button Bar {Alt, a, i}.

   Note: *The Insert Columns/Rows dialog box displays.*

3. Select the desired Insert option.

For example, check that the Rows option is selected and that the number displayed in the Rows box is highlighted. If necessary, select Rows {r}.

4. Type the number of rows to be inserted {type desired number of rows}.

    For example, type 2.

5. Select the desired Placement option.

    For example, check that **Before** is selected {press Tab *or* b}.

6. Select OK {press Enter}.

    ***Note:** Two new rows display at the top of the table.*

Finish-Up Instructions

- If necessary, press **Shift** and **Tab** to move the insertion point to the first cell in the table.
- Type the following text into the new cells as shown. (Remember: Press the **Tab** key to move from cell to cell and row to row.)

Semiannual Sales		
Names	Divisions	Sales

- Use the *new* filename **5drill1.ins** and save the file again (select **File**, **Save As**; if necessary, click in the Drives box and click on the drive letter where the file disk is located; type the new filename, select **OK**).

Start-Up Instructions

- The file named **5drill1.ins** should be displayed in the document window.

Steps to Join Table Cells

1. Select the cells to be joined by moving the mouse pointer to the left line of the first cell to be joined until the left selection arrow displays (see Figure 5.5). Double-click to highlight the desired row of cells {place the insertion point in the first and/or left cell to be selected; press and hold the Shift key and tap F8 and then tap the End key; continue to hold the Shift key and press the right or down arrow key to extend the highlighting}.

    For example, select the cells in row one.

2. Select Table, Join {Alt, a, j}.

Left selection arrow

Semiannual Sales		
Names	Divisions	Sales
Emma Croft	Western	155575.25
Tan Nguyen	Central	155295.95
Lloyd Guevara	Southern	155333.75

FIGURE 5.5

Table with left selection arrow

3. Select **Cell** {c}.

   Note: All cells in row 1 are now one cell. Continue with the following Steps to Change Justification in Multiple Cells.

Shortcut

1. With the cells to be joined selected, click the *right* mouse button to display the QuickMenu.
2. Select **Join Cells**.

Start-Up Instructions

- The table named **5drill1.ins** should be displayed in the document window.

Steps to Change Justification for Multiple Cells

1. Select the cells where justification is to be changed by moving the mouse pointer to the left line of the top left cell to be selected until the left selection arrow displays. Press and hold the left mouse button while dragging to highlight the desired cells and rows {see Step 1 in the Steps to Join Table Cells on page 109}.

   For example, select all cells in rows 1 and 2.

2. Move the mouse pointer to the **Justification** button. Press and hold the mouse button while dragging the mouse pointer to the desired justification. Release the mouse button {Alt, a, o *or* Ctrl and F12; e, j, press the down arrow key until Center displays, press Enter}.

   For example, select **Center**.

Finish-Up Instructions

- If necessary, click once to deselect the table cells.
- Use the *new* filename **5drill1.jus** and save the file again (select **File**, **Save As**; if necessary, click in the Drives box and click on the drive letter where the file disk is located; type the new filename, select **OK**).

Start-Up Instructions

- The file named **5drill1.jus** should be displayed in the document window.

Steps to Insert a Table Column

1. Place the insertion point in the column that will be located before or after the inserted column.

   For example, place the insertion point in any cell in column C.

   Note: Check that the cell address in the middle of the Status bar displays with a "C" followed by a number, e.g., TABLE A Cell C3).

2. Select the **Tbl Insert** button on the Tables Button Bar {Alt, a, i}.

   Note: The Insert Columns/Rows dialog box displays

3. Select **Columns** {c}.

Note: The number in the Columns box is highlighted.

4. Type the number of columns to be inserted.

For example, check that "1" is displayed. If necessary, type "1."

5. Select the desired Placement option {press Tab}.

For example, check that the **Before** option is chosen. (If necessary, select **Before**.)

6. Select **OK** {press Enter once}.

Finish-Up Instructions

❖ Type the following information into the new column cells.

Office
Los Angeles
Kansas City
Atlanta

Note: The original Center justification is in effect in the cell containing the column heading, while the remaining column cells are left aligned.

❖ Save the file again using the same filename **5drill1.jus** (select the **Save** button).

Start-Up Instructions

❖ The file named **5drill1.jus** should be displayed in the document window.

Steps to Change Table Row Height

1. Select and highlight the rows where the row height is to be changed. (If necessary, see Step 1 of the Steps to Join Table Cells on page 109.)

For example, select the first two table rows.

2. Select the **Format Tbl** button on the Tables Button Bar {Alt, a, o *or* Ctrl and F12}.

Note: The Format dialog box displays.

3. Select the desired Format option.

For example, check that **Row** is selected. (If necessary, select **Row** {o}.)

4. Select the **Row Height Fixed** option {x}.

Note: The figures in the Fixed box are highlighted.

5. Type the desired row height.

For example, type .4. (Do not type the final period.)

6. Select **OK** {press Enter once}.

Note: Rows 1 and 2 are increased in height.

Finish-Up Instructions

- Click or press the down arrow key to deselect the table rows.
- Use the *new* filename **5drill1.hig** and save the file again (select **File**, **Save As**; if necessary, click in the Drives box and click on the drive letter where the file disk is located; type the new filename, select **OK**)

Start-Up Instructions

- The file named **5drill1.hig** should be displayed in the document window.

Steps to Change Column Widths

1. Move the mouse pointer to a line between table columns (or at the left or right side of the table) until a double-headed arrow displays {place the insertion point in the column where the width is to be changed}.

   For example, point to the table column line between column A and B until the double-headed arrow displays.

2. *To decrease the column width,* press and hold the left mouse button while dragging the mouse to the left {press and hold the Ctrl key while tapping the less than (<) key}.

   For example, visually estimate and drag the mouse approximately ½" to the left.

3. *To increase the column width,* press and hold the left mouse button while dragging the mouse to the right {press and hold the Ctrl key while tapping the greater than (>) key}.

Finish-Up Instructions

- Move the mouse pointer to the table column line between columns B and C. Visually estimate and drag the column line left until the column width is approximately 1¼".

  Hint: *Use your first finger and bend your finger at the joints. Place the flat area of your finger (between the two joints) against the screen to estimate approximately one inch, or if desired, use the ruler provided in the back of this book.*

- Repeat Steps 1 and 2 of the Steps to Change Column Widths to decrease the widths in columns C and D. Visually estimate that the column widths are approximately the same.

  Note: *Your table column widths should be approximately the same size. The column decimals will be aligned after using the following Steps to Set and Customize the Number Type.*

- Use the *new* filename **5drill1.wid** and save the file (select **File**, **Save As**; if necessary, click in the Drives box and click on the drive letter where the file disk is located; type the new filename, select **OK**).

Start-Up Instructions

- The file named **5drill1.wid** should be displayed in the document window.

Steps to Set and Customize the Number Type

1. Select the cell(s) where the number type is to be set. (If necessary, see Step 1 in the Steps to Join Table Cells on page 109.)

   For example, move the mouse pointer to the left side of cell D4 until the left selection arrow displays. Press and hold while dragging downward to highlight cells D4 and D5. Release the mouse button.

2. Select the **Tbl # Type** button on the Tables Button Bar {Alt, a, u or Alt and F12}.

   Note: The Number Type dialog box displays.

3. Choose the desired Select Type For option.

   For example, select the **Column** option {o}.

4. Select the desired Available Types option.

   For example, select **Commas** {m}.

5. Select **Custom** {u}.

   Note: The Customize Number Type dialog box displays.

6. Change the desired option(s).

   For example, in the Digits After Decimal box, click on the down triangle twice to display a zero (0) {d, type 0 (zero)}.

7. Select **OK** twice {press Enter twice}.

   Note: The comma displays in the cell figures but no cents display.

Finish-Up Instructions

- Select and highlight cell D3.
- Set the Number Type to Currency and zero digits after the decimal. (Select the **Tbl # Type** button, check that Cell is selected, select **Currency**, select **Custom** in the Digits After Decimal box, click on the down triangle twice to display a zero, select **OK** twice.)
- Save the file again using the same filename **5drill.wid** (select the **Save** button).

Steps to Align Figures at the Decimal Point

1. Select the desired cell(s) in the column where the decimals are to align.

   For example, select cells D3 to D5 in column D. (If necessary, see Step 1 in the Steps to Join Table Cells on page 109.)

2. Move the mouse pointer to the **Justification** button in the Power Bar. Press and hold the left mouse button while dragging the mouse pointer downward to highlight the **Decimal** option. Release the mouse button {Alt a, o *or* Ctrl and F12; j, press the down arrow key repeatedly until Decimal Align displays, press Enter once}.

   Note: The dollar amounts in column D are aligned at the right digit since no decimal point is displayed. If decimal digits display, use the Steps to Set and Customize the Number Type to change the digits after decimal option. Your table should look similar to Figure 5.6.

Semiannual Sales			
Names	Divisions	Office	Sales
Emma Croft	Western	Los Angeles	$155,575
Tan Nguyen	Central	Kansas City	155,296
Lloyd Guevara	Southern	Atlanta	155,344

FIGURE 5.6

Table with decimal alignment and changed column widths

Finish-Up Instructions

- Use the *new* filename **5drill1.dec** and save the table on the file disk (select **File**, **Save As**; if necessary, click in the Drives box and click on the drive letter where the file disk is located; type the filename; select **OK**).

Start-Up Instructions

- The file named **5drill1.dec** should be displayed in the document window.

Steps to Center a Table Horizontally

1. Place the insertion point in any cell in the table.
2. Select the Format Tbl button on the Tables Button Bar {Alt, a, o *or* Ctrl and F12}.
3. Select Table {a}.
4. In the Table Position option box, move the mouse pointer to Left, press and hold the left mouse button, and drag the mouse pointer to Center; release the mouse button {press Alt and t, press Tab twice, press the down arrow key until Center displays}.
5. Select OK {press Enter}.

   Note: *To display the table centered horizontally on the screen, select the* ***Page Zoom Full*** *button. Select the* ***Page Zoom Full*** *button again to return to the normal view.*

Finish-Up Instructions

- Save the file again using the same filename, **5drill1.dec** (select the **Save** button).
- Print one copy (select the **Print** button; choose **Print**).
- Close the document (select **File**, **Close**).

Convert Tabbed Text to a Table

Text that is separated by tabs and hard returns can be converted easily to a table. Once the tabbed text is typed, select the columns. The Convert Table dialog box dis-

FIGURE 5.7

Text to be converted to a table

Tab

Telecommunications → TTH → 108 (Press Enter)
Word Processing → MW → 110 (Press Enter)
Local Area Networks → MWF → 145 (Do not press Enter)

plays after selecting the **Table** button on the Tables Button Bar or after choosing **Table, Create**.

Once the text is converted to a table, the information that was once horizontally separated by tabs is now contained in individual cells and surrounded by table lines. The information in the cells can be formatted and the structure of the table modified by using the buttons on the Tables Button Bar or by selecting the desired options from the **Table** drop-down menu.

Start-Up Instructions

- Type the text to be converted to a table. Press the **Tab** key once between each item and press the **Enter** key at the end of the first two lines. Do not press Enter after typing the last line.
- Type the information shown in Figure 5.7.

Steps to Convert Tabbed Text to a Table

1. Select all lines of the tabbed text.

   For example, select all three lines of text by choosing **Edit, Select, All** {Alt, e, e, L}.

2. Select the **Table** button on the Tables Button Bar {Alt, a, c *or* F12}.

   Note: *The Convert Table dialog box displays.*

3. The Tabular Column option should be selected. (If necessary, select **Tabular Column** {t}.)

4. Select **OK** {Enter}.

   Note: *The table lines display and the third column cell lines extend to the right margin. Text may wrap around in the first two cells of the last row.*

Finish-Up Instructions

- Change the column widths for columns B and C. (If necessary, see the Steps to Change Column Widths on page 112 for additional information on changing column widths.) For example, visually estimate to change the widths of columns B and C to approximately 1". If necessary, widen column A so that text in each cell displays on a single line.
- Center the table horizontally (select **Format Tbl, Table, Table Position, Center, OK**).
- Use the filename **5drill2** and save the file on your file disk (select **Save** button; type the filename; if necessary, click in the Drives box and click on the drive letter where the file disk is located; select **OK**).

Change Table Borders and Lines and Fill (Shade) Cells

The lines and borders that display around the table cells can be changed by choosing a border, line, or fill style. The default line style for all the table lines (left, right, top, bottom, inside, and outside) is "Single." The preset border line style is "No Border." There are various types of line and border styles, such as dashed, dotted, thick, thin-thick, etc. (see Figure 5.8). The line styles can be designated to print around all table cells or only specific cells, and table border can be designated to print around an entire table. Lines can also be omitted (see Chapter 6).

The fill style is a pattern (or gradient) that includes foreground and background colors (see Figure 5.8). The foreground or background colors are shaded percentages of a color. For example, the 10% Shaded Fill appears light gray. A sample of the selected fill displays in a sample box in the Table Line/Fill dialog box. If a color monitor is being used, various colors or shades can be chosen and displayed on the screen.

If the table lines are changed to "None," the table structure can still be shown in the document by selecting the **TblGrid** button on the Tables Button Bar or by choosing **View**, **Table Gridlines.** The table gridlines visually replace the border, line, and fill styles and display as small dots around all table cells. The table gridlines do not print.

Start-Up Instructions

- Open the file named **5drill3.wpd** located on the data disk (select the **Open** button; if necessary, click in the Drives box and click on the drive letter where the file disk is located; double-click on the filename).

Steps to Change the Table Border

Note: When changing the table border, the insertion point can be located in any table cell.

1. Select the **TblLineFill** button on the Tables Button Bar {Alt, a, L *or* Shift F12}.

   Note: The Table Lines/Fill dialog box displays showing the options for changing a cell border line or fill style.

2. Select the desired option.

   For example, select **Table** {a}.

   *Note: When **Table** is selected, different options display in the Table Lines/Fill dialog box.*

3. Click on the NO BORDER button in the Border Lines box {Alt and b, Spacebar}.

   Note: A palette of border styles displays (see Figure 5.8).

4. Move the mouse pointer to the desired border style and click once {press the arrow keys until the desired border style is selected; Enter}.

   For example, move the mouse pointer to the double border (first border in the third row) and click once.

5. Select **OK** {press Enter}.

   Note: The table displays with double borders on the top, bottom, left, and right sides.

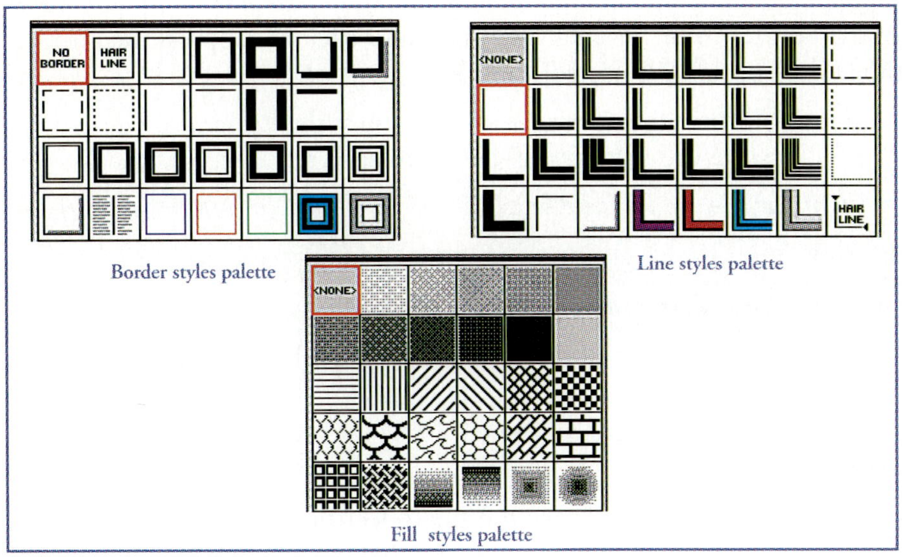

FIGURE 5.8

Line, Border, and Fill styles palettes

Steps to Change Table Lines

1. Select the cell(s) where the line(s) is to be changed. (If necessary, see Step 1 of the Steps to Join Table Cells on page 109 for selecting cells.)

   For example, select all cells in row 2 where the column headings are located.

2. Select the **TblLineFill** button on the Tables Button Bar {Alt, a, L *or* Shift and F12}.

   Note: The current Cell or Selection option is chosen.

3. Click once on the desired Line Styles option button.

   For example, click on the **Bottom** button {Alt and b, Spacebar}.

   Note: A palette of line styles displays (see Figure 5.8).

4. Move the mouse pointer to the desired line style and click once {press the arrow keys until the desired line style is selected; Enter}.

   For example, move the mouse pointer to the double line option (first row, to the right of "None") and click once.

5. Select **OK** {press Enter}.

   Note: The bottom line of row 2 displays with a double line.

Steps to Fill (Shade) Table Cells

1. Select the cells to be shaded. (If necessary see Step 1 in the Steps to Join Table Cells on page 109.)

   For example, select all cells with money amounts.

2. Select the **TblLineFill** button on the Tables Button Bar {Alt, a, L *or* Shift and F12}.

3. Click on the NONE button in the Fill Options box {Alt and f, Spacebar}.

   Note: A palette of fill options displays (see Figure 5.8).

4. Move the mouse pointer to the desired fill option and click once {press the arrow keys until the desired option is selected; Enter}.

   For example, move the mouse pointer to the lightest shaded sample, 10% fill (first row, to the right of <NONE>) and click once.

   Note: A 10% fill displays in the Fill style box.

5. Select OK {Enter}.

   Note: Click once to deselect the cells and display the 10% fill.

Finish-Up Instructions

- Select the title and column headings in rows 1 and 2 and change the font to Swiss721 BlkEx BT, 14-point.
- Use the *new* filename **5drill3.fil** and save the file (select **File**, **Save As**; type the filename; if necessary, click in the Drives box and click on the drive letter where the file disk is located; select **OK**).

Center a Table or Text Vertically

Table rows or lines of text can be centered vertically on a page between the top and bottom margins. On an 8½ by 11-inch sheet of paper, approximately 66 lines (6 lines per inch) or approximately 33 table rows (3 lines per inch) can be printed. Text that occupies fewer than 54 lines (66 – 12 = 2" top/bottom margins) and tables that occupy fewer than 27 rows will usually display more attractively on a page if the lines/rows are centered between the top and bottom margins. The tables typed in this book will be fewer than 20 rows; therefore, vertical centering will be useful.

Start-Up Instructions

- The file named **5drill3.fil** should be displayed in the document window.

Steps to Center a Table or Text Vertically

1. With the insertion point located in any table cell, select Layout, Page, Center {Alt and L, p, c}.
2. Select the Current Page {p}.
3. Select OK {Enter}.

   *Note: Select the **Page Zoom Full** button to view the table centered vertically on the page. Select the **Page Zoom Full** button again to return to the normal view. Select **View, Draft** to display the table at the top of the document window.*

Finish-Up Instructions

- Save the file again using the same filename **5drill3.fil** (select the **Save** button).
- Print one copy (select the **Print** button; choose **Print**).
- Close the document (select **File**, **Close**).

The Next Step

Chapter Review and Activities

Self-Check Quiz

T F 1. A table can be created using the **Tables Quick Create** button on the Power Bar.

T F 2. The intersection of each column and row is called a cell.

T F 3. The **Enter** key is pressed in a cell in order to insert a new table row.

T F 4. Formatting a table can include increasing or decreasing the table column widths.

T F 5. Text that is separated by tabs and hard returns can be converted to a table.

6. When the **Decimal** justification option is selected, figures are aligned
   a. at the left digit.
   b. at the right digit.
   c. at the decimal point.
   d. either b or c.

7. To use the **Tab** key to indent text in a cell, press
   a. Tab.
   b. Shift and Tab.
   c. Ctrl and Tab.
   d. none of the above.

8. A table or text can be centered vertically on a page by selecting **Layout**, **Page**, **Center**, and choosing
   a. **Current Page**.
   b. **Current and Subsequent Pages**.
   c. **Center Page(s)**.

9. State the primary purpose for formatting a table.

10. Give one reason for joining table cells.

Enriching Language Arts Skills

Spelling/Vocabulary Words

initiative readiness to begin action.
strategic pertaining to the importance of accomplishing a plan.
alliances a joining together to meet a common goal.

Dollar Amounts Formats

Use a comma to separate the number digits into groups of thousands. No space is placed between a number and the dollar sign. If even numbers are used in the body of a document or if a column of numbers has even dollar amounts, the zeros are omitted. Even dollar amounts can either be right justified or decimal justified in a column in order to align the numbers on the right.

Example:

$28,655,342
1,389
10,843

Activities

Activity 5.1—Create and Format a Table and Change Table Number Type

1. Create a table with 3 columns and 4 rows (select the **Table Quick Create** button on the Power Bar, press and hold the mouse button and drag to highlight a 3 x 4 table, release the mouse button).
2. Type the unformatted text as shown.

Federated Growth Trust	Yearly increase	1453.55
Colonial Growth Shares	Bi-annual increase	675.67
Fidelity Set Energy	Quarterly increase	420.25
Global Income Trust	Yearly increase	1600.75

3. Use the filename **5act1.tbl** and save the file.
4. Use the following instructions to format the table:
   a. Change the justification for the text in column B to **Right**. (Select all cells in column B. Select the **Justification** button and choose **Right**. Click once to deselect the cells.)
   b. Change the justification for the figures in column C to **Decimal**. (Select all cells in column C. Select the **Justification** button and choose **Decimal**. Click once to deselect the cells.)
   c. Change the number type for cell C1 to **Currency**. (Select cell C1, choose the **Tbl # Type** button, and select **Currency, OK**.)
   d. Change the number type for cells **C2** through **C4** to **Commas**. (Select cells **C2** through **C4**, choose the **Tbl # Type** button, and select **Commas, OK**.)
   e. Visually estimate and decrease columns B and C to approximately 2 inches wide each. (Place the mouse pointer on the column line between columns B and C until the double-headed arrow displays. Press

and hold the mouse button while dragging the line to the left. Release the mouse button. Repeat for the column line at the right of the table.)

f. Position the table centered horizontally on the page (select **Format Tbl, Table, Table Position, Center, OK**).

*Note: Your table should look **similar** to the following:*

Federated Growth Trust	Yearly increase	$1,453.55
Colonial Growth Shares	Bi-annual increase	675.67
Fidelity Set Energy	Quarterly increase	420.25
Global Income Trust	Yearly increase	1,600.75

5. Use the same filename, **5act1.tbl**, and save the file again (select the **Save** button).
6. If desired, select the **Page Zoom Full** button to view the table horizontally centered. Select the **Page Zoom Full** button again to return to the normal view.
7. Print one copy (select the **Print** button; choose **Print**).
8. Close the document (select **File, Close**).

Activity 5.2—Create and Format a Table, Insert Rows, Join Cells, Change Table Number Type, and Change Row Height

1. Create a table with 2 columns and 5 rows (select the **Table Quick Create** button on the Power Bar, press and hold the mouse button while dragging to highlight a 2 x 5 table, release the mouse button).
2. Type the unformatted text as shown.

Alaska	402500
Iowa	2993000
New York	18499500
Oklahoma	3188000
Texas	14555000

3. Change the number type for column B to Commas and set the digits after the decimal to zero. (Select cells **B1** through **B5**. Choose the **Tbl # Type** button and select **Commas**, select **Custom**, click twice on the down triangle beside the Digits after Decimal box to display zero (0), and select **OK** twice.)
4. Change the justification of column B to Decimal. (With column B selected, move the mouse pointer to the **Justification** button, press and hold the mouse button while dragging to select **Decimal**. Release the mouse button.)
5. Click to deselect the formatted figures.

6. Insert three rows (place the insertion point in either cell in row 1, select the **Tbl Insert** button, click on **Rows**, type **3**, select **OK**).
7. Join the row 1 cells (select the cells in row 1; select **Tables**, **Join**, **Cell**).
8. Join the second row cells.
9. Center all cells in rows 1, 2, and 3. (Select all cells in rows 1, 2, and 3. Move the mouse pointer to the **Justification** button, press and hold the mouse button while dragging to select **Center**. Release the mouse button. Click once to deselect the cells.)
10. Change the row height for the first two rows to **.5**. (Select the first two rows, select the **Format Tbl** button, select **Row Height**, select **Fixed**; type .5; **OK**. Click once to deselect the cells.)
11. In row 1, type the title **State Populations** in the top row. Notice that the text is centered.
12. In row 2, type the subtitle **(Approximately)**.
13. Type the column headings **State** and **Population** in the third row cells.
14. Visually estimate and decrease the width of columns A and B to approximately 2". (Place the mouse pointer on the column line between columns B and C until the double-headed arrow displays. Press and hold the mouse button while dragging the line to the left. Release the mouse button. Repeat for the column line at the right of the table.).

    Note: *Your table should look similar to the following table:*

State Populations	
(Approximately)	
State	Population
Alaska	402,500
Iowa	2,993,000
New York	18,499,500
Oklahoma	3,188,000
Texas	14,555,000

15. Center the table horizontally on the page (select the **Format Tbl** button; select **Table**, **Table Position**, **Center**, **OK**).
16. Use the filename **5act2.spa** and save the file (select the **Save** button; type the filename; if necessary, click in the Drives box and click on the drive letter where the file disk is located; select **OK**).
17. Print one copy (select the **Print** button; choose **Print**).
18. Close the document (select **File**, **Close**).

Activity 5.3—Create and Format a Table, Insert a Column, Shade Cells, and Change Table Number Type

1. Create a table with 2 columns and 5 rows (select the **Tables Quick Create** button on the Power Bar, press and hold the mouse button while dragging to highlight a 2 x 5 table, release the mouse button).
2. Type the unformatted text as shown.

Mortgage Affordability	
Annual Income	Mortgage Amount
25000	55000
45000	115000
65000	166000

3. Use the following information to format the table shown:
   a. Select and join the cells in row 1 (select **Table, Join, Cell**).
   b. Select and center the title and column heading cells in rows 1 and 2. (With rows 1 and 2 selected, move the mouse pointer to the **Justification** button, press and hold the mouse button while dragging to select **Center.** Release the mouse button.)
   c. With all cells in rows 1 and 2 selected, shade the cells. (Select the **TblLineFill** button, click on the **None** button in the Fill Options box, click on the lightest fill style, **OK.**)
   d. Select all cells that contain dollar amounts and set the number type to **Commas** and the digits after the decimal to zero. (Select the **Tbl # Type** button, select **Commas**; select **Custom**, click twice on the down triangle twice beside the Digits after Decimal box to display zero (0), select **OK** twice.)
   e. With the cells containing amounts highlighted, select the **Justification** button and choose **Decimal**. Click once to deselect the cells.
   f. Insert one new table column between columns A and B (place the insertion point in column B, select the **Tbl Insert** button, select **Columns, OK**).
   g. Type the following information into the new column cells:

Home Price
68,500
136,700
205,200

   h. Visually estimate and adjust each table column width to approximately 2". (Move the mouse pointer to the desired column line until the double-headed arrow displays, press and hold the mouse button and drag the mouse left to decrease the column width.)

i. Change the number type for all cells in row 3 to Currency and change the digits after the decimal to zero. (Select the cells in row 3, select the **Tbl#Type** button, choose **Currency**; select **Custom**, click twice on the down triangle beside the Digits after Decimal box to display zero (0), and select **OK** twice).

j. Center the table horizontally (select the **Tbl Fmt** button on the Tables Button Bar, choose **Center** in the Table Position box, **OK**).

Note: Your table should look similar to the following:

Mortgage Affordability		
Annual Income	Home Price	Mortgage
$25,000	$68,500	$55,000
45,000	136,700	115,000
65,000	205,200	166,000

4. Use the filename **5act3.mag** and save the file (select the **Save** button; type the filename; if necessary, click in the Drives box and click on the drive letter where the file disk is located; select **OK**).
5. Print one copy (select the **Print** button; choose **Print**).
6. Close the document (select **File**, **Close**).

Activity 5.4—Create and Format a Table, Change Table Lines

1. Create a table with 4 columns and 6 rows (select the **Table Quick Create** button Power Bar, press and hold the mouse button while dragging to highlight a 4 x 6 table, release the mouse button).
2. Type the unformatted text as shown.

Daily Summary of Sales Calls			
July 21	General	Agency	Total
Calls offered	5393	971	6364
Calls lost	121	10	131
Inquiries	1877	896	2773
Bookings	650	251	901

3. Use the following information to format the table:

   a. Select and join the cells in row 1 (select **Table**, **Join**, **Cell**).

   b. Center the title in row 1. (Move the mouse pointer to the **Justification** button, press and hold the mouse button while dragging to select **Center**. Release the mouse button.)

c. Select cells B2 through D6 and use **Right** justification. (Move the mouse pointer to the **Justification** button, press and hold the mouse button while dragging to select **Right**. Release the mouse button.)

d. Visually estimate and decrease the column width of columns B, C, and D to approximately 1.25". (Move the pointer to the desired column line until the double-headed arrow displays, press and hold the mouse button and drag the mouse left to decrease the column width.)

e. Select all table cells and set the row height to .5". (Select the **Format Tbl** button, select **Row**, select **Row Height**, select **Fixed**; type .5, select **OK**. Click to deselect the cells.)

f. Center the table horizontally (select the **Format Tbl** button, select **Table**, choose **Center** in the Table Position box, select **OK**).

g. Select all cells in row 2 and choose double lines for the top and bottom. (Select the **TblLineFill** button, click on the line style button beside the word **Top**, click on the double-line style; click on the line style button beside the word **Bottom**, click on the double-line sample; select **OK**.)

h. Center the table vertically (select **Layout**, **Page**, **Center**, **Current Page**, **OK**).

*Note: If desired, select the **Page Zoom Full** button on the Power Bar to view the centered table. Select the **Page Zoom Full** button again to return to normal view. Your table should look similar to the following:*

Daily Summary of Sales Calls			
July 21	General	Agency	Total
Calls offered	5,393	971	6,364
Calls lost	121	10	131
Inquiries	1,877	896	2,773
Bookings	650	251	901

4. Use the filename **5act4.dss** and save the file (select **Save** button; type the filename; if necessary, click in the Drives box and click on the drive letter where the file disk is located; select **OK**).

5. Print one copy (select the **Print** button; choose **Print**).

6. Close the document (select **File**, **Close**).

Challenge Your Skills

Skill 5.1—Create and Format a Table, Insert a Column, Change Row Height, and Shade Cells

1. Create a table with 3 columns and 12 rows.
2. Type the unformatted text as shown.

Parts List		
Item	Description	Part No.
A	Left upright	3307-6
B	Right upright	3308-4
C	Top shelf	3310-5
D	Rail	3311-7
E	Bottom shelf	3314-2
F	Adjustable shelf	4400-1
G	Kick panel	4415-8
H	Back panel	4418-2
I	Screw	4420-2
J	Dowel	4422-6

3. Use the following information to format the table:
   a. Join the cells in row 1.
   b. Select and center the title and column heading cells in rows 1 and 2.
   c. Use **Center** justification in all cells of column A except the title and column heading. Use **Right** justification in all the cells of column C except the column heading.
   d. Insert a column between columns B and C.
   e. Set **Center** justification for all cells of the new column C, including the column heading.
   f. Use a light fill (shading) for rows 1 and 2.
   g. Set the row height for rows 1 and 2 to .4".
   h. Type the text as shown into the new column.

Quantity
1
1
1
3

1
2
1
1
8
12

i. Change the font for the entire table to **Arrus BT, 14-point.**

j. Adjust the widths of the columns so that the table information is appealing and easy to read.

k. Center the table horizontally and vertically.

4. Use the filename **5skill1.pal** and save the file.
5. Print one copy.
6. Close the document.

Skill 5.2—Create and Format a Table and Insert Rows and a Column

1. Create a table with 2 columns and 8 rows and type the unformatted text as shown.

Cost/Expense Items	Amount Budgeted
Salaries, programmers	96000
Salaries, system designers	106000
Salaries, computer operators	120000
Salary, manager	68000
Computer supplies	35000
Miscellaneous expenses	5500
Insurance	12500

2. Use the following information to format the table:

a. Insert a row at the top of the table. Join the cells in row 1. Set the row height for row 1 to .5".

b. Type the title **R & A Consulting Services** and use **Center** justification.

c. Select cells B2 through B9 and set **Decimal** justification (including the column heading cell).

d. Insert a new row above "Miscellaneous expenses."

e. Type the following information into the new row:
Depreciation, furniture; 6,500

f. Insert a column between columns A and B.

g. Type the following information into the new column cells: Actual Amount Spent; 95060.25; 85081.16; 129882.43; 73247.20; 43463.50; 6500.00; 6700.00; 13240.00

3. Make decisions regarding number type format and the digits after the decimal for the cells containing figures.
4. Make decisions regarding border, line, and fill styles for cells, font changes, table lines, and column widths so that the table information appears pleasing and easy to read.
5. Use the filename **5skill2.rac** and save the file.
6. Print one copy.
7. Close the document.

Skill 5.3—Create and Format a Memorandum with a Table; Language Arts

1. Use Memorandum—Style 1 and the following information:
   a. The memo should be sent to Abby Foods Group from Helen Millard.
   b. The subject of the memo is New Vice President.
   c. Use the current date; include your reference initials.
   d. Correct three spelling errors, one punctuation error, and one dollar amount format error.
   e. After creating the table, format cells as desired (e.g., increase or decrease column widths, change the justification of column headings, choose fill style for desired cells, change table lines, and set the number type, digits after decimal, and justification for dollar amounts.
   f. The memorandum body text follows:

Douglas Bartlett has been appointed to the position of Vice President, Business Development and National Accounts--Grocery, Sales & Integrated Logistics Division.

The role of Business Development continues to grow in importance as the cornerstone of Sales & Integrated Logistics' intiative to pursue strategic customer aliances. In this new position Douglas will be responsible for developing and directing startegic programs and partnership alliances with national and regional account grocery customers. He will report to Gayleen Kirkland, Senior Vice President, Sales & Integrated Logistics Division, Abby Foods Group.

Reporting to Douglas are:

Name	Accounts	Account Value
Santiago Cruz	Business Development & National Accounts	390000
Veronica Johnson	Business Development & Eastern Region	135000
Richard Epstein	Business Development & Midwestern Region	96000
Connie Jimenez	Business Development & Southern Region	78000.00

Douglas assumes his new responsibilities from the position of Regional Vice President, Broker Sales, Central Region. His office is located at 2022 Oakton Street, Des Plaines, IL 60018, and the telephone number is (708) 555-9009.

---

2. Use the filename **5skill3.nat** and save the file.
3. Print one copy.
4. Close the document.
5. If you have completed your work, exit WordPerfect.

CHAPTER 6

Edit a Table

Features Covered

- Move a row and column
- Delete a row and column
- Change table row margins
- Copy a table
- Delete a table
- Calculate column and row totals
- Copy a formula
- Omit table lines and borders
- Print double underlines

Chapter Objectives and Introduction

After successfully completing this chapter, you will be able to move and delete a table row and column, change table row margins, and copy and delete a table. You will also be able to calculate a column or row total, set the number type and digits after the decimal, omit table lines and borders, and use double underlines. Once a table has been typed and printed, the table information can be edited. Changes can include moving or deleting columns and rows, changing row margins, and omitting table lines. A formula can be used to total a column or row, and can be copied to other cells. An entire table can also be copied or deleted.

Move a Table Column or Row

A table column or row can be moved to another column or row location within a table. When a column or row is moved, the column or row is deleted from the original location and relocated. When a column or row is copied, the column or row displays in the original location *and* the new location.

FIGURE 6.1

Table with up selection arrow displayed

Top selection arow

Product Data				
Product name	Disk Size	Part No.	List Price	Discount Price
WinPro 3.5	5.25" or 3.5"	1269	$150	$85
Matrix 1.0	3.5"	1270	$175	$95
ArtFree Design 2.0	3.5"	4688	$495	$299

The column or row to be moved must be selected before the move process can be started. After selecting the **Cut** button, the column or row is deleted from the screen and placed in the Clipboard. Before inserting a cut (delete) column, the insertion point is placed in any cell in the column that will be located to the right of the moved column. Before inserting a cut (deleted) row, the insertion point is placed in any cell in the row that will be located below the moved row. After placing the insertion point in the desired column or row, select the **Paste** button to display the deleted (moved) column or row in the new location.

Start-Up Instructions

❖ Open the file named **6drill1.pro** located on the data disk.

Steps to Move a Table Column

1. Select the column to be moved by moving the mouse pointer to the top line of any cell in that column until the up selection arrow displays (see Figure 6.1). Double-click to highlight the desired column {place the insertion point in the first cell of the column to be moved, press and hold the Shift key while tapping the down arrow key}.

   For example, obtain the up selection arrow in column C and double-click.

2. Select the Cut button on the Power Bar {Alt, e, t *or* Ctrl and x}.

   Note: *The Table Cut/Copy dialog box displays (see Figure 6.2).*

3. Select the Column option {c}.
4. Select OK {Enter}.

FIGURE 6.2

Table Cut/Copy dialog box

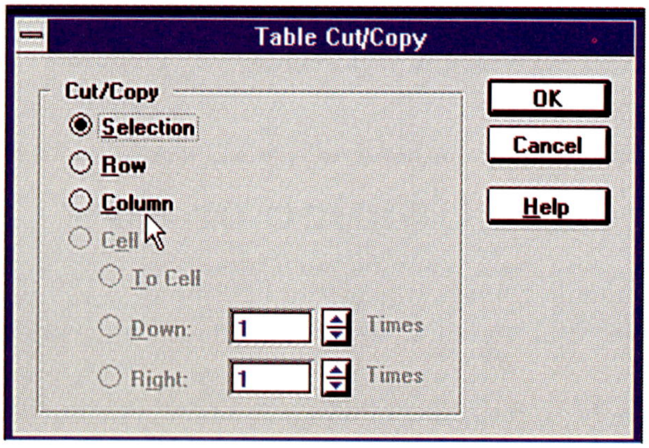

Note: The selected column is removed from the table and placed in the Clipboard.

5. Move the insertion point to any cell in the column that will be located to the right of the moved column.

   For example, place the insertion point in any cell in column B.

6. Select the **Paste** button on the Power Bar {Alt, e, p *or* Ctrl and v}.

   Note: When the deleted (cut) column is inserted at the new location, the cells in row 1 will no longer be joined. That's OK.

Chapter 6
Edit a Table

Finish-Up Instructions

- Rejoin the cells in row 1 (select row 1 and select **Table, Join, Cell**).
- Use the *new* filename **6drill1.mov** and save the file on the file disk (select **File, Save As**; type the filename; if necessary, click in the Drives box and click on the drive letter where your file disk is located; select **OK**).
- Print one copy (select the **Print** button; choose **Print**).

Start-Up Instructions

- The file named **6drill1.mov** should be displayed in the document window.

Steps to Move a Table Row

1. Select the row to be moved by moving the mouse pointer to the left line of any cell in the row to be moved until the left selection arrow displays. Double-click to highlight the desired row {place the insertion point in the first cell of the row to be moved, press and hold the Shift key and press F8, then press the right arrow key}.

   For example, obtain the left selection arrow in row 4 and double-click. (Check the Status bar to confirm the cell address.)

2. Select the **Cut** button on the Power Bar {Alt, e, t, *or* Ctrl and x}.
3. Select the **Row** option {r}.
4. Select **OK** {press Enter}.

   Note: The selected row is removed from the table and placed in the Clipboard.

5. Move the insertion point to any cell in the row that will be located below the moved row.

   For example, place the insertion point in any cell in row 3.

6. Select the **Paste** button on the Power Bar {Alt, e, p *or* Ctrl and v}.

Finish-Up Instructions

- Use the *new* filename **6drill2.row** and save the file on the file disk (select **File, Save As**; type the filename; if necessary, click in the Drives box and click on the drive letter where your file disk is located; select **OK**).
- Print one copy (select the **Print** button; choose **Print**).

Delete a Table Column or Row

When editing a table, a column or row can be deleted. A column or row is deleted by first placing the insertion point in the column or row to be deleted and then choosing the **Delete Tbl** button on the Tables Button Bar and selecting **Rows** or **Columns**. A row or column can also be deleted by selecting the row or column and choosing the **Cut** button on the Power Bar.

If a column or row is deleted by mistake, **Edit**, **Undo** can be selected (or select the **Undo** button on the Power Bar) to retrieve and display the deleted column or row. However, **Edit**, **Undo** must be selected before another action is performed.

Start-Up Instructions

- The file named **6drill2.row** should be displayed in the document window.

Steps to Delete a Table Column

1. Place the insertion point in any cell in the column to be deleted.

   For example, place the insertion point in any cell in column B. (Check the Status bar to confirm the cell address.)

2. Select the **Delete Tbl** button on the Tables Button Bar {Alt, a, d}.

   Note: The Delete dialog box displays.

3. Select the desired delete option.

   For example, select **Columns** {c}.

   Note: The number "1" displays.

4. Select **OK** to delete one column {press Enter}.

   *Note: If a table column is deleted by mistake, select the **Undo** button to retrieve the deleted column.*

Finish-Up Instructions

- Use the *new* filename **6drill2.del** and save the file on the file disk (select **File**, **Save As**; type the filename; if necessary, click in the Drives box and click on the drive letter where your file disk is located; select **OK**).
- Print one copy (select the **Print** button; choose **Print**).

Start-Up Instructions

- The file named **6drill2.del** should be displayed in the document window.

Steps to Delete a Table Row

1. Place the insertion point in any cell in the row to be deleted.

   For example, place the insertion point in any cell in row 3.

2. Select the **Delete Tbl** button on the Tables Button Bar {Alt, a, d}.

3. Select the desired delete option.

For example, check that Rows is selected and that the number "1" displays.

4. Select OK {Enter}.

Note: If a table row is deleted by mistake, select the ***Undo*** *button to retrieve the deleted row.*

Finish-Up Instructions

- Use the *new* filename **6drill2.dtr** and save the file on the file disk (select **File**, **Save As**; type the filename; if necessary, click in the Drives box and click on the drive letter where your file disk is located; select **OK**).
- Print one copy (select the **Print** button; choose **Print**).

Change Table Row Margins

Another WordPerfect editing feature is the capability to change any or all table row margins. The row margins are the spaces that are placed between the cell text and the top, bottom, left, and right table cell lines. For example, the space placed between the top table line and the cell text is the top row margin. The cell margins are measured in fractions of inches. An example of a top row margin is .1 inches.

Row margins are changed by using the Table Format dialog box. Before setting row margins, select the cell(s) where margins are to be changed. The **Row** option is chosen to display the Row Margin options. The desired row margins can be typed or the up and down triangles can be selected to increase or decrease the amount displayed in the Top/Bottom option boxes.

Start-Up Instructions

- The file named **6drill2.dtr** should be displayed in the document window.

Steps to Change Table Row Margins

1. Select the row(s) where the row margin is to be changed.

   For example, select all table cells by moving the mouse pointer to the top or left side of any cell until the top or left selection arrow displays and triple-click {place the insertion point in the first table cell, press and hold the Shift key, then press the down arrow key until all rows are highlighted}.

2. Select the Format Tbl button on the Tables Button Bar {Alt, a, o *or* Ctrl and F12}.

3. Select Row {o}.

   Note: The Format dialog box changes to display only the row format options.

4. Double-click in the desired Row Margins box.

   For example, double-click in the **Top** option box {p}.

5. Type the desired margin for the table row(s).

   For example, type .2. (Do not type the final period.)

6. Double-click in the desired Row Margins box.

   For example, double-click in the **Bottom** option box {press Tab}.

7. Type the desired margin for the table row(s).

   For example, type .2. (Do not type the final period.)

   Note: *Check that the* ***Auto*** *option is selected in the Row Height box.*

8. Select OK {press Enter}.

   Note: *The top and bottom cell margins in all cells are changed. If desired, click once to deselect the table cells.*

Finish-Up Instructions

- Use the *new* filename **6drill2.mar** and save the file on the file disk (select **File**, **Save As**; type the filename; if necessary, click in the Drives box and click on the drive letter where your file disk is located; select **OK**).
- Print one copy (select the **Print** button; choose **Print**).
- Continue with the following Steps to Copy a Table or close the document.

Copy a Table

An entire table can be copied to another window or to another location within the current document window. A table is often copied for the purpose of making changes to the copied table without changing the original table, for the purpose of saving paper by placing two items on a page, or for the purpose of using the table information in another letter, memorandum, or report.

Start-Up Instructions

- The file named **6drill2.mar** should be displayed in the document window.

Steps to Copy a Table

1. Select the entire table by moving the mouse pointer to the top or left of any cell to obtain the up or left selection arrow and triple-click {place the insertion point in the first cell of the table, press and hold the Shift key while tapping the down arrow key}.
2. Select the Copy button on the Power Bar {Alt, e, c *or* Ctrl and x}.

   Note: *The Table Cut/Copy dialog box displays.*

3. Select Column or Row {c or r}.
4. Select OK {Enter}.

   Note: *A copy of the table is placed in the Clipboard.*

5. Locate the insertion point at the desired position.

For example, move the mouse pointer below the table and click once {press the down arrow key repeatedly}. Press the **Enter** key once to place a hard return after the table.

6. Select the **Paste** button on the Power Bar {Alt, e, p *or* Ctrl and v}.

   Note: *A copy of the table is inserted at the location of the insertion point.*

Finish-Up Instructions

- Use the *new* filename **6drill3.cop** and save the file on the file disk (select **File**, **Save As**; type the filename; if necessary, click in the Drives box and click on the drive letter where your file disk is located; select **OK**).
- Optional. Print one copy (select the **Print** button; choose **Print**).
- Continue with the Steps to Delete a Table or close the document.

Chapter 6
Edit a Table

Delete a Table

A table can be deleted by selecting the entire table. If a table is deleted by mistake, select the **Undo** button on the Power Bar to retrieve and display the table on the screen again. The **Undo** button must be selected before any other operation is performed.

Start-Up Instructions

- The file named **6drill3.cop** should be displayed in the document window.

Steps to Delete a Table

1. Select the table to be deleted.

   For example, select the first table by moving the mouse pointer to the top or left of any cell in the table until the up or left selection arrow displays and triple-click {place the insertion point in the first cell of the table, press and hold the Shift key while tapping the down arrow key}.

2. Select the **Delete Tbl** button on the Table Button Bar {Alt, a, d}.

   Note: *The Delete Table dialog box displays with the Entire Table option selected.*

3. Select **OK** {Enter}.

Finish-Up Instructions

- Close the document and do not save the file.

Calculate a Column or Row Total

Table cells containing numbers (values) can be calculated by using formulas to add, subtract, multiply, or divide. A value number is a number used to obtain a mathematical result. A text number is a number that will not be used to compute a result. Examples of text numbers are a social security number or a year (e.g., 1995).

Columns and rows are totaled by using a table formula. Table formulas are easily created in the Edit Formula box located in the Table Formula Feature Bar. The Tables Formula Feature Bar is displayed by selecting the **TblFormBar** on the Tables Button Bar. The insertion point is first placed in the cell that will contain the column or row sum and then is placed in the Edit Formula box. The formula is typed or selected from the list of table functions. The table cells to be summed are typed or selected using the mouse. An example of a formula to add a column is *SUM(B3:B7)*.

A shortcut for summing a column is to locate the insertion point in the desired cell, then click in the Edit Formula box and select the **Sum** button. The Sum button shortcut method can also be used to total a single row; however, the row must be the first row containing numbers in the table.

With the Tables Button Bar displayed, a formula is deleted from a cell by placing the insertion point in the cell and selecting **Delete Tbl** and choosing **Cell Contents.** Also, a formula can be deleted by selecting the cell and choosing **Edit**, **Cut** or by selecting the **Cut** button on the Power Bar.

If numbers (values) are changed in the table cells, the cells that contain formula results will need to be recalculated. One method to recalculate is to select the **Calculate** button on the Tables Formula Feature Bar. When the **Calculate** button is selected on the Tables Formula Feature Bar, all formulas in every table in the document are recalculated.

A second method to recalculate is to select the **Calculate** button on the Tables Button Bar. When the **Calculate** button on the Tables Button Bar is chosen, the Calculate dialog box displays. The **Calc Table** button is selected to recalculate the formula(s) in the current table or the **Calc Document** button is selected to recalculate the formulas in every table in the document.

Also in the Calculate dialog box, the **Calculate Table** and **Calculate Document** options can be used to turn on the automatic recalculate feature. If the **Calculate Table** option is selected, the formula(s) in the current table are automatically recalculated. If the **Calculate Document** option is selected, formulas in every table in the document are automatically recalculated. The automatic recalculation takes place after a number is changed and the insertion point is moved to another cell.

Start-Up Instructions

- Open the file named **6drill4.exp** located on the data disk.

Steps to Use a Formula to Calculate the Sum of a Column

1. Select the TblFormBar button on the Tables Button Bar {Alt, a, r}.

   ***Note:** The Table Formula Feature Bar displays below the Power Bar (see Figure 6.3).*

2. Place the insertion point in the cell where the calculated sum will be placed.

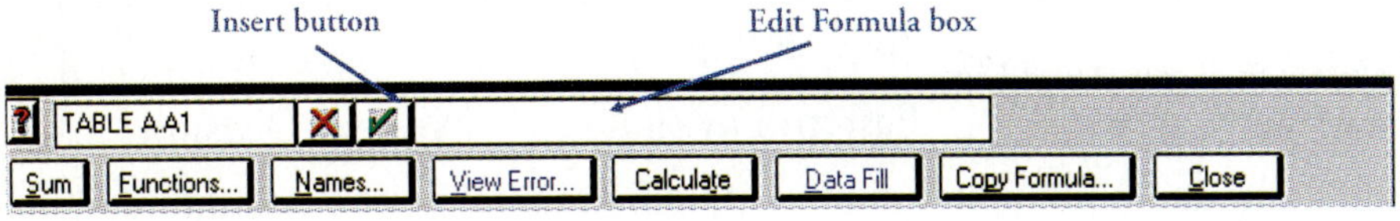

FIGURE 6.3

Table Formula Feature Bar

For example, place the insertion point in cell B8. (Check the Status bar to confirm the cell address.)

3. Move the mouse pointer to the Edit Formula box in the Table Formula Feature Bar and click once {Alt and Shift and e}.

   Note: *The insertion point displays in the Edit Formula box. The message "Formula Edit mode is on" displays in the right side of the Table Formula Feature Bar.*

4. Select the **Functions** button located in the Table Formula Feature Bar {Alt and Shift and f}.

   Note: *The Table Functions dialog box displays.*

5. Click on the scroll box in the Function box to scroll down until the desired function displays. Move the mouse pointer to the desired function and double-click {type the letters of the desired function until the function name is highlighted}.

   For example, scroll down the list of functions until SUM(List) displays. Move the mouse pointer to **SUM(List)** and double-click {type sum, press Enter}.

   Note: *The SUM(List) function displays in the Edit Formula box with the word List highlighted.*

6. Select the cells to be calculated {type the cell addresses to be calculated separated by a colon or period.

   For example, select cells B3 through B7 {type B3:B7}.

   Note: *When the mouse is used to select the cells, the cell addresses B3:B7 display in the Edit Formula box and the cells are highlighted in the table.*

7. Select the **Insert** button (✓) located to the left of the Edit Formula box to insert the formula and results in the current cell (where the insertion point is located) {press Enter}.

   Note: *The Column sum displays in cell B8. The formula for cell B8 displays in the Status bar at the bottom middle of the document window, e.g., TABLE A Cell B8 = SUM(B3:B7). TABLE A indicates that this is the first table in a document.*

Shortcut

1. With the Table Formula Feature Bar displayed, place the insertion point in the cell where the calculated sum will be placed.
2. Click once in the Edit Formula box to locate and display the insertion point.
3. Click on the **SUM** button on the Table Formula Feature Bar.

Finish-Up Instructions

❖ Place the insertion point in cell C8 and use the shortcut to total the values in column C.

FIGURE 6.4

Edited table

Division Expenses		
Expense Category	Eastern Division	Western Division
Indirect labor	$34,500	$38,600
Materials	14,800	15,200
Supplies	15,800	16,200
Utilities	17,400	18,200
Insurance	12,500	13,700
TOTALS	$95,000	$101,900

- Use the filename **6drill4.cal** and save the file on the file disk (select **File, Save As**; type the filename; if necessary, click in the Drives box and click on the drive letter where your file disk is located; select **OK**).

Start-Up Instructions

- The file named **6drill4.cal** should be displayed in the document window.
- The Table Formula Feature Bar should be displayed (if necessary, select the **TblFormBar** button on the Tables Button Bar).
- Edit the table as shown in Figure 6.4.

Steps to Edit Table Figures and Recalculate

1. After the table figures have been changed, place the insertion point in any table cell.

   Note: *To change any number, select the original number, then type the revised number.*

2. Select the Calculate button on the Table Formula Feature Bar to automatically recalculate the table column totals {Alt, e, a}.

   Note: *If the* ***Calculate*** *button is selected on the Tables Button Bar, the Calculate dialog box displays. Select the* ***Calc Table*** *button to automatically update the column totals.*

3. If desired, select Close on the Table Formula Feature Bar.

Finish-Up Instructions

- Use the *new* filename **6drill5.rev** and save the file on the file disk (select **File, Save As**; type the filename; if necessary, click in the Drives box and click on the drive letter where your file disk is located; select **OK**).
- Print one copy (select the **Print** button; choose **Print**).

Start-Up Instructions

- The file named **6drill5.rev** should be displayed in the document window.
- Insert one table column after column C (place the insertion point in any cell in column C, select the **Tbl Insert** button, select **Columns**, select **After, OK**).
- Select and join the cells in row 1 (select **Table, Join, Cell**).

❖ Type the column heading **Total Expenses** in cell D2. Visually estimate and decrease the column widths so they appear approximately the same width. The first row total will be calculated in the following Steps to Total a Row.

Steps to Total a Row

1. Place the insertion point in the cell where the row total is to be inserted.

   For example, place the insertion point in cell D3.

2. If necessary, select the **TblFormBar** button on the Tables Button Bar {Alt, a, r}.

   Note: *The Table Formula Feature Bar displays below the Power Bar.*

3. Move the mouse pointer to the Edit Formula box in the Table Formula Feature Bar and click once {Alt and Shift and e}.

   Note: *The insertion point displays in the Edit Formula box.*

4. Select the **Functions** button located in the Table Formula Feature Bar {Alt and Shift and f}.

5. Click on the scroll box in the Function box to scroll down until the desired function displays. Move the mouse pointer to the desired function and double-click {type the letters of the desired function until the function name is highlighted}.

   For example, scroll down the list of functions until SUM(List) displays. Move the mouse pointer to **SUM(List)** and double-click {type sum, press Enter}.

6. Select the cells to be calculated {type the cell addresses to be calculated separated by a colon or period}.

   For example, select cells B3 through C3.

   Note: *When the mouse is used to select cells, the cell addresses B3:C3 display in the Edit Formula box and the cells are highlighted in the table.*

7. Select the Insert button (✓) located to the left of the Edit Formula box to insert the formula and results in the current cell {press Enter}.

   Note: *The row sum displays in cell D3. The formula for cell D3 displays in the Status bar, e.g., TABLE A Cell D3 = Sum (B3:C3). TABLE A indicates that this is the first table in a document.*

8. Select **Close** on the Table Formula Feature Bar {Alt and Shift and c}.

Finish-Up Instructions

❖ Use the *new* filename **6drill6.tro** and save the file on the file disk (select **File, Save As**; type the filename; if necessary, click in the Drives box and click on the drive letter where your file disk is located; select **OK**).

❖ Continue with the Steps to Copy a Formula.

Copy a Formula

After a formula is placed in a table cell, the formula can be copied to one or more cells. A formula can be copied to a single cell, down a column, or right across a row. A formula is copied to multiple cells by indicating direction (down or right) and the desired number of cells in which the formula should appear. For example, to copy a formula to five rows, the **Down** option is selected and the number 5 is placed in the Down option box.

After the formula is copied, the results are displayed immediately in the cell(s) where the formula was copied. When a formula is copied, the row and column cell addresses in the formula are automatically changed to reflect the cell addresses where the formula was copied.

Start-Up Instructions

- The file named **6drill6.tro** should be displayed in the document window.
- The Table Formula Feature Bar should be displayed. (If necessary, select the **TblFormBar** button on the Tables Button Bar.)

Steps to Copy a Formula

1. Place the insertion point in the cell that contains the formula to be copied.

   For example, place the insertion point in cell D3.

2. Select the **Copy Formula** button on the Table Formula Feature Bar {Alt and Shift and m}.

   Note: The Copy Formula dialog box displays. The Source box and the To Cell box both display the cell address, i.e., D3.

3. Select the Destination option.

   For example, select **Down** {Alt and d}.

   Note: The number "1" is highlighted in the Down box.

4. Select the up triangle to display the number of cells in which to copy the formula {type the desired number}.

   For example, click on the up triangle repeatedly until the number 5 displays.

   Note: The number in the Down option box will not accept a figure greater than the number of empty cells below the cell to be copied.

5. Select **OK** {press Enter}.

   Note: WordPerfect immediately copies the formula into each cell in column D and displays the total results for each row.

6. Select the **Close** button on the Table Formula Feature Bar {Alt and Shift and c}.

Finish-Up Instructions

- If necessary, visually estimate and change the column widths to appear approximately the same width.

- Use the *new* filename **6drill6.for** and save the file again (select **File**, **Save As**; type the filename; if necessary, click in the Drives box and click on the drive letter where your file disk is located, select **OK**).
- Print one copy (select the **Print** button; choose **Print**).

Chapter 6
Edit a Table

Omit Table Lines

The single lines that display around each cell are defaulted (preset) to print. The table lines and/or border can be omitted from table rows and cells. After the table lines or border are omitted, the table's row and column structure remains in effect.

Start-Up Instructions

- The file named **6drill6.for** should be displayed in the document window.

Steps to **Omit All Table Lines**

1. Place the insertion point in any table cell.
2. Select the TblLineFill button on the Tables Button Bar {Alt, a, L *or* Shift and F12}.

   Note: *The Table Lines/Fill dialog box displays.*
3. Select the Table option {a}.

   Note: *The Table Lines/Fill options display.*
4. Select the button to the right of the Line Style option {Alt and L, Spacebar}.

   Note: *A palette of available line styles displays.*
5. Click on <NONE> {press the arrow keys until NONE is selected; Enter}.
6. Select OK {press Enter}.

   Note: *The table lines no longer display in the document window; however, the table's column and row structure remain in effect.*

Finish-Up Instructions

- Select the row that contains the column headings; choose the **Underline** button on the Power Bar.
- Use the *new* filename **6drill6.omt** and save the file on the file disk (select **File**, **Save As**; type the filename; if necessary, click in the Drives box and click on the drive letter where your file disk is located;. select **OK**).
- Optional. Print one copy (select the **Print** button; choose **Print**).

Print Double Underlines Below the Total Amount

Double underlines are placed under a column total amount in order to emphasize the total. Generally, if double underlines are used, table lines are not printed. When a column is totaled, a single underline is used to separate the last column amount from the total amount.

The single underline traditionally has been formatted to extend the width of the total amount. Therefore, one or more spaces were placed to the left of the last column number in order to extend the underline. Because WordPerfect's number type format feature does not allow a space(s) to be used to extend the underline, the additional space(s) will not be effective unless the General number format is used.

Traditionally, the dollar sign ($) in the first figure and the last figure of a column have been formatted to align. Since there is often an additional digit(s) in the total amount, an extra space(s) would be placed between the dollar sign and the first digit in the first column entry. However, WordPerfect's Table Number type feature does not allow a space to be placed between a dollar sign and an amount when the Currency format is selected.

Once the column total has been calculated, the amount is selected and the **Double Underline** attribute is selected in the Cell Format dialog box. An example of text with double underlines displays at the bottom of the Format dialog box.

Start-Up Instructions

- The file named **6drill6.omt** should be displayed in the document window.
- Select cells B7 to D7 in the row above the row containing the total amounts. Select the **Underline** button on the Power Bar.

Steps to Print Double Underlines

1. Select the cells that contain the total amounts.

   For example, select cells **B8, C8,** and **D8**.

2. Select the Format Tbl button on the Tables Button Bar {Alt, a, o *or* Ctrl and F12}.
3. Select the desired option.

   For example, check that **Cell** is selected. If necessary, select **Cell** {e}.

4. Select the Double Underline option in the Appearance box {d}.

   ***Note:** An X displays beside the Double Underline option. Also, a sample of text with double underlines displays at the bottom of the Format dialog box.*

5. Select OK {Enter}.

Finish-Up Instructions

- If necessary, click once to deselect the selected row.
- Use the *new* filename **6drill6.und** and save the file on the file disk (select **File, Save As**; type the filename; if necessary, click in the Drives box and click on the drive letter where your file disk is located; select **OK**).

- ❖ Print one copy (select the **Print** button; choose **Print**).
- ❖ Close the document (select **File**, **Close**).

The Next Step

Chapter Review and Activities

Self-Check Quiz

T F 1. A table row or column can be moved.

T F 2. Before deleting a table column, place the insertion point in any cell in the column to be deleted.

T F 3. An entire table can be copied to another document window or another location in the current document window.

T F 4. If table cell values or formulas are changed, the column or row totals can be recalculated and updated by selecting the **Calculate** button on the Table Formula Feature Bar.

5. A row or column can be deleted by choosing the ______ button on the Tables Button Bar and selecting **Rows** or **Columns**, **OK**.
   a. **Format Tbl**
   b. **TblCellForm**
   c. **Delete Tbl**
   d. **Tbl # Type**

6. A moved column is deleted from the original location and _______ a new location.
   a. duplicated in
   b. relocated to
   c. copied to
   d. reproduced in

7. When using the Table Formula Feature Bar, the _____ button is used to create a formula to total cells.
   a. **Sum**
   b. **Function**
   c. **Calculate**
   d. Either a or b.

8. The _______ table lines are defaulted to print.
   a. Single
   b. Double
   c. Thick/Thin 1
   d. None of these.

9. Write down the formula for adding three cells in row 4. The cells are located in columns C, D, and E.

10. Describe a table row margin.

Enriching Language Arts Skills

Spelling/Vocabulary Words

adversely having an unfavorable effect.

per diem an amount allowed for daily expenses.

reimbursement money repaid for expenses incurred.

Single and Double Underlines for Dollar Amounts

Place a single underline between the last column amount and the total amount. Traditionally, the single underline extended the width of the amount with the most characters, including the dollar sign. However, if any of WordPerfect's number type options (other than General) is used, the spaces cannot be added to extend the single underline. In a table without lines or borders, a total amount is usually emphasized by placing double underlines beneath the total amount. *Both of the following* examples are acceptable.

Examples:

Formatted using the General number type	Formatted using the Currency and Commas number types
$110,550	$110,550
3,600	3,600
2,820	2,820
$116,970	$116,970

Activities

Activity 6.1—Calculate the Total of the Columns and Rows and Set Number Type and Digits After the Decimal

1. Create a table with 4 columns and 7 rows.
2. Type the following unformatted information into the table cells:

General Fund Expenditures			
Fund	June	July	Totals
Remodeling	55000	30500	
Equipment	50000	25000	
Interfund transfers	48000	12460	
Capital outlays	95000	72680	
Totals			

3. Use the following instructions to format the table:

a. Select and join the cells in row 1(select **Table**, **Join**, **Cell**).

b. Select and center the title and column headings in rows 1 and 2 (move the mouse pointer to the **Justification** button, press and hold the mouse button while dragging to select **Center**, release the mouse button).

c. Select the **TblFormBar** button on the Tables Button Bar.

d. Calculate the sum for columns B and C (place the insertion point in cell B7, click in the Edit Formula box, select the **Sum** button). Move the insertion point to cell C7 and repeat the instructions.

e. Calculate the sum for row 3 (place the insertion point in cell D3, click in the Edit Formula box, select the **Function** button, choose **SUM(List)**, select cells **B3** and **C3**, select the Insert [✓] button).

f. Copy the formula from row 3 to rows 4 through 7 (select the **Copy Formula** button, select **Down**, **4**, **OK**).

g. Close the Table Formula Feature Bar (select the **Close** button on the Table Formula Feature Bar).

h. Select cells **B3** through **D7** and set **Decimal** justification (move the mouse pointer to the **Justification** button, press and hold the mouse button while dragging to select **Decimal**, release the mouse button).

i. Select cells **B4** through **D6** and set the number type to **Commas** with zero digits after the decimal (select the **Tbl # Type** button, select **Commas**, select **Custom**, click twice on the down triangle beside the Digits after Decimal box, select **OK** twice).

j. Select cells **B3** through **D3** and set the number type to **Currency** with zero digits after the decimal (select the **Tbl # Type** button, select **Currency**, select **Custom**, click twice on the down triangle beside the Digits after Decimal box, select **OK** twice). Select cells **B7** through **D7** and repeat the instruction.

4. Visually estimate and adjust the column widths so that the columns containing figures are approximately the same width.

5. Center the table horizontally (select the **Format Tbl**, **Table**, **Table Position**, **Center**, **OK**).

Note: Your table should look similar to the following table:

General Fund Expenditures			
Fund	June	July	Totals
Remodeling	$55,000	$30,500	$85,500
Equipment	50,000	25,000	75,000
Interfund transfers	48,000	12,460	60,460
Capital outlays	95,000	72,680	167,680
Totals	$248,000	$140,640	$388,640

6. Save the file on the file disk; use the filename **6act1.gen**.

7. Print one copy and close the document.

Activity 6.2—Move Columns, Change Row Margins, Copy a Table and Delete a Table

1. Create a table with 4 columns and 8 rows.
2. Type the following unformatted information into the table cells as shown. (Remember: Text will automatically wrap around in cells.)

Norton Products			
Annual Conference Costs			
Item	1992	1993	1994
Conference facilities	3600	4000	5000
Demonstration materials	2500	3400	4000
Accommodations	35500	36800	37600
Meals	25000	26000	26700
Travel	31900	32300	35400

3. Use the following instructions to format the table:
   a. Move column D (i.e., 1994 information) between columns A and B (move the mouse pointer to the top of any cell in column D to obtain the top selection arrow, double-click, select the **Cut** button, select **Column**, **OK**; place the insertion point in any cell in column B, select the **Paste** button).
   b. Move the now column D (1993 information) between columns B and C (see step 3a, if necessary).
   c. Select and join the cells in row 1.
   d. Select and join the cells in row 2.
   e. Select rows 1 and 2 and center the title and subtitle.
   f. Increase the width of column A so the words display on one line.
   g. Select the entire table and change the top and bottom row margins to **.15** (move the mouse pointer to the top or left of any cell until the up or left selection arrow displays, triple-click; select the **Format Tbl** button, select **Row**, double-click in the **Top** Row Margins option box, type **.15**, double-click in the **Bottom** Row Margins option box, type **.15**, select **OK**).
   h. Select cells **B3** through **D8** and set **Decimal** justification (move the mouse pointer to the **Justification** button, press and hold the mouse button while dragging to select **Decimal**, release the mouse button).
   i. Select cells **B4** through **D4** and set the number type to **Currency** and the digits after the decimal to zero (select the **Tbl # Type** button, se-

lect **Currency**, select **Custom**, click twice on the down triangle beside the Digits after Decimal box, select **OK** twice).

j. Select cells **B5** through **D8** and set the number type to **Commas** and the digits after the decimal to zero (select the **Tbl # Type** button, select **Commas**, select **Custom**, click twice on the down triangle beside the Digits after Decimal box, select **OK** twice).

Note: *Your table should look similar to the following table:*

Norton Products			
Annual Conference Costs			
Item	1994	1993	1992
Conference facilities	$5,000	$4,000	$3,600
Demonstration materials	4,000	3,400	2,500
Accommodations	37,600	36,800	35,500
Meals	26,700	26,000	25,000
Travel	35,400	32,300	31,900

4. Copy the table.

   a. Select the entire table by moving the mouse pointer to the top or left of any cell in the table until the up or left selection arrow displays and triple-click.

   b. Select the **Copy** button.

   c. Move the mouse pointer below the table and click once; press the **Enter** key twice.

   d. Select the **Paste** button.

   Note: *To view both tables on the screen, select the* ***Page Zoom Full*** *button. Select the* ***Page Zoom Full*** *button again to return to the normal view.*

5. Save the file on the file disk; use the filename **6act2.nor**.

6. Print one copy.

7. Delete the first table.

   a. Repeat step 4a and select the entire table.

   b. Select the **Delete Tbl** button; select **OK**.

   Note: *Select the* ***Page Zoom Full*** *button to view the single remaining table. Select the* ***Page Zoom Full*** *button again to return to the normal view.*

8. Optional. Print the single table.

9. Close the document (do not save the modified file).

Activity 6.3—Copy a Formula, Delete a Row and Column and Omit Table Lines

1. Open the file named **6act3.mac** located on the data disk.
2. Calculate the sum of column B (select the **TblFormBar** button, place the insertion point in cell B10, click in the Edit Formula box, select **Sum**).
3. Copy the formula in cell B10 to C10 and D10 (place the insertion point in cell B10, select the **Copy Formula** button, select **Right**, type **2**, **OK**). Select the **Close** button on the Table Formula Feature Bar.
4. Select cells **B10** through **D10** and set the number type to **Currency** and set the digits after the decimal to zero (select the **Tbl # Type** button, select **Currency**, select **Custom**, click twice on the down triangle beside the Digits after Decimal box, select **OK** twice).

   Note: *Your table should look similar to the following table:*

MAINTENANCE COSTS			
Ardenwood Condominiums			
Job	April	May	June
Landscaping	$1,500	$1,500	$1,500
Pool cleaning	300	450	700
Roof repairs	8,670	4,200	3,700
Light fixtures	50	50	50
Deck repairs	5,000	4,600	4,950
Tennis courts	175	225	380
TOTALS	$15,695	$11,025	$11,280

5. Use the new filename **6act3.ard** and save the file on the file disk.
6. Print one copy.
7. Edit the table as follows:
   a. Delete row 8 (i.e., Deck repairs). (Place the insertion point in any cell in row 8, select the **Delete Tbl** button, check that **Rows** is selected, **OK**).

      Note: *The total amounts are automatically recalculated.*

   b. Delete column D (place the insertion point in any cell in column D, select the **Delete Tbl** button, select **Columns**, **OK**).
   c. Select the entire table and omit table lines (select the **TblLineFill** button, select **Table**, select the **Line Style** button, select **None**, **OK**).
   d. Select row 3 and underline the column headings (select the **Underline** button on the Power Bar).

e. Select and underline the figures in cells B8 and C8 (select the **Underline** button on the Power Bar).

f. Select and double underline the total amounts in cells B9 and C9 (select the **Format Tbl** button, select **Double Underline**, **OK**).

g. Center the table horizontally on the page (select the **Format Tbl** button, select **Table**, **Table Position**, **Center**, **OK**).

8. Use the *new* filename **6act3.con** and save the file on the file disk.

9. Print one copy and close the document.

Challenge Your Skills

Skill 6.1—Create a Table and a Formula

1. Create a two-column table using the following information:

   a. The title of the table is TOTAL PRINTER STAND COST.

   b. The price of the Premium Printer Stand is $99.99.

   c. Shipping and Handling will be $5.50.

   d. The charge for Express Delivery is $15.00.

   e. Calculate the total amount due.

2. Make decisions regarding:

   Justification for table columns
   Row margins
   Column widths
   Placement of the table on the page (vertically and horizontally)
   Table lines and border
   Shading cells
   Single and double underlines

3. Use the filename **6skill1.tot** and save the file.

4. Print one copy and close the document.

Skill 6.2—Calculate Column Totals; Language Arts Skills

1. Use the traditional style letter and the following information:

   a. The letter should be addressed to Mr. N. G. Specht, Branch Manager, Tucker-Haynes Corporation, 206 Midvale Blvd., Madison, WI 53705.

   b. The letter is from Loreen K. Faulkner, District Manager.

   c. Make decisions regarding:

      Margins
      Justification
      Date
      Salutation

Closing
Justification for table columns
Number type and digits after the decimal
Formulas
Table lines and border
Shading cells
Reference initials
Document identification

d. Correct three spelling, two punctuation, and one dollar amount format errors.

e. Letter body text follows:

Changes in our corporate travel reimbursement rates are necessary because of increased capital expenditures. The current travel rates remain in effect until the first of next month.

The following table shows the current and new rates.

Per Diem Amounts		
Item	Current Rate	New Rate
Lodging	95.00	105.00
Breakfast	9.00	6.00
Lunch	10.50	8.75
Dinner	28.00	23.00
Car rental	36.00	28.00
Total Per Deim		

As you will note while the amount allowed for lodging has been increased by $ 10, the amount allowed for meals and car rental has decreased. Please let me know by the first of the month if you feel that these changes will adverseily affect your personnel.

Please remind all employees that receipts for every item must be submitted before a reinbursement check can be written. As of the first of the month, no out-of-pocket expenses will be reimbursed unless preapproved by a branch manager.

If you have any questions regarding these rate changes please call me.

2. Use the filename **6skill2.per** and save the file.
3. Print one copy.
4. If you have completed your work in WordPerfect, exit the program.

CHAPTER 7

Create a Résumé

Features Covered

- Insert special characters
- Convert case
- Use a hard space
- Change margins using the Ruler Bar
- Set tabs

Chapter Objectives and Introduction

After successfully completing this chapter, you will be able to insert special WordPerfect characters, change the case for characters to all lowercase, all uppercase, or initial capitals, use a hard space to keep words on the same line, change left and right margins using the Ruler Bar, and set tabs in order to format an attractive, easy-to-read résumé.

A résumé is a document that summarizes a person's education, work experience, and work skills. A résumé is submitted to a prospective employer when applying for a job. Because a résumé serves as a person's introduction to a prospective employer, it is important that the résumé be attractive and easy to read. A résumé may be formatted using the Tab and Indent features, or the Table feature may be used to arrange information in parallel columns.

Tab settings can be changed so that paragraphs can be indented in an attractive manner. Emphasis can be added to text by using text attributes such as bold, underline, and italics. Special characters, such as the accent marks in résumé, can be inserted into a document. In addition, special emphasis can be given by placing symbols in front of desired paragraphs. (See Figure 7.1.)

Special Characters

Special text characters, such as the é's in résumé, and symbols, such as ❖ and ✰, can be inserted into a document by accessing WordPerfect's character sets. The Word-

FIGURE 7.1

Completed résumé

Résumé
Will Swanson
45 Frederick Court
Belmont, CA 94002
(415) 555-8743

EDUCATIONAL BACKGROUND

A.A. Information Processing, DeAnza College 6/94
❖ Studied microcomputer courses--WordPerfect, MS/DOS, Telecommunications, and Desktop Publishing

Certificate, City College of Chicago 9/92
❖ Obtained a Certificate in BASIC programming

Completed U.S. Navy correspondence course 4/91

EMPLOYMENT EXPERIENCE

<u>U.S. Navy--4 years</u>
Have experience as a member of the flight crew for the P3 Orion; also worked as a shipboard navigator and computer operator.

<u>Stanford Linear Accelerator--1 year</u>
Operated a 20-ton forklift, oscilloscope, and vacuum systems and was a machine operator.

<u>Kentucky Fried Chicken--1 year</u>
Managed employees, handled inventory, and supervised kitchen operations.

REFERENCES

Available upon request.

Perfect character sets contain characters that are not on the computer keyboard, such as mathematical symbols, foreign letters, and graphics symbols. There are fourteen character sets available, containing over 1,500 characters and symbols.

Start-Up Instructions

- Type an **R** (to begin typing the word Résumé).

Steps to Insert Special Characters

1. Place the insertion point at the location where the special character should be inserted.

   For example, the insertion point should be located immediately following the letter *R*.

2. Select **Insert, Character** {Alt, i, c *or* Ctrl and w}.

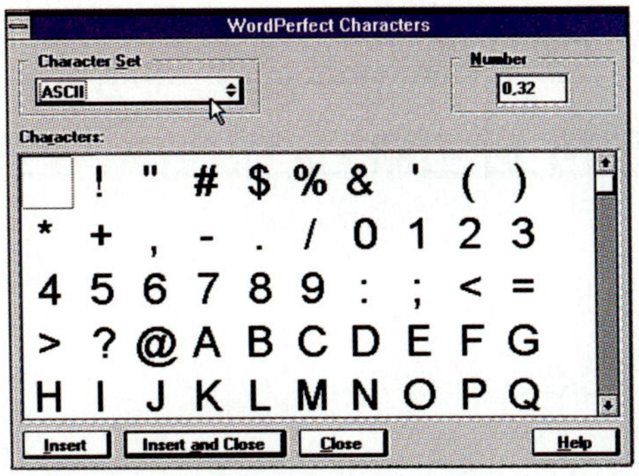

FIGURE 7.2

WordPerfect Characters dialog box

Note: The WordPerfect Characters dialog box displays (see Figure 7.2).

3. Move the mouse pointer to the triangles in the Character Set box. Press and hold the left mouse button to drop down the list of available character sets {Alt and s}.

4. Drag the mouse pointer to the desired character set and release the mouse button {press the down or up arrow key until the desired character set displays, Enter}.

   For example, point to **Multinational** and release the mouse button.

5. If necessary, use the scroll bar in the WordPerfect Character dialog box to display the desired character. Move the mouse pointer to the desired special character. Click to select the character {Alt and r; use the arrow keys to locate the outline around the desired character}.

   For example, use the scroll bar to display the é character. Move the mouse pointer to the é character and click once.

   Note: A blinking outline displays around the selected character.

6. Select **Insert** to copy the selected special character into the document at the location of the insertion point {a}.

   Note: When using the mouse, the WordPerfect Characters dialog box remains on the screen, and the selected special character is placed in the document. However, if keystrokes are used, the WordPerfect Characters dialog box must be removed from the screen by using the Insert and Close option.

7. Move the mouse pointer to the desired location in the document, click to display the insertion point, and type additional text as desired.

   For example, move the mouse pointer to the right of the é, click to display the insertion point, and type **sum**. (Do not type the final period.)

8. Move the mouse pointer to the WordPerfect Characters dialog box. If necessary, use the scroll bar to display the desired character. Move the mouse pointer to the desired character and click once {repeat steps 1–5 to obtain the desired WordPerfect characters}.

   For example, check that the outline displays around the é.

9. To insert a special character and close the WordPerfect Characters dialog box, select **Insert and Close** {a}.

Finish-Up Instructions

❖ Press the **Enter** key several times to insert some blank lines below the word Résumé.

FIGURE 7.3

Selecting a special character in the text

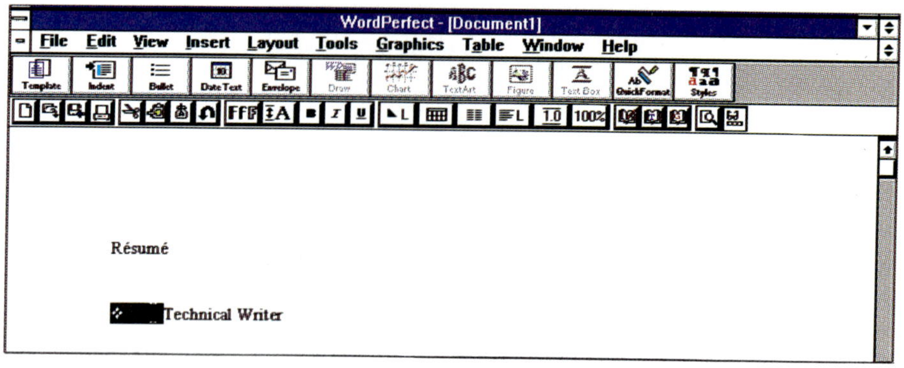

- ❖ Repeat steps 2–4 of the Steps to Insert Special Characters to display the WordPerfect Characters dialog box and select the **Iconic Symbols** character set.
- ❖ Use the scroll bar in the WordPerfect Characters dialog box to locate the ❖ character. Click on the ❖ character and choose **Insert and Close**.
- ❖ Select the **Indent** button on the Button Bar to indent the text that follows the bullet character.
- ❖ Type the words **Technical Writer** and press **Enter** once.
- ❖ Select the bullet character and the blank space *(Hd Left Ind)* before the letter *T* (see Figure 7.3).
- ❖ Select the **Copy** button on the Power Bar.
- ❖ Move the insertion point to the location where the bullet character should be inserted, e.g., place the insertion point in the blank line below the words Technical Writer.
- ❖ Select the **Paste** button on the Power Bar.
- ❖ Type the words **Copyeditor** and press **Enter** once.
- ❖ Select the **Paste** button to insert the ❖ character and indent code again.
- ❖ Type the words **Assistant Copyeditor** and press **Enter** once.
- ❖ Use the filename **7drill1.spe** and save the file on your file disk.

Upper/Lowercase Change

After text has been typed, the WordPerfect program can automatically convert the case of the text to all uppercase characters, all lowercase characters, or initial capitals. First, the text to be converted is selected, and then the **Edit**, **Convert Case** option is chosen.

Start-Up Instructions

- ❖ The file named **7drill1.spe** should be displayed in the document window.

Steps to Convert the Case of Characters

1. Select the text to be converted to uppercase or lowercase letters.

For example, select the word **Résumé**.

2. Select **Edit, Convert Case** {Alt, e, v}.
3. Select **Uppercase, Lowercase,** or **Initial Capitals.**

   For example, select **Uppercase** to convert all selected text to uppercase characters {u}.
4. Click once to deselect the text.

Finish-Up Instructions

- Save the file again using the same filename, **7drill1.spe**.

Hard Space

Sometimes two words, such as dates or a person's first and last names, are dependent on each other to be a complete thought and should be printed on the same line. A hard space can be inserted between the words to instruct WordPerfect to always print the word(s) on the same line. For example, the date September 25, 199x, should print on the same line; therefore, a hard space is placed between September and 25 and between the comma and 199x. A hard space is also referred to as a nonbreaking space.

Start-Up Instructions

- The file named **7drill1.spe** should be displayed in the document window.
- Place the insertion point at the end of the document.
- Type the following information on a new line:

  Assisted with the copyediting of the company newsletter, sales brochures, and procedures manuals. After eighteen months as an Assistant Copyeditor, I received a promotion to Copyeditor on May 1, 1993.

Steps to Insert a Hard Space

***Note:** If the numeric keypad is used, Num Lock must be turned off in order for a hard space to be inserted. If necessary, press the Num Lock key to turn off Num Lock.*

1. Move the insertion point to the location where the hard space should be inserted.

   For example, place the insertion point immediately after the *y* in *May*.
2. Press the **Delete** (Del) key once to delete the space between letters.
3. Press and hold the **Ctrl** key and then press the **Spacebar** once (**Ctrl** and **Spacebar**) to insert a hard space.

Finish-Up Instructions

- Place the insertion point immediately after the comma that follows the number *1*. Repeat Steps 2 and 3 to insert a hard space.

- Turn on Reveal Codes to view the hard space (*HSpace*) code (**Alt** and **F3**). Turn off Reveal Codes (**Alt** and **F3**).
- Save the document again using the same filename, **7drill1.spe**.

The Ruler Bar

A Ruler Bar containing margin, paragraph indent, and tab markers can be displayed below the Power Bar. The Ruler Bar shows measurement in inches (see Figure 7.4). The left and right margins, paragraph indents, and tab locations can be set by using the mouse to move the appropriate markers on the Ruler Bar.

Steps to Display the Ruler Bar

1. Select **View, Ruler Bar** {Alt, v, r *or* Alt and Shift and F3}.

   Note: *The Ruler Bar displays below the Power Bar. The triangles displayed every ½" represent left-aligned tabs. Margin markers display above the 1" and 7.5" marks (see Figure 7.4).*

Steps to Remove the Ruler Bar

1. Select **View, Ruler Bar** {Alt, v, r *or* Alt and Shift and F3}.

Start-Up Instructions

- The file named **7drill1.spe** should be displayed in the document window.
- The Ruler Bar should be displayed on the screen.

Steps to Change the Left and Right Margins Using the Ruler Bar

1. Place the insertion point at the location in the document where the margin change is to take effect.

   For example, place the insertion point at the beginning of the document.

2. Move the mouse pointer to the left margin marker located in the Ruler Bar (see Figure 7.4).

   Note: *Be sure to place the mouse pointer on the black margin marker.*

FIGURE 7.4

The Ruler Bar

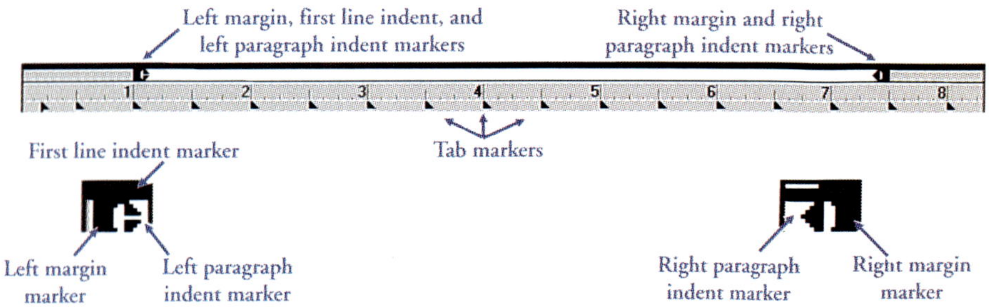

3. Press and hold the mouse button and drag the left margin marker to the desired location. Release the mouse button.

   For example, drag the left margin marker to **1.5**" on the Ruler Bar.

   Note: *The text moves to the new left margin.*

4. Move the mouse pointer to the right margin marker located in the Ruler Bar (see Figure 7.4).

   Note: *Be sure to place the mouse pointer on the black margin marker.*

5. Press and hold the mouse button and drag the right margin marker to the desired location. Release the mouse button.

   For example, drag the right margin marker to 7" on the Ruler Bar.

Finish-Up Instructions

- Use the new filename **7drill1.mar** and save the file on your file disk.
- Print one copy.

Tabs

By default, tabs are set every one-half inch. If desired, tabs can be changed to indent information at a position other than the preset tabs. There are eight types of tabs available: left, center, right, decimal, dot left, dot center, dot right, and dot decimal. Dot leader tabs contain dots which are periods that display between tabbed information. Tabs can be set in the Tab Set dialog box or by choosing the desired tab locations on the Ruler Bar.

Tab locations can be measured from the left margin (relative) or from the left edge of the page (absolute). The default is relative tabs. With relative tabs, if the left margin is changed, the location of all tab(s) will also be changed. Therefore, the distance between the left margin and the tab location(s) will always remain the same. With absolute tabs, the location of the tabs does not change when the left margin is changed. Therefore, the distance between the left margin and the tab locations will change if the left margin is changed. If a change is made to the right margin, it may be necessary to adjust some of the tab locations to accommodate the new right margin.

When tabs are set using the Ruler Bar, tab locations are measured from the left edge of the page (the left edge of the page is zero). When tabs are set using the Tab Set dialog box, tab locations are measured from the left margin (the left margin is zero). For example, if a tab is to be set at .75 inches from the left margin and the left margin is set at 1.25 inches, the tab is set at 2 inches on the Ruler Bar. However, if the Tab Set dialog box is used to set a tab, the tab is set at .75 inches. (It is not necessary to know where the left margin is set because the left margin is always zero in the Tab Set dialog box.)

When creating a document, type the text and press the **Tab** key once between each section (column) of information. Once all the text is typed, tab settings can be adjusted to create a more readable and attractive presentation. Also, the WordPerfect

Tables feature can be used to type and format each column of information (see Chapter 5 for information on converting existing tabbed text into a table).

After tabs are changed, the new tab settings can be viewed by turning on Reveal Codes. If necessary, all tab set codes can be deleted to return to the default tab settings.

Start-Up Instructions

- The file named 7**drill1.mar** should be displayed in the document window.
- The Ruler Bar should be displayed on the screen.

Steps to Set Tabs Using the Ruler Bar

Note: A mouse must be used to set tabs using the Ruler Bar.

1. Place the insertion point at the location where the tabs are to be set, or select the text for which tabs are to be set.

   For example, select the three bulleted items.

2. To clear all existing tabs, move the mouse pointer to a tab marker on the Ruler Bar, click the *right* mouse button once and select Clear All Tabs.

3. Check the letter that displays in the Tab Set button on the Power Bar. (If necessary, select a different tab type by pressing and holding the mouse button and dragging to select the desired tab type; release the mouse button.)

   For example, check that **L** displays in the Tab Set button.

4. Move the mouse pointer to the bottom of the Ruler Bar at the desired tab location and click once.

   For example, move the mouse pointer to **1.75"** on the Ruler Bar and click.

Note: A left tab marker displays on the Ruler Bar.

Insert a New Tab with Dot Leaders

5. Move the mouse pointer to the Tab Set button on the Power Bar. Press and hold the mouse button and drag to select the desired dot leader type.

   For example, select the **...Right** tab type.

Note: The Dot Right tab type displays in the Tab Set button on the Power Bar.

6. Move the mouse pointer to the bottom of the Ruler Bar at the desired tab location and click once.

   For example, move the mouse pointer to 7" and click.

Note: A right tab marker with dot leader characters displays on the Ruler Bar. Continue with the following Finish-Up Instructions to complete the typed information.

Finish-Up Instructions

- Place the insertion point to the right of the last character in the word *Writer*. Press the **Tab** key once.

- ❖ Technical Writer . . . . June 199x
- ❖ Copyeditor . . . . May 1993
- ❖ Assistant Copyeditor . . . . November 1990

FIGURE 7.5

Document with dot leader characters

Note: Dot characters display from the end of the word ***Writer*** *to the right margin, and the insertion point is located at the right margin.*

- ❖ Type **June 199x.**
- ❖ Move the insertion point to the right of the last character in the next line, *Copyeditor*. Press the **Tab** key and type **May 1993.**
- ❖ Move the insertion point to the right of the last character in the final line, *Assistant Copyeditor*. Press the **Tab** key and type **November 1990**.
- ❖ The last several lines of your document should look similar to Figure 7.5.
- ❖ Use the *new* filename **7drill1.tab** and save the file on your file disk.
- ❖ Close the document. If necessary, remove the Ruler Bar from the screen (select **View**, **Ruler Bar**).

Start-Up Instructions

- ❖ Open the file named **7drill2.wpd** located on the data disk.

Steps to Set Tabs Using the Tab Set Dialog Box

1. Place the insertion point where tabs are to be set, or select the text for which tabs are to be set.

   For example, place the insertion point in the blank line after the title.

2. Select Layout, Line, Tab Set {Alt, L, L, t}.

   Note: The Tab Set dialog box displays (see Figure 7.6).

3. Select the Clear All button to delete all the preset tabs {Alt and a}.

4. To set a tab, move the mouse pointer to the Position box and double-click. Type the desired tab location {Alt and p, type the desired tab location}.

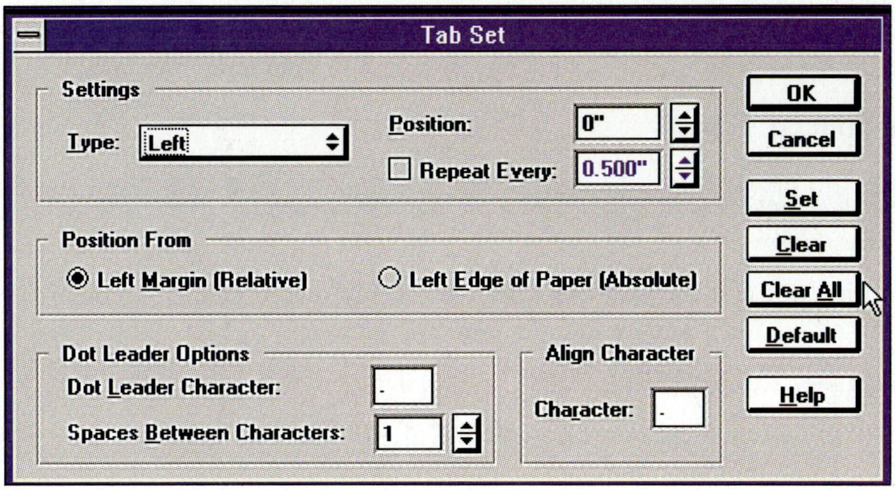

FIGURE 7.6

Tab Set dialog box

For example, type .25. (Do not type the final period.)

Note: Check that Left displays in the Type box.

5. Select Set {Alt and s}.
6. Repeat step 4 and type the desired tab location {Alt and p, type the desired tab location}.

    For example, type 2.5. (Do not type the final period.)

7. To select a different tab type, move the mouse pointer to the Type box, press and hold the mouse button, and drag to select the desired type; release the mouse button {Alt and t, press the up or down arrow keys until the desired tab type displays}.

    For example, select the **Center** tab type.

8. Select Set {Alt and s}.
9. Repeat step 4 and type the desired tab location {Alt and p, type the desired tab location}.

    For example, type 4.5. (Do not type the final period.)

10. Repeat step 7 to select the desired tab type.

    For example, select the **Right** tab type.

11. Select Set {Alt and s}.
12. Repeat step 4 and type the desired tab location {Alt and p, type desired tab location}.

    For example, type 5.5. (Do not type the final period.)

13. Repeat step 7 to select the desired tab type.

    For example, select the **Decimal** tab type.

14. Select Set {Alt and s}.
15. Select OK to exit the Tab Set dialog box {Enter}.

    Note: The columns are aligned at each tab.

Finish-Up Instructions

- Use the *new* filename **7drill2.set** and save the file.
- Print one copy
- Close the document.

Steps to Create Evenly Spaced Tabs

Note: The following Steps to Create Evenly Spaced Tabs and the Steps to Delete Tab Set Code are for your information.

1. Place the insertion point at the location where the evenly spaced tabs are to be in effect.
2. Select Layout, Line, Tab Set {Alt, L, L, t}.
3. Select Clear All to delete all existing tabs {Alt and a}.

4. Select the Repeat Every option {Alt and v}.
5. Double-click in the Repeat Every box and type the spacing desired between tabs {press Tab and type the desired spacing}.
6. Select OK {press Enter}.

Steps to Delete Tab Set Code

1. Turn on Reveal Codes (**Alt** and **F3**).
2. Place the red or shaded block to the left of the tab set code *(Tab Set).*
3. Press Delete.

Create a Résumé

- Use the following information to create the résumé shown in Figure 7.1 on page 154.
- Change the font to **Arrus BT, 12-point**, or **make a font choice of your own**. Use bold, italic, and underline text attributes as shown.
- Use the Ruler Bar and change the left margin to 1.25" and the right margin to 7.25".
- Use the Ruler Bar and set a left tab at 1.5" and a right tab with dot leaders at 7.25".
- Use special text and bullet characters as shown. The *é* is found in the Multinational character set and the (❖) is found in the Iconic Symbols character set.
- Remember to use the **Indent** button to indent paragraphs.
- Save the file on your file disk; use the filename **7drill3.swa**.
- Print one copy.
- Close the document.

Create a Résumé Using the Table Feature

A résumé can also be created using the Table feature to format the information in two columns. Sideheads, such as EMPLOYMENT EXPERIENCE, EDUCATIONAL BACKGROUND, HONORS, and REFERENCES, can be typed in the first column and related information can be placed in the second column. The widths of the table columns can be adjusted to accommodate headings and text. Some of the advantages of using a table to format a résumé are ease of setup and formatting, ease of reading, and visual attractiveness.

Steps to Create a Résumé Using the Table Feature

- Use the following information to create the résumé shown in Figure 7.7.

- Change the font to **Arrus BT, 10-point**, or **make a font choice of your own**. Use bold and italic text attributes as shown.
- Type and center the heading information.
- Create a table with two columns and seven rows. Decrease the width of column 1 and increase the width of column 2. Omit all table lines. (If necessary, see Chapters 5 and 6 for information on changing the width of table columns and omitting table lines.)
- Save the file on your file disk; use the filename **7drill4.wen**.
- Print one copy and close the document.

FIGURE 7.7

Résumé created using the Table feature

RÉSUMÉ
MAXINE WENRICH
45 BLACKSTONE DRIVE
AVENEL, NJ 07001
(201) 555-4828

EMPLOYMENT EXPERIENCE	*Berkhard Newsletter*, Hillside, New Jersey. Full-time editor/reporter. Responsible for reporting and editing several industry newsletters. March 1991 to present.
	The Trentonian, Trenton, New Jersey. Part-time reporter. Responsibilities included covering municipal meetings and developing feature articles. November 1988 to March 1991.
EDUCATIONAL BACKGROUND	Camden Community College, Cherry Hill, New Jersey. A.A. Communications; specialized in journalism. Computer courses studied: Microsoft Word for Windows, WordPerfect, PageMaker, and Paradox.
	High School Diploma, Camden High School, Cherry Hill, New Jersey.
HONORS	Dean's Scholar, 1988. Member Beta Gamma, Honorary Scholastic Society.
REFERENCES	Available upon request.

The Next Step

Chapter Review and Activities

Self-Check Quiz

T F 1. Tabs are set by default every inch.

T F 2. The eight tab types are left, center, decimal, right, dot left, dot center, dot right, and dot decimal.

T F 3. A hard space between words instructs WordPerfect to always print both words on the same line.

T F 4. When a relative tab is set, the tab location changes when the right margin is changed.

T F 5. The WordPerfect Characters dialog box is accessed by selecting **Font, Character**.

6. WordPerfect can convert the case of letters to
   a. all uppercase.
   b. all lowercase.
   c. initial capitals.
   d. any of the above.

7. The Ruler Bar can be used to
   a. set left and right margins.
   b. set top and bottom margins.
   c. set tabs.
   d. both a and c.

8. List two advantages of using a table when creating a résumé.

9. In which WP character set are the following symbols found?

   é ❖ ➟ ✐ ©

10. What is the difference between a relative and an absolute tab?

Enriching Language Arts Skills

Spelling/Vocabulary Words

implement to carry out; to set in motion.

incentive that which inspires action; motivation.
promotional a way of publicizing a product or service.
wholesalers people who sell in large amounts to retailers.

Commas Used in a Series

Words and/or ideas listed in a series are separated by commas.

Example:

The mailing list was sent to Karen Smith, Georgia Cain, and Perry Arnston.

Activities

Activity 7.1—Create a Résumé, Set Tabs, and Insert Special Characters

1. Use the following information and type the résumé shown.
   a. Use the Margins dialog box to change the left and right margins to **1.25"** and to change the top margin to **1.5"** (select **Layout**, **Margins**, type desired margins, **OK**).
   b. Clear all existing tabs and set a left tab at **.3** and a right tab with dot leaders at **6** (select **Layout**, **Line**, **Tab Set**, **Clear All**; double-click in the Position box and type **.3**, select **Set**; double-click in the **Position** box, type **6**, select **Dot Right** tab type, select **Set**, select **OK**).
   c. Change the font to **Arrus**, **10-point**, or **make a font choice of your own**.
   d. Use bold and italic text attributes as shown.
   e. Use special characters for the *é*'s in Résumé and the ✦ characters (select **Insert**, **Character**). The *é* is found in the Multinational character set. The ✦ character is found in the Iconic Symbols character set.

Résumé
Olivia R. Norton
2634 Mississippi Avenue
Ft. Pierce, FL 33451

EDUCATIONAL BACKGROUND

A.A. Business, Indian River Community College 1/93
✦ Major courses: Accounting, Business Law, Office Management, Word Processing, and Telecommunications.

G.E.D., Tampa, Florida 1991

SPECIAL SKILLS

Shorthand: *100* words per minute; typing: *80* words per minute; WordPerfect and Microsoft Word on an IBM PC. Experience with Windows and Microsoft Excel.

EMPLOYMENT EXPERIENCE

Delcon Corporation, Ft. Pierce, Florida

✦ *Office Assistant* 3/93-Present

General backup support for sales department. Responsibilities include answering phones, typing correspondence using WordPerfect, maintaining files, processing mail, making travel arrangements, and entering expense data into an Excel spreadsheet.

Indian River Community College, Ft. Pierce, Florida

✦ *Clerk Typist* (part-time) 12/91-1/93

Responsible for keyboarding notices of faculty meetings, board minutes, and special reports. Filed office materials using alphanumeric system.

REFERENCES

Available upon request.

---

2. Use the filename **7act1.nor** and save the file.
3. Print one copy.
4. Close the document.

Activity 7.2—Create and Edit a Résumé Using the Tables Feature

1. Use the Tables feature and the following information to type the résumé shown.
   a. Use bold and italic text attributes as shown.
   b. Select a font of your own choice in a point size of 10 or 12.
   c. Use special text characters for the *É*'s *in RÉSUMÉ*. The *É* is found in the Multinational character set.

RÉSUMÉ
W. KEVIN KINCAID
172 VINE STREET, APT. 12
ATLANTA, GA 30314

Education	Georgia State, Atlanta, Georgia *B.S. Business Administration,* Minor in Psychology Studied microcomputer applications: Lotus, dBase IV, WordPerfect, and Ventura. Also studied BASIC, PASCAL, and C programming languages. 5/93
Experience	Goldman Research, Hapeville, Georgia (part-time) Responsible for interviewing prospective panel members for the firm. Handled public relations as a host and supervised numerous focus groups. 9/92-4/93
	GTE Service Corporation, Macon, Georgia Worked with a small group of individuals on a project to develop a computer-based *Vertical Services* costing model used to develop costs of a new company telephone service. Summer 1992
	Southern National Bank, Atlanta, Georgia (part-time) Worked in the *Customer Service Department.* Answered phones, distributed mail, and researched microfiche documents to verify answers to customer questions. 10/89-5/92
Activities	Member of Voyagers Club, Newton Math Society, and Tau Sigma Kappa (Computer Honor Society).
References	Available upon request.

2. Use the filename **7act2.kin** and save the file.
3. Use the following information and edit the résumé.
   a. Change the sideheadings to all uppercase letters.
   b. Insert and center the phone number (404) 555-2438 beneath the city, state, and zip code.
   c. Delete the words "Available upon request" that follow the References sideheading.
   d. Insert the following two references:

Cynthia Bates, Office Supervisor
Goldman Research
390 Walker St.
Hapeville, GA 30354
(404) 555-8901

Rubin Cortez, Bank Manager
Southern National Bank
2012 Spring NW
Atlanta, GA 30318
(404) 555-2200

4. Use the filename **7act2.rev** and save the file.
5. Print one copy and close the document.

Activity 7.3—Create Your Own Résumé

1. Create your own résumé using Figure 7.1 or Figure 7.7 as a guide.
2. If necessary, use margin changes to increase or decrease the amount of text that will fit on a page. For example, if your résumé is short, it may be desirable to increase the left, right, and top margins. If your résumé is long, decrease the top, bottom, left, and right margins.
3. Remember to insert special characters for the word *résumé*.
4. Use one or two fonts to enhance the appearance of your résumé.
5. Use the Speller and proofread carefully.
6. Use the filename **7act3.res** and save the file.
7. Print one copy and close the document.

Challenge Your Skills

SCANS

Skill 7.1—Create a Résumé, Set Tabs, and Insert Special Characters

1. Use the following information to type the résumé shown.
   a. Change the top margin to .75" and the bottom margin to .5"; reduce the left and right margins by .25" each.
   b. Clear all tabs. Use the Ruler Bar to set a left tab at 1" and set a dot right tab at the right margin.
   c. Use the bold and italic text attributes as shown.
   d. Select a symbol from the Iconic Symbols character set. Insert the chosen symbol in front of each job title.

Résumé
Randall McChesney
3845 West 23rd Place
Chicago, IL 60623
(312) 555-3841

EDUCATIONAL BACKGROUND

Northwestern University, Evanston, Illinois 6/93
Candidate for *Masters of Management degree.* Concentration in marketing and finance. Member of the Finance Club and Black Management Association.

B.A. Economics, Spelman College, Atlanta, Georgia 5/91
Sun Oil Scholar, Avon Scholar, and recipient of four-year Honors Program Scholarship. President of Economics Club.

EMPLOYMENT EXPERIENCE

Wyle Services, Inc., Chicago, Illinois
Corporate Planning Assistant 8/93-Present
Review and analyze the strategic plans, prepare presentations for senior management, and evaluate Wyle's presence in Japan with respect to imports, exports, and net income.

Stein, Roe & Farnham Mutual Funds, Inc., Chicago, Illinois
Summer Intern 1991
Prepared new account reports and analyzed the flow of dollars into the funds. Utilized Microsoft Excel and MacDraw microcomputer programs for the Macintosh computer.

Prudential Insurance Co., Chicago, Illinois
Claims Representative 6/88-8/90
Initiated correspondence between the company and municipalities, made arrangements for outside adjusters to inspect cars and homes, and settled claims over the telephone.

REFERENCES

Mrs. Roberta Anzac, Manager
Prudential Insurance Co.
1290 Michigan Ave.
Chicago, IL 60600
(312) 555-5000 ext. 3423

Mr. Benjamin Harpreet
Wyle Services, Inc.
121 Adams West
Chicago, IL 60604
(312) 555-6200

2. Use the filename 7**skill1.rmc** and save the file.
3. Print one copy.
4. Close the document.

Skill 7.2—Create a Résumé with Special Characters; Language Arts Skills

1. Create a résumé for Carlene Quevedo using the following information.
   a. Make decisions regarding:
      Résumé format
      Margins
      Tab settings and indentions
      Fonts
      Hard spaces
      Uppercase and lowercase headings
      Bold and italic text attributes
      Special characters
      References
   b. Correct four spelling and two punctuation errors
   c. Carlene lives at 570 Betner Dr., Mansfield, OH 44907 (419) 555-8387.
   d. Carlene graduated in 1988 with a B.A. in Political Science from Ohio State University, Columbus, OH. She is currently a master's degree candidate in Business Administration at Ohio State University, Columbus, OH.
   e. Carlene's work experience is as follows:

      Hayden Services, Network Services Department, Mansfield, OH
      Product Developer
      7/90-Present
      Job responsibilities include: develop and impliment the insentive program for the Smart Ring product line. Specifically, develop the tracking systems and implementation booklet for the program.

      J.M. Smucker Company, Orrville, OH
      District Sales Manager
      9/88-6/90
      Job responsibilities included managing food brokers over a five-state region, including training for office and sales staff. Assisted in sales presentations and customer relations. Responsible for personal selling to large restaurants, hotels and food service chains.

      Also at J.M. Smucker Company, Carlene worked as a part-time sales representative in the Columbus district from 6/86-9/88. Her responsibilities were: direct contact with grocery retailers and wholesalors; introduction of new products, presentation of promottional deals, and maintenance of customer relations.

f. Carlene's references are:

Marly Lawson, Hayden Services, 30 Park Ave. West, Mansfield, OH 44902 (419) 555-4550

Norman P. Costello, Jr., J.M. Smucker Company, 689 Main St., Orrville, OH 44667 (216) 555-8799

2. Use the filename **7skill2.cq** and save the file.
3. Print one copy.
4. If you have completed your work, exit WordPerfect.

CHAPTER 8

Create Newspaper and Parallel Text Columns

Features Covered

- Newspaper-style columns
- The Columns Define button
- Change column definitions
- Balanced newspaper columns
- Column breaks
- Hyphenation
- Parallel columns
- Convert text in parallel columns to a table

Objectives and Introduction

After successfully completing this chapter, you will be able to use the **Columns Define** button to format text in newspaper-style columns and to use the Columns feature or the Table feature to create parallel columns. In addition, you will also learn how to control the flow of text in newspaper columns using the balanced newspaper column feature and column breaks, and how to use the hyphenation feature to improve the look and readability of columnar text.

Columns of text can be arranged in newspaper style or parallel style. Text in newspaper columns wraps around from line to line, column to column, and page to page. Paragraphs of related text can be arranged in parallel columns so that information can be read from left to right. The Hyphenation feature can be used to improve the readability of columnar text by reducing the amount of space at the end of lines.

Newspaper Columns

Newspaper columns are created by placing a column definition code at the beginning of the text that will be arranged in columns either before or after the text is typed. The simplest method for creating columns is to place the code in the document *after* the text is typed. When the column code is inserted, the column arrangement displays instantly on the screen.

A quick way to create columns using WordPerfect's default column settings (equal width newspaper column with .5 inch space between columns) is to select the **Columns Define** button on the Power Bar and choose the desired number of columns. WordPerfect automatically calculates even column widths based on the page margins, inserts a .5-inch gutter (blank space between columns), and displays the text in columns in the document window.

If column settings different from the default are desired, select **Layout**, **Columns**, **Define** or select the **Columns Define** button on the Power Bar and choose the **Define** option. The Columns dialog box displays and the column type, number of columns, space between columns and column widths can be specified (see Figure 8.3).

The *Type* section is used to specify newspaper, balanced newspaper, or parallel columns (the default is newspaper). The *Number of Columns* box is used to specify the number of desired columns (the default is 2). Parallel columns are discussed later in this chapter.

The *Spacing Between Columns* box in the Columns dialog box is used to specify the amount of space (in inches) to be placed between the columns. The default setting is .5 inches and can be changed. (The distance between columns is often referred to as the gutter space.)

Once the number of columns is specified, WordPerfect automatically calculates equal widths for each column and determines the left and right margins for each column. The width of each column and the distance between each column displays in the *Custom Widths* box. If the number of columns or distance between columns is changed, the column margins are automatically recalculated when **OK** is selected.

A border line can be placed between columns or borders can be placed around text by selecting **Layout**, **Columns**, **Border/Fill** and choosing the desired border style. WordPerfect provides many styles of borders including a single line between columns, hairline, double, dashed, and extra thick. In this chapter, we will work with the single line between columns style. Borders are also discussed in chapters 5 and 13.

Once all the column settings are set, **OK** is chosen and the text displays in columns on the screen. Turn on Reveal Codes to view the column definition code *Col Def.* When the red or shaded block is located to the left of the column definition code, the code expands to show the column type and number of columns, e.g., *Col Def: Newspaper, Total: 2, Col[Adj], Gut [0.5"], Col[Adj].*

When newspaper columns have been defined, the text flow can be controlled by inserting a column break to force text to the next column or page. A column break is inserted by pressing **Ctrl** and **Enter**. Once newspaper columns are turned on, pressing **Ctrl** and **Enter** moves the insertion point and any text that follows the insertion point to the top of the next column. If the insertion point is located in the final column of the page when **Ctrl** and **Enter** are pressed, the text is forced to the top left column of the next page.

Text in newspaper and balanced newspaper columns automatically flows from the bottom of one column to the top of the next column and flows from the bottom of one page to the top left column of the next page (see Figure 8.2). The term *snaking* is often used to describe columnar text that wraps from column to column and page to page.

When the **Balanced Newspaper** type is selected, the flow of text is adjusted so that each column is approximately the same length. This method provides a more balanced appearance on the page and is often used when text does not completely fill the last column on a page.

After newspaper columns are typed, extra space may display at the end of lines, making the columnar information difficult to read. Hyphenation can be used to align words more evenly at the margin and to improve the appearance and readability of the columnar text.

A column off code can be placed at the end of the columnar text in order to change the number of columns, e.g., to return to a single-column layout. To end a multicolumn layout, insert a column off code by selecting the **Columns Define** button on the Power Bar and choosing the **Columns Off** option.

Start-Up Instructions

- Open the file named **8drill1.wpd** located on the data disk.

Steps to Create Newspaper Columns

1. Place the insertion point to the left of the first character in the text to be placed in columns.

   For example, place the insertion point to the left of T in the word "The" (first word of the first paragraph).

2. Move the mouse pointer to the **Columns Define** button on the Power Bar. Press and hold the mouse button {Alt, L, c, d}.
3. Move the mouse pointer to the desired number of columns and release the mouse button {type desired number of columns, Enter}.

   For example, select **2 Columns.**

   Note: The text is displayed in columns on the screen.

Finish-Up Instructions

- Turn on Reveal Codes (select **View**, **Reveal Codes**). Move the red or shaded block in the Reveal Codes window to the left of the column definition code, *Col Def,* to display the expanded code. Turn off Reveal Codes (select **View**, **Reveal Codes**).
- Use the *new* filename **8drill1.new** and save the file on your file disk.

Start-Up Instructions

- The file named **8drill1.new** should be displayed in the document window.

Steps to Place a Border Line Between Newspaper Columns

1. With the insertion point located anywhere in the newspaper columns, select **Layout, Columns, Border/Fill** {Alt, L, c, b}.

   Note: The Column Border dialog box displays.

2. Select the **Border Style** button {Alt and b, Spacebar}.

FIGURE 8.1

Column Border dialog box

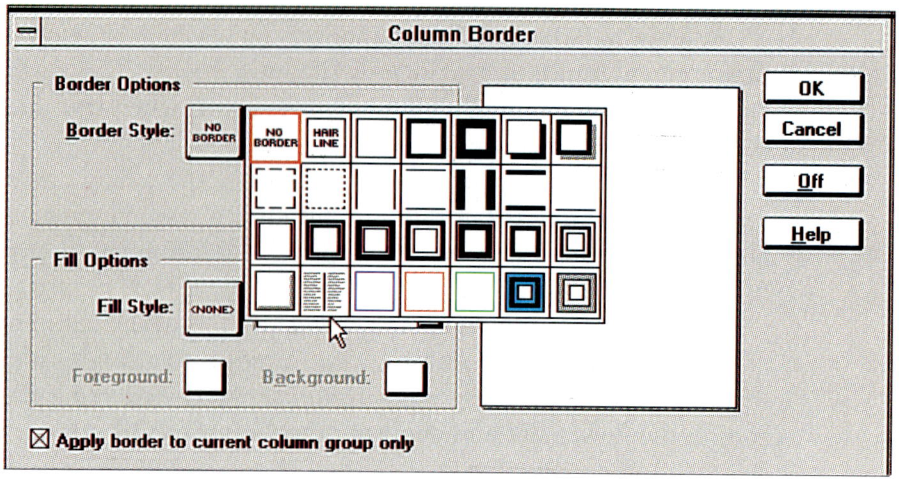

Note: A palette of available border styles displays (see Figure 8.1).

3. Move the mouse pointer to the desired border style and click the mouse button once {press the arrow keys until the desired border style is selected; Enter}.

   For example, click on the **Column Between** (the second button in the bottom row) border style.

   Note: A sample of the border style displays on the Border Style button and on the right side of the Column Border dialog box. Also, the words "Column Between" displays in the box to the right of the Border Style button.

4. Select OK to exit the Column Border dialog box {Enter}.

   Note: Your document should look similar to Figure 8.2. Select the ***Page Zoom Full*** *button on the Power Bar to view the entire page; select the* ***Page Zoom Full*** *button again to return to the normal view.*

Finish-Up Instructions

- Save the file again using the same filename, **8drill1.new**.
- Print one copy.

Start-Up Instructions

- The file named **8drill1.new** should be displayed in the document window.

Steps to Change the Column Definition

1. Place the insertion point at any location in the newspaper columns.

   Note: The insertion point must be located to the right of the Col Border and Col Def codes. If necessary, turn on Reveal Codes and position the insertion point after the column codes.

2. Move the mouse pointer to the Columns Define button in the Power Bar. Press and hold the mouse button {Alt, L, c}.
3. Move the mouse pointer to Define and release the mouse button {d}.

FIGURE 8.2

Text arranged in multiple columns

SAVING AND INVESTING TRENDS

The pattern for saving and investing money during the next ten years will be drastically different than in the years past. Several distinct areas are the driving forces of the changes predicted for the next decade.

Healthy Savings Attitudes

Americans' attitudes towards saving and investment are improving. During the past few years, the average savings rate for Americans was 5% of after-tax income--far less than the previous decade. However, last year Americans had a healthy increase in savings to 6.5%

Demographics

The baby boom generation is fast approaching middle age. They are planning for their children's education, their own retirement, and their own leisure activities. In addition, Americans have increased their wealth dramatically and are recognizing the need to save and invest wisely.

Products

During the past decade, Americans began to achieve their savings goals by investing in nontraditional products. For example, mutual funds, money market funds, and annuities have been selected for investments because they provide an opportunity for higher returns with limited risks. In the next decade, demand for unconventional investments will be even more noticeable.

Demand for Change

The American people are telling the financial institutions that they want more products, more security, and honest advisors. Such requests are driving financial institutions to look inward and re-evaluate their philosophies in order to make primary changes in the way they conduct business.

Financial Institutions

Traditionally, individuals have used Savings and Loan associations for many of their savings needs and turned to brokerage firms for investments. Since the Savings and Loan industry has experienced great difficulties, many people have lost confidence and seek a more secure place for their savings.

***Note:** The Columns dialog box displays (see Figure 8.3).*

4. Make the desired changes to the type of columns, number of columns, distance between columns, etc.

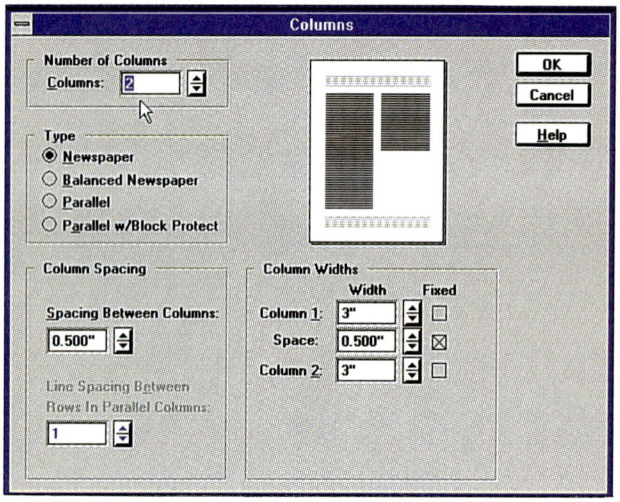

FIGURE 8.3

Columns dialog box

For example, type **3** in the Number of Columns box. Double-click in the **Spacing Between Columns** box and type **.35** {Alt and s, type .35}.

5. Select OK {Enter}.

Note: The text is changed to three columns.

Steps to Move the Insertion Point in Newspaper Columns or Parallel Columns

Note: The text must first be typed and arranged in either newspaper or parallel columns.

1. To move the insertion point quickly from one column to another, place the mouse pointer in the desired column and press the mouse button once {press Alt and the left or right arrow key}.

Finish-Up Instructions

- Use the *new* filename **8drill1.3c** and save the file on your file disk.
- Print one copy.
- Close the document.

Start-Up Instructions

- Open the file named **8drill1.wpd** located on the data disk.

Steps to Create Balanced Newspaper Columns

1. Place the insertion point to the left of the first character in the text to be placed in columns.

   For example, place the insertion point to the left of the **T** in the word "The" (first word of the first paragraph).

2. Move the mouse pointer to the **Columns Define** button on the Power Bar. Press and hold the mouse button {Alt, L, c}.
3. Move the mouse pointer to **Define** and release the mouse button {d}.

Note: The Columns dialog box displays.

4. Type the number of columns desired in the Number of Columns box {type desired number of columns}.

   For example, if necessary, type **2**.

5. Select **Balanced Newspaper** located in the Type box {Alt and b}.

6. To change the amount of space between columns, double-click in the **Spacing Between Columns** box and type the desired amount {Alt and s, type desired amount}.

   For example, type **.35**. (Do not type the final period.)

7. Select **OK** {press Enter}.

   Note: The text is displayed in columns in the document window and the text columns end at approximately the same line on the page.

Steps to Insert a Column Off Code

1. Place the insertion point at the end of the columns after the last column entry.

   For example, press **Ctrl** and **End** to move the insertion point to the end of the document.

2. Move the mouse pointer to the **Columns Define** button in the Power Bar. Press and hold the mouse button {Alt, L, c}.

3. Move the mouse pointer to **Columns Off** and release the mouse button {o}.

   *Note: The insertion point moves to the left margin below the text. Text typed after the **Column Def: Off** code will no longer be formatted in columns.*

Finish-Up Instructions

- Press **Enter** twice. Type and center the following sentence:

  START YOUR SAVINGS PLAN TODAY!

  Note: The one-column format is in effect.

- Use the *new* filename **8drill1.bal** and save the file on your file disk.
- Print one copy.
- Close the document.

Start-Up Instructions

- Open the file named **8drill2.fre** located on the data disk.
- Place the insertion point below the subtitle to the left of the **G** in the word *Gerald* in the first paragraph. Create two newspaper columns (select the **Columns Define** button on the Power Bar and choose **2 Columns**).

Steps to Insert a Column Break to Control the Flow of Columnar Text

1. Locate the insertion point to the left of the first character of text to be placed in another column.

For example, place the insertion point at the beginning of the third paragraph to the left of the **B** in the word *Before.*

2. Press **Ctrl** and **Enter**.

   Note: *The text following the insertion point is immediately moved to the second column.*

Finish-Up Instructions

- Center the text vertically on the page (select **Layout**, **Page**, **Center**, **Current Page**, **OK**).
- Use the *new* filename **8drill2.brk** and save the file on your file disk.
- Print one copy.
- Close the document.

Hyphenation

Hyphenation is the process of dividing a word at the right margin so that the first part of the word prints at the end of the line and the remainder of the word prints at the beginning of the next line. Hyphenating words is used to make line endings at the right margin look more even (less ragged) or to avoid large gaps between words in a line with full justification. Hyphenation can be controlled by using the Prompt for Hyphenation *When Required* or Prompt for Hyphenation *Always* options.

When text is typed, regular, soft, and hard hyphens and hyphenation soft returns can be inserted. Regular hyphens break compound words at the right margin when necessary. For example, the hyphenated word *well-qualified* will split after the hyphen if the hyphen is at the right margin.

A hard hyphen, such as the hyphen in the compound name *Jones-Meyer*, is inserted between words that should always appear on the same line of text. A hard hyphen is inserted by pressing the **Ctrl** and hyphen (-) keys (**Ctrl** and -). The hard hyphen is also referred to as a required hyphen.

A soft hyphen can be inserted by placing the insertion point to the left of the character that will follow the hyphen, pressing and holding the **Ctrl** and **Shift** keys while tapping the hyphen key once. When a word that contains a soft hyphen does not break at the end of line, the hyphen is hidden. In other words, a soft hyphen will display in the document window only if the hyphenated word needs to break at the end of the line. However, the soft hyphen code always displays in the Reveal Codes window.

A hyphenation soft return is used for words that are separated by slashes, e.g., administrator/director. If the words separated by a slash reach the right margin, WordPerfect separates the words after the slash only if a hyphenation soft return has been inserted after the slash. The hyphenation soft return is actually a code, *Hyph Srt*, and, similar to a soft hyphen, affects the document only when words separated by slashes need to be broken at the right margin.

WordPerfect uses a hyphenation zone to determine which words need to be hyphenated. The hyphenation zone includes an area to the left of the right margin and also an area to the right of the right margin. If a word begins before the left area and extends beyond the right area, hyphenation of the word is desirable. The default hyphenation zone is 10 percent left and 4 percent right. This means that WordPerfect

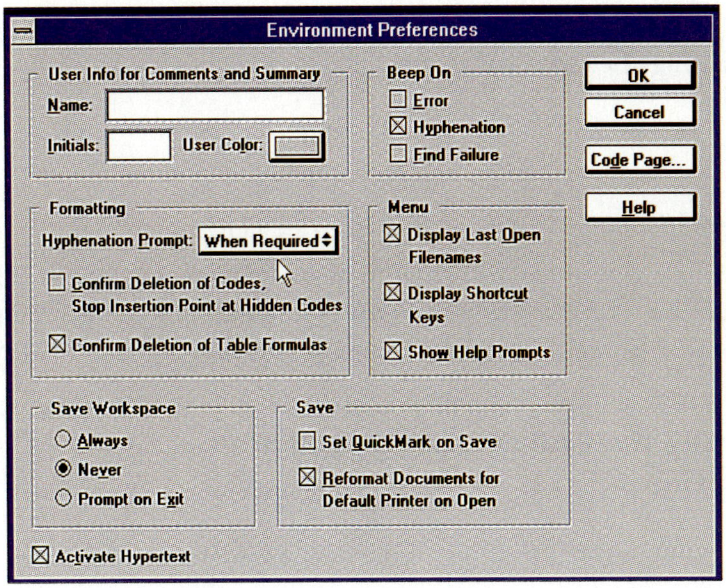

FIGURE 8.4

Environment Preferences dialog box

will determine an area that is 10 percent of the line length as the left area and 4 percent of the line length as the right area. A small hyphenation zone will produce more hyphenated words; a larger hyphenation zone will reduce the number of hyphenated words. Generally, the default hyphenation zone will produce a visually acceptable hyphenation area.

There are three options for controlling the hyphenation process. The hyphenation options are found in the Hyphenation Prompt section of the Environment Preferences dialog box (see Figure 8.4). The Environment Preferences dialog box is displayed by selecting **File**, **Preferences**, and double-clicking on **Environment**.

The three hyphenation options, *Never*, *When Required*, and *Always*, are used to control how and when WordPerfect will hyphenate words. The default setting is Hyphenation Prompt When Required. With *When Required* in effect, words found in the WordPerfect main dictionary are automatically hyphenated. However, if a word is not found in the dictionary, the program will pause and ask the user to select the appropriate hyphenation point.

When Hyphenation Prompt *Never* is selected, WordPerfect hyphenates words found in the main dictionary without pausing. However, if a word is not found in the dictionary, WordPerfect determines a hyphenation point and does not pause to allow the user to make a hyphenation decision. The Hyphenation Prompt *Never* and *When Required* settings are not recommended, because the main dictionary words may not include all the words that need to be hyphenated and the hyphenation decisions made by WordPerfect may not follow basic word division guidelines (see page 182).

If Hyphenation Prompt *Always* is selected, WordPerfect will pause at each word to be hyphenated and allow you to to confirm the displayed hyphenation suggestion. The hyphenation point can be changed if desired by pressing the left or right arrow keys.

Turn on hyphenation only after a document has been proofread, edited, and is being prepared for final form. Use one of the hyphenation procedures only if there are gaps between words or large spaces at the right margins. If the gaps or spaces are small, hyphenation may be unnecessary.

Once hyphenation has been turned on, WordPerfect begins looking for words that can be hyphenated. Typically, WordPerfect decides where to divide a word, then separates the word and places the hyphen at the end of the line. Depending on the Hyphenation Prompt setting selected, WordPerfect may or may not pause for hyphenation confirmation.

Start-Up Instructions

- Open the filename **8drill1.new** created earlier in this chapter.
- Check that the Hyphentation Prompt **When Required** setting is selected. Select **File, Preferences,** double-click on **Environment, Hyphenation Prompt, When Required, OK, Close** {Alt, f, e; Alt and e, Enter; Alt and p, w; Enter, Alt and c}.

Steps to Hyphenate Text Using the Prompt for Hyphenation When Required Option

1. Place the insertion point at the beginning of the document (**Ctrl** and **Home**).
2. Select **Layout, Line, Hyphenation** {Alt, L, L, e}.

   Note: *The Line Hyphenation dialog box displays.*
3. Click in the box located beside the word **Hyphenation On** {o}.

   Note: *An X should display in the Hyphenation On box.*
4. Select **OK** {Enter}.

   Note: *If WordPerfect does not recognize a word that needs to be hyphenated, a Position Hyphen dialog box displays. If necessary, press the left or right arrow keys to position the hyphen at the appropriate location. Select* ***Insert Hyphen*** *{Alt and i}. If a word should not be hyphenated, select* ***Ignore Word*** *{Alt and w}.*
5. When the entire document has been reviewed for possible words to be hyphenated, any words that were hyphenated display with a hyphen at the end of the text line(s).

   Note: *Depending on the selected font and point size (see Chapter 3), the hyphenation zone settings, and the words in the document, there may not be any words hyphenated.*

Finish-Up Instructions

- Use the *new* filename **8drill3.hyp** and save the file on your file disk.
- Print one copy.
- Close the document.

Start-Up Instructions

- Open the file named **8drill2.brk** created earlier in this chapter.

Steps to Hyphenate Text Using the Hyphenation Prompt Always Option

1. Read the following guidelines for correct word division before proceeding to step 2.
   a. Hyphenate only between syllables. Use a dictionary, if necessary.
   b. Avoid hyphenating words of five characters or less, e.g., *often.*

c. Hyphenate a word so that at least three characters remain on the line, e.g., *in-* or *ly.*, but not *i-* or *ly* without the period.

d. Place a hyphen after a vowel, e.g., *initi-ate.*

e. Place a hyphen between double consonants, e.g., *accom-modate.*

f. Do not hyphenate the last word of a paragraph; do not hyphenate the last word in the first line of a document.

g. Avoid hyphenating words at the end of two consecutive lines.

h. Do not hyphenate proper nouns, e.g., Apprenticeship Council.

Note: *Once a document has been checked for possible words to be hyphenated, there may not be any words hyphenated.*

2. Select File, Preferences, double-click on Environment {Alt, f, e; Alt and e, Enter}.
3. Move the mouse pointer to the Hyphenation Prompt box. Press and hold the mouse button to display the available choices {Alt and p}.
4. Move the mouse pointer to the Always option and release the mouse button {a}.
5. Select OK, Close {press Enter, Alt and c}.
6. With the insertion point at the beginning of the document, select Layout, Line, Hyphenation {Alt, L, L, e}.
7. Click in the box to the left of the words Hyphenation On {o}.

   Note: *An X should display in the Hyphenation On box.*
8. Select OK {Enter}.
9. When the Position Hyphen dialog box displays, make appropriate hyphenation decisions.

   Note: *The following hyphenation decisions are based on your text being set for Times New Roman Regular, 12 point. If a different font is used, the words to be hyphenated may be different.*

   a. The word *analyst* displays in the Position Hyphen dialog box. The hyphen displays between the *n* and *a.* Press the right arrow key once to move the hyphen between the *a* and *l.* Select **Insert Hyphen** {Alt and i}.

   b. The word *associates* displays in the Position Hyphen dialog box. The hyphen displays between the two *s*'es. This is a correct and desirable hyphenation; select **Insert Hyphen** {Alt and i}.

   c. The word *contract* displays with correct hyphenation; select **Insert Hyphen** {Alt and i}.

   d. The word *construction* displays with correct hyphenation; select **Insert Hyphen** {Alt and i}.

Note: *When the hyphenation process is completed, the Position Hyphen dialog box no longer displays.*

Finish-Up Instructions

- Scroll down to view the hyphenated text. The last word of the first paragraph is hyphenated. Delete the hyphen in the word *analyst* because the last word of a paragraph should not be hyphenated.
- Use the *new* filename **8drill4.hyp** and save the file on your file disk.
- Print one copy and close the document.

Parallel Columns

Parallel columns are blocks of related information placed next to each other in rows so that the information can be read across the page from left to right. Text in parallel columns wraps in each column, similar to newspaper columns. The main difference between newspaper and parallel columns is that in parallel columns, the information does not wrap from the bottom of the first column to the top of the second column. With parallel columns, the information in the first column and the related information in the second column may vary in length. For example, the information in the first column might include only one or two lines of text while the related information in the second column might include three or more lines of text. (See Figure 8.5.) Either the Columns or Table feature can be used to create parallel columns.

When using the Columns feature, the Parallel or Parallel w/Block Protect option is chosen for the type of columns desired. Either of these options creates parallel columns; however, the Parallel w/Block Protect option will keep all lines of related information (one block) together on the same page. The Line Spacing Between Rows option is used to specify the amount of blank space to be inserted between rows (blocks) of text in parallel columns. Generally, one blank line is placed between blocks of text.

When typing text in parallel columns, press **Ctrl** and **Enter** to move the insertion point from column to column. When the insertion point is located in the right column and **Ctrl** and **Enter** are pressed, the insertion point moves back to the left column and inserts a vertical blank line space above the insertion point.

Parallel columns can also be created using the Table feature (see Figure 8.6). A table is often the most efficient way to set up parallel columns, because it is easier to move, insert, and delete columns and rows, and the **Tab** key is used to move the insertion point between columns and rows. To create a table with the desired number of columns and rows, see Chapter 5. When typing, text automatically wraps around in each cell. The table lines can be omitted if desired (see Chapter 6).

Parallel columns that have been created using the Columns feature can be converted to a table. This is useful if additional columns or rows are needed or if lines around or between columns are desired.

Start-Up Instructions

- Type and center the title of the document shown in Figure 8.5 and press **Enter** three times. Use the following steps to type the remainder of the document.

FIGURE 8.5

Parallel text columns

COMPUTER TERMINOLOGY

ASCII (Ctrl and Enter)	The acronym ASCII stands for American Standard Code for Information Interchange (pronounced *ask-kee*). This standard code enables computers to convert keyboard symbols, such as letters, numbers, and punctuation, into binary code. (Ctrl and Enter)
BUG (Ctrl and Enter)	An error or problem that prevents the proper execution of a computer task. A bug can be a hardware or software error. (Ctrl and Enter)
COMPUTER GRAPHICS (Ctrl and Enter)	Pictures that are created by using a computer with graphics software. Today, graphics software is capable of producing movies, animation, color illustrations, and three-dimensional drawings. (Ctrl and Enter)
DOWN (Ctrl and Enter)	A computer that is "down" is not operating, usually because of software or hardware failure. (Ctrl and Enter)

Steps to Create Parallel Columns Using the Columns Feature

1. Move the mouse pointer to the **Columns Define** button on the Power Bar. Press and hold the mouse button {Alt, L, c}.
2. Move the mouse pointer to **Define** and release the mouse button {d}.

   ***Note:** The Columns dialog box displays.*
3. Type the number of columns desired in the Number of Columns box {type desired number of columns}.

   For example, if necessary, type 2.
4. Select **Parallel w/Block Protect** located in the Type box {Alt and a}.
5. To change the amount of space between columns, double-click in the **Space Between Columns** box and type the desired amount {Alt and s, type desired amount}.

   For example, type .35. (Do not type the final period.)
6. Select **OK** {press Enter}.

Note: The column definition code has been inserted into the document. If you wish to view the expanded code, turn on Reveal Codes and move the red or shaded block to the left of the ***Col Def*** *code.*

7. Type the information for the first entry in the left column.

   For example, type **ASCII**.

8. Press **Ctrl** and **Enter** to move the insertion point to the right column.

   Note: A hard column break code, ***Hcol,*** *is inserted into the document. The code can be viewed by turning on Reveal Codes.*

9. Type the information for the first entry in the right column.

   For example, type **The acronym ASCII . . .**

10. Press **Ctrl** and **Enter** to move the insertion point back to the left column.

    Note: A vertical blank line space is inserted automatically above the insertion point.

Finish-Up Instructions

- Continue to type each block of information shown in Figure 8.5 using steps 7–10.
- Use the filename **8drill5.par** and save the file on your file disk.
- Print one copy.
- Close the document.

Start-Up Instructions

- The text shown in Figure 8.6 will be used to create parallel columns using the Table feature.

Steps to Create Parallel Columns Using the Table feature

1. Move the mouse pointer to the Tables Quick Create button on the Power Bar. Press and hold the mouse button while dragging to highlight the desired number of columns and rows. Release the mouse button {Alt a, c, type number of columns, Tab, type number of rows, Enter}.

   For example, drag to highlight a 3 x 3 table.

2. Type the text for column A.

   For example, type **Performance Expectations: Achieves . . .** (see Figure 8.6).

   Note: The text wraps around within each cell; do not press Enter.

3. Press the Tab key to move the insertion point to column B.
4. Type the text for the first paragraph in column B.

   For example, type **Distinguished Rating**.

5. Press the Tab key to move the insertion point to column C.
6. Type the text for the first paragraph in column C.

   For example, type **102.0 and higher**.

FIGURE 8.6

Parallel columns created using the Table feature

Performance Expectations: Achieves total business objective within division for the most recent 12 periods	Distinguished Rating	102.0 and higher
Achieves division annual management objective	Distinguished Rating	101.0 and higher
Maintains or increases total dollar market share	Distinguished Rating	+1.5 and greater

7. Press the Tab key to move the insertion point back to column A.

Finish-Up Instructions

- Repeat steps 2–7 to type the remaining information in Figure 8.6.
- If desired, omit all table lines (see Steps to Omit Table Lines, Chapter 6, page 143).
- Save the file on your file disk; use the filename **8drill6.tbl**.
- Print one copy.
- Close the document.

Start-Up Instructions

- Open the file named **8drill5.par** created earlier in this chapter.

Steps to Convert Parallel Columns to a Table

1. Select all the text typed in parallel columns. (Do not select the title.)
2. Select Tables, Create {Alt, a, c}.

   ***Note:** The Convert Table dialog box displays.*
3. Check that the Parallel Columns option button is selected {p}.
4. Select OK {press Enter}.

Finish-Up Instructions

- Visually estimate and decrease the width of column A to approximately 2".
- Insert a new column after column B (place the insertion point in any cell in column B, select **Table**, **Insert**, **Column**, **After**, **OK**).
- Visually estimate and increase the width of column B to approximately 3".
- Type the following information into the empty cells in column C:

See page 20.
See page 34.
See page 18.
See page 25.

- Save the file on your file disk; use the new filename **8drill5.con**.
- Print one copy.
- Close the document.

The Next Step

Chapter Review and Activities

Self-Check Quiz

T F 1. When typing parallel columns that have been created using the Columns feature, press **Ctrl** and **Enter** to move the insertion point to the next column.

T F 2. Parallel columns require that the number of lines of text in the left column equal the number of lines of text in the right column.

T F 3. Newspaper-style columns can be defined before *or* after text is typed.

T F 4. The amount of blank space between newspaper columns cannot be changed.

T F 5. The Table feature can be used to create parallel columns.

6. Balanced newspaper columns are created by selecting the **Columns Define** button,
   a. choosing **Define**, and selecting the **Balanced Newspaper** type.
   b. and choosing the number of columns.
   c. choosing **Define**, and selecting **Parallel w/Block Protect**.

7. Which of the following guidelines should be remembered when hyphenating text?
   a. Avoid hyphenating words of fewer than five characters.
   b. Place hyphens between double consonants.
   c. Hyphenate between syllables.
   d. All of the above.

8. List three reasons why it may be more efficient to create parallel columns using the Table feature instead of the Columns feature.

9. When and why should hyphenation be used?

10. Show the correct hyphenation points for the following words.

attitude unkempt offensive

Enriching Language Arts Skills

Spelling/Vocabulary Words

prompt done at once without delay; on time.
unkempt in a messy or untidy condition.
offensive undesirable; highly annoying.
antagonistic behaving in a hostile or unfriendly manner.
attitude a manner toward or feeling about something or someone.

Using the Abbreviations *e.g.* and *i.e.*

The abbreviation *e.g.* is used in place of "for example" and is often used when one or more of many examples are listed. The abbreviation *i.e.* is used in place of "that is" and is used when all potential conditions are listed. A period follows each initial with no space between the period and the initials. The final period is followed by a comma.

Examples:

There are many word processing programs that include desktop publishing features, e.g., WordPerfect, Microsoft Word, and AmiPro.

When the president's name is typed in the signature line, use the first name initial and include Sr., i.e., J. Thomas-Meyers, Sr.

Activities

Activity 8.1—Create Balanced Newspaper Columns

1. Type the following unformatted information with the spacing and bold as shown:

UPDATES FOR THE EMPLOYER

Report Corporate Changes

Any changes in corporate status (e.g., mailing addresses, corporate name, and organizational form) should be reported on the new corporate change form. The form should be attached to your quarterly reports return envelope. There are four parts to the corporate change form.

I. Part I is for a mailing address change.

II. Part II is used for reporting changes in the corporation name.
III. Part III is used to report the dissolution of the corporation. If Part III is filed, you may also need to complete Part IV.
IV. Part IV requires specific information on all parties involved in the changes.

If you have questions about the corporate change form, call the Corporate Employer department.

New Wage Reporting (Public Works)

As of the last quarter, all contractors and subcontractors performing public works construction projects must use the new payroll reporting guidelines. In accordance with the new guidelines, certified payroll records must be submitted within 15 days of the payment of the wages.

Contractors and subcontractors can be assessed a penalty of up to $250 per day for failure to provide the required payroll records.

Quarterly Wage Reports

Over half of all employers submit quarterly wage reports on magnetic tape. For smaller operations or where magnetic tape is not available, employers can use personal computers to submit their wage reports on disks. An IBM-compatible program, WageReps, can be used to generate the wage information in the format necessary for submission to the Corporate Employer department. Two versions of WageReps are available: 1.1 for employers with fewer than 250 employees and 2.0 for employers with 250 or more employees.

Employer Seminars

A series of seminars for employers will be held to introduce new programs and services of the Corporate Employer department. One-day seminars are offered at convenient locations, and a small registration fee is required. For more information about these seminars, call (619) 555-3030.

---

2. Center the title.
3. Create balanced newspaper columns:
   a. Place the insertion point at the left of (or under) the **R** in the first word of the first sidehead, Report.
   b. Move the mouse pointer to the **Columns Define** button on the Power Bar. Press and hold the mouse button.
   c. Move the mouse pointer to **Define** and release the mouse button.
   d. Select **Balanced Newspaper** in the Type box. Select **OK**.
4. Use the filename **8act1.bnp** and save the file.
5. Print one copy.
6. Close the document.

Activity 8.2—Create Parallel Columns Using the Columns Feature

1. Type, center, and bold the title, **PEOPLE IN THE NEWS.** Press **Enter** three times.
2. Create and keyboard parallel columns:
   a. Move the mouse pointer to the **Columns Define** button on the Power Bar. Press and hold the mouse button.
   b. Move the mouse pointer to **Define** and release the mouse button.
   c. Select **Parallel w/Block Protect** Type box.
   d. Check that **2** displays in the Number of Columns box.
   e. Select **OK.**
   f. Continue typing each entry from left to right.

PEOPLE IN THE NEWS

Sherry Osborne Enter Branch Manager Enter Astoria, Oregon Ctrl and Enter	Sherry received the 1992 Woman of Achievement Award. North Bay United Bank nominated her for the award because of her exceptional leadership and community activities. Ctrl and Enter
David Mathiesen Enter Customer Service Representative Enter Eugene, Oregon Ctrl and Enter	David raised $1,340 selling T-shirts at the Jet Fan Fly Air Show. The proceeds from the sale were used to provide grocery gift certificates for homeless families in the Eugene area. Ctrl and Enter
Bennett Dobson Enter Director of Foreign Currency Enter Portland, Oregon Ctrl and Enter	Bennett's department handles wholesale trading of foreign currency for corporations, hotels, and travel agencies. Bennett's time is divided between currency trading and business development. Ctrl and Enter

---

3. After the final character in the last column is typed, move the mouse pointer to the **Columns Define** button on the Power Bar. Press and hold the mouse button. Move the mouse pointer to **Columns Off** and release the mouse button.
4. Use the filename **8act2.par** and save the file.
5. Print one copy.
6. Close the document.

Activity 8.3—Create Parallel Columns Using the Table feature

1. Change the left and right margins to .75".
2. Create a table with 3 columns and 6 rows. (If necessary, see Chapter 5, Steps to Create a Table.)
3. Join the cells in row 1 (select the cells in row 1, select **Table, Join, Cell**).
4. Type the following information into the table cells as shown. Remember to use the **Tab** key to move from column to column and row to row.

DAILY SCHEDULE		
Times	Names	Tasks
8:30 a.m.-10:30 a.m.	Clyde Rice Caroline Pyle	Call title companies to request open deeds of trust information. Follow up on calls made to title companies the previous day.
10:30 a.m.-12:00 noon	Cary Fong Clyde Rice	Update property information on the computer using the Daily Sales report, Lender Field Representative report, and information received from the title companies.
1:00 p.m.-3:30 p.m.	Gus Lynch Caroline Pyle Cary Fong	As newspapers are delivered, record the date of the newspaper in the Newspaper Log. Cut out all Notice of Trustee Sales. Enter information on new notices into the computer database. Print the Fresh Cut report and deliver it to the department manager.
3:30 p.m.-5:00 p.m.	Caroline Pyle Clyde Rice	Generate a daily sales report for the next day. Contact trustees and verify status of all scheduled sales. Record this information on the Daily Sales report.

5. Use the filename **8act3.tbl** and save the file.
6. Print one copy.
7. Close the document.

Challenge Your Skills

Skill 8.1—Create Newspaper Columns

1. Open the file named **8skill1.wpd** located on the data disk.
2. Change the text to a two-column newspaper format and make decisions regarding:

   Newspaper or balanced newspaper type
   Space between columns
   Border between columns
   Justification
   Appropriate use of bold, underline, and spacing for title and sidehead
   Fonts
   Hyphenation

3. Save the file as **8skill1.new**.
4. Print one copy.
5. Close the document.

Skill 8.2—Create Parallel Columns

1. Create parallel columns for the following information and make decisions regarding:

   Method to create the parallel columns (i.e., Columns feature or Table feature)
   Fonts
   Hyphenation
   Justification

Water Waste Prevention

Kitchen and Laundry	Use the automatic dishwasher and washing machine only when fully loaded.	
	When washing dishes by hand, don't leave the water running.	Use two different containers: one for washing the dishes and one for rinsing the dishes.
	Check faucets and pipes for leaks.	Leaks waste water 24 hours a day, 7 days a week.

Outside Water Use	Water lawns and plants during the cool part of the day.	Early morning watering is generally better than watering at dusk, because it helps prevent the growth of fungus.
	Don't water the street.	Position sprinklers to water the lawn or garden and not the paved areas.
	Use a broom instead of a hose to clean the driveway and decks.	
	Don't have the water hose on while washing a vehicle.	Clean the car with a pail of soapy water and use the hose only for rinsing.

2. Use the filename **8skill2.wwp** and save the file.
3. Print one copy and close the document.

Skill 8.3—Create Parallel Columns; Language Arts

1. Type and center the title. Press **Enter** three times.
2. Create parallel columns and make decisions regarding:

   Method to use to create the parallel columns (i.e., Columns feature or Table feature)
   Margins
   Justification
   Amount of space between parallel columns
   Fonts
   Bold
3. Correct five spelling errors and two punctuation errors.

Interview Tips

Do's	Don'ts
Inquire prior to the interview whether any tests will be given.	Don't drink alcoholic beverages before the interview.
Learn about the company before the interview.	Don't show up in unkept attire.

Travel to the interview location a day before the interview in order to determine travel times, bus schedules, parking availability, etc.	Don't be late.
Take a copy of your résumé and the names, addresses, and phone numbers of personal and business references.	Don't sit down before the interviewer sits down.
Dress appropriately, e.g. business attire--skirts or suits for women and sports coats or suits for men.	Don't chew gum.
Be prommpt; leave an extra half hour for unexpected delays.	Don't smoke even if a cigarette is offered to you.
Be well groomed.	Don't be antegonistic to the interviewer.
Use good eye contact.	Don't discuss unnecessary personal issues or views.
Answer interviewer's questions briefly and concisely.	Don't give lengthy answers to the interviewer's questions.
Be honest about your past experience and education.	Don't exaggerate your past job experiences.
If you can't make your appointment, call to cancel and reschedule.	Don't go to an interview with ofensive odors, ie., bad breath, body odor, heavy perfumes/colognes, smoky clothing or breath.
Maintain a positive atitude during the interview.	

4. Use the filename **8skill3.inv** and save the document. Print one copy.
5. If you have completed your work, exit WordPerfect.

Part 2
Checking Your Step

Production Skill Builder Activities
Chapters 5-8

Production Activity 2.1—Create and Copy Table Formulas, Insert a Row, and Recalculate

1. Create the table shown. Type the following unformatted information into the table cells.

   Note: *The text may wrap around in the cells differently than shown because of the fonts and point sizes selected on your computer.*

PROPERTY SALES			
1st Quarter			
Location	Original Purchase Price	Appraised Value	Price Realized
30661 W. Elliot Ave.	145000	185000	182950
895 Garden Rd.	108000	191000	193450
309 Talco Ave.	220000	259000	256500
73 Walnut St.	179000	299000	293750
Totals			

2. Block and join the cells in row 1. Also join the cells in row 2.
3. Make decisions regarding:

   Justification for title, subtitle, and column heading cells
   Justification for columns containing dollar amounts
   Table lines
   Shading cells
   Column widths

4. Insert a formula into cell B8 to calculate the column total.

5. Copy the formula in cell B8 to cells C8 and D8.
6. Set the number type format for cells B4 through D4 to **Currency**. Set the number of digits after the decimal to zero.
7. Set the number type format for cells B5 through D7 to **Commas**. Set the number of digits after the decimal to zero.
8. Set the number type format for cells B8 through D8 to **Currency**. Set the number of digits after the decimal to zero.
9. Insert a row between row 6 and 7. Type the following information into the new row table cells: 652 Parkland; 89000; 169000; 168200. Recalculate the table column totals.
10. Save the file; use the filename **2pact1.tbl**.
11. Print one copy.
12. Close the document.

Production Activity 2.2—Create a Résumé, Set Tabs, and Insert Special Characters

1. Use the following information to type the résumé shown.
   a. Change the top margin to .75" and the bottom margin to .5".
   b. Use the Tab Set dialog box and clear all tabs; set left tabs at .5 and .75 and set a right tab with dot leaders at 6.
   c. Make decisions on the use of bold, underline, and italic text attributes.
   d. Select a font of your own choice in a point size of 12.
   e. Use special characters to create the é's in Résumé.
   f. Choose an appropriate bullet character to replace the asterisks shown.

Résumé
Robert N. Ortiz
341 Maple Ave.
Paterson, NJ 07509
(201) 555-4582

EMPLOYMENT EXPERIENCE

Crowe Communications, Inc., Wyckoff, New Jersey
* Technical Writer 10/91-Present
Write and edit technical journals and procedure manuals for computer systems and applications on a contract basis.

Newpark Software, Boston, Massachusetts
* Copyeditor 5/87-10/91
Copyedited documentation for software applications.

* Assistant Copyeditor 8/86-5/87
   Assisted with the copyediting of company newsletters, internal procedure manuals, and some advertising information. Was promoted to Copyeditor on May 1, 1987.

Law Offices of Adam T. Cusick, Takoma Park, Maryland
* Clerical Assistant (part-time) 1/85-5/86
   Duties included typing, photocopying, faxing, and mail distribution.

EDUCATIONAL BACKGROUND

Rutgers University, Newark, New Jersey (part-time) 2/91-Present
A.A. English, Montgomery Jr. College, Takoma Park, Maryland 9/84-5/86
High School Diploma, Denbigh High School, Denbigh, Virginia 6/84

REFERENCES

Jason Heller, Supervisor
Newpark Software
230 Franklin St., Suite 25
Boston, MA 02110
(617) 555-6721

Tom Yim, Paralegal
Law Offices of Adam T. Cusick
7629 Carroll Ave.
Takoma Park, MD 20912
(301) 555-3990

---

2. Use the filename **2pact2.res** and save the file.
3. Print one copy and close the document.

Production Activity 2.3—Create Parallel Columns

1. Create the following document using parallel columns. Make decisions regarding:

   Margins
   Justification
   Fonts
   Method to use to create the parallel columns (i.e., Columns feature or Table feature)
   Width of columns
   Bold/underline/capitalization of title, subtitle, and sideheads
   Hyphenation

Engineer's property inspection report
306 West 98th St.
July 18, 199x

general	The property is known as 306 West 98th Street and is located on the north side of West 98th Street.
construction	The building was built in 1920 under the new building application NB-584. It is constructed of wood floors and roof beams of masonry bearing and is classified as Class 3, non-fireproof construction, under the Indianapolis City Administrative Building Code.
occupancy	The building is classified as a Class A multiple dwelling. The occupancy, room, and apartment counts have not changed since the building was constructed.
street	The front building abuts West 98th Street, which is a publicly owned and maintained street with a single sidewalk on the north side of the street. The street is paved with asphalt and is in good condition.
utilities	Water is supplied to the building from an Indianapolis City water main in the bed of 98th Street from a curb box at the edge of the sidewalk at the south property line. Gas for domestic cooking ranges is supplied from a main in the bed of 98th Street maintained by the Consolidated Gas Co. The gas is metered and billed to each occupant separately. Electricity is supplied and individually metered and billed to each apartment occupant from a main line in the bed of 98th Street maintained by Consolidated Gas Co.

2. Save the file; use the filename **2pact3.pir**.
3. Print one copy.
4. Close the document.

Production Activity 2.4—Create Newspaper Columns; Language Arts Skills

1. Open the document with the filename **2pact4.txt** located on the data disk.
2. Use newspaper columns and the following information to complete the document.

a. Make decisions regarding:

   Margins and font size to fit document on one page
   Number of columns
   Type of columns
   Space between columns
   Border line between columns
   Justification
   Fonts
   Spacing before and after sideheadings
   Bold/underline/capitalization of title, subtitle, and sideheads

b. Correct two spelling errors and four punctuation errors.

3. Use the filename **2pact4.fin** and save the file.

4. Close the document.

Part 3
A Step Up

Create Reports and Special Documents

Chapters 9-12

- Document information
- Change vertical line spacing
- Thesaurus
- Grammatik
- Standard paragraphs
- Copy text between windows
- Print page numbers
- Create headers and footers
- Keep text together (widow/orphan)
- Create footnotes and endnotes
- Search for codes
- Print specific pages
- Create form files and data files
- Determine field names
- Merge files
- Edit data files and form files
- Mark a record(s)
- Create an envelope address
- Create an envelope definition
- Create mailing labels
- Sort table data file records

CHAPTER 9

Create a One-Page Document

Features Covered

- Document information
- Thesaurus
- Grammatik
- Standard paragraphs
- Copy text between windows
- Change vertical line spacing

Objectives and Introduction

After successfully completing this chapter, you will be able to create a one-page document with vertical line spacing of one and left justification and use Document Information to determine the word count. You will also be able to create a one-page document with vertical line spacing of two and full justification and use the Thesaurus to find alternative words (synonyms). In addition, you will learn to assemble personalized documents using standard paragraphs, to copy text between document windows, and to use the Grammatik program to check a document for correct grammar.

A one-page document can be an article, essay, minutes, agenda, report, or any type of document that describes an event or provides information. Investment, insurance, sales, real estate, and medical documents are examples of one-page business documents.

Create a One-Page Document

A document can be created with vertical line spacing of one (single spacing) or vertical line spacing of two (double spacing). If a document is typed with vertical line spacing of one, the paragraphs begin at the left margin with one blank line space between paragraphs (see Figure 9.1). If a document is typed with vertical line spacing of two, the first line of each paragraph is indented approximately one-half inch from the left margin (see Figure 9.3). Either left justification or full justification can be used in a one-page document, depending on the writer's preference and the appearance of the document.

Format a Document

A standard 8½ by 11-inch sheet of paper using the default 1" top and bottom margins has 9 vertical inches available for printed text. Normally, the default margins will be used when creating a one-page document; however, if desired, the margins can be changed.

The document title is centered and often typed bold and/or printed in a different font. If a subtitle is used, one blank line follows the title. A subtitle is typed in lowercase letters with the first letter of each main word capitalized. *Initial caps* is the phrase used to indicate words/phrases typed with the first letter of each main word capitalized.

When the vertical line spacing of one is used in a document, two blank lines precede the first paragraph and one or two blank lines precede a sidehead (see Figure 9.1). When the vertical line spacing of two is used in a document, one or three blank lines precede the first paragraph and one or three blank lines precede a sidehead (see Figure 9.3).

One blank line follows a side head when vertical line spacing of one or two is used. Also, when line spacing of two is used, the **Tab** key is pressed to indent the first line in a paragraph.

Start-Up Instructions

- Use the default left, right, top, and bottom margins and the default left justification.
- After reviewing the Steps to Create a One-Page Document with Vertical Line Spacing of One and Left Justification, type the information in Figure 9.1.

Steps to Create a One-Page Document with Vertical Line Spacing of One and Left Justification

1. Center the title and use the bold text attribute.
2. Press **Enter** three times after the title.
3. Press **Enter** twice after typing each sidehead.
4. Press **Enter** two or three times after each body text paragraph.

   For example, **Enter** is pressed twice after each body text paragraph in Figure 9.1.
5. Type the body text paragraphs with line spacing of one.
6. If desired, make the sidehead bold.

Finish-Up Instructions

- Use the filename **9drill1.tsm** and save the file.

FIGURE 9.1

One-page document with vertical line spacing of one and left justification

TSM Staff Profiles ← Report title

3 Enters

Cynthia Runyan, President ← Sidehead

2 Enters

Cynthia initiates and manages the textbook and trade series books. Prior to establishing TSM, she founded and managed Hegstrom Press and Bay Publishing. Her previous experience includes acting as Editor-in-Chief of Engineering and Computer Books for Stanton Hill and Marketing Director and Vice President for Ross & Collins Publishers. Cynthia has developed and published hundreds of technical, reference, and trade books. ← Body text paragraph

2 Enters

William Donovan, Director of Production

2 Enters

Bill supervises book production for TSM, organizes projects, sets and maintains schedules, and manages the internal and freelance staff. His 25 years in publishing include acting as Regional Editor, Production Editor, Production Manager, and Director of Marketing Operations for Ross & Collins, Los Angeles, and, most recently, Director of Composition and Graphics Services, and Publisher, Hartman Publications. His experience covers text, trade, reference, and professional books, as well as magazine and journal publishing.

2 Enters

Samuel Clayworth, Marketing Services Director

2 Enters

Sam creates and administers marketing programs, including implementing and analyzing direct mail and advertising campaigns. His prior positions at TSM include Account Executive, Production Manager, and Operations Manager. At Jay Marketing Services, Colonial Publications, and the Crown Institute, Sam developed expertise in sales promotion, advertising, book and print production, financial management, budget control, and telemarketing.

2 Enters

Becky Rodriguez, Senior Account Manager

2 Enters

Becky manages books and media projects in computer applications, health sciences, and vocational/technical curricula. A former Vice President at Winston House, she was responsible for all operations of the Health Sciences Division, including their best-selling nursing list. She has developed and marketed texts in the health sciences, biology, mathematics, and more.

2 Enters

Leo Sandoval, Account Manager

2 Enters

Leo manages book and media projects in business education and other vocational areas. Before joining TSM, he was with Mills Corporation managing the development and production of unauthored, heavily illustrated, complex books. At Appleby, Leo was Director of Sales and Marketing, Executive Editor for Business Education, and Senior Editor for Business and Economics. In addition, he published "how-to" books at Sullivan.

- Print one copy.

Document Information

WordPerfect compiles various statistics for a document or partial document. These statistics are listed in the Document Information dialog box (see Figure 9.2) and in-

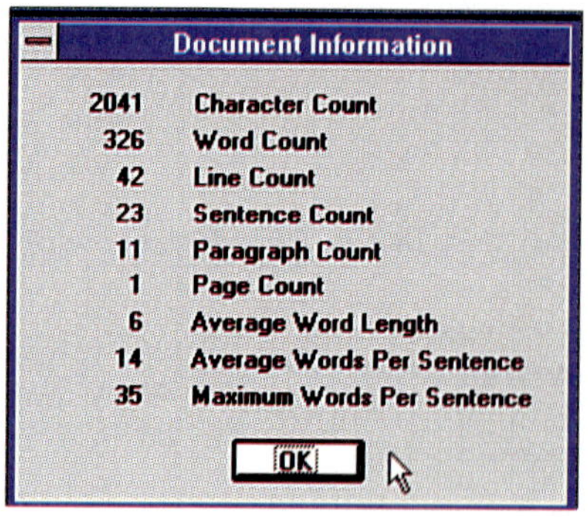

FIGURE 9.2

Document Information dialog box

clude total the number of characters, words, lines, sentences, paragraphs, and pages contained in a document or selected text. The average word length, average words per sentence, and maximum words per sentence also display in the Document Information dialog box.

When a portion of a document is selected and the statistics are listed, the statistics displayed in the dialog box relate only to the selected text. A total word, character, or line count is useful when preparing a document that must meet specific guidelines, for example, a school research paper or an article submitted for publication.

Start-Up Instructions

- The file named **9drill1.tsm** should be displayed in the document window.

Steps to Use Document Information

1. Select File, Document Info {Alt, f, i}.

   Note: A Document Information dialog box similar to Figure 9.2 displays.

2. Select OK to return to the document window {Enter}.

Finish-Up Instructions

- Optional. At the top of the printed document, handwrite the total number of words.
- Optional. If any changes are made to the document, save the file again using the same filename, **9drill1.tsm**.
- Close the document.

Change Vertical Line Spacing

Additional space can be created between lines of text by changing the vertical line spacing. The added space can be used, for example, to accommodate handwritten changes to draft letters or reports. Also, a report set for line spacing of two may be easier to read.

The **Line Spacing** button on the Power Bar can be used to change the line spacing to 1 (single), 1.5, or 2 (double). The **Other** option in the **Line Spacing** button drop-down list is selected to display the Line Spacing dialog box. In the Line Spacing dialog box, a specific line spacing amount can be typed or selected by clicking on the up or down triangles to display the desired line spacing amount.

When the line spacing is changed, a line spacing code is inserted in the document. In Reveal Codes, the line spacing code is shown as *Ln Spacing*. When the insertion point is located to the left of the line spacing code, the expanded code displays with the amount of line spacing selected (e.g., *Ln Spacing: 2.0*).

Start-Up Instructions

❖ Open the file named **9drill2.ann** located on the data disk.

Steps to Change the Vertical Line Spacing

1. Place the insertion point at the beginning of the text where the vertical line spacing is to be changed.

   For example, place the insertion point at the beginning of the document.

2. Move the mouse pointer to the **Line Spacing** button [1.0] on the Power Bar. Press and hold the mouse button and drag to select the desired line spacing option. Release the mouse button {Alt, L, L, s; delete the existing line spacing amount, type the desired line spacing amount, Enter}.

   For example, move the mouse pointer to the **Line Spacing** button, press and hold the mouse button and drag to select **2**. Release the mouse button.

Finish-Up Instructions

❖ Move the mouse pointer to the left of the first character in the first paragraph and select **Full** justification (move the mouse pointer to the **Justification** button on the Power Bar, press and hold the mouse button and drag to select **Full**, release the mouse button).

Note: Your document should look similar to Figure 9.3.

❖ Use the filename **9drill2.v2** and save the file.

❖ Print one copy.

Chapter 9
Create a One-Page Document

Use the Thesaurus

A list of words that have the same or similar meaning (synonyms) are stored in the WordPerfect Thesaurus. An author writing a letter or other information attempts to use words that will effectively communicate ideas. A thesaurus assists a writer by providing synonyms that may more clearly convey his/her message. The WordPerfect Thesaurus can be used during the writing process or after a document is written.

When the Thesaurus command is selected, a dialog box displays containing a list of synonyms with subgroups of nouns, verbs, and/or adjectives. Words marked with a bullet character are called "headwords." By double-clicking on a headword, additional synonyms can be displayed. A list of *antonyms* (words with opposite meanings) may display at the bottom of the synonyms list.

FIGURE 9.3

One-page document with vertical line spacing of two and full justification

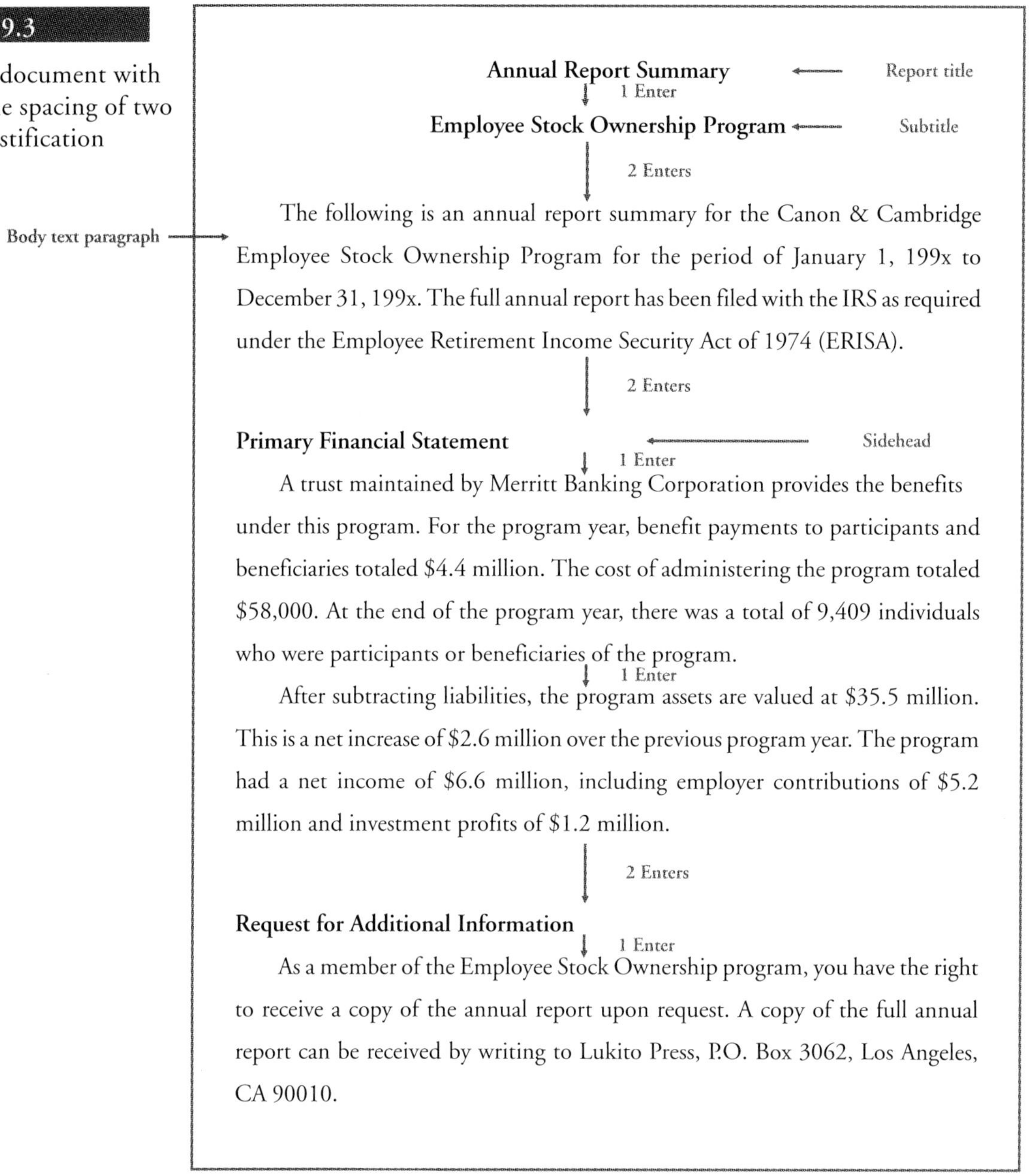

Annual Report Summary

Employee Stock Ownership Program

The following is an annual report summary for the Canon & Cambridge Employee Stock Ownership Program for the period of January 1, 199x to December 31, 199x. The full annual report has been filed with the IRS as required under the Employee Retirement Income Security Act of 1974 (ERISA).

Primary Financial Statement

A trust maintained by Merritt Banking Corporation provides the benefits under this program. For the program year, benefit payments to participants and beneficiaries totaled $4.4 million. The cost of administering the program totaled $58,000. At the end of the program year, there was a total of 9,409 individuals who were participants or beneficiaries of the program.

After subtracting liabilities, the program assets are valued at $35.5 million. This is a net increase of $2.6 million over the previous program year. The program had a net income of $6.6 million, including employer contributions of $5.2 million and investment profits of $1.2 million.

Request for Additional Information

As a member of the Employee Stock Ownership program, you have the right to receive a copy of the annual report upon request. A copy of the full annual report can be received by writing to Lukito Press, P.O. Box 3062, Los Angeles, CA 90010.

In the Thesaurus, the author can replace the word, look up a listed word, view the text in the document window, or close. (If the selected word cannot be found, the message "Word not found..." displays at the bottom left of the Thesaurus dialog box.) The author can choose a word from the displayed list, type a different word to be looked up, or double-click on a listed word that is marked with a bullet.

After double-clicking on a marked word, a list of related synonyms and antonyms displays in the next column in the Thesaurus dialog box. Words that are not marked with a bullet are not included in the WordPerfect Thesaurus or are not included in the form requested (e.g., the word *seasonal* that displays for the requested adjective *season* is not marked because the requested word is for an adjective, not a noun). However, if you double-click on an unmarked word, another form of the word may display (e.g., *face* displays after double-clicking on the unmarked word *facing*).

Start-Up Instructions

❖ The filename **9drill2.v2** should be displayed in the document window.

Steps to Select Synonyms From the Thesaurus

1. Place the insertion point between any characters in the word to be looked up in the Thesaurus.

   For example, place the insertion point between any character in the word *full* in the second sentence of the first paragraph.

2. Select the **Thesaurus** button on the Power Bar {Alt, t, t *or* Alt and F1}.

   Note: The Thesaurus dialog box displays (see Figure 9.4).

3. Place the mouse pointer on the down arrow in the scroll bar to the right of the listed words. Press the left mouse button repeatedly to scan through the listed words until the desired word displays {press the Tab key four times, then press the down arrow keys repeatedly until the desired word displays}.

   For example, press the left mouse button repeatedly until the word *complete* displays.

4. Move the mouse pointer to the desired replacement word and click once {press the up or down arrow key to highlight the desired word}.

5. Select **Replace** {Alt and r}.

6. Place the insertion point between any character in the next word to be looked up.

   For example, place the insertion point between any characters in the word *benefit* in the second sentence of the second paragraph.

7. Select the **Thesaurus** button on the Power Bar {Alt, t, t *or* Alt and F1}.

8. Scan through the words listed on the screen and determine if there is a suitable replacement. If no suitable replacement word displays, select **Close** {Alt and c}.

   For example, because there is no suitable replacement for the word *benefit,* select **Close.**

9. Place the insertion point in the next word to be looked up.

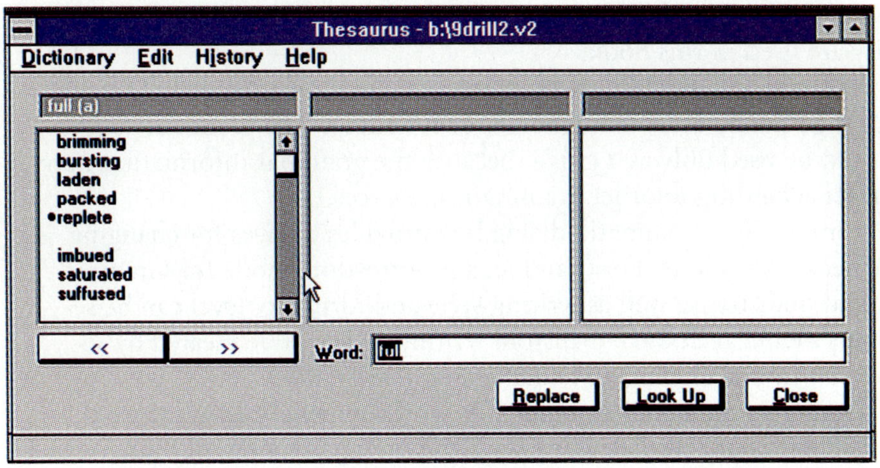

FIGURE 9.4

Thesaurus dialog box

For example, place the insertion point between any character in the word *administering* in the third sentence of the second paragraph.

10. Select **the Thesaurus** button and scan the listed words. If a suitable replacement word exists, select the word and choose **Replace** {Alt and r}.

For example, choose the word **manage**. Select **Replace.**

Note: *The Thesaurus does not include the "ing" suffix when the word administering is replaced. Continue with the Finish-Up Instructions.*

Finish-Up Instructions

- Delete the **e** in *manage* and type **ing**.
- Place the insertion point in the word *assets* in the first sentence of the third paragraph; select the **Thesaurus** button and scroll down the list of words until the word *holdings* displays; select **holdings**; select **Replace**.
- Place the insertion point in the word *receive* in the first sentence of the fourth paragraph; select the **Thesaurus** button and scan the list of words. Select **obtain**; choose **Replace**.

  Note: *Normally, the file with the new synonyms is saved and, if desired, renamed.*
- Use the *new* filename **9drill2.the** and save the file.
- Print one copy.
- Continue to the Steps to Use the Grammatik program or close the document.

Use the Grammatik Program

Grammatik (rhymes with *dramatic*) is a grammar-checking program that checks a document for grammatical, spelling, and writing-style errors. When the **Grammatik** button is selected, the text is checked against a list of grammar rules such as passive voice, subject-verb agreement, double negatives, repetitive expressions, and capitalization.

The grammar rules used to check text can be viewed or changed by selecting **Options, Writing Style** in the Grammatik dialog box. Select a writing style option such as Business Letter, Memo, or Report. The formality level (*i.e.,* Standard, Formal or Informal) can be selected also. The default settings for the General writing style and Standard Formality are used in this book.

When Grammatik checks a document, suggested changes are displayed. The suggested grammar change can be accepted, ignored, or rewritten. The grammar suggestions provided should be used only as a guide, because the grammar information may or may not be correct according to other grammatical sources.

The Options menu in the Grammatik dialog box provides choices for changing various grammar-checking defaults. For example, a proofreading mode for Grammar, Mechanics, Style, and Statistics as well as writing style and formality level can be selected in the Options menu. If desired, a custom writing style can be created by selecting the Edit button in the Writing Style dialog box (see Figure 9.5).

If Statistics is selected in the list of Options, the word, syllable, paragraph, and sentence (long and short) count display along with the average number of sentences

Rule Classes		Styles	
Grammar	Uses rules relating to the correct use of parts of speech, e.g., subject and verb agreement, possessive forms, homonyms, etc.	Business Letter	For writing that requires a formal tone and precise use of grammar and style rules.
Mechanical	Uses rules relating to errors in spelling, capitalization, transposed letters, punctuation, etc.	Memo	Appropriate for informal, interoffice correspondence.
Style	Uses rules relating to style and word choice, such as passive voice, jargon, wordiness, etc.	Report	Appropriate for formal business reports and college papers

FIGURE 9.5

Custom writing style options

in a paragraph, words per sentence, and syllables per word. Also listed in the statistics is the Flesch Reading Ease readability number. The number displayed by the Flesch Reading Ease option indicates a grade level in school, for example, a number under 30 is considered college level while a number over 90 is considered fourth grade level. Any readability number between 50 and 80 is considered an effective reading level for most individuals.

Start-Up Instructions

❖ The file named **9drill2.the** should be displayed in the document window.

Steps to Use the Grammatik Program

Note: Using the mouse is the most effective way to perform the Steps to Use the Grammatik Program. A mouse must be available to perform the following steps.

1. The document to be grammar checked must be saved and displayed on the screen.
2. Select the **Grammatik** button on the Power Bar.

   Note: The Grammatik dialog box displays.
3. Select **Start**.

   *Note: The first occurrence of a word, phrase, or sentence to be checked is displayed. The item to be checked is highlighted in the document window. For example, **for the period of** and the advice, "Simplify," displays in the Rule Class box (see Figure 9.6).*
4. View the suggested words listed in the bottom left of the dialog box. Double-click on the desired replacement option.

   For example, double-click on **from**.

   Note: The next item to be checked (ERISA) is highlighted.
5. Select the **Ignore Word** button because the acronym (ERISA) is spelled correctly.

   *Note: The next item to be checked is highlighted, e.g., **has been filed**.*

FIGURE 9.6

Grammatik window

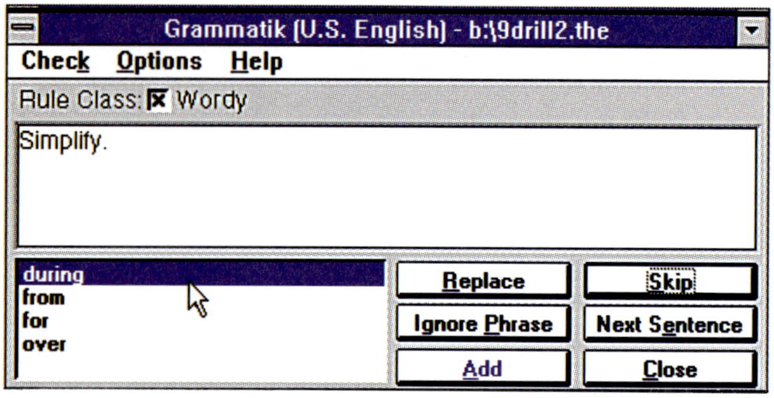

6. Select the Skip button because "has been filed" is grammatically correct.

   Note: The next item to be checked is highlighted, e.g., ***with the IRS . . .***

7. Click in the document screen and change one of the prepositional phrases.

   For example, click once to dehighlight the text; place the insertion point in front of *Employee*, press the **Spacebar** once, and type **1974**. Delete the prepositional phrase "of 1974" at the end of the sentence.

8. Select the **Resume** button.

   Note: The next item to be checked is highlighted, e.g., ***has been filed.***

9. Select the **Next Sentence** button twice.

   Note: The next item to be checked is highlighted, e.g., ***are valued.***

10. Select the **Next Sentence** button since the sentence is grammatically correct.

    Note: The next item to be checked is highlighted, e.g., ***Lukito.***

11. Select the **Ignore Word** button because *Lukito* is a proper name and is spelled correctly.

    Note: The next item to be checked is highlighted, e.g., ***can be received.***

12. Select the **Skip** button.

    Note: A box displays with the message, "Grammar check completed. Close Grammatik?".

13. Select **Yes**.

Finish-Up Instructions

- Use the new filename **9gram.tik** and save the file.
- Print one copy.
- Close the document.

Use Standard Paragraphs to Assemble Individualized Documents

Text that is used repeatedly as part of personalized documents can be saved and opened when needed. For example, a will created by a lawyer contains many standard paragraphs that are common to all wills. The standard paragraphs are saved in a separate document, and the desired paragraph(s) is retrieved to assemble a document created for a specific individual.

The first part of the process to assemble documents using standard paragraphs is to create and save a document that contains the standard paragraphs. The second part of the process is to open a new document and type the information that is specific to the personalized document, for example, date, name, address, and nonstandard paragraphs.

The final process to assemble documents using standard paragraphs is to copy text from the standard paragraphs document to the personalized document. WordPerfect is capable of having nine document windows open (in memory) at a time. Each document is placed in a separate document window. For example, the standard paragraphs document and the personalized document are both open and each is in a separate window. With the standard paragraphs document displayed, the desired standard paragraph(s) is copied to temporary memory. After switching to the personalized document window, the text is pasted in the personalized document at the location of the insertion point.

Text can be copied from a file displayed in the Viewer window and then pasted in a document that is open in a document window. To copy text from the Viewer, select the **Open** button on the Power Bar, highlight the desired filename, and select **View**. With the chosen document displayed in the Viewer window, select the text to be copied. Press the *right* mouse button, select **Copy to Clipboard**, and choose **Cancel** in the Open dialog box. With the insertion point at the desired location in the open document, select the **Paste** button to insert the copied text.

Steps to Create the Standard Paragraphs Document

1. Type the standard paragraphs.

   For example, type the information shown in Figure 9.7.

2. Save the file that contains the standard paragraphs.

   For example, save the file on your file disk; use the filename **9drill3.stn**.

Steps to Create the Personalized Document

1. Create a new document by selecting the **New Document** button on the Power Bar {Alt and f, n *or* Ctrl and n}.

   Note: A new document window displays on the screen. The file named ***9drill3.stn*** *is still open in memory but is currently hidden.*

2. Type the information that is specific to the personalized document.

FIGURE 9.7

Standard paragraphs document (9drill3.stn)

Standard Seminar Information

Seminar Locations and Dates

March 5-6, 199x--Park Plaza, Boston, Massachusetts
March 14-15, 199x--Four Ambassadors, Miami, Florida
March 19-20, 199x--Hyatt Regency, Phoenix, Arizona
March 21-22, 199x--Seattle Hilton, Seattle, Washington

Session Descriptions

New Technologies--This session provides a preview of new technologies, including wireless communications and interactive television. Hand-held pen devices and voice user interfaces will be demonstrated.

Electronic Distribution--This session discusses the best way to distribute sophisticated print documents in electronic form that can be viewed on a screen and printed out when needed.

The Future of Electronic Delivery--This session includes the impact of developments that are predicted to take place over the next decade: online delivery using telephone, cable, and satellite services.

Telecommunications for Print Production--This session begins with a summary of the status of high-speed digital communications around the world. Specific user examples illustrating methods in which print publishers are using the technology will be discussed.

Advertising in a Digital World--This session will be a panel discussion on the impact of online interactive services and the effect the digital world will have on advertising.

For example, type the current date, inside address, salutation, and first two paragraphs of the letter shown in Figure 9.8. Press **Enter** twice after the second paragraph.

3. Save the personalized document.

   For example, save the file on your file disk; use the filename **9nunes.ltr**.

Steps to Copy Text Between Windows

1. Select Window {Alt, w}.
2. Select the name of the document that contains the standard paragraphs {press the down arrow key as many times as needed to highlight the desired filename, press Enter}.

   For example, click once on the file named **9drill3.stn**.

   Note: *The file containing the standard paragraphs displays on the screen. The file containing the new document is still open in memory but is currently hidden.*
3. Select the desired text to be copied to the personalized document.

FIGURE 9.8

Personalized document assembled using standard paragraphs (9nunes.ltr)

(Use current date)

Mr. Theodore Nunes
4808 Cameron Creek, Apt. 8
Fort Worth, TX 76132

Dear Mr. Nunes:

Your registration has been received to attend the upcoming Communications Conference.

The conference date, location, and description of your selected session(s) is as follows:

Copy the following paragraphs from the list of Standard Seminar Information (**9drill3.stn**).

March 19-20 conference date and location information

New Technologies

Telecommunications for Print Production

If you need additional information about the seminar or hotel accommodations, please call 1-800-555-1800.

Sincerely,

Howard Walsh
Seminar Coordinator

HW/xx
nunes.ltr/disk1

Chapter 9 Create a One-Page Document

For example, select **March 19-20, 199x--Hyatt Regency, Phoenix, Arizona.**

4. Select the **Copy** button on the Power Bar {Alt, e, c *or* Ctrl and c}.

   Note: *A copy of the selected text has been placed in the clipboard.*

5. Select **Window** {Alt, w}.

6. Choose the filename of the personalized document.

   For example, click once on the file named **9nunes.ltr**.

   Note: *In the personalized letter, the insertion point should be located at the left margin one blank line space below the second paragraph.*

7. Select the **Paste** button on the Power Bar {Alt, e, p *or* Ctrl and v}.

   Note: *The copied text is retrieved from the clipboard and displays on the screen.*

8. If necessary, press the **End** key to locate the insertion point at the end of the line, and press **Enter** one or two times in order to locate the insertion point one blank line space below the copied text.

9. Select **Window** {Alt, w}; choose the filename of the document that contains the standard paragraphs.

   For example, choose **9drill3.stn.**

10. Select the text to be copied to the personalized document.

    For example, select the paragraph that begins **New Technologies--.**

11. Select the **Copy** button on the Power Bar {Alt, e, c *or* Ctrl and c}.

12. Select **Window** {Alt, w}. Choose the filename of the personalized document.

    For example, choose **9nunes.ltr.**

    Note: *The insertion point should be located at the left margin one blank line below the conference date information.*

13. Select the **Paste** button on the Power Bar {Alt, e, p *or* Ctrl and v}.

14. If necessary, place the insertion point at the end of the paragraph. Press **Enter** one or two times to locate the insertion point one blank line space below the copied paragraph.

Finish-Up Instructions

- Repeat steps 9–14 and copy the paragraph that begins **Telecommunications for Print Production--**.
- Type the final paragraph, complimentary closing, typed signature, title, reference initials, and document identification as shown in Figure 9.8.
- Save the personalized document file using the same filename, **9nunes.ltr**.
- Print one copy.
- Close the document

The Next Step

Chapter Review and Activities

Self-Check Quiz

T F 1. A Tab is used to indent the first line of a paragraph for a document with vertical line spacing of one.

T F 2. A thesaurus contains synonyms that assist a writer in communicating clearly.

T F 3. A document typed with vertical line spacing of two is always printed with full justification.

T F 4. The advice presented by the Grammatik program should always be used to correct the grammar in a document.

5. The standard paragraphs file must be ____ before copying text that will be pasted in an individualized document.
   a. open in a document window
   b. displayed in the Viewer window
   c. closed
   d. either a or b

6. If a document is typed with vertical line spacing of two, one or _____ blank lines precede the first paragraph.
   a. three
   b. two
   c. one
   d. none of these

7. A document title is often centered and printed in ____.
   a. italic
   b. a different font
   c. uppercase letters
   d. both a and c

8. The text copied from an open document or from the Viewer window is placed in the _____.
   a. clipboard
   b. Viewer window
   c. document window
   d. Page Zoom window

9. List the names of the menu and submenu selected in order to display the Document Information dialog box.

10. State one purpose for using standard paragraphs to assemble individualized documents.

Enriching Language Arts Skills

Spelling/Vocabulary Words

partnership a legal association of individuals joined together, often for business purposes.

accrual method an accounting technique that reports income when earned. In contrast, the cash accounting method records income when payment is received.

maturity the date when a financial exchange is due, e.g., the day a promissory note or bond is to be paid.

depreciation reduction in the value of an asset; decrease in price.

liability a debt owed; a disadvantage.

amortized the method of distributing the cost of an asset over the life of the debt.

Speller Hint

The Speller approves words that are correctly spelled; however, a correctly spelled word can be incorrectly used in a sentence. After using the Speller, proofread the document for words used incorrectly.

Examples:

of, off	you, your, you're	is, it, in, if	to, too, two	its, it's
no, not	for, from, form	a, as, an	there, their	used, sued

Activities

Activity 9.1—Create a One-Page Document and Use Document Information

1. Type the following document with vertical line spacing of one and left justification.
2. Use the default left, right, top, and bottom margins.

Telephone System

Enhanced Phone System

Flextex Health Care has improved its telephone system. The phone changes enhance previous improvements made to the system and, as a result, have increased ease of use for our customers' convenience.

The new system features direct dial access to the Client Services Department for all client inquiries. Client representatives are available to provide information and assistance Monday through Friday from 9:00 a.m. to 4:00 p.m. and on Saturday from 9:00 a.m. to 3:00 p.m.

Who to Call

All questions should be directed to the Client Services Department. If the staff is unable to answer your particular question at the time of your call, they will research the answer and call you with a response.

Where to Call

Next week you will be provided with a list of numbers to call for specific inquiries. One set of numbers is for claims and referral information; the other is for benefits information. It is important that you use the new department extension numbers because the new phone system replaces all previous telephone extension numbers. All calls to Client Services will be answered in the order that the calls are received.

Clients calling Flextex's main phone number, (505) 555-2310, will reach the automated phone system with a current list of options. Callers can access the list by using a touch-tone telephone. Clients with rotary telephones can remain on the line for an operator's assistance.

Current Telephone Numbers

Please use the following information about the current telephone numbers.

Call 1 + (800) 555-4554 or (505) 555-7878 for information concerning bills, medical referrals, reimbursements, and third-party liability.

Call 1 + (800) 555-8322 or (505) 555-4849 for information concerning copayments, benefits, changing a primary care physician, replacing identification cards, enrollment eligibility information, group coverage, and notification of address or telephone changes.

---

3. Use the filename **9act1.tel** and save the file.
4. Print one copy.
5. Select **File, Document Info** to determine the total number of words in the document. Handwrite the number of words at the top of your printed copy. Select **OK**.
6. Close the document.

Activity 9.2—Create Personalized Letters Using Standard Paragraphs

1. Open the file named **9drill3.stn** that was created previously in this chapter, or create the standard paragraphs document shown in Figure 9.7.
2. Create a new file and type the following personalized letter. Copy the standard paragraphs from the file named **9drill3.stn** as indicated.

(Use current date)

Ms. Mary Sinclair
951 David Ross Road
W. Lafayette, IN 47906

Dear Ms. Sinclair:

Thank you for your interest in attending our Communications Conferences. Below is a listing of the upcoming conference dates and a description of the two seminars in which you have expressed an interest.

> Copy the following standard paragraphs from the list of seminar information in the file named **9drill3.stn**.
>
> Copy all four seminar locations and dates.
>
> Copy the paragraph that begins "Advertising in a Digital World."
>
> Copy the paragraph that begins "The Future of Electronic Delivery."

If you need additional information about the seminars or hotel accommodations, please call 1-800-555-1800.

Sincerely,

Howard Walsh
Seminar Coordinator

HW/xx
sinclair.ltr/disk3

---

3. Save the file as **9sincl.ltr.**
4. Print one copy.
5. Create a new file and type the following personalized letter. Copy the paragraphs indicated from the file named **9drill3.stn**.

(Use current date)

Ms. Pamela R. Parkins
Professional Technologies
3007 College Oak St.
Sacramento, CA 95841

Dear Ms. Parkins:

We appreciate your request for information regarding our upcoming West Coast seminars. Currently, the following two seminars are scheduled for the Western Region:

> Copy the seminar location and date information for the Phoenix, Arizona, and Seattle, Washington, seminars from the list of standard seminar information in the file named **9drill3.stn**.

With regard to your interest in future electronic distribution systems, the following seminar is recommended:

> Copy the paragraph that begins "The Future of Electronic Delivery" from the list of standard seminar information in the file named **9drill3.stn**.

I hope to see you at one of our Western Region seminars.

Sincerely,

Howard Walsh
Seminar Coordinator

HW/xx
parkins.ltr/disk2

---

6. Save the file as **9parkin.ltr**.
7. Print one copy and close the documents (close both personalized letter files and the standard paragraphs file).

Activity 9.3—Format a One-Page Document and Use the Thesaurus

1. Open the file named **9act3.rus**.
2. Set the vertical line spacing to two and use left justification; use the default left, right, top, and bottom margins.
3. Use the Thesaurus to find synonyms for the underlined words (select the **Thesaurus** button on the Power Bar). Boldface the replaced synonyms and remove the underlining.

   Note: *There may not be appropriate synonyms for all underlined words.*
4. Use the new filename **9act3.syn** and save the file.
5. Print one copy and close the document.

Activity 9.4—Create a One-Page Document and Use Grammatik

1. Type the following document using the default margins, vertical line spacing of two, and full justification.

One solution is to ensure that the system increases the user's capability by delivering professional results and functions needed for the job. For example, voice has been overlooked in many systems; telephone integration and voice mail are being added to some office systems.

A second solution is to give the user more control over the system resources by providing personal tools. Personal computers are turning out to be a most powerful motivator for office personnel. People also feel more in control if they can choose their own furnishings, selecting desks and filing components that fit their work style.

Individual satisfaction and motivation are the critical components of working life quality and productivity improvement. Designs that address users' personal concerns by providing intuitive and efficient interfaces, needed functions, and resource control can improve job satisfaction and motivation.

---

2. Save the file; use the filename **9act4.sys.**

3. Use Grammatik to check the document using the following information:

   a. Select the **Grammatik** button on the Power Bar; select **Start.**

   b. The first highlighted words "has been overlooked" are grammatically correct; select **Skip.**

   c. The word "Personal" is highlighted and is correctly used; select **Skip.**

   d. The advice for the highlighted word "motivator" is helpful. Change the subject to a *singular* subject by locating the insertion point at the beginning of the sentence and then change "Personal computers are" to **A personal computer is** (click once in the document to dehighlight; click beside the "P" in Personal at the beginning of the sentence, type the correction; select **Resume**).

   e. The message displays "Usually a paragraph should be more than one sentence." (select **Next Sentence**).

   Note: The message displays "Grammar check completed. Close Grammatik?".

   f. Select **Yes.**

4. Use the new filename **9act4.gra** and save the corrected file.

5. Print one copy and close the document.

Challenge Your Skills

Skill 9.1—Create and Edit a One-Page Document

1. Open the file named **9skill1.tec.**

2. Make decisions regarding:

   Margins
   Justification
   Bold

3. Edit the document as follows:

   a. Delete the last sentence of paragraph two; combine paragraphs one and two into a single paragraph.

   b. Add the sideheads:

   Add Technical Training Program above the now paragraph two.

   Add Management Trainee Program above the now paragraph three.

   Add Employee Support Program above the now paragraph five.

   c. Make decisions about spacing and bolding for the sideheads.

4. Use the filename **9skill1.fin** and save the file.

5. Print one copy and close the document.

Skill 9.2—Create a One-Page Document and Use the Thesaurus

1. Create the following document using vertical line spacing of two. Do not underline the underlined words. Make decisions regarding:

   Indents
   Margins
   Justification
   Title alignment and capitalization
   Bold
   Sidehead spacing and capitalization

2. Use the Thesaurus to make decisions for replacing (or *not* replacing) the bolded words. Bold the substituted words.

Transfer and Servicing Disclosure

When applying for a mortgage loan, the Real Estate Settlement Procedures Act (RESPA) specifies certain rights granted under federal law. This statement indicates that the servicing for this loan may be transferred to a different loan servicer. "Servicing" refers to collection of the principal, interest, and escrow account payments. If the loan servicer changes, there are certain **procedures** that must be followed.

Transfer practices and requirements

If the loan servicing is assigned, sold, or transferred to a new servicer, written notice must be given describing the transaction. The **present** loan servicer must send a written notice of the transfer not fewer than fifteen (15) days before the date of transfer.

Complaint resolution

Section 6 of RESPA **gives** certain consumer rights. If a qualified written request is sent to the loan servicer regarding the loan servicing, the servicer must **provide** a written acknowledgment within twenty (20) business days of receipt of the request. A "qualified written request" is written correspondence other than notice on a payment coupon that includes the mortgagee's name, account number, and **reasons** for the request. The loan servicer must take action on the qualified written request within sixty (60) days after receiving the request.

---

3. Save the file; use the filename **9skill2.ser**.
4. Print one copy and close the document.

Skill 9.3—Create Standard Paragraphs and Assemble Individual Documents; Language Arts

Part I

1. Type the following standard list of accounting policies as shown.
2. Correct three spelling errors, three misused words, and four punctuation errors.

Standard List of Accounting Policies

Accounting Method

The partnership maintains its records on the accural method of accounting for financial reporting and Federal and State income tax purposes.

Cash Equivalents

For purposes of the statements of cash flows the partership considers all highly liquid debt instruments purchased with an original maturity of three months or less to be cash equivalents.

Depreciation

The partnership records depreciation on the building and improvements using the straight-line method over an estimated useful life of 30 years.

Income Taxes

The entity is treated as a partnership for income tax purposes and any taxable income or loss realized is that of the individual partners. Therefore there is not libility for income taxes. There can be no assurance that the partnership and its partners will receive the benefits of being taxed as a partnership rather than as a corporation.

Loan Restructuring Fees

Loan restructuring fees are amortized on a straight-line basis over the term off the respective trust deed note payable.

Net Income (Loss) Per Limited Partnership Unit

Net income (loss) per limited partnership unit was based on the weighted average number of limited partnership units outstanding of 2,000 during 1990 1991, and 1992.

Reclassification

Certain amounts in the 1990 and 1991 financial statements have been reclassified two conform with the 1992 presentation.

Revenue Recognition

Sales of golf course club memberships were recorded upon acceptance of membership applications and receipt of corresponding membership fees. Membership dues were recorded as earned on a monthly basis.

---

3. Save the standard list as **9skill3.std**.
4. Print one copy.

Part II

1. If necessary, open the file named **9skill3.std**.

2. The standard list of accounting policies will be used to construct two one-page documents reporting the accounting policy for the two limited partnerships.
3. For each document, make decisions regarding:

   Line spacing (one or two)
   Justification
   Margins
   Bold
   Fonts

4. Create a new file and type the following individualized document:

CORONADO RANCH, LTD.
A Limited Partnership
Accounting Policy Notes

> Copy the following paragraphs in the order listed below from the standard list of accounting policies (**9skill3.std**).
>
> Accounting Method
> Cash Equivalents
> Depreciation
> Income Taxes
> Net Income (Loss) Per Limited Partnership Unit
> Reclassification

---

5. Save the personalized document as **9skill3.cor**. Print one copy.
6. Create a new file and type the following individualized document:

YUMA FIELD BUSINESS PARK, LTD.
A Limited Partnership
Accounting Policy Notes

> Copy the following paragraphs in the order listed below from the standard list of accounting policies (**9skill3.std**).
>
> Accounting Method
> Cash Equivalents
> Income Taxes
> Net Income (Loss) Per Limited Partnership Unit
> Revenue Recognition
> Loan Restructuring Fees

---

7. Save the personalized document as **9skill3.yum**.
8. Print one copy.
9. If you have completed your work, exit WordPerfect.

CHAPTER 10

Create a Multiple-Page Document

Features Covered

- Print page numbers
- Create headers and footers
- Keep text together (widow/orphan)
- Create footnotes and endnotes
- Search for codes
- Print specific pages

Objectives and Introduction

After successfully completing this chapter, you will be able to create a multiple-page document, print page numbers on each page, and use the widow/orphan feature. Also, you will be able to create and edit headers, footers, footnotes, and endnotes as well as print a specific page(s) and search for codes.

A multiple-page document is comparable to a one-page report and can be an article, essay, minutes, agenda, or any type of document that describes an event or provides information. A multiple-page document consists of two or more pages. Examples of multiple-page business documents are investment, insurance, legal, medical, and sales documents.

Create a Multiple-Page Document

Like a one-page document, a multiple-page document can be created with vertical line spacing of one (single spacing) or two (double spacing). Pages of a multiple-page document are formatted the same as a one-page document with 1-inch top, bottom, left, and right default margins. (See Chapter 9, Figures 9.1 and 9.3.)

Each page of a multiple-page document is separated by a soft page break. When the number of available vertical lines on the page are filled, the text automatically

FIGURE 10.1

Hard page break in Page view mode

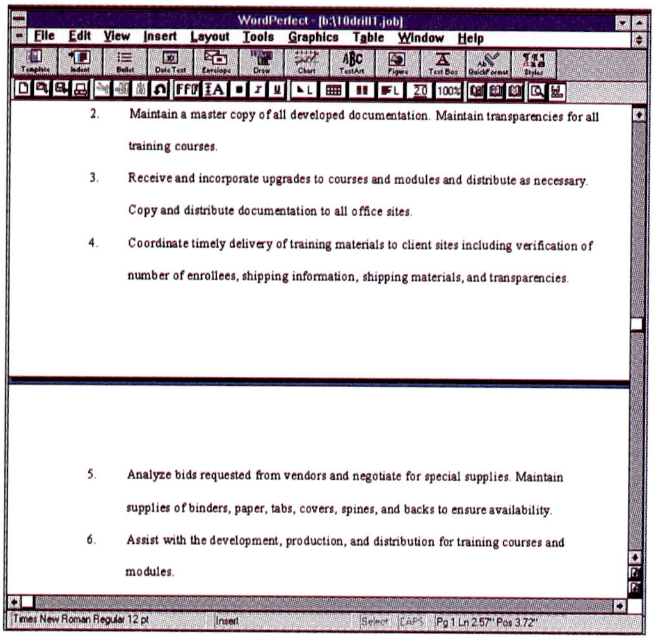

wraps to the next page. The soft page break is also referred to as an automatic page break. In Reveal Codes, a soft page break is identified with an *SPg* code.

If a new page is desired before the available lines on the page are filled, a hard page break is used to create the new page. A hard page break is placed in a document by pressing the **Ctrl** and **Enter** keys. The hard page break is also known as a required page break. In Reveal Codes, a hard page break is identified with an *HPg* code.

WordPerfect provides several modes to view text in the document window, namely, Page, Two Page, and Draft views. The Page view mode is referred to as a WYSIWYG (what you see is what you get) display because the page elements such as margins, fonts, text attributes, headers/footers, and footnotes display in the document window as they will print. A graphical representations of the top and bottom of each page and space that indicates margins display in the document window (see Figure 10.1).

The Two Page view mode, similar to the Page view mode, displays two consecutive pages side by side in the same document window. The Two Page view mode is useful for evaluating the page layout and the text is usually too small to read.

The Draft view mode is also similar to the Page view mode; however, headers/footers, footnotes, and top and bottom margins do not display in the document window. A soft page break displays as a single horizontal line placed across the width of the document window. A hard page break may display as two single horizontal lines or as a thick single line.

The pages of a multiple-page document can be viewed on the screen to see the placement of the lines and page numbers. The current page is viewed by using either the Page View or the Page Zoom Full feature. In Page View, additional pages can be viewed by pressing the **Page Up** and **Page Down** keys. Also, in Page Zoom Full, additional pages can be viewed by selecting the **Previous Page** and **Next Page** buttons, which are located at the bottom of the vertical scroll bar (see Figure 1.7 in Chapter 1). If desired, two pages can be displayed on the screen at one time by selecting **View, Two Page.**

Print Page Numbers

Each page of a multiple-page document should be numbered. If the pages are numbered at the bottom, number 1 is printed at the bottom of the first page. If pages are numbered at the top, the first page may or may not be numbered. WordPerfect's default is to print with no page numbers.

Page numbers can be instructed to print at the top or bottom of the page and at the left margin, centered, or at the right margin as well as alternating on the top or bottom of pages. The default position for page numbers is 1 inch from the top of the page or 1 inch from the bottom of the page. The **Position** option in the Page Numbering dialog box is used to indicate the placement of page numbers. The **Options** button in the Page Numbering dialog box can be selected to format the page numbers and to specify text that will be included with the page number. For example, the page numbering format could be changed to uppercase Roman numerals or the word *Page* can be printed along with the page number (e.g., Page 1).

Page numbers can be set to print as lowercase letters (a, b, c, etc.) or uppercase letters (A, B, C, etc.), lowercase Roman numerals (i, ii, iii, etc.), uppercase Roman numerals (I, II, III, etc.), or numbers (1, 2, 3, etc.). If text will accompany the page number, type the desired text in the Format and Accompanying Text box before or after the page number code (*[Pg#]*).

A different beginning page number can be set by selecting the **Value** button in the Page Numbering dialog box. For example, to begin numbering pages with page 4, type 4 in the New Page Number box in the Page Settings category.

A header or footer can also be used to print page numbers. (See Headers and Footers later in this chapter.)

Start-Up Instructions

- Open the file named **10drill1.job** located on the data disk.

Steps to Number Pages

1. With the insertion point located at any position on page one, select Layout, Page, Numbering {Alt, L, p, n}.

   Note: The Page Numbering dialog box displays.

2. Move the mouse pointer to the Position box, press and hold the mouse button and drag to select the desired page number position option {Alt and p, press the up or down arrow keys until the desired position option is highlighted}.

   For example, move the mouse pointer to the Position box, press and hold the mouse button and drag to select **Bottom Center**; release the mouse button.

   ***Note:** A sample of the page number location displays below the Position box (see Figure 10.2).*

3. Select OK {press Enter}.

   ***Note:** Select **View, Two Page** to display both pages on the screen. Select **View, Page** to return to the normal view.*

FIGURE 10.2

Page Numbering dialog box

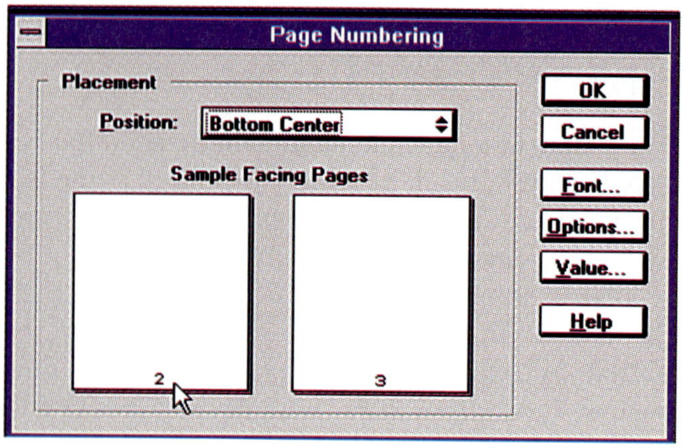

Finish-Up Instructions

- Turn on Reveal Codes (select **View, Reveal Codes**). With the insertion point located at the beginning of the document, place the red or shaded block to the left of the *Pg Num Pos* code and view the expanded page numbering code, e.g., *Pg Num Pos: Bottom Center.* Turn off Reveal Codes (select **View, Reveal Codes**).
- Use the *new* filename **10drill1.num** and save the file.
- Print one copy.

Start-Up Instructions

- The file named **10drill1.num** should be displayed in the document window.

Steps to Change the Page Numbering Method

1. With the insertion point located at any position on page one, select **Layout, Page, Numbering** {Alt, L, p, n}.
2. Select **Options** {o}.
3. Move the mouse pointer to the Page box; press and hold the mouse button and drag to select the desired number type. Release the mouse button {Alt and p, press the up or down arrow until the desired option displays}.

   For example, select **Uppercase Roman.**
4. Select **OK** to return to the Page Numbering dialog box {Enter}.
5. Select **OK** {press Enter}.

Finish-Up Instructions

- Turn on Reveal Codes (select **View, Reveal Codes**). With the insertion point at the beginning of the document, place the red or shaded block to the left of the *Pg Num Meth* code and view the expanded page numbering method code, e.g., *Pg Num Meth: Lev 1;4.* Turn off Reveal Codes (select **View, Reveal Codes**).
- Use the filename **10drill1.rom** and save the file.
- Print one copy.

Start-Up Instructions

- The file named **10drill1.rom** should be displayed in the document window.

Steps to **Delete Page Numbers by Deleting the Page Numbering Position Code**

1. If necessary, turn on Reveal Codes (select **View, Reveal Codes**).
2. Place the red or shaded block to the left of the page number code.

   For example, place the red or shaded block to the left of the code *Pg Num Pos: Bottom Center.*
3. Press the Delete key.
4. Turn off Reveal Codes (select **View, Reveal Codes**).

Finish-Up Instructions

- In Page View, scroll to the bottom of each page. Notice that the page numbers no longer display at the bottom of the document pages.
- Close the document. Do not save the file.

Headers and Footers

Generally, a multiple-page document includes headers or footers. A header is a title or information that prints in the top margin of the second and following pages (see Figures 10.3 and 10.5). A footer is a title or information that prints in the bottom margin of each page (see Figure 10.5). Headers and footers can consist of more than one line of text. Once created, headers and footers can be edited, suppressed for a single page, discontinued, or deleted.

When a header is used, the header information is normally not printed on the first page of a document but prints at the top of the second and following pages. When a footer is used, the title information along with the page number (optional) prints at the bottom of every page. The default position for headers is 1" from the top of the page, and the default position for footers is 1" from the bottom of the page. A header or footer can be viewed by selecting **View, Page** or by choosing the **View, Two Page** option.

Two different headers or footers can be created. Header A & B and Footer A & B are options available in the Headers/Footers dialog box. Usually, only Header A or Footer A is used. However, if a document is set up to display different headers/footers on left and right pages, Header/Footer A would be used to create a left-page header or footer and Header/Footer B would be used to create a right-page header or footer. The footers in this textbook are examples of different left- and right-page footers.

If the format of a document is changed, the format of the header or footer must also be altered to match the changed document format. For example, if the margins or fonts are changed for the entire document, the margins or fonts for the header and/or footer must also be changed.

FIGURE 10.3

Two sample styles of headers

Right Moves Presentation
Page 2
March 25, 199x

Header for two-page memorandum or report

This process will not fail if made a part of the presentation format discipline. In addition, remember that no more than three recommended changes should be presented at one time. The recommendations should be presented in a concise and informative manner.

Header for two-page letter

Ms. Holly Pierce	Page 2	March 25, 199x

Costs included in this invoice are for final preparation by a Senior Engineer, review by a Principal, geotechnical drafting and typing, and reproduction of the Distress Investigation report. Expenses are for film purchase, developing, and printing.

When a one-line header or footer is typed, a one-row table with two or three columns can be created to make formatting and aligning the text easier. For example, in the one-line header displayed in the second sample in Figure 10.3, "Page 2" is centered in the middle column and the date is right aligned in the right column. The table border and table lines are omitted.

Start-Up Instructions

- Open the file named **10drill1.job** located on the data disk.
- If necessary, select the Page view mode (select **View**, **Page**).

Steps to Create a Header and Insert a Page Number

1. With the insertion point located at any position on page one, select **Layout, Header/Footer** {Alt, L, h}.

   Note: The Headers/Footers dialog box displays with Header A selected. (If necessary, select Header A.)

2. Select **Create** {c}.

   Note: The Header/Footer Feature Bar displays below the Power Bar (see Figure 10.4) and the Title bar displays "Header A" following the document filename (e.g., 10drill1.job - Header A).

3. Type the header information.

FIGURE 10.4

Header/Footer Feature Bar

For example, type **Coordinator for Support Services**. Press **Alt** and **F7** to move the insertion point to the right margin.

4. Select the **Number** button, select **Page Number** {Alt and Shift and m, p}.

   Note: The page number 1 displays at the right margin.

5. Select **Close** on the Header/Footer Feature Bar to exit the Header A window {Alt and Shift and c}.

   Note: Turn on Reveal Codes to display the Header A code. Turn off Reveal Codes.

Suppress the Header on Page One

6. Select **Layout, Page, Suppress** {Alt, L, p, u}.
7. Select the box located beside the **Header A** option {e}.

   Note: An X displays in the Header A box.

8. Select **OK** {press Enter once}.

Finish-Up Instructions

- Select **View, Two Page** to view the header on page 2 of the document.
- Use the *new* filename **10drill1.hdr** and save the file.
- Print one copy.

Start-Up Instructions

- The file named **10drill1.hdr** should be displayed in the document window.

Steps to Edit Headers/Footers

1. Select **Layout, Header/Footer** {Alt, L, h}.
2. Select the desired **Header** or **Footer** option {press the desired letter a, b, f, or o}.

   For example, check that **Header A** is selected.

3. Select **Edit** {e}.

   Note: The insertion point moves to the first occurrence of the header or footer and the Header/Footer Feature Bar displays.

4. Make the desired changes to the header or footer text using the customary editing methods.

   For example, delete the page number and type **Job Description**.

   *Note: The text **Job Description** should be aligned flush right (see Figure 10.5).*

5. Select **Close** {Alt and Shift and c}.

Finish-Up Instructions

- In Page view mode, select the **Previous Page** or **Next Page** buttons located at the bottom of the vertical scroll bar to view the changed header.
- Use the *new* filename **10drill1.edi** and save the file.

Start-Up Instructions

- ❖ The file named **10drill1.edi** should be displayed in the document window.

Steps to Create a Footer

1. With the insertion point located at any position on page one, select **Layout, Header/Footer** {Alt, L, h}.

   Note: The Headers/Footers dialog box displays.

2. Select **Footer A** {f}.
3. Select **Create** {c}.

   Note: The Footer A window displays on the screen. The footer window is exactly like the header window, except Footer A displays in the Title bar. The insertion point displays at the bottom of the screen.

4. Type the footer information.

   For example, type **Revision date: 11/9x**. Press **Alt** and **F7** to move the insertion point to the right margin. Type **Page** and press the **Spacebar** once.

5. Select the **Number** button; select **Page Number** {Alt and Shift and m, p} .
6. Select **Close** {Alt and Shift and c}.

   *Note: If necessary, select **View, Two Page** to view the footer. Also, if desired, turn on Reveal Codes to display the Footer A code.*

Finish-Up Instructions

- ❖ Use the *new* filename **10drill1.ftr** and save the file.
- ❖ Print one copy.

Steps to Delete Headers/Footers

Note: These steps are for your information only.

1. Turn on Reveal Codes (select **View, Reveal Codes**).
2. Locate the red or shaded block to the left of the header or footer code in the Reveal Codes screen.
3. Press the **Delete** key.

Keep Text Together (Widow/Orphan)

WordPerfect's Keep Text Together feature is used to keep a block of text, two lines, or a specific number of lines together on one page. Widow/orphan lines are controlled by keeping a minimum of two lines of a paragraph at the bottom and top of a page. In other words, the first two lines or last two lines of a paragraph will not be separated from one page to another.

Coordinator for Support Services Job Description

4. Coordinate timely delivery of training materials to client sites, including verification of number of enrollees, shipping information, shipping materials, and transparencies.
5. Analyze bids requested from vendors and negotiate for special supplies. Maintain supplies of binders, paper, tabs, covers, spines, and backs to ensure availability.
6. Assist with the development, production, and distribution for training courses and modules.
7. Provide software training, support, and troubleshooting via phone for all administrative office personnel.
8. Develop and maintain consultant orientation/training programs, quick WordPerfect training materials, and style sheets for Ventura.
9. Assist with evaluation of new and upgraded software and new office machines prior to purchase.

Duties and responsibilities may be added, deleted, or changed at any time at the discretion of management, formally or informally, either verbally or in writing.

Revision date: 11/9x Page 2

FIGURE 10.5

A document with a header and footer

Block protect is used to keep selected text or table(s), or chart(s) from being divided between two pages. (The selected text to be block protected must be less than one page in length.)

The conditional end of page is used to keep a specific number of lines together on one page. For example, a sidehead and the first two lines of the paragraph that follows the sidehead should be kept together on one page.

Start-Up Instructions

- The file named **10drill1.ftr** should be displayed in the document window.

Steps to Keep Text Together Using Widow/Orphan

1. With the insertion point at any position on page one, select **Layout, Page, Keep Text Together** {Alt, L, p, k}.
2. In the Widow/Orphan area, move the mouse pointer to the **Prevent the first and last lines of paragraphs from being separated across pages** option and click once {Alt and p}.

   Note: *An X displays in the box under Widow/Orphan.*

3. Select **OK** {press Enter once}.

Finish-Up Instructions

- Check that the insertion point is located at the beginning of the document. Turn on Reveal Codes to view the widow/orphan code, *Wid/Orph.* Turn off Reveal Codes.
- Save the file again using the same filename, **10drill1.ftr.**
- Print one copy.
- Close the document.

Create Footnotes and Endnotes

A multiple-page document can include footnotes or endnotes. The footnote or endnote reference information provides the name, date, and page number of the source from which the information being discussed was obtained (see Figure 10.6). Footnotes and endnotes are also referred to as reference notes or sources.

Once a footnote or endnote is created, WordPerfect automatically places the footnote or endnote reference number in the document text. The reference number is superscripted (raised slightly above the text line).

Codes for the footnote and endnote references are placed in the document text and can be displayed by using Reveal Codes. The footnote and endnote reference information can be displayed in the document window by selecting **View**, **Page** or **View**, **Two Page**.

Footnote reference information is printed at the bottom of the page where the footnote reference number is located. A 2-inch separator line is placed above the footnote reference information. The first line of the footnote reference information is indented, the footnote reference number is superscripted, and the information is printed with vertical line spacing of one (see Figure 10.6). The footnote separator line's style, length, line position, and the spacing above and below the line can be changed by selecting the Separator option in the Footnote Options dialog box.

Endnotes are automatically placed at the end of the document text. A hard page break (**Ctrl** and **Enter**) is inserted after the last line of text in the document so that endnotes will print on a separate page. A title such as *Notes* is usually placed at the top of the endnote page. Depending on the requested design/style, the first line of the endnote reference information may either be typed at the left margin or indented, and the information may be printed with line spacing of one or two.

To change the numbering method or the format for footnotes or endnotes, the Options selection is chosen in the Footnote or Endnote menu. Roman numerals as well as any character supplied in the WordPerfect character sets can be designated as the numbering method. The note format for footnotes and endnotes can be changed by altering the amount of space between notes. The amount of a footnote or endnote (measured in inches) to be kept together is increased or decreased in the Continued Footnote or Continuous Notes options in the Footnote Options or Endnote Options dialog box.

The numbering style (such as indents, fonts, and line spacing) for footnotes and endnotes can be changed by selecting the **Edit Numbering Style In Note** option in the Footnote or Endnote Options dialog box to display the Styles Editor. (See Chap-

FIGURE 10.6

Partial document with footnotes

four-year scholarships have been established for children of firefighters who have died in the line of duty. Other Lieberman Enterprises scholarship programs have been for graduates of West City Community College, city employees, and Norfolk high school teachers. In response to the need for more qualified science teachers, Lieberman Enterprises offers training in computer science to high school teachers. A Science Seminar Program provides science teachers with updated teaching materials and methods.[2]

---

[1]J. Russell Mason, The President's Report to the Board of Directors, Spring 1990, p. 2.

[2]Ibid., p. 3.

ter 15 for additional information on the Styles Editor.) The numbering style for footnote or endnote reference numbers can be changed by selecting the **Edit Numbering Style In Text** option and making the desired changes in the Styles Editor.

Footnotes or endnotes can be manually renumbered by selecting **Footnote** or **Endnote** from the **Insert** menu and choosing **New Number.** After typing the new number, select **OK.**

If endnotes are desired in a location other than at the end of the document, the Placement option is used. Place the insertion point at the desired location, then select **Insert, Endnote, Placement.** Choose **Insert Endnote at Insert Point** or **Insert Endnote at Insertion Point and Restart Numbering** and select **OK**. Changing the location of endnotes is useful when the endnotes are to be placed at the end of each chapter in a book and multiple chapters are included in a document. A hard page break is inserted automatically after the endnotes (before the next page of text).

Start-Up Instructions

- Open the file named **10drill2.foo** located on the data disk.
- If necessary, select the **Page** view mode (select **View, Page**).

Steps to Create Footnotes

1. Place the insertion point to the right of the text to be referenced.

   For example, place the insertion point after the period in the last sentence of the first paragraph that ends with the word *annually.*

2. Select Insert, Footnote, Create {Alt, i, f, c}.

   Note: A divider line and footnote number display at the bottom of the current page. The insertion point is located to the right of the footnote number. The Footnote/Endnote Feature Bar displays below the Power Bar.

3. Type the footnote information.

For example, type **J. Russell Mason, The President's Report to the Board of Directors, Spring 1990, p. 2.**

4. Select **Close** on the Footnote/Endnote Feature Bar {Alt and Shift and c}.

   Note: *The footnote number displays at the location of the insertion point. To display the footnote, select* ***View, Two Page*** *and/or scroll to the bottom of the page.*

Finish-Up Instructions

- Place the insertion point after the last period in the third paragraph that ends with the word *methods.*
- Use steps 2-4 to create the following footnote:

  Ibid., p. 3.
- Place the insertion point after the last period in the final paragraph that ends with the word *centers.*
- Use steps 2-4 to create the following footnote:

  Lois Hodges, "Contribution to Community Education," ***The Times Crier*****, 3 May 1991, p. 10.**
- Use the *new* filename **10drill2.fnt** and save the file.
- Print one copy.

Start-Up Instructions

- The file named **10drill2.fnt** should be displayed in the document window.

Steps to Edit a Footnote or Endnote

Note: *The same method is used to edit footnotes and endnotes. For information on creating endnotes, see page 241.*

1. Select **Insert, Footnote** or **Endnote, Edit** {Alt, i, f or e, e}.

   For example, select **Insert, Footnote, Edit** {Alt, i, f, e}.

   Note: *The Edit Footnote dialog box displays.*
2. Type the number of the footnote/endnote to be edited.

   For example, check that the number **3** displays. If necessary, type **3**.
3. Select **OK** to locate the insertion point at the beginning of the footnote/endnote {Enter}.
4. Make corrections using the customary edit methods.

   For example, change p. 10 to **p. 24.**
5. Select **Close** on the Footnote/Endnote Feature Bar {Alt and Shift and c}.

Finish-Up Instructions

- Save the file again using the same filename, **10drill2.fnt**.

Start-Up Instructions

- The file named **10drill2.fnt** should be displayed in the document window.

Steps to Delete a Footnote or Endnote

Note: The same method is used to delete footnotes and endnotes. For information on creating endnotes, see the following Steps to Create Endnotes.

1. Select the footnote or endnote reference number in the document.

   For example, select the footnote reference number 2 that displays after the third paragraph.

2. Press the Delete key once. The footnote/endnote number and the footnote/endnote information are both deleted.

   Note: If other footnotes/endnotes follow the deleted footnote or endnote, the remaining footnotes/endnotes are automatically renumbered.

Finish-Up Instructions

- Use the *new* filename **10drill2.fin** and save the file.
- Print one copy.
- Close the document.

Start-Up Instructions

- Open the file named **10drill2.foo** located on the data disk.

Steps to Create Endnotes

1. Place the insertion point to the right of the text to be referenced.

   For example, place the insertion point to the right of the period after the last sentence in the first paragraph that ends with the word *annually*.

2. Select **Insert, Endnote, Create** {Alt, i, e, c}.

   Note: The Endnote Feature Bar displays below the Power Bar, and the endnote number is shown at the bottom of the screen after the last paragraph in the document.

3. Press the Tab key once; type the endnote information.

   For example, type **J. Russell Mason, The President's Report to the Board of Directors, Spring 1990, p. 2.**

4. Select the Close button on the Endnote Feature Bar {Alt and Shift and c}.

   Note: The insertion point returns to the referenced text, and the number 1 displays at the end of the paragraph. In Page view mode, scroll down to display the last page of the document and view the endnote.

Finish-Up Instructions

- Place the insertion point after the last period in the third paragraph that ends with the word *methods.*
- Use steps 2-4 to create the second endnote:

  Ibid., p. 3.
- Place the insertion point after the last period in the final paragraph that ends with the word *centers.*
- Use steps 2-4 to create the third endnote:

  Lois Hodges, "Contribution to Community Education," ***The Times Crier*****, 3 May 1991, p. 24.**

  Note: If necessary, select **Close** *on the Endnote Feature Bar.*
- With the insertion point to the right of the footnote number located after the last paragraph that ends with the word *centers,* press **Ctrl** and **Enter** to create a hard page break.
- Type the title **Notes**; press **Enter** once.
- Select and center the title.
- Use the *new* filename **10drill2.end** and save the file.
- In order to view all endnotes in Page view mode, it may be necessary to scroll down the page.
- Print one copy.

Search for Codes

To quickly locate a specific place in a document, the user can search for text or codes. Searching for codes is quite similar to searching for specific text (see Chapter 4). Locating a code is useful for deleting or moving a code or for finding a specific area of the document.

A code can be located by matching a code listed in the Codes dialog box. A code can also be found by designating a specific value or a specific code such as *Font, Just* or *Bot Mar.*

To find a code that has been assigned a specific value (e.g., a font size code), choose **Type** in the Find Text dialog box, select **Specific Codes,** double-click on **Font Size**, select the up or down triangles to increase or decrease the number until the desired size displays and select **Find Next**; select **Close** (or move the Find Font Size box to the top of the document window—see Chapter 16). Turn on Reveal Codes to display the found code. The red or shaded block is located to the right of the found code.

Start-Up Instructions

- The file named **10drill2.end** should be displayed in the document window.

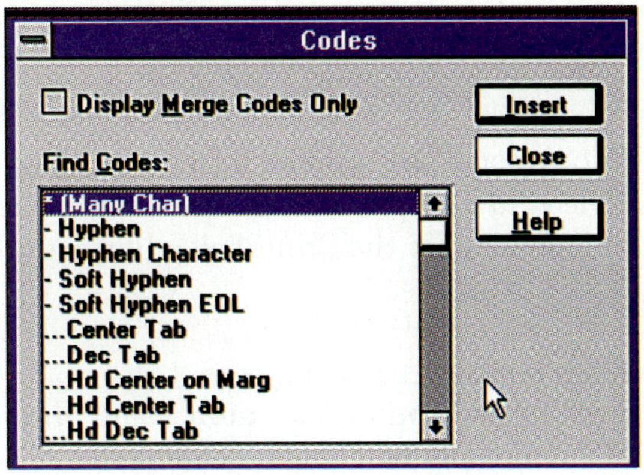

FIGURE 10.7
Codes dialog box

Steps to Search for a Code

Note: The insertion point should be located at the top of the document to be searched.

1. Select Edit, Find {F2}.
2. Select Match, Codes {Alt and m, o}.

   Note: The Codes dialog box displays (see Figure 10.7).
3. Begin typing the desired code or use the scroll bars to display the desired code.

   For example, type **Endn.**

   *Note: The code Endnote is highlighted after typing **endn**.*
4. Double-click on the desired code {press Enter}.

   For example, double-click on the **Endnote** code.

   Note: The code Endnote is placed in the Find box in the Find Text dialog box.
5. Select Find Next in the Find Text dialog box {Alt and f}.

   Note: The endnote number is highlighted in the text.
6. Select Close {Alt and c}.

Finish-Up Instructions

- Press the **Backspace** key to delete the endnote code in the document.

  Note: The endnotes are automatically renumbered in the document but are not renumbered on the last page of the document.
- Select **Insert**, **Endnote**, **Edit**, select **OK** or type **1**, press the **Delete** key, type **1**, select **Close**.

  Note: If desired, scroll to the end of the document to view the renumbered endnote(s).
- Save the file again using the same filename, **10drill2.end**.

Print Specific Pages

After printing a multiple-page document, one or more of the pages may need to be edited and only those pages will need to be reprinted. To specify the exact pages to print, the Multiple Pages option is selected in the Print dialog box, and the desired pages are entered as follows:

- Place a comma or space between nonconsecutive pages, e.g., 1,3 or 2 4 6.
- Place a dash between the beginning and ending page numbers to print a consecutive range of pages, e.g., 5-9.
- Place a dash after the beginning page number to print from a specific page to the end of the document, e.g. 5-.
- Place a dash before the page number to print from the beginning of a document up to a specific page, e.g., -6.

A combination of these methods can be used, e.g., 4,5, 8-11 *or* 2-4 6. Page numbers must be typed in numerical order. If, for example, the specified pages are 8, 2-5, only page 8 will print.

Also, a single page can be printed by typing the page number in the Page(s) box or by placing the insertion point anywhere on the page, selecting the **Print** button on the Power Bar, choosing the **Current Page** option, and selecting **Print**. When the **Current Page** option is selected, only the page where the insertion point is located will print.

Start-Up Instructions

- The document containing the pages to print should be displayed in the document window. For example, the file named **10drill2.end** should be displayed in the document window.

Steps to Print Specific Pages

1. Select the Print button on the Power Bar {Alt, f, p *or* F5}.
2. Select the Multiple Pages option in the Print dialog box {Alt and m}.
3. Select Print {Alt and p}.

   Note: The Multiple Pages dialog box displays with the word ***all*** *highlighted in the Page(s) box (see Figure 10.8).*
4. In the Page(s) box, type the page numbers to be printed.

FIGURE 10.8

Multiple Pages dialog box

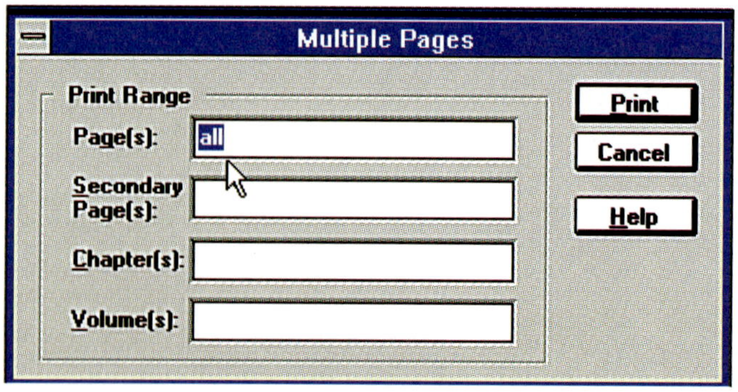

For example, type **1,3** to print pages 1 and 3 only.

5. Select **Print** {Alt and p}.

   Note: A message, "Preparing document for printing," displays briefly.

Finish-Up Instructions

- Close and do not save the document.

The Next Step

Chapter Review and Activities

Self-Check Quiz

T F 1. A multiple-page report is printed with vertical line spacing of one or two.

T F 2. A footer is typed once but prints on all pages of a multiple-page document.

T F 3. A header is normally printed on all pages of a document.

T F 4. Footnotes are consecutively numbered and printed on the page where the information is referenced.

5. Press _____ and **Enter** to place a hard page break in a document.
   a. **Ctrl**
   b. **Alt**
   c. **Shift**
   d. **Home**

6. Using the Page Numbering options, numbers can be set to print as ______
   a. lowercase or uppercase letters.
   b. lowercase or uppercase Roman numerals.
   c. numbers (1, 2, 3, etc.).
   d. any of these.

7. The _____ feature of the keep text together function can be used to prevent a table or chart from being printed on two pages.
   a. widow/orphan
   b. block protect
   c. conditional end of page
   d. none of the above

8. A code in a document can be found by ________________
   a. matching a code listed in the Codes dialog box.
   b. designating a specific value.
   c. indicating a specific code such as *Bot Mar.*
   d. any of these.

9. State the difference between a footnote and a footer.

10. List two reasons for searching for a code.

Enriching Language Arts Skills

Spelling/Vocabulary Words

phenomenon an event perceived and/or felt by one's senses; sensation; spectacle.

biosphere region of the earth that provides a self-sustaining ecological system.

analysis the study of and inquiry into the nature of something; investigation; evaluation.

profound intense; extreme; significant.

euphoria a feeling of well-being, usually not based on reality.

Quotation Marks with Punctuation

Always place a comma or period inside a closing quotation mark.

Example:

"I wonder," said Joan to herself, "how I got myself into this situation."

Place a question mark or exclamation point inside closing quotation marks if the question or exclamation pertains only to the quoted information. Place a question mark or exclamation point outside the closing quotation marks if the question or exclamation pertains to the entire sentence.

Example:

Jan said, "Help me!" (The exclamation pertains only to the quoted information.)

Was the returned check marked "Insufficient Funds"? (The question pertains to the entire sentence.)

Semicolons and colons are placed outside closing quotation marks.

Example:

The following items were in a package marked "Fragile": an antique bowl, four glasses, and a pitcher.

Activities

Activity 10.1—Create a Multiple-Page Document with Page Numbers

1. Type the following report and use vertical line spacing of two.

Compusoft Modular for Windows and OS/2

Compusoft Modular is a fresh new design of communications software for all categories of users. Modularity and profiling strengths provide the user with the ability to "customize" and "personalize" Compusoft for precise functions.

Compusoft Modular offers more LAN/Gateway connectivity and terminal emulations than any other product in today's market. Uniform support for both Windows and OS/2 platforms is included in every package; the user simply chooses the appropriate installation diskette.

Compusoft's simulated reasoning capability lets users create a mental model compatible with their own thinking process, and it makes expanded and advanced use occur without conscious effort. Once users successfully configure a task, they never need to configure that particular task again. Over time, users achieve a higher level of user interaction.

By the end of the next quarter, Compusoft Modular will support over 50 terminal emulations. By the end of the third quarter, an additional 10 terminal emulations will be available. Another standard Compusoft module will enable the user to utilize Telenet to run multisessions with integrated file transfer protocols. Users can download these new modules at no charge from Corbin's bulletin board service as they are made available.

Compusoft Modular also includes all of the features that users of the Compusoft PC Classic have been accustomed to during the past eight years, such as an extensive number of file transfer protocols, dynamic keyboard remapping, an extensive script language, keyboard macros, multinational keyboard/emulation support, session scrollback, and preconfigured sessions for most online services.

Even though Compusoft has numerous features and functionality, it is extremely easy to manage and run. An excess of features is eliminated by removing functions that are not needed during the installation process, leaving only the desired modules. Compusoft Modular's dynamic graphics user interface displays only the functionality chosen by the user.

Compusoft Modular, version 1.0, costs $315 per user. For more information about Compusoft Modular, call (800) 555-5050.

---

2. Set the widow/orphan control (with the insertion point on page one, select **Layout**, **Page**, **Keep Text Together**, **Prevent the first and last lines of paragraphs from being separated across pages**, **OK**).
3. Use page numbering to print numbers at the bottom center of each page (select **Layout**, **Page**, **Numbering**, move the mouse pointer to the Position box, press and hold the mouse button and drag to highlight **Bottom Center**, release the mouse button, select **OK**).
4. Use the filename **10act1.mod** and save the file. Print one copy.
5. Close the document.

Activity 10.2—Create a Header for a Two-Page Memorandum

1. Open the memorandum with the filename **10act2.mem**.
2. Select **Layout**, **Header/Footer**, **Header A**, choose **Create** and insert a header that contains the following information:

   Right Moves Presentations
   Date
   Page (select the **Number** button, **Page Number**, select the **Close** button).

3. Suppress the header on the first page (select **Layout, Page, Suppress, Header A, OK**).
4. Use the new filename **10act2.fin** and save the file. Print one copy.
5. Close the document.

Activity 10.3—Create a Header and Footer for a Multiple-Page Document

1. Open the report with the filename **10act3.mag** located on the data disk.
2. Set vertical line spacing of two.
3. Set the widow/orphan control (with the insertion point located on page one, select **Layout, Page, Keep Text Together, Prevent the first and last lines of paragraphs from being separated across pages, OK**).
4. Select **Layout, Header/Footer, Header A**, and create a header:

   Everyday Magic **(Current Date)**

5. Suppress the header on the first page (select **Layout, Page, Suppress, Header A, OK**).
6. Select **Layout, Header/Footer, Footer A**, choose **Create** and insert a footer:

   Bill Pearce **Page (insert page number code)**

7. Use the new filename **10act3.fin** and save the file. Print one copy.
8. Close the document.

Activity 10.4—Create a Header and Footnote for a Multiple-Page Document

1. Open the report with the filename **10act4.dtp** located on the data disk.
2. Set the widow/orphan control (with the insertion point located on page one, select **Layout, Page, Keep Text Together, Prevent the first and last lines of paragraphs from being separated across pages, OK**).
3. Optional. Set the vertical line spacing to two.
4. Select **Layout, Header/Footer, Header A**, choose **Create** and insert a header:

   Desktop Publishing and Graphic Design **Page (insert page number code)**

5. Suppress the header for the first page (select **Layout, Page, Suppress, Header A, OK**).
6. Create a footnote:

   a. Place the insertion point after the last character in the document, select **Insert, Footnote, Create**, and type the following footnote:

      LaVaughn Hart and Katie Layman, "Desktop Publishing and Graphic Design," ***The California Business Teacher*****, Spring 1990, pp. 22–23.**

7. Use the filename **10act4.fin** and save the file. Print one copy.
8. Close the document.

Challenge Your Skills

Skill 10.1—Create a Header and Format a Two-Page Memorandum and Table

1. Use Memorandum—Style 1 and the following information to complete the memorandum.

    a. Make decisions regarding:

        Margins
        Justification
        Fonts
        Table format
        Widow/Orphan control
        Reference initials

    b. The memo should be sent to Noah Demello, Vice President, Field Sales.

    c. The memo is from Joyce S. Greiner, Regional Vice President.

    d. The memo should be dated June 22, 199x.

    e. The subject of the memo is Weekly Business Conditions Report.

    f. Copies of the memo should be sent to:

        T. W. Hakinson, Ellen Harrell, Alvin Lai, and Region Staff.

    g. The memorandum body text follows:

Regional Sales Performance

Period: 6
Week: 4
Week ending: 6/19/9x

Dollar Sales				
(in thousands)				
	1993 Actual	1993 Objectives	Difference in Dollars	Percent Change
Week Ending	8,244	7,473	771	10.3
Period Ending	28,695	29,099	(404)	(1.4)

General Business Conditions

The Northwest Region delivered 26.4% of its Period 6 objectives in Week 4, which reduced the deficit by $771,229 to finish the period down ($404,065). This Week 4 push enabled three divisions, Portland, Seattle, and San Francisco, to exceed their objectives.

This week's business was primarily driven by retailers seeking to maximize overlay payout potentials, some sales teams striving to achieve consistency bonuses, and preshipment of Cheesecake Yummies inventory prior to Week 1, Period 7's ad feature activity.

Significant Competitive Activity

<u>Whitehouse</u>

If a customer buys Mom's Tasties, Bite Size Fudge Chips are free!

Whitehouse will introduce their 7 oz. Ponderosa Munch'ems to the Portland Division during Period 7, and the new Deluxe Crispies will arrive Period 8.

The Seattle Division reports coupons being distributed in stores offering a free pound of bananas with the purchase of one package of Heart Wafers.

<u>Lucky Star</u>

The price for Super Snack Cookies 12 oz. or larger is $.45.

In the San Francisco Division, Lucky Star is hosting a "Grocery Giveaway Contest" that customers can enter to win $60 worth of groceries.

Other Information

The current issue of <u>FOOD SNACKS</u> profiles Milano, a Seattle, Washington, snack supplier plotting a course towards retail expansion by emphasizing quality, competitive pricing, innovative products, and dedicated service. Although its roots are in the bulk/industrial snack trade, Milano knows they will have to decide whether to concentrate on being a retail snack supplier or continue to emphasize re-packers' demands. This is an example of a lower-priced, "less fancy" snack variety entering the growing "All Other" cracker category.

2. Create a two-line header:

Weekly Business Conditions	June 22, 199x
Northwest Region	Page (insert page number code)

Note: Remember to suppress the header on the first page.

3. Use the filename **10skill1.fin** and save the file.
4. Print one copy.
5. Close the document.

Skill 10.2—Create a Header and Footnotes; Format a Multiple-Page Document with Table

1. Open the multiple-page document with the filename **10skill2.sto** located on the data disk.
2. Make decisions regarding:

   Margins
   Line spacing
   Justification
   Fonts
   Table format
   Widow/Orphan control
   Header format and placement
   Spacing before and after, capitalization, and bold for title and sideheads
3. Create the following footnotes in the document.
   a. Place the first footnote reference after the closing quotation mark in the first paragraph "... which includes national and international listing." Footnote text: The Southwest Stock Exchange Bulletin, p. 6.
   b. Place the second footnote reference in the third paragraph after the closing quotation mark that ends "... prices and trades on a daily basis." Footnote text: EITAK Commodities Annual Report, p. 2.
   c. Place the third footnote reference at the end of item number 3, "... inquiries by account executive." Footnote text: Ibid.
4. Create an appropriate header including the page number.
5. Use the *new* filename **10skill2.fin** and save the file.
6. Print one copy and close the document.

Skill 10.3—Create a Footnote and Page Numbering for a Multiple-Page Document; Language Arts

1. Open the multiple-page document with the filename **10skill3.boo** located on the data disk.
2. Make decisions regarding:

   Margins
   Line spacing
   Justification
   Hyphenation
   Headers and footers
   Widow/Orphan control
3. Correct four spelling and three punctuation errors
4. Create the following footnote in the document.
   a. Place the footnote reference after the period in the last sentence of the document. Footnote text: "Book Review--The Overview Effect: Space

Exploration and Human Evolution," *Spacefaring Gazette*, August 1988, p. 9.

5. Number the document pages at the top right corner.
6. Use the *new* filename **10skill3.fin** and save the file.
7. Print one copy.
8. If you have completed your work, exit WordPerfect.

CHAPTER 11

Create a Form Letter and Mailing List

Features Covered

- Create a form (primary) file
- Create a data (secondary) file
- Merge files
- Determine field names
- Edit data files and form files
- Mark a record(s)

Objectives and Introduction

After successfully completing this chapter, you will be able to create and merge a data file with a form file. You will also understand fields and records and learn how to remove the blank line that results from an empty field. In addition, you will be able to edit data and form files, mark records, and sort by fields.

A form letter is a standard letter that is sent to many individuals or companies. The same letter can be typed once, merged with a list of names and addresses, and printed. A form letter can be used for collecting overdue accounts, requesting donations, presenting product information, etc. The form letter is referred to as the form file. The list of names and addresses is referred to as the data file.

Create a Data File

The *data file* is a group of variables and field names. A variable is the information that changes in each form letter and can include names, addresses, dollar amounts, dates, special comments, etc. The variable information is referred to as data. The data file can be either a text or a table file. If a text data file is used, each variable displays on a separate line followed by a code. If a table data file is used, the variable information displays in table cells (see Figure 11.1). A table data file is recommended,

FIGURE 11.1

A data file with field names and data

title	first	last	co	address	city	state	zip	acct#
Ms.	Roxanne E.	Peterson		P.O. Box 96	Cathlamet	WA	98516	4182
Mr.	Mark	Koch, Jr.	Abby, Inc.	25 Jones Lane	Mt. Juliet	TN	37122	3198
Ms.	Esther	Emerson		40 E. 56th St., #5	New York	NY	10022	2186

because it is easier to create, proofread, and edit. (In earlier versions of WordPerfect the data file was called the secondary file.)

A *field* is the name given to a variable; for example, a dollar amount field can be named "dollar." A field name should be determined for each unit of information before beginning the process to create a data file. The field names in the data file must correlate exactly with the field names in the form file. A collection of all desired units (fields) is a record. In other words, a record is a single "set" of information that pertains to one entity, for example, one individual's first name, last name, company, address, city, state, and zip code.

When the table data file and records are created and displayed on the screen, the Merge Feature Bar automatically shows below the Power Bar. The Merge Feature Bar is used to insert fields, the Date code, and merge codes, and to display the Merge dialog box. If the data file is displayed, the **Go to Form** button shows on the Merge Feature bar. This button provides a quick way to create or open a form letter.

Steps to Create a Table Data File

1. Select Tools, Merge {Alt, t, e *or* Shift and F9}.

   Note: The Merge dialog box displays (see Figure 11.2).

2. In the Data File area, select Place Records in a Table option {p}.

   Note: An X displays in the box beside the Place Records in a Table option.

FIGURE 11.2

Merge dialog box

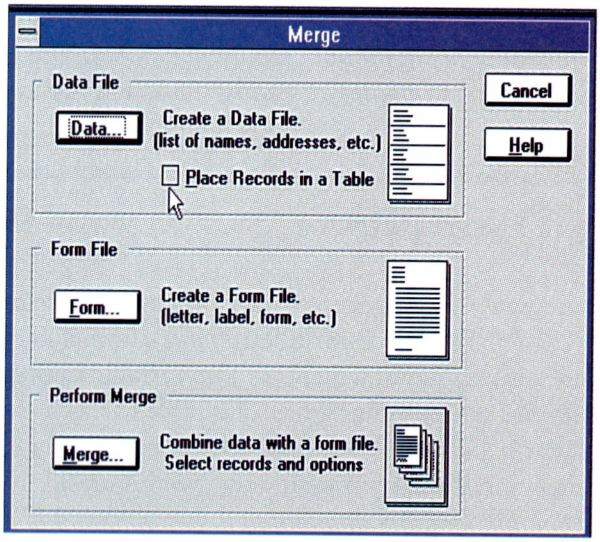

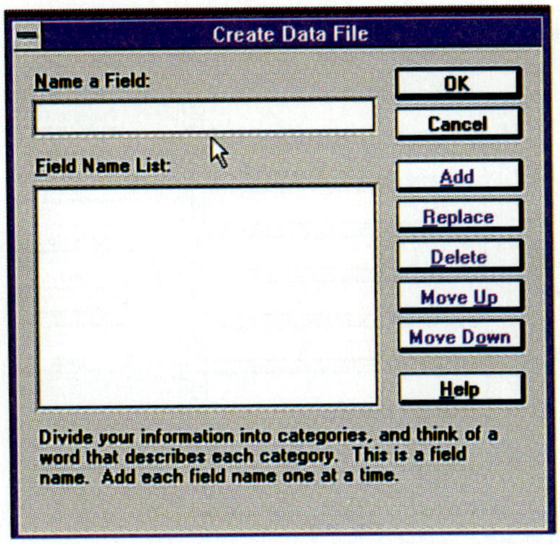

FIGURE 11.3

Create Data File dialog box

3. Select the **Data** button {d}. The Create Data File dialog box displays (see Figure 11.3).

   *Note: If the Create Merge File dialog box displays, select the **New Document Window** option.)*

4. Decide on a name for each data file field.

   For example, **title, first, last, co, address, city, state, zip,** and **acct#.**

5. Create each field name as follows:

   a. Type the name of the first field in the Name a Field box.

      For example, type **title**. (Do not type the final period.)

   b. Select **Add** or press **Enter** to display the field name in the Field Name List box.

   c. Type the next field name in the Name a Field box.

      For example, type **first**. (Do not type the final period.)

   d. Select **Add** or press **Enter** to display the field name in the Field Name List box.

6. Repeat steps 5a-b to add the remaining field names.

   For example, type the field names **last, co, address, city, state, zip,** and **acct#**. (Do not type the final period.)

   Note: If changes are desired, move the mouse pointer to the field name to be changed in the Field Name List box and click once. Use the Add, Replace, Delete, Move up, or Move down button options.

7. Select **OK** {Enter once}.

   Note: The Quick Data Entry dialog box with a list of the first eight field names displays for one record (see Figure 11.4). Also, a table with the field names displays in the document window.

8. With the insertion point in the first field name box, type the variable information.

   For example, type the recipient's title: **Ms.** (Type the final period.)

9. Press the **Tab** key to move the insertion point to the next field name box.

FIGURE 11.4

Quick Data Entry dialog box

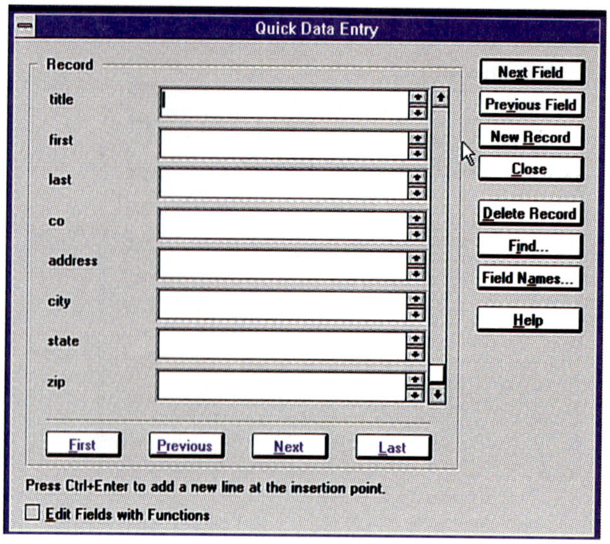

Note: If desired, point to the desired field name box and click once.

10. Type the the second field name data.

    For example, type the recipient's first name and, if available, middle initial: **Roxanne E.** (Type the final period.)

11. Press the Tab key to move the insertion point to the next field name box.
12. Type the third field name data.

    For example, type the recipient's last name: **Peterson**. (Do not type the final period.)

13. Press the Tab key to move the insertion point to the next field name box.
14. Type the the next field name data.

    For example, type the company name. No company name is available; therefore, press the Tab key.

    *Note: When information for a field is not available, press the **Tab** key to skip to the next field name box.*

15. Type the next field name data and press the Tab key.

    For example, type **P.O. Box 96** and press the Tab key.

16. Repeat step 17 and type the remaining data for the record.

    For example, type the following data:

Cathlamet	Tab
WA	Tab
98612-0096	Tab
4182	Do not press Tab.

17. Select the New Record button {Alt and r}.

    *Note: When the **New Record** button is selected, the data for the record just completed displays in the table in the document window.*

18. Repeat steps 8-17 and enter the field data for the following two records.

Mr.	Tab
Mark	Tab
Koch, Jr.	Tab
Abby, Inc.	Tab
25 Jones Lane	Tab
Mt. Juliet	Tab
TN	Tab
37122	Tab
3198	Select New Record.
Ms.	Tab
Esther	Tab
Emerson	Tab
	Tab
40 E. 56th St., #5	Tab
New York	Tab
NY	Tab
10022	Tab
2186	Do not press Tab.

19. When all the records have been completed, select Close {Alt and c}.
20. A message displays, "Save the changes to disk?" Select Yes {Enter}. Type the drive letter where the disk is located followed by the filename.

    For example, type **a:11drill1.dat**; select **OK**.

    Note: The data displays in a table; the first row contains the field names. The Merge Feature bar displays below the Power Bar (see Figure 11.5).

Finish-Up Instructions

❖ Continue with the Steps to Create a Form File.

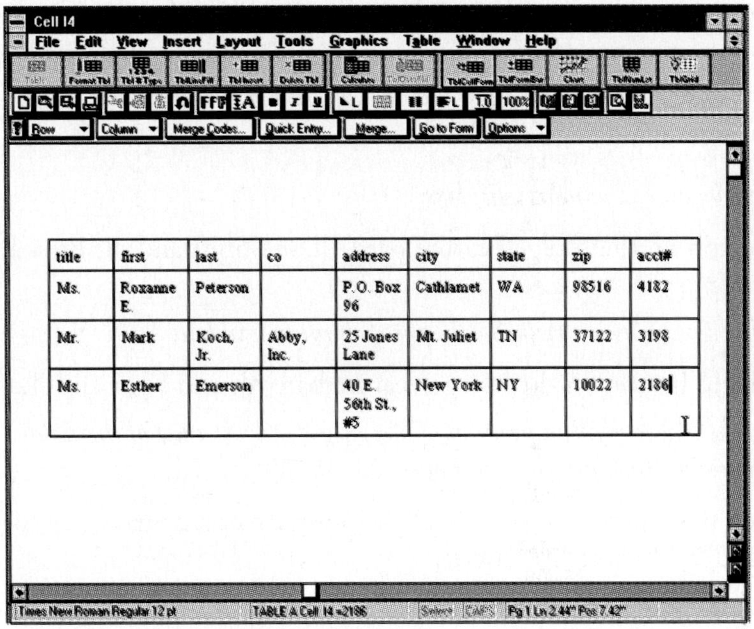

FIGURE 11.5

Table Data File with Merge Feature Bar displayed

Create a Form File

A *form file* is a document containing the information that remains the same in each letter (see Figure 11.7). The form file also includes the *field names* that correspond to the variable information that will print in each letter. Field names that exactly match the data file field names are placed in the form file to indicate the specific location for each field. In earlier versions of WordPerfect, the form file was called a primary file.

Because field information in a data file can vary, WordPerfect has provided special instructions that give the user more control over the varied information. Some fields in a data file can be empty; for example, a company field may not be needed in all form letters. Blank cells in the table data file indicate the fields that contain no data. When the data file and form file are prepared for merging, **Options** can be selected in the Perform Merge dialog box (see Steps to Merge a Form File and Data File later in this chapter). When the **Remove Blank Line** option is chosen, the hard returns that ordinarily result from a blank field will not be placed in the merged letter.

A form letter can be used over and over again with the date set up to change with each use. The Date code is inserted in the form file at the location where the current date is to print. When the **Date** button in the Merge Feature bar is selected, the current date is automatically displayed in the letter. The word DATE displays in the form letter file. The date code *MRG: DATE* can be viewed in Reveal Codes.

When a field name is inserted in a document, the word FIELD displays in all red uppercase letters (or in another color). The field name is enclosed in red/color parentheses.

Start-Up Instructions

❖ The data file named **11drill1.dat** should be displayed in the document window.

Steps to Create a Form File

1. With the table data file and Merge Feature Bar displayed in the document window, select the **Go to Form** button on the Merge Feature Bar {Alt and Shift and g}.

   Note: The Associate dialog box displays with the message "No Associated File."

2. Select **Create** {c}.

   Note: A new, empty document window displays.

3. Select the **Date** button on the Merge Feature bar {Alt and Shift and d}. Press **Enter** five times.

   Note: The word DATE displays in red/color in the document window.

4. Select the **Insert Field** button on the Merge Feature bar {Alt and Shift and i}.

   Note: The Insert Field Name or Number dialog box displays with a list of the field names that were created in the data file (see Figure 11.6).

5. Point to the desired field name and double-click {press the down arrow key to highlight the desired field name, Alt and i}.

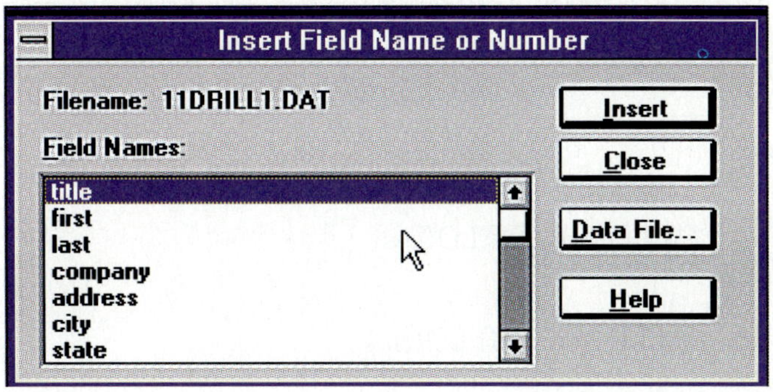

FIGURE 11.6

Insert Field Name or Number dialog box

For example, double-click on the field name **title** and press the **Spacebar** once.

Note: The code FIELD(title) displays in the document window.

6. In the Insert Field Name or Number dialog box, double-click on the desired field name {Alt and Shift and i, press the down arrow key to highlight the desired field name, Alt and i}.

   For example, double-click on **first** and press the **Spacebar** once.

7. Repeat step 6 and double-click on the desired field name.

   For example, double-click on the field name **last** and press **Enter** once.

8. Repeat step 6 and double-click on the desired field name.

   For example, double-click on **co** and press **Enter** once.

9. Repeat step 6 and double-click on the desired field name.

   For example, double-click on **address** and press **Enter** once.

10. Repeat step 6 and double-click on the desired field name.

    For example, double-click on **city**, type a comma (,), and press the **Spacebar** once.

11. Repeat step 6 and double-click on the next field name.

    For example, double-click on **state**. Press the **Spacebar** once.

12. Repeat step 6 and double-click on the next field name.

    For example, in the Insert Field Name or Number dialog box, point to the down scroll arrow in the scroll box and click until the field name **zip** displays. Double-click on **zip**, press **Enter** twice, type **Dear**, and press the **Spacebar** once.

13. Repeat step 6 and double-click on the next field name.

    For example, in the Insert Field Name or Number dialog box, point to the up scroll arrow in the scroll box and click until the field name **title** displays. Double-click on **title** and press the **Spacebar**.

14. Repeat step 6 and double-click on the next field name.

    For example, double-click on **last**, type a colon, and press **Enter** twice.

FIGURE 11.7

Form file

(DATE)

FIELD(title) FIELD(first) FIELD(last)
FIELD(co)
FIELD(address)
FIELD(city), FIELD(state) FIELD(zip)

Dear FIELD(title) FIELD(last):

Thank you for your World Club card membership. Your account number is FIELD(acct#).

I want to take this opportunity to inform you of our new service, Account Registry. With this service, we will inform all of your card issuers in the event that your wallet is lost or stolen. You will only have to make one phone call.

A brochure describing the Account Registry program features and costs as well as an enrollment form are enclosed.

I urge you to take advantage of this convenient service and sign up today.

Sincerely,

Frazer M. Horwitz
Vice President

FMH/xx
11drill1.frm/diska

Enc.

Finish-Up Instructions

- Continue to type the first paragraph of the letter body text shown in Figure 11.7. Repeat step 12 to create a field for **acct#**. Remember to place a space before the account field and to type a period after the account field. Press **Enter** twice before typing the second paragraph.
- In the Insert Field Name and Number dialog box, select **Close** {Alt and Shift and i, Alt and c}.
- Type the remaining letter body text.
- Place the insertion point at the top of the document and change the top margin to **1.5**"; change the left and right margins to **1.25**".
- Use the filename **11drill1.frm** and save the file.
- Continue with the Steps to Merge a Form File and Data File.

Merge a Form File and Data File

Once the form file and data files are created and saved, the files are combined by selecting **Merge** in the Perform Merge dialog box. If desired, the **Options** button in the Perform Merge dialog box is selected in order to choose the **Remove Blank Line** option. If a blank field is encountered in the data file and the **Remove Blank Line** option is selected, no blank line will display in the merged letter when the form file and data file are merged. When the form file and data file are merged, all the merged letters display in the new document window with each letter on a separate page.

In the Form File box of the Perform Merge dialog box, the option <Current Document> is defaulted to display. This means that the form file that is currently displayed in the document window is the file used for merging. If no file is displayed or if a different form file is to be used, select the left triangle beside the Form File box, choose **Select File**, and select the desired form filename.

If an addressed envelope is desired for each merged letter, select the **Envelopes** option in the Perform Merge dialog box. (See Chapter 12 for information on how to print mailing labels and envelope addresses.) The Envelope dialog box displays. To display the Insert Field Name or Number dialog box, select the **Field** button. Double-click on the desired field names and use the spacing and type the punctuation desired. A sample of the field names to be included in the mailing address are displayed in the Mailing Addresses box and in the sample envelope, which displays at the bottom of the Envelope dialog box. If changes are needed, point to the desired location in the Mailing Addresses box and click. Make the needed editing changes. Select **OK** to return to the Perform Merge dialog box

Once the form file and data file have been merged, check each of the merged letters for accuracy. If there are any errors in any of the merged letters, close (but do not save) the merged file and access the form and/or data file to make corrections. Once the necessary corrections have been made, the form and/or data file is saved, and the form file and data file are merged again. If desired, the merged letters can be saved; however, saving the merged letters is not recommended because the same information has been saved previously in the form file and data file.

A copy of each letter is printed using the normal print feature. Because a hard page break is placed between each letter, each letter will print on a separate page. If only one or two of the merged letters are to be printed, see Steps to Mark and Merge Specific Records beginning on page 265.

After the form file is merged with the data file, printed copies of the form and data files can be very useful for filing or reference purposes. If desired, the table data file text and structure can be changed to display the information in a more attractive and readable manner. For example, widening the columns, selecting a smaller font, and/or changing the table position to Full will assist in making the table easier to read.

Start-Up Instructions

- The form file **11drill1.frm** and the secondary file **11drill1.dat** must have been created and saved before beginning the Steps to Merge a Form File and Data File.
- The form file named **11drill1.frm** should be displayed in the document window.

FIGURE 11.8

Perform Merge dialog box

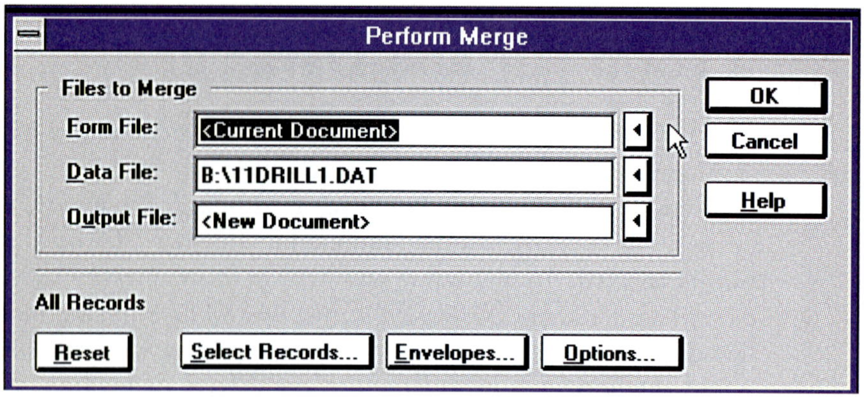

Steps to Merge a Form File and Data File

1. Select the Merge button on the Merge Feature bar {Alt and Shift and m}.
2. Select Merge {m}.

   Note: The Perform Merge dialog box displays (see Figure 11.8). Check that ***11drill1.dat*** *displays in the Data File box. If necessary, select or type the filename* ***11drill1.dat****; select* ***OK****. Also check that the Output File option is <New Document>. If necessary, click on the left triangle in the Output File box and select* ***<New Document>****.*
3. In the Perform Merge dialog box, select the Options button.

   Note: The Peform Merge Options dialog box displays (see Figure 11.9).
4. Check that Remove Blank Line displays at the If Empty Field in Data File option box. If necessary, move the mouse pointer to the down triangle beside the If Empty Field in Data File option box; press and hold the mouse button and drag until the option Remove Blank Line is highlighted; release the mouse button {press Tab twice, press the down arrow once}.
5. Select OK {Enter}.

   Note: The Perform Merge dialog box displays.
6. Select OK to begin the merge process {Tab, Enter}.

   Note: A message in the Status bar briefly displays, "Merging Record 1, 2," etc. After a few moments, all merged letters display on the screen. The insertion point is located after the last letter. A hard page break displays between each letter. Each letter will print on a separate page.

FIGURE 11.9

Perform Merge Options dialog box

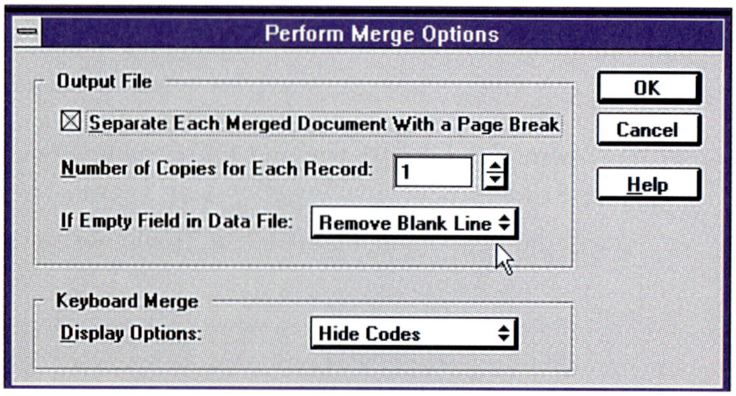

Finish-Up Instructions

- Select the Page Up button and/or the Page Down button at the bottom of the vertical scroll bar to display each letter. Proofread the letters to check that the addresses, names, and variable information are placed correctly in the letter.
- Select the **Print** button on the Power bar to print the merged letters. (A copy of each letter will be printed.)
- Close the merged letter document. If desired, use the filename **11merged.ltr** and save the document.
- Continue with the Steps to Edit a Table Data file or close the form file document and data file.

Edit Data Files and Form Files

Often the information in a table data file and/or form file must be updated or altered. The data file is changed by adding and/or deleting a record(s) or field(s). Also, the data in any field can be changed. A form file is changed by deleting or inserting fields and/or by changing the text of the document. The record information in the table data file and the text in the form file can be altered using normal editing procedures.

To add or delete a field(s) in a table data table file, use the same procedures as used to edit tables (see Chapters 5 and 6). An edited form and/or data file should be saved again before merging.

After a form file or data file is changed, all or specific data file records can be merged with the form file. The records can be viewed by field name and the modified records marked and merged. If a specific range of records is to be merged, the **Specify Record Number Range** option is selected in the Select Records dialog box. Then the record (row) number of the first record to be merged is typed or selected in the From box and the record (row) number of the last record to be merged is typed or selected in the To box. For example, if only records 2–4 are to be merged from a data file containing eight records, 2 is typed in the From box and 4 is typed in the To box.

Start-Up Instructions

- The form file **11drill1.frm** and the data file **11drill1.dat** must be available on a disk before beginning the Steps to Edit a Table Data File.

Steps to **Edit a Table Data File**

1. The table data file to be edited should be displayed in the document window.

   For example, select the **Window** menu and click on the filename **11drill1.dat** or open the data file named **11drill1.dat**.

2. Place the insertion point in the cell of the column or row to be edited.

   For example, place the insertion point in any cell in the column with the field name **co**.

3. Select the **Delete Tbl** button on the Tables Button bar or choose **Table, Delete** {Alt, a, d}.

Note: The Delete dialog box displays.

4. Select the desired option in the Delete dialog box.

   For example, select **Columns** {c}.

   Note: The number 1 displays in the Columns option box.

5. Select OK {Enter}.

   *Note: The column is immediately deleted. If a mistake is made, select **Edit, Undo** before performing another action.*

6. Add records to the table data file as needed.

   For example, place the insertion point in any cell in the last row. Select the **Quick Entry** button on the Merge Feature Bar {Alt and Shift and q}. Select **New Record** {Alt and r}. Type the following record information into the new row cells: **Mr. A.D. Simmons, 2064 Maria Ave., Northbrook, IL 60062, 3956.**

7. When the new record(s) is complete, select Close {Alt and c}.

8. Select Yes to save the changes to the disk {Enter}.

   Note: The Save Data File As dialog box displays.

9. Select OK {Enter} to accept the displayed filename or type a new filename.

   For example, check that **11drill1.dat** displays in the Filename box and select **OK**.

10. If the message "Do you want to replace it?" displays, select Yes {y}.

    Note: Continue with the Steps to Edit a Form File.

Steps to Edit a Form File

*Note: If a data file is not in the document window, open the desired file, **11drill1.frm**, and skip to Step 2.*

1. Select the Go to Form button on the Merge Feature bar.

   *Note: If the Associate dialog box displays, choose the **Select** button and select the desired filename in the Select Form File dialog box.*

2. Delete or insert the desired text and/or fields.

   For example, select and delete **FIELD(co)** and the following hard return in the second line of the letter address fields.

3. When all the editing is complete, save the form file again using the same filename.

   For example, save the file named **11drill1.frm**.

Finish-Up Instructions

- Continue with the Steps to Mark and Merge Specific Records.

Steps to Mark and Merge Specific Records

1. With the form file and data file each available in a separate window, select **Tools, Merge** {Alt, t, e *or* Shift and F9}.

   For example, with the form file **11drill1.frm** and the data file **11drill1.dat** each available in a separate window, select **Tools, Merge.**

2. Select the **Merge** button {m}.

   Note: *The Perform Merge dialog box displays.*

3. Choose the **Select Records** option {Alt and s}.

   Note: *The Select Records dialog box displays.*

4. Choose the desired option.

   For example, select the **Mark Records** option in the Selection Method area {Alt and a}.

5. Move the mouse pointer to the desired record(s) in the Record List and click once {Alt and L, press the up or down arrow keys to place the outline around the desired filename, press the Spacebar once}.

   For example, select the **A.D. Simmons** and **Mark Koch, Jr.** records.

6. Select **OK** {Enter}.

   Note: *The Perform Merge dialog box displays again.*

7. Select **OK** {Enter}.

   Note: A message displays briefly, "Merging Record . . ."

Finish-Up Instructions

- Select the Page Up and/or Page Down buttons at the bottom of the vertical scroll bar to view the letters.
- Optional. Print the merged letters.
- Close the merged letters and do not save.
- Close the data and form files and, if requested, save the file(s).

The Next Step

Chapter Review and Activities

Self-Check Quiz

T F 1. A form letter is usually sent to more than one individual or company.

T F 2. A data file usually contains the field names and the records for each recipient.

T F 3. A field name is the filename given to the data file.

T F 4. The form file contains the variable information for each record.

T F 5. To print the current date each time the form file is merged with the table data file, select the **Date** button on the Merge Feature bar.

6. The _____ option in the Perform Merge options dialog box omits a blank line that results from an empty data file field.
   a. Leave Blank Line
   b. Remove Blank Line
   c. Hide Codes
   d. none of these

7. The form file contains the letter text, ___________, spacing, and any other information that remains the same in each letter.
   a. filenames
   b. data file
   c. field names
   d. both a and b

8. An example of variable information is _____.
   a. a company name
   b. an acct #
   c. a street address
   d. all of these

9. State the difference between a record and a field.

10. List one reason why the Date button on the Merge Feature Bar is used when creating a form file.

Enriching Language Arts Skills

Spelling/Vocabulary Words

confirmation the act of validating; establishing accuracy.

prime rate the interest rate that banks use when loaning money to corporations.

virtually just about; almost.

Nonrestrictive Clause

A nonrestrictive clause is a clause that is not essential to the meaning of the sentence and is, therefore, set off by a comma or commas.

Examples:

We will meet Tuesday at 1:30 for our monthly sales meeting, which was postponed last month.

Jim Clemens, who has good English and computer skills, can obtain well-paying jobs.

Activities

Activity 11.1—Create a Data File and Form File and Merge

1. Use the following information to create a table data file.
   a. Select **Tools, Merge**; select **Place Records in a Table**; select **Data.**
   b. Type each of the following field names and press **Enter** after each field name: **name, address, city, state, zip, salutation, child's name,** and **birthdate.**
   c. Select **OK.**
   d. Type the data for each record using the following information.
   Hint: *Remember to select **New Record** to obtain empty field name boxes. After entering the data for the last record, select **Close.***

Mr. and Mrs. Bob Otis	Ms. Carol A. Weber	Philip and Dawn Celaya
38 Nicholson Ave.	280 Winton Ave., #6	4806 Mission St.
San Leandro	Hayward	Fremont
CA	CA	CA
94577	94545	94539
Mr. and Mrs. Otis	Ms. Weber	Philip and Dawn
Benjamin	Christine	Ernest
May 8	May 10	May 5

2. Select **Yes** to save the changes to disk; use the filename **11act1.dat.**
3. Select the **Go to Form** button on the Merge Feature bar.
4. Select **Create** in the Associate dialog box.
5. Use the following information to create a form file.
   a. Change the top margin to **1.75"**; change the left and right margins to **1.5"**.
   b. Insert the date (select the **Date** button on the Merge Feature Bar). Press the **Enter** key five times.
   c. To insert field codes, select the **Insert Field** button on the Merge Feature Bar. Double-click on the desired field names. Type the following form letter and insert field codes where shown.

(DATE)

FIELD(name)
FIELD(address)
FIELD(city), **FIELD**(state) **FIELD**(zip)

Dear **FIELD**(salutation):

I have read with interest the recent article in the newspaper about the birth of **FIELD**(child's name) on **FIELD**(birthdate) and extend to you my warmest best wishes and congratulations.

I would like to take this opportunity to join your family and friends in wishing you and **FIELD**(child's name) the best of health and much personal happiness in the years ahead.

If my office can be of service to you at any time, please contact me or my staff.

Sincerely,

Raymond T. Fletcher
Senator, 12th District

RTF/xx

6. Save the form file; use the filename **11act1.frm**.
7. Select the **Close** button in the Insert Field Name or Number dialog box.
8. Select the **Merge** button in the Merge Feature Bar; select the **Merge** button in the Merge dialog box.
9. If necessary, type or select the Form File or Data File name(s) needed in the Perform Merge dialog box; select **OK**.
10. Print one copy of each merged letter.
11. Optional. Save the file of merged letters; use the filename **11act1.mer**.
12. Close all documents (select **File, Close** until a clear document window displays).

Activity 11.2—Create Data/Form Files and Merge; Edit and Mark Specific Records to Print

1. Use the following information to create a table data file.
    a. Select **Tools, Merge**; select **Place Records in a Table**; select **Data**.
    b. Type each of the following field names and press **Enter** after each field name: **first/mid**, **last**, **address**, **city**, **state**, **zip**, **title**, and **amount**.

c. Select **OK.**

d. Type the data for each record using the following information.

*Hint: Remember to select **New Record** to obtain empty field name boxes. After entering the data for the last record, select **Close**.*

Wanda B.	Lawrence	Ali R.
Chung	Aames	Ignacio
82 Main St., Apt. 16	6200 Baker Pl.	38 Sixth St.
Mesa	Seattle	Tenafly
AZ	WA	NJ
85201	98102	07670
Ms.	Mr.	Mr.
$5,000	$6,000	$6,000

2. Select **Yes** to save the changes to disk; use the filename **11act2.dat**.
3. Select the **Go to Form** button on the Merge Feature bar.
4. Select **Create** in the Associate dialog box.
5. Use the following information to create a form file.
   a. Change the left, right, and top margins to **1.5"**.
   b. Insert the date (select the **Date** button on the Merge Feature bar). Press the **Enter** key five times.
   c. To insert field codes, select the **Insert Field** button on the Merge Feature bar. Double-click on the desired field names. Type the following form letter and insert field codes where shown.

(DATE)

FIELD(first/mid) **FIELD**(last)
FIELD(address)
FIELD(city), **FIELD**(state) **FIELD**(zip)

Dear **FIELD**(title) **FIELD**(last):

Your UniCard credit line has been increased to **FIELD**(amount). You are a valued card member and because of your outstanding payment record, you have earned this additional purchasing power.

Your satisfaction with your UniCard is our highest priority. To help you get the most from your UniCard, our professional Customer Service representatives are available toll-free 24 hours a day to assist you and provide information about our exclusive card member services.

We appreciate the opportunity to serve you.

Sincerely,

Ginger T. Adams
President & CEO

GTA/xx

---

6. Save the form file; use the filename **11act2.frm**.
7. Select the **Close** button in the Insert Field Name or Number dialog box.
8. Select the **Merge** button on the Merge Feature bar, select the **Merge** button in the Merge dialog box.
9. If necessary, type or select the Form File or Data File name(s) needed in the Perform Merge dialog box; select **OK**.
10. Print one copy of each merged letter.
11. Optional. Save the file of merged letters; use the filename **11act2.mer**.
12. Close the file containing the merged letters.
13. To edit the data file, use the following information:
    a. To display the data file named **11act2.dat**, select the **Go to Data** button on the Merge Feature Bar.
    b. Change Wanda Chung's last name to Davis.
    c. Change the amount in Ali Ignacio's record to $7,000.
    d. Add a new record (place the insertion point in any cell of the last row, select the **Quick Entry** button on the Merge Feature Bar; select **New Record**. Type the new record information: **Keith J., Castro, 2390 New York Ave., Whiting, IN, 46394, Mr., $5,000**. Select **Close**.
    e. Save the edited table data file to disk using the same filename, **11act2.dat** (select **Yes**, **OK**, **Yes**).
14. Use the following information to view the records by field name and mark data records to be merged.
    a. Select the **Merge** button on the Merge Feature bar; select **Merge**.
    b. Check that the form file filename **11act2.frm** and the data file filename **11act2.dat** display in the Form File and Data File boxes of the Perform Merge dialog box.
    c. Choose the **Select Record** option.
    d. Select **Mark Records**.
    e. In the Record List, select **Keith Castro** and **Ali Ignacio**.
    f. Select **OK**.

g. Select **OK**.

   Note: *Only the letters to Keith Castro and Ali Ignacio display.*

h. Print one copy of the merged letters.

   Note: *It is not necessary to save the merged letters for Keith Castro and Ali Ignacio.*

15. Close all documents (select **File**, **Close** until a clear document window displays).

Activity 11.3—Create and Merge a Form File and Data File with Blank Fields; Edit the Form File and Data File and Merge

1. Use the following information to create a table data file.

   a. Select **Tools, Merge;** select **Place Records in a Table**; select **Data**.

   b. Type each of the following field names and press **Enter** after each field name: **first**, **last**, **company**, **address**, **city**, **state**, **zip**, **title**, **vendor**, **date**, and **amount**.

   c. Select **OK**.

   d. Type the data for each record using the following information.

   Hint: *Remember to select **New Record** to obtain empty field name boxes. After entering the data for the last record, select **Close**.*

Roy E.	Sharon	D. L.
Dunhill	Gaffney	Ibbaro
	McClure's Carpets	
6309 Clemens Ave.	7600 Third St.	2 S. Tenth Ave.
Ft. Lauderdale	Raleigh	Jacksonville
FL	NC	FL
36092	39016	33125
Mr.	Ms.	Mr.
Casual Foods	Timberline Associates	Abbey Shoes
October 25, 1994	December 31, 1994	November 20, 1994
15,000	8,000	12,000

2. Select **Yes** to save the changes to disk; use the filename **11act3.dat**.
3. Select the **Go to Form** button on the Merge Feature Bar.
4. Select **Create** in the Associate dialog box.
5. Use the following to create a form file.

   a. Change the left and right margins to **1.5**"; change the top margin to **2**".

   b. Insert the date (select the **Date** button on the Merge Feature Bar). Press the **Enter** key five times.

   c. To insert field codes, select the **Insert Field** button on the Merge Feature bar. Double-click on the desired field names. Type the following form letter and insert field codes where shown.

(DATE)

FIELD(first) **FIELD**(last)
FIELD(company)
FIELD(address)
FIELD(city), **FIELD**(state) **FIELD**(zip)

Dear **FIELD**(title) **FIELD**(last):

It is a pleasure to answer your recent letter requesting current information about **FIELD**(vendor). Credit was extended to **FIELD**(vendor) on **FIELD**(date),with a limit of $**FIELD**(amount).

Their invoices have always been paid promptly, many times taking advantage of the cash discount.

This information is to be held in strict confidence. We are glad to be of service to you. If you have any further questions, please do not hesitate to contact us.

Sincerely,

T. W. Loyden
Credit Division Manager

TWL/xx

---

6. Save the form file; use the filename **11act3.frm**.
7. Select the **Close** button in the Insert Field Name or Number dialog box.
8. Select the **Merge** button on the Merge Feature bar, select **Merge**.
9. If necessary, type or select the Form File or Data File names(s) needed in the Perform Merge Dialog box.
10. Select **Options**, check that Remove Blank Line displays. If necessary, press and hold the mouse button and drag to highlight **Remove Blank Line**. Release the mouse button. Select **OK**.
11. Select **OK** to Perform Merge.
12. Print one copy of each merged letter.
13. Optional. Save the file of merged letters; use the filename **11act3.mer**.
14. Close the file containing the merged letters.
15. To edit the data file, use the following information:
    a. To display the data file named **11act3.dat**, select the **Go to Data** button on the Merge Feature Bar.

b. Change D. L. Ibbaro's initials to **Daniel Louis.**

c. Add the company name **Foodland, Inc.** to Roy E. Dunhill's record.

d. Delete the column that contains dollar amounts (place the insertion point in the desired column, select **Table, Delete,** select **Columns, OK).**

e. Save the edited data file using the same filename, **11act3.dat.**

16. To edit the form file, use the following information:

a. To display the form file named**11act3.frm**, select the **Go to Form** button on the Merge Feature Bar.

b. Delete **FIELD(amount)** and replace with **14,000.**

c. Save the file using the same filename, **11act3.frm.**

17. Merge **11act3.frm** with **11act3.dat.** (If necessary, see steps 8, 9, and 11 for specific instructions.)

18. Print one copy of each merged letter.

19. Optional. Save the file of merged letters; use the filename **11act3.me2.** Close all documents.

Challenge Your Skills

Skill 11.1—Create, Merge, and Edit a Form File and Data File; Mark Specific Data Records to Print

1. Use the following information to create a table data file.

a. The field names for the table data file are: first, last, address, city, state, zip, title, date, and amounts

b. The information for each record follows:

Lowell S.	Sharlene	Rudolph P.
Grizoffi	Kelterman	Lehman
72 Cobbs Creek Circle	572 Tiyunga Blvd.	1370 North Avenue
New Gloucester	North Hollywood	Miami
ME	CA	FL
04260	91600	33139
Mr.	Ms.	Mr.
October 24, 199x	November 5, 199x	September 12, 199x
$15,000, $40,000, or $65,000	$25,000, $60,000, or $100,000	$10,000, $25,000, or $50,000

2. Save the tabe data file; use the filename **11skill1.dat.**

3. Create the following form file. Make decisions regarding:

Margins
Justification
Fonts
Tab settings for indention of enumerated items

(DATE)

FIELD(first) **FIELD**(last)
FIELD(address)
FIELD(city), **FIELD**(state) **FIELD**(zip)

Dear **FIELD**(title) **FIELD**(last):

Thank you for your request for information on our special group term life plans. A brochure describing the special group life plans and an application for coverage are enclosed. In order for you to be eligible for the special group life rates, the enclosed application must be received by **FIELD**(date). After that date, this special group plan will no longer be available.

Based on your age, there are three amounts of group term life insurance that you can apply for--**FIELD**(amounts). With the special group plan, you are guaranteed:

1. **No medical exam.** A medical exam is not automatically required--your insurability can usually be determined based on the information in your application.

2. **Personal rate protection.** Once your application has been accepted, the only time your rates will change is when you move into a different age group.

3. **Credit card convenience.** Your monthly premiums can be conveniently billed to your UniCard account. You will never have to worry about paying the premium on time.

Please fill out, sign, and return the enclosed application in the postage-paid envelope. Remember, the signed application must be received in our office by **FIELD**(date).

Sincerely,

Marshall K. Piazzola
Executive Vice President

MKP/xx

Enc.

4. Save the form file; use the filename **11skill1.frm**.
5. Merge **11skill1.frm** with **11skill1.dat**.
6. Print one copy of each merged letter.
7. Optional. Save the file of merged letters; use the filename **11skill1.mer**.
8. Edit the table data file using the following information:
   a. Delete the **amounts** field column.

b. Use the following information to add two new records to the table data file named **11skill1.dat:**

Peter N.	Art
Hurtado	Mansano
1469 Wilshire Blvd.	887 Hardow Drive
Los Angeles	Las Vegas
CA	NV
90023	89106
Mr.	Mr.
November 2, 199x	October 1, 199x

c. Save the changed table data file.

9. Edit the form file using the following information:

   a. Delete the first sentence of the second paragraph that begins "Based on . . ."

   b. Delete the last sentence in the last paragraph that begins "Remember . . ."

   c. Save the changed form file.

10. Mark and merge the two new records.

11. Print a copy of the two new merged letters and close all documents.

Skill 11.2—Create and Merge a Form File and Data File with Blank Fields; Language Arts

1. Use the following information to create a table data file.

   a. The field names for the data file are: title, first, lastname, address1, address2, city, state, zip, name, and amount

   b. The information for each record follows:

Mr.	Ms.	Mr.	Mrs.
Yohannes	Paige	Joseph R.	June A.
Wohlenberg	Ybarra	Nevitt	Penning
Gardenwood Terrace			Shore Apartments
36 Hill Rd., #16	2606 Auburn Way	313 36th St.	28 Addison Way, #6
York	Weatherford	Arlington	Springfield
PA	TX	VA	NJ
17403	76087	22203	07081
Yohannes	Paige	Joseph	June
5,000	7,000	6,000	5,000

2. Save the table data file; use the filename **11skill2.dat**.

3. Create the following form file. Make decisions regarding:

   Margins
   Justification
   Fonts
   Reference initials, document identification, and enclosure notation

4. Correct three spelling errors, two misused words, and two punctuation errors.

(DATE)

FIELD(title) **FIELD**(first) **FIELD**(lastname)
FIELD(address1)
FIELD(address2)
FIELD(city), **FIELD**(state) **FIELD**(zip)

Dear **FIELD**(title) **FIELD**(lastname):

First things first, **FIELD**(name). You can receive a credit card that is free forever.

You have been pre-approved to receive a Continental Omni card with a credit line of $**FIELD**(amount). All you need to do is use the card at least once a year and its yours--free from annual fees for life. Simply apply by the expiration date on the enclosed confirmation card.

That's not the only savings you will receive. You can save on interest, to. Ninety million people are currently paying 16% or more in credit card interest. The Continental Omni card offers a variable Annual Percentage Rate that is only 15.4% (prime rate plus 9.4%). And if the prim rate drops, your interest rate drops, too.

Your Continental Omni card which includes your picture, is accepted worldwide. So you can shop, dine, travel and make calls--with one card. You will also have the only Omni card that comes with the TWT Customer Service network. You can reach us anytime--24 hours a day, 365 days a year--from virtualy anywhere. And you will receive the responsive, personal service you would expect from TWT.

The fastest way to receive your card is to call 1-800-555-8222 or complete and return the enclosed confirnation card in the postage-paid envelope provided.

Sincerely,

Rachael G. Hunsberger
President

---

5. Save the form file; use the filename **11skill2.frm**.
6. Merge **11skill2.frm** with **11skill2.dat**.

   ***Hint:** Remember to use the **Remove Blank Line** option.*
7. Print one copy of each merged letter.
8. Optional. Save the file of merged letters; use the filename **11skill2.mer**.
9. If you have completed your work, exit WordPerfect.

CHAPTER 12

Create and Print Mailing Labels

Features Covered

- Create an envelope address
- Create an envelope definition
- Create mailing labels
- Sort records in a table data file

Objectives and Introduction

After successfully completing this chapter, you will be able to create envelope addresses, an envelope definition, and mailing labels using predefined labels. In addition, you will be able to sort records in a table data file.

Once a form file is merged with a data file, envelope addresses or mailing labels can be created for each document. Using existing data file addresses or letter addresses to create envelope addresses or mailing labels can assist in expediting the process of setting up and printing addresses on envelopes or labels.

Create Envelope Addresses

Envelope addresses are easily created by selecting the **Envelope** button on the WordPerfect Button Bar or by using the **Layout**, **Envelope** command. WordPerfect reviews the file in the current document screen and automatically identifies the address information.

Once WordPerfect has identified the address information, the Envelope dialog box displays (see Figure 12.1). The address information displays in the Mailing Addresses box. If WordPerfect has incorrectly identified the address information, the correct address can be typed. If no address information is found in the current file, the Mailing Addresses box of the Envelope dialog box will be empty.

A previously typed return address may display in the Return Addresses box. Return or mailing addresses can be typed and added to a list of addresses. The list of return or mailing addresses is displayed by selecting the down arrow below the Return/Mailing Addresses option boxes. Also, the font for the return or mailing addresses can be changed easily by selecting the **Font** button located below the Return/Mailing Addresses option boxes. If an X displays in the Print Return Address option box, the return address displays in the Return Addresses option box and in the sample envelope, which displays at the bottom of the Envelope dialog box. The return address will print when the mailing address is printed. If no X displays in the Print Return Address option box, no return address displays in either the Return Addresses option box or the sample envelope, and the return address will not print.

The U.S. Postal Service requests that mailing addresses be typed with vertical line spacing of one and no italic text or indented lines. For a large No. 10 envelope, the address is placed approximately 2 to 2½ inches from the top edge and 4 to 4½ inches from the left edge of the envelope. For many years, the Postal Service preferred addresses to be typed in all uppercase letters with no punctuation; however, the main concern of the Postal Service now is that the typed address be placed in an area easily read by OCR (optical character recognition) equipment. OCR equipment scans addresses electronically and sorts mail quickly, thus expediting the mail service. WordPerfect automatically prints the envelope address in the appropriate location.

Using uppercase letters and no punctuation or using lowercase letters with initial capitals and punctuation are now both considered acceptable forms for mailing addresses. Typing mailing labels in uppercase letters with no punctuation is recommended, however, because it is more efficient to type characters in one case and keystrokes are saved when punctuation is omitted.

The position of the return or mailing addresses can be changed by selecting the **Options** button in the Envelope dialog box. If desired, the horizontal and/or vertical position can be adjusted. WordPerfect also has the capability of creating the USPS bar code for any zip code. (The USPS bar code is used by the U.S. Postal Service to expedite the routing of mail.) The **Options** button in the Envelope dialog box is chosen to display the Envelope Options dialog box. The three USPS Bar Code options are: **None**, **Include and Position Above Address**, and **Include and Position Below Address.**

Start-Up Instructions

- Open the file named **12drill1.ltr** located on the data disk.

Steps to Create an Envelope Address

1. With the insertion point located at any position in the letter, select the Envelope button on the WordPerfect Button Bar {Alt, L, v}.

   Note: The Envelope dialog box displays (see Figure 12.1). Check that the address for the letter displays in the Mailing Addresses box. If a return address was typed at a prior time, the return address may also display in the Return Addresses box. If a letter address is not displayed, click in the Mailing Addresses box and type the desired address.

2. Click in the **Return Addresses** box {r}.
3. Type the desired return address.

   For example, type your name and return address information.

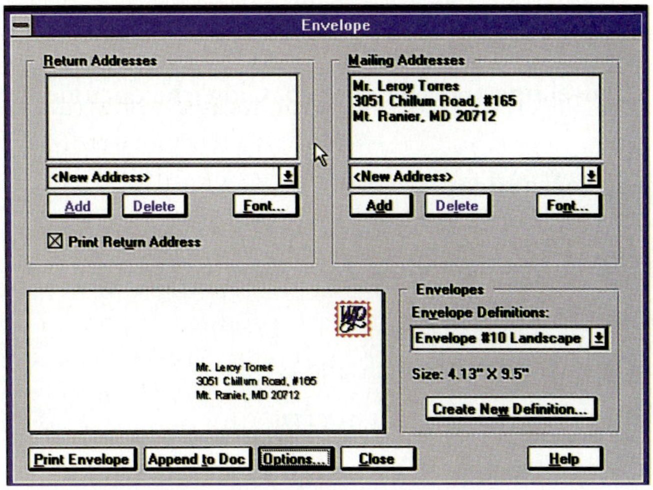

FIGURE 12.1

WordPerfect Envelope dialog box

Note: If a return address displays that is not your address, select all lines of the address and then type your address.

4. Select the **Options** button at the bottom of the Envelope dialog box {Alt and o}.

   Note: The Envelope Options dialog box displays.

5. Select the desired USPS Bar Code option. Select **OK** to return to the Envelope dialog box

   For example, in the USPS Bar Code Options area, check that Include and Position Below Address is selected. If necessary, select **Include and Position Below Address**. Select **OK**.

6. Check that an Envelope Definition displays. If necessary, select **Envelope Definitions**, click on the down arrow at the right of the Envelope Definition box, and click once on the desired envelope definition {Alt and v, press the up and down arrows until the desired envelope is highlighted}.

   For example, if necessary, check with your instructor for an envelope definition or make a selection of your own .

7. Select **Append to Document** {Alt and t}.

   *Note: The envelope information is placed (appended) at the end of the letter after a page break. To view the letter and the envelope, press **Ctrl** and **Home** to locate the insertion point on page one of the file and select **View, Two Page**. Select **View, Page** to return to the normal view.*

To Print an Envelope

8. The insertion point should be located on the page containing the envelope address and bar code.

9. Select the **Print** button {Alt, f, p *or* F5}.

10. Select **Current Page** {u}.

11. Select **Print** {Enter}.

    Note: The printer pauses, allowing an envelope to be inserted in the printer or paper tray. Use of plain paper is OK for this practice activity. The address prints on the paper in the appropriate area.

Finish-Up Instructions

- Use the *new* filename **12envel.ope** and save the file. Close the document.

Steps to Create a New Envelope Definition

Note: The following steps are for your information and use if needed.

1. Select the **Envelope** button {Alt, L, v}.
2. Select the **Create New Definition** button {Alt and w}.

   Note: The Create Envelope definition dialog box displays.
3. In the Paper Name box, type a descriptive name for the new envelope.
4. Check that **Envelope** displays in the Paper Type box.
5. In the Size box, click on the down triangle to display the current envelope definitions. Scroll down the list of envelope definitions and click on User Defined Size {Alt and s, press the down arrow key to display User Defined Size or other}.
6. Type the dimensions of the new envelope in the boxes below the Size box, e.g., 6.5 by 3.5.
7. In the Paper Location area, check that the desired paper location is displayed. If necessary, click on the down arrow to the right of the Location box and click on the correct paper location.
8. Select the desired **Orientation** option {Alt and f}.
9. Select **OK** {Enter}.
10. If desired, select **Print Envelope** {Alt and p} or select **Close** {Alt and c}.

Mailing Labels

Mailing labels are short forms on which names and addresses are printed. Mailing labels come in various sizes. Two commonly used sizes are 4 by 1⅓ inch and 2⅝ by 1 inch. Generally, the labels are self-adhered to backing paper that is 11 inches in length. The self-adhesive mailing label is removed from the backing paper and placed on an envelope.

The mailing labels are usually designed with one, two, or three columns per page. Preferably the address is printed two to three spaces from the left edge of the form and starts on the second or third line.

Create Mailing Labels Using Predefined Labels

WordPerfect provides predefined label formats to create mailing labels, for example, label size, number of labels per page, etc. The format for many common Avery and 3M labels can be selected from the Labels dialog box (see Figure 12.2).

Once the mailing label format is chosen, the mailing labels are created by typing the recipient's address information followed by a hard page break. In the Page view, the typed labels display in the document window in the same format as the labels will print. The **Page Zoom Full** button can also be used to view the layout of the mailing labels on the page. If a laser printer is selected, the mailing labels will appear with a dotted horizontal line placed between each row of labels. With a dot matrix (tractor feed) printer, each row of labels will appear with a light and dark line between each row.

Based on the label and font chosen, WordPerfect determines the number of lines available on each label. If the typed lines reach the last available line of the label, the insertion point moves automatically to the top line of the next label when the **Enter** key is pressed.

Mailing labels can also be created by using the Merge feature (see Chapter 11). The data file used to create form letters can be merged with a new form file that has been formatted using a predefined label format to create mailing labels.

Start-Up Instructions

❖ The Page view mode should be selected. If necessary, select **View**, **Page**.

Steps to Create Mailing Labels Using a Predefined Label

1. Select **Layout, Labels** {Alt, L, b}.

   Note: The Labels dialog box displays (see Figure 12.2).

2. Check that **Both** is selected; scroll down the list of labels until the desired label name is displayed; double-click on the desired name {press the down arrow key repeatedly until the desired label name is highlighted}.

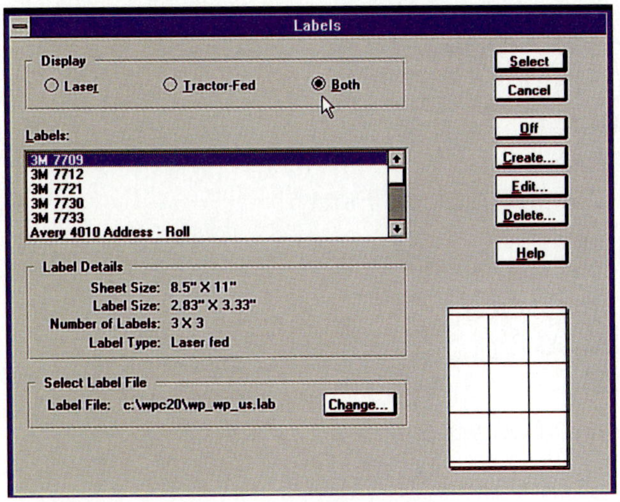

FIGURE 12.2

Labels dialog box

FIGURE 12.3

Label for in the document window

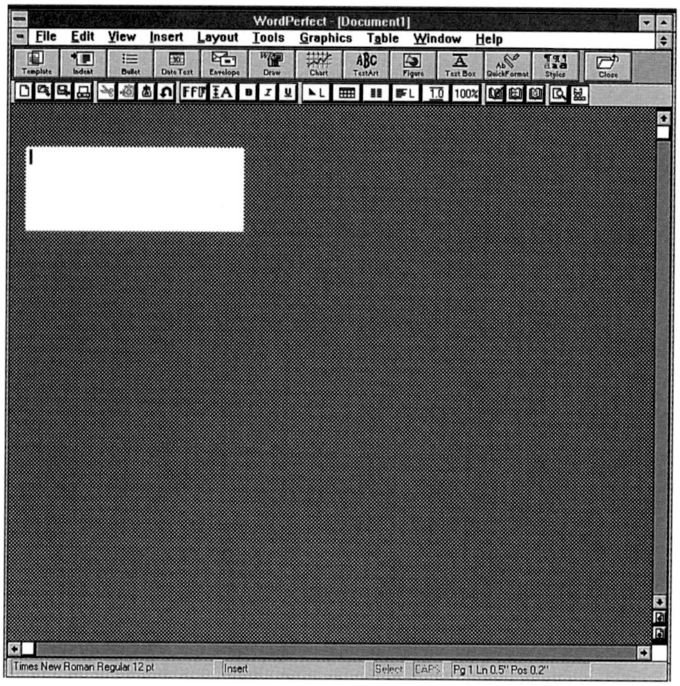

For example, *if using a dot matrix printer,* double-click on **Avery 4144 Address**. *If using a laser printer,* double-click on **Avery 5260 Address**.

3. Choose Select {Enter}.

   Note: *The first label form displays in the document window (see Figure 12.3).*

4. Type the label information.

   For example, type the following label:

   NORA MARIE MURRAY
   220 N BOSWORTH APT 7
   CHICAGO IL 60613 {press **Ctrl** and **Enter**}.

5. Repeat step 4 to type the remaining labels.

   For example, type the following labels:

   STACEY L NAGATA
   P O BOX 543
   PLATTSBURG NY 12901 {press **Ctrl** and **Enter**}.

   RICHARD MCDANIEL
   MCDANIEL'S GARAGE
   1050 BRANHAM LANE
   SAN JOSE CA 95123 {press **Ctrl** and **Enter**}.

   LAUREL T KIRK
   NATIONAL TECHNOLOGY
   TWO INDUSTRIAL AVE
   LOWELL MA 01851

Note: *It is not necessary to press* ***Ctrl*** *and* ***Enter*** *after the last zip code.*

Finish-Up Instructions

- Use the filename **12drill2.lab** and save the file.
- Select the **Page Zoom Full** button to display the labels on a full page.
- Print one copy (using plain paper is OK).

  Note: *The printer may pause waiting for mailing labels to be manually placed in the tray. If necessary, press the printer button to activate the printer.*
- Close the document.

Create Mailing Labels Using a Form File and Data File

Mailing labels can be easily created using existing form file and data file. The inside address field names are copied to a new file from an existing form file (see Figure 12.4). A new document screen is obtained, the copied inside address field names are pasted, and a label definition is inserted. The new label form file is saved. A new document screen is obtained, and the new label form file is merged with an existing data file.

The Sort feature can be used to arrange the data file records in an assigned order. For example, the mailing label records can be presorted by zip codes in order to receive discounts on mail rates. To use the Sort feature, determine which field is to be used to sort the records. When sorting a data file, the number of the column is used to determine the number of the Sort field. After determining the column number of the Sort field, **Tools**, **Sort** is selected and the sort criteria are specified (see Figure 12.5). The Sort feature is discussed further in Chapter 15.

To obtain the sorted mailing labels, save the sorted data file and merge with the desired form file. Labels can be viewed in the chosen label format either in Page view or by selecting the **Page Zoom Full** button.

Start-Up Instructions

- The files named **11drill1.frm** and **11drill1.dat** created in Chapter 11 must be available.

Steps to Create Mailing Labels Using an Existing Form File and Data File

1. Open the form file that contains the inside address field names.

   For example, open **11drill1.frm.**
2. Select the inside address field names (see Figure 12.4) and click once on the Copy button {Alt, e, c *or* Ctrl and c}.
3. Select the New Document button to obtain a new document screen {Alt, f, n}.
4. Select the Paste button to insert the copied inside address field names {Alt, e, p *or* Ctrl and v}.

FIGURE 12.4

Field names selected in a form file

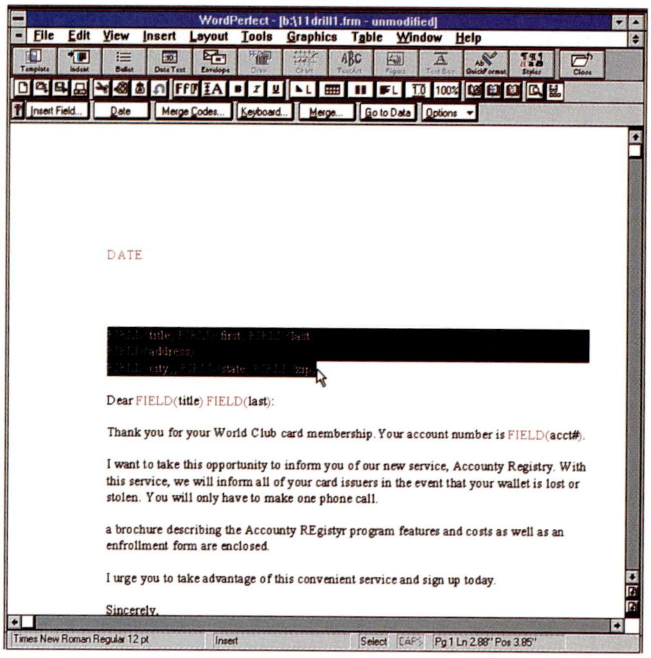

5. Use the following information and repeat steps 1–3 in the Steps to Create Mailing Labels Using a Predefined Label on pages 281–282.

   a. If using a dot matrix printer, select **3M 7721** label.

   b. If using a laser printer, select **Avery 5161 Address** label.

   Note: The field names display in the label outline.

6. Save the new label form file.

   For example, use the filename **12drill3.frm** and save the form file.

Start-Up Instructions

❖ The label form file named **12drill3.frm** and the data file named **11drill1.dat** must be available.

Steps to Sort the Records in a Data File

1. Open the data file that contains the records to be sorted.

   For example, open the file named **11drill1.dat.**

2. Determine the number of the column that will be used to sort records.

   For example, zip is column number 7.

   Note: The insertion point can be located in any table cell.

3. Select **Tools, Sort** {Alt, t, r *or* Alt and F9}.

   Note: The Sort dialog box displays.

4. In the Sort By box, check that Table Row is selected.

5. Select the desired type, i.e., **Alpha** or **Numeric** {Tab four times, n or a}.

   For example, point to the Type box, press and hold the mouse button and drag to highlight **Numeric**; release the mouse button.

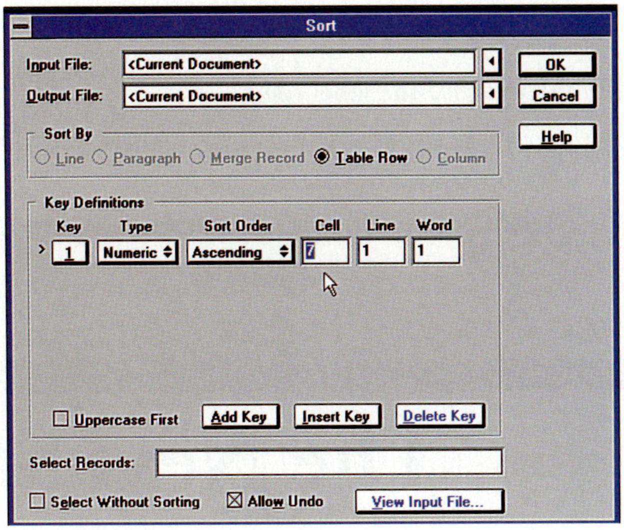

FIGURE 12.5

Sort dialog box with sort criteria

6. Select the desired sort order, i.e., **Ascending** or **Descending** {Tab to highlight the Sort Order box, a or d}.

   For example, check that **Ascending** is selected. If necessary, point to the Sort Order box, press and hold the mouse button and drag to highlight **Ascending**; release the mouse button.

7. Select **Cell** and type the number of the column to be used for sorting records {Tab to highlight the Cell box, type column number}.

   For example, select **Cell** and type 7.

   Note: Your Sort dialog box should look similar to the one shown in Figure 12.5.

8. Select **OK** {Enter}.

   Note: A Sort Status box displays briefly.

9. Save the sorted data file.

   For example, use the filename **12drill3.dat** and save the file.

Merge a Label Form File and Sorted Data File

10. Select the **Merge** button on the Merge Feature Bar {Alt, t, e *or* Shift and F9}.

    Note: The Merge dialog box displays.

11. Select **Merge** {Alt and m}.

12. Type or select the name of the label form file.

    For example, type **a:12drill3.frm** or select the left triangle beside the Form File box, choose **Select File**, and double-click on the filename **12drill3.frm**.

13. Check that the correct data file name displays in the Data File box. If necessary, select or type the name of the existing data file.

    For example, if necessary, type **a:12drill3.dat**. (Do not type the final period.)

14. Select **OK** {Enter}.

    Note: The labels display with the insertion point located at the end of last label, and the labels are arranged in ascending order by zip code.

Finish-Up Instructions

- Use the filename **12drill3.lbl** and save the label file.
- Print one copy. If the printer pauses to allow you to insert labels, press the necessary button(s) on the printer to begin printing. (Plain paper is OK.)
- Close all documents (select **File**, **Close** until a clear document window displays).

The Next Step

Chapter Review and Activities

Self-Check Quiz

T F 1. Mailing labels are short forms that are self-adhered to backing paper.

T F 2. The inside address field names from an existing form file can be copied and pasted in a new file to begin creating a form file for labels.

T F 3. When typing information in a mailing label using a predefined label, a hard page break (**Ctrl** and **Enter**) is inserted after each recipient's zip code.

T F 4. The letter address must be selected before the **Envelope** button is chosen.

T F 5. The records of a data file can only be sorted by the company name.

6. U.S. Postal Service regulations require that no mailing labels be printed with ___________
   a. line spacing of one.
   b. line spacing of two.
   c. no indented lines.
   d. both a and c.

7. The ____ button in the Envelope dialog box is selected to change the position of the return or mailing addresses.
   a. **Append to Doc**
   b. **Options**
   c. **Font**
   d. **Create New Definition**

8. A standard large business envelope is referred to as a No. ____ envelope.
   a. 6
   b. 8
   c. 10
   d. 12

9. List two of the five options that can be selected in the Return Addresses area of the Envelope dialog box.

10. List the three USPS Bar Codes Options.

Enriching Language Arts Skills

Spelling/Vocabulary Words

warranty a written agreement between a customer and manufacturer guaranteeing that the manufacturer will repair or replace a defective item or part.

components individual parts of an item.

reliable trustworthy; credible; dependable.

Subject-Verb Agreement

Verbs must agree in number with their subject. If a subject is singular (one), use a singular verb; if a subject is plural (more than one), use a plural verb.

Examples:

***Bill** and **Cindy are** co-owners of the condominium.*

*Our **president**, as well as all staff members, **is** looking forward to developing a good relationship with new clients.*

To determine if a subject and verb are in agreement, omit the words between the subject and verb.

Examples:

*The **legs** of the chair **were** damaged.*
*(The **legs were** damaged.)*

***Anna**, together with her two daughters, **is** to arrive on an evening flight.*
*(**Anna is** to arrive on an evening flight.)*

Activities

Activity 12.1—Create Mailing Labels Using Predefined Labels

1. Select **Layout, Labels.**
2. Use the following information to select the desired label.
   a. *If using a dot matrix printer,* highlight the **Avery 4031** label.
   b. *If using a laser printer,* highlight the **Avery 5161** label.
3. Type the following names and addresses in uppercase letters with no punctuation. After each zip code, press **Ctrl** and **Enter** to obtain a hard page break.

MR NEIL LEONARD
4110 WEST 21ST PLACE
CHICAGO IL 60623

MS NICOLE OTTO
6500 E PRENTICE AVE
ENGLEWOOD CO 80171

MR GARTH KAHN
42 OLIVE STREET
ARLINGTON HEIGHTS IL 60005

MRS PAULA LANGENBERG
185 EAST ROCKS ROAD
NORWALK CT 06851

MR BERT ROTCHFORD
P O BOX 595
COLORADO SPRINGS, CO 80901-0595

4. Use the filename **12act1.pre** and save the address labels.
5. Print the address labels.
6. Close the document.

Activity 12.2—Create Mailing Labels Using Existing Form and Data Files

*Note: The files named **11act1.frm** and **11act1.dat** must be completed from Chapter 11, Activity 11.1.*

1. Open the file named **11act1.frm**.
2. Select and copy the inside address field names.
3. Create a new document and paste the inside address information into the new document.
4. Select **Layout**, **Labels**, and use the following information to select the desired label.
   a. *If using a dot matrix printer*, highlight the **Avery 4032** label.
   b. *If using a laser printer*, highlight the **Avery 5161** label.
5. Use the filename **12act2.frm** and save the new label form file.
6. Merge **12act2.frm** with **11act1.dat** to create mailing labels. (Select **Tools**, **Merge**, select **Merge**. Type or select the form file named **a:12act2.frm** in the Form File box. Type or select the data file named **a:11act1.dat** in the Data File box. Select **OK**.)
7. Optional. Use the filename **12act2.lab** and save the mailing labels.
8. Print one copy and close all documents.

Activity 12.3—Create an Envelope Address

1. Type the following letter:

(Use current date)

Mr. Dennis Collins
200 Ramona St.
Yuma, AZ 85364

Dear Mr. Collins:

Recently you received a policy renewal notice. Now is a good time to review your insurance coverage limits and available optional coverages and deductibles.

Give me a call at 555-7007 or stop by the office. I look forward to seeing you.

Sincerely,

Alma Gossett

AG/xxx
collins.ltr/disk5

2. Use the filename **12act3.den** and save the file.
3. Select the **Envelope** button.
4. Check that the recipient's address is correct in the Mailing Addresses dialog box.
5. In the **Return Addresses** box, type your name and address.
6. Select the **Options** button; check that the **Include and Position Below Address** option is selected in the USPS Bar Code Options area.
7. In the Envelope Definition box, select a choice given to your by your instructor or make a selection of your own. (If necessary, select the down arrow to locate the desired envelope definition.)
8. Select **Append to Doc** to place the envelope information at the end of the letter.
9. Optional. Print the envelope.
10. Use the *new* filename **12act3.env** and save the file. Close the document.

Challenge Your Skills

Skill 12.1—Create Three-Column Mailing Labels Using Predefined Labels

1. Use the **Avery 4062** label (dot matrix) or **Avery 5260** label (laser) and create a label file using the information shown below.

GEORGETTE HANSEN PERSONNEL MANAGER 1330 GREENWOOD PLACE LAKEWOOD CO 80226	LAURA RADDING INVERNESS INC 6534 75TH AVE FT COLLINS CO 80525	CHARLES CIMINO PERSONNEL DIRECTOR S & T SYSTEMS P O BOX 229 LAKE CITY FL 32056
DONG PHOUNG NGUYEN VICE PRESIDENT MICROCOMPUTER INC 460 UNIVERSITY AVE WESTERBURY NY 11590	MORT DEL SECCO P O BOX 7214 NASHVILLE TN 37221	DENNIS SUTTER 1023 POWERS TERRACE MARIETTA GA 30067
AMY R GONSALVES BUDGET DIRECTOR WESTERN SALES INC 445 S GRAND AVE LOS ANGELES CA 90071	RHONDA PLUMMER 160-20 91ST STREET HOWARD BEACH NY 11414	GARY ALMANZA 55 MARSHALL STREET ST PAUL MN 55102
DALE R ENGLEMAN P O BOX 502 HATTIESBURG MS 39401	SHANNON ANN TUNG 4030 PERSHALL DR #6B ST LOUIS MO 63131	DELOIS W TRUONG DWT INC P O BOX 60 LINCOLN NE 68588

2. Use the filename **12skill1.ave** and save the file.
3. Print the mailing labels.
4. Close the documents.

Skill 12.2—Create Form and Data Files; Sort and Merge Mailing Labels; Language Arts

1. Read the following information, including the form letter below, and make decisions regarding the number of fields needed and the field names.
2. Create a table data file using the following information. Make a decision regarding a filename for the data file.
   a. Ms. Bonnie Avakian purchased a microwave range on the 15th of last month. The standard warranty will expire three years from the date of

purchase. Ms. Avakian's mailing address is Box 168, Cobleskill, NY, 12043.

b. Joseph L. Brownell, who resides at 310 Concord Street, Apt 8, Bloomfield, MI, 48304, purchased a refrigerator on the 20th of last month. The standard warranty will expire two years from the date of purchase.

c. Russ Atkinson purchased a garbage compactor on the 24th of last month. The standard warranty will expire one year from the date of purchase. Mr. Atkinson resides at 2100 Indian Creek, Hood River, Oregon, 97031.

d. Kip R. Carrillo, who resides at 68 Moorepark Ave., Tuscon, AZ, 85730, purchased a dishwasher on the 29th of last month. The standard warranty will expire three years from the date of purchase.

e. Sort the table data file in ascending order by zip code.

f. Use an appropriate filename; save the data file.

3. Use the traditional block style letter and create the following form file. Make decisions regarding:

   Margins
   Justification
   Fonts
   Reference initials
   Filename for form file

4. Correct three spelling errors, two misused words, and four punctuation/grammatical errors.

DATE

{Inside
address
fields}

Dear {salutation field}:

Congratulations on the purchase of your new Vista {appliance field}. Thank you for placing your confidence in Vista products and service.

Years of Vista experience and quality workmanship has been built into your new {appliance field}, so you can expect many years of excellent performance.

Please take a few minutes to look through the Use and Care manual included with your purchase. It was written to address the questions most frequently asked by our customers about there new appliances. If you have additional service needs or questions we have also listed some phone numbers for your convenient reference.

Of course, the standard warrenty covering your appliance remains in force until {expiration field}. Should service be needed, repairs will cost you absolutely nothing while the warranty are in effect.

When your standard warranty runs out, you can continue protecting your {appliance field} with Vista's "Service Plan Plus". It covers all expenses for replacement parts and labor on repairs to operating componants that fail due to normal use. When you choose our extended service contract, you receive prompt, relieble service from our experienced personal as often as you need it.

We are proud that you are a Vista customer. Thank you again for giving us the opportunity to serve you!

Sincerely,

Trudy J. Carrigan
Director, Service Plan Plus

---

5. Merge the letter form file and data file to create a personalized letter for each customer.
6. Optional. Print the merged letters.
7. Create a form file for labels (you determine an appropriate, predefined label number to be used).
8. Merge the label form file and the data file to create a mailing label for each customer.
9. Optional. Print the mailing labels.
10. If you have completed your work, exit WordPerfect.

Part 3
Checking Your Step

Production Skill Builder Activities
Chapters 9-12

SCANS

Production Activity 3.1—Create Standard Paragraphs and Assemble Personalized Letters

1. Create a document that contains the following standard paragraphs:

Allied Health Plan

Allied Health is an individual practice health maintenance organization (HMO). It provides health care directly to its members through hospitals, physicians, and other health care providers who have entered into agreements with Allied Health and who are located in your community.

Health Care Solutions Plan

Health Care Solutions, a statewide HMO, offers its members access to a comprehensive network of respected medical groups and independent practice associations. It provides a health care delivery system that cares for the individual needs of all members. Chiropractic care and prescription drug coverage are also included.

Ready-Care Health Plan

Ready-Care Health is a fee-for-service plan that contracts with private practice physicians and community hospitals to provide quality care to all members. They work diligently with their doctors to help ensure that members receive consistent, high-quality care. The provider network is currently comprised of over 1,700 highly respected physicians and specialists and 26 community hospitals.

Zion-Care Health Plan

Zion-Care Health is a fee-for-service health plan that allows its members to manage their own health care through the selection of physicians, hospitals, and other specialists. When selecting a physician or hospital provider, Zion-Care provides a higher level of reimbursement when the provider is a member of the Zion-Care physician network. This statewide network includes 270 hospitals, 36,000 physicians, and 30,000 related health professionals.

---

2. Save the standard paragraphs document; use the filename **3pact1.stn.**
3. Use the following information and the standard paragraphs document to create personalized letters for the following individuals:
   a. Ms. Mary Ann Weinstein
      85 Main Street, #4
      University Park, PA 16802
      Ms. Weinstein is interested in HMO plans.
   b. Mr. Irvin H. McCarthy
      P.O. Box 568
      Philadelphia, PA 19104
      Mr. McCarthy is interested in fee-for-service plans.
   c. Kenneth and Judy Chitwood
      2403 State Street
      Philadelphia, PA 19106
      Mr. and Mrs. Chitwood are interested in both the HMO and the fee-for-service plans that offer statewide health coverage.
   d. The letters are from Virginia A. Velasquez, Health Care Broker.
   e. Make decisions regarding:
      Letter style
      Margins
      Justification
      Fonts
      The health care plan descriptions (2 or 3) that should be copied into each letter
      Reference initials/document identification/enclosure notation
      Filename for saving each letter
   f. The body of the letter follows:

      Thank you for contacting Health Care Referral Network regarding health care programs in your area. Based on our conversation, below are brief descriptions of several programs I feel will provide the health care you desire.

      Copy the health care program descriptions that address each individual's interest from the file named **3pact1.stn.**

      Please call me after you have reviewed the enclosed brochures on each of these programs. I will be happy to answer any additional questions you may have and to enroll you and your family in the program that best meets your needs.

4. Print one copy of each letter.
5. Close all documents.

Production Activity 3.2—Create Multiple-Page Report with Footnotes and Page Numbering; Use Thesaurus

1. Open the report with the filename **3pact2.han** located on the data disk.
2. Make decisions regarding:

   Margins
   Vertical line spacing
   Justification
   Fonts
   Widow/Orphan control
   Spacing before and after sideheads
   Bold/underline/capitalization of title and sideheads
   Spacing before, between, and after enumerated items
   Possible replacement words from the Thesaurus for underlined words
   Page numbering using the page number feature or a header
   Page number position on the page

   Note: *If the page number is placed at the top of the page, the page number should be suppressed on the first page.*

3. Create the following footnotes in the document:
   a. Place the first footnote reference after the period in the first sentence in the second paragraph. Footnote text: Tony S. Carr, "Five Hundred Invest in Credit Union," *The Times*, 8 September 1992, sec. B, p. 1.
   b. Place the second footnote reference after the period in the second sentence in the second paragraph. Footnote text: Ibid.
   c. Place the third footnote reference after the period at the end of item number six. Footnote text: Norma H. Ames, "Historical Perspective of Credit Unions," presented at the National Association of Credit Unions Annual Conference, February 8, 1991.
4. Use the *new* filename **3pact2.fin** and save the file.
5. Print one copy.
6. Close the document.

Production Activity 3.3—Create and Merge Form File and Data File; Create Mailing Labels; Sort the Data File

1. Create a table data file using the following information:
   a. The field names are: title, first, mid, last, jr/sr, address1, address2, city, state, zip, employee type, contact name, phone.
   b. The information for each recipient follows.

   Note: *Remember, each record must contain the same number of fields. Be sure to create blank fields where no data are available.*

Mr. Allen H. Nakakura, Sr.
Gardenwood Terrace
703 N. Durant, Apt. 105
Santa Ana, CA 92706
Mr. Nakakura is *an active* employee. The contact name is *Carlos Lang* who can be reached at *555-4004.*

Mr. Rick Mitchell
The Villages Community
20150 Burbank Blvd.
Woodland Hills, CA 91367
Mr. Mitchell is *a retired state* employee. The contact name is *Beth Adams* who can be reached at *555-6730.*

Ms. Edith J. Montero
780 Debra Ave.
Sepulveda, CA 91343
Ms. Montero is *a public agency* employee. The contact name is *John Montalvo* who can be reached at *555-6800.*

Mrs. Rose Marie Xavier
4500 Atlantic Blvd.
Long Beach, CA 90807
Mrs. Xavier is *a public agency* employee. The contact name is *John Montalvo* who can be reached at *555-6800.*

2. Use the filename **3pact3.dt** and save the file.
3. Sort the table data file by zip codes.
4. Use the same filename and save the file again.
5. Create the following letter form file. Make decisions regarding:

   Margins
   Justification
   Fonts
   Bullet type and spacing for bulleted list
   Reference initials/document identification/enclosure notation

---

(Use date code)

FIELD(title) **FIELD**(first) **FIELD**(mid) **FIELD**(last) **FIELD**(jr/sr)
FIELD(address1)
FIELD(address2)
FIELD(city), **FIELD**(state) **FIELD**(zip)

Dear **FIELD**(title) **FIELD**(last):

In response to the excessive premium increase presented by Diablo last month, the SERS (State Employees Retirement System) Board of Directors has elected to freeze new enrollments in the Basic Diablo North/South Health Plans. This freeze applies to active as well as retired state and public agency employees. This freeze does not affect employees and retirees who are currently enrolled in Diablo Health Plans.

The following types of transactions are **not** permitted:

- New enrollments in the basic Diablo Health Plans effective August 1, 199x.

The following types of enrollment transactions **are** permitted:

- New enrollments in a Diablo basic plan effective July 1, 199x, or earlier.
- Enrollment changes in the Diablo Supplement to Medicare plans.
- Additions and deletions of eligible family members.

Refer to your Health Plans booklet for additional information about the state's Health Benefit Program.

As **FIELD**(employee type) employee, please direct your inquiries to your health benefit officer, **FIELD**(contact name), at **FIELD**(phone).

Sincerely,

Catherine L. Hawley
Assistant Executive Officer
Health Benefits Services

---

6. Use the filename **3pact3.frm** and save the file.
7. Merge the letter form file and the data file to create personalized letters.
8. Print one copy of each letter.
9. Create a 2- or 3-column form label file. Select an appropriate label for your printer.

   ***Hint:** Copy the inside address field codes from the letter form file.*
10. Use the filename **3pact3.lab** and save the label form file.
11. Merge the label form file and the data file to create a mailing label for each recipient. Print one copy of the mailing labels.
12. Close the documents.

Production Activity 3.4—Create a Letter and an Envelope; Language Arts

1. Use the traditional block letter style and create the following letter. Make decisions regarding:

   Margins
   Justification
   Fonts
   Date of letter
   Capitalization and punctuation for the letter address
   Salutation
   Text attributes
   Correct four spelling errors, one misused word, and two punctuation/grammatical errors
   Reference initials/document identification/enclosure notation
   Capitalization and punctuation for the letter address

a. Send the letter to Mr. Francisco T. Ayala, who resides at 210 Richneck Road, Williamsburg, VA 23185, and should receive a 15% One-Day Savings Pass. Mr. Ayala's authorization must be received no later than 20 days after the date of the letter.

Dear (provide an appropriate salutation):

Once a year we choose a limited number of people to receive a pre-approved Armstrong Credit Card. You are one of those select people.

Armstrong Credit Card rates are among the lowest in the industry. Our rates are 3.5% above the prrime rate. Our company has instant and reliabel services that is provided through our toll-free number, 24 hours a day, and seven days a week.

To claim your card, simply sign and mail the enclosed Armstrong certificate. Because this offer is a special pramotion, we need your authorization by (supply the date).

With your new card, you will receive excellent service, a low interest rate, and a (supply percent discount) One-Day Savings Pass. Also you will get a free desk-top calculator when you make your first credit purchase.

If you send in your pre-approved certificate today, you no-annual-fee Armstrong Credit Card will be mailed to you within one week.

Sincerely,

Jamila R. Maldonado
Manager, Special Services

---

2. Print the letter.
3. Create and print an envelope for the letter (using a return address is optional).
4. Use a filename of your choice and save the file.
5. Close the document.
6. If you have completed your work, exit WordPerfect.

Part 4
A Step in the Right Direction

Advanced Documents and Features

Chapters 13-16

- Create graphic lines
- Retrieve graphic images
- Position and size graphic images
- Create page borders
- Overlay text with a graphic image
- Use WP Draw
- Mirror (flip) a graphic image
- Contour the flow of text around graphic images
- Create TextArt
- Kerning, word spacing, and letterspacing
- Leading adjustment
- Document initial font
- Append
- Superscripts and subscripts
- Equation Editor
- Sort
- Use macros
- Use QuickFormat
- Format document using styles
- Use ExpressDoc Templates
- Tile, cascade, maximize, minimize, move, and size document windows
- Document summary information
- Use File Options
- QuickList
- Convert files
- Passwords
- Use DOS without exiting WordPerfect
- Insert an existing file into a document on the screen.
- Use QuickMenus
- Use Print Manager

CHAPTER 13

Create a Letterhead, Flier, and Newsletter

Features Covered

- Create graphic lines
- Retrieve graphic images
- Position and size graphic boxes
- Create page borders
- Overlay text with a graphic image
- Use the WP Draw program to edit a graphic image
- Copy graphic images
- Create Text boxes
- Mirror (flip) a graphic image
- Contour the flow of text around a graphic image
- Create TextArt
- Position and size a graphic box using the mouse

Objectives and Introduction

After successfully completing this chapter, you will be able to use horizontal graphic lines to create a letterhead; to retrieve, position, and size graphic images; and to place borders around an entire page in order to create a flier. You will also learn how to overlay text with a graphic image. In addition, you will be able to use the WP Draw program to edit, rotate, and reduce a graphic image and to contour the flow of text around a graphic image.

WordPerfect's graphic features are used to illustrate an idea by means of a picture or to present text or data in an interesting and appealing manner. In addition, horizontal and vertical graphic lines can be used to separate text for a more pleasing appearance and to assist with easier reading.

FIGURE 13.1

Graphic boxes

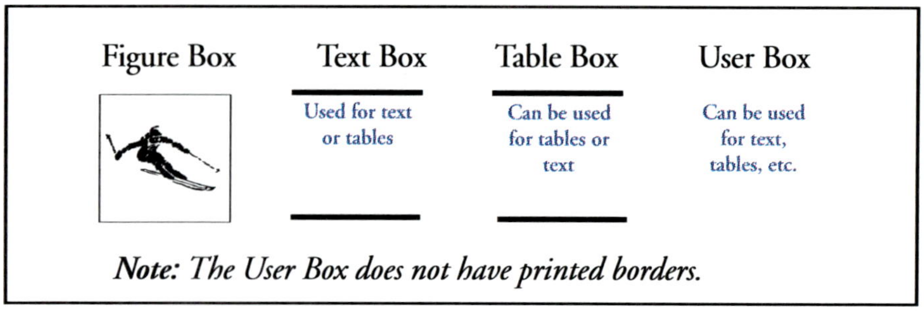

Nine types of graphic boxes are available in WordPerfect: Figure, Text, Table, User, Button, Watermark, Equation, Inline Equation, and OLE. Each type of box is designed for a specific purpose and includes default settings for size, shading, and borders. Figure 13.1 shows samples of the border settings for Figure, Text, Table, and User graphic boxes. Although the predesigned graphic boxes are designated to be used for a specific item, most of the boxes can be used for other contents. For example, Table and User boxes can contain graphics, text, a table, or an equation.

WordPerfect provides 135 graphic images that can be retrieved into a document. When a graphic image is retrieved, WordPerfect automatically places the graphic image in a Figure box. In addition to the graphic images provided by WordPerfect, graphic files created using many other graphic programs can also be retrieved into WordPerfect documents. Graphic images from other graphic programs must be saved in a format that can be interpreted by WordPerfect, such as PCX (PC Paintbrush) or PIC (Lotus 1-2-3).

Create a Letterhead with Graphic Lines

A letterhead can be created using different fonts, point sizes, and borders. Type the text for the letterhead unformatted. Once the letterhead text is typed, the fonts, point sizes, graphic lines, and alignment are selected.

To enhance the appearance of letterhead text, different fonts and point sizes as well as text attributes such as bold and italic can be used. The placement of letterhead text can be changed using the justification options. In addition, horizontal graphic lines can be placed above, below, or around the letterhead text.

Horizontal and vertical graphic lines can be created easily by selecting the **Graphics** menu and choosing the **Horizontal Line** or **Vertical Line** option. The default settings for horizontal and vertical lines is Single, Full, with no space above or below the line. Different styles of lines can be created by selecting the **Custom Line** option on the Graphics menu. When the **Custom Line** option is selected, the Create Graphics Line dialog box displays. The line style, line type (horizontal or vertical), position, length, color, thickness, and additional space above and/or below the line can be specified.

Once a graphic line has been created, the line settings can be edited. Move the mouse pointer to the graphic line and click once to select the line. Black handles display at the ends and center of the graphic line to indicate that the line is selected. The line settings can be changed as follows:

- *To change the length of the selected line,* move the mouse pointer to a black handle at either end of the line until a double-headed arrow displays; press and hold the mouse button and drag left or right to resize the line. Release the mouse button when the desired length is reached.

- *To change the thickness of the line,* move the mouse pointer to either of the black handles in the center of the selected line until a double-headed arrow displays; press and hold the mouse button and drag up or down to increase or decrease the width of the line. Release the mouse button when the desired thickness is reached.

- *To change the line style, line type, color, or spacing above or below the line,* move the mouse pointer to the selected line and double-click to access the Edit Graphics Line dialog box. Make the desired changes and select **OK**.

Start-Up Instructions

❖ Open the file named **13drill1.txt** located on the data disk.

Steps to Create Graphic Lines

1. Place the insertion point at the location where the graphic line should be inserted.

   For example, check that the insertion point is located in the blank line above the company name.

2. Select Graphics, Horizontal Line {Alt, g, h *or* Ctrl and F11}.

   ***Note:** A single horizontal line displays above the company name.*

Create a Horizontal Graphic Line Using the Custom Line Option

3. Place the insertion point at the location where the graphic line should be inserted.

   For example, place the insertion point in the first blank line below the company name.

4. Select Graphics, Custom Line {Alt, g, L}.

   ***Note:** The Create Graphics Line dialog box displays (see Figure 13.2).*

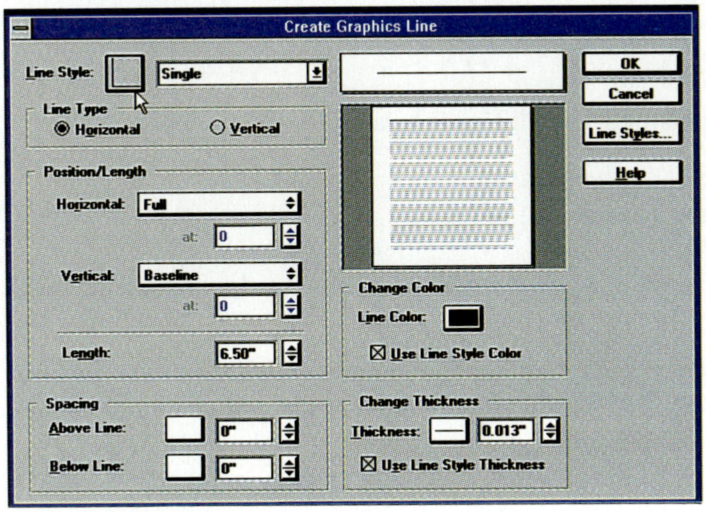

FIGURE 13.2

Create Graphics Lines dialog box

FIGURE 13.3

Sample letterhead with graphic line

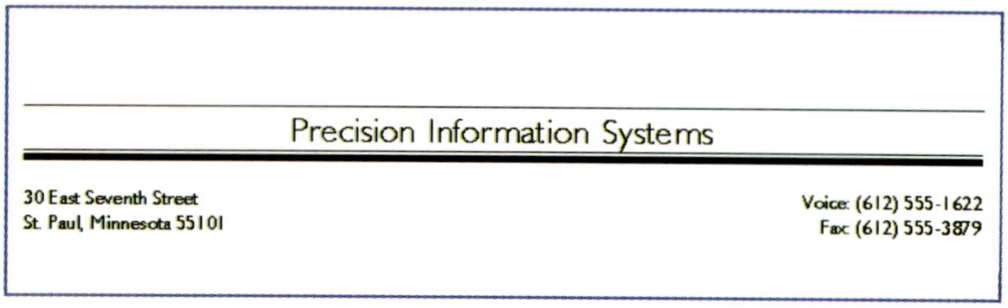
Precision Information Systems

30 East Seventh Street
St. Paul, Minnesota 55101

Voice: (612) 555-1622
Fax: (612) 555-3879

5. Move the mouse pointer to the button to the right of the words "Line Style" and click once to display the Line Style palette {Alt and L, Spacebar}.
6. Move the mouse pointer to the desired line style and click once {press the arrow keys until the desired line style is selected; Enter}.

   For example, move the mouse pointer to the **Thick/Thin 2** line style (fourth line style on the second row) and click once.

   Note: *A sample of the Thick/Thin 2 line displays beside the Line Style box.*
7. Select OK {Enter}.

   Note: *Your letterhead should look similar to Figure 13.3.*

Finish-Up Instructions

- Use *new* the filename **13drill1.lth** and save the file.
- Print one copy and close the document.

Create a Flier with a Graphic Image

Creating a flier in WordPerfect is similar to creating a flier on a typewriter. The flier, however, can include graphic lines, graphic images, and text printed in different font styles and point sizes (see Figure 13.4 on page 306).

Once the flier text is typed, the text is formatted with the desired fonts, point sizes, justification, and appearance. When a graphic image is retrieved, the image is placed in a graphic Figure box. Graphics can be sized or repositioned on the page, the border lines around the graphic Figure box can be removed or changed, and a border can be placed around the entire page.

Start-Up Instructions

- Open the file named **13drill2.wpd** located on the data disk.

Steps to Retrieve a Graphic Image

1. With the insertion point located at the beginning of the document, select the Figure button on the Button Bar {Alt, g, f}.

   Note: *The Insert Image dialog box displays. A list of graphic files with the filename extension .wpg displays. The graphic files are stored in the default WordPerfect graphics directory (e.g., c:\wpwin60\graphics).*

2. Scroll through the list of files and click on the desired filename {Alt and n, Tab, press the down arrow key to highlight the desired filename}.

   For example, click once on **hotair.wpg**.

3. To view the graphic image before retrieving the image into the document, select the View button {Alt and w}.

   Note: *The hot air balloon graphic image displays in the Viewer window.*

4. Select OK to retrieve the selected graphic image {Enter}.

   Note: *The hot air balloon graphic image is placed in a graphic Figure box and displays in the right corner of the document window. A border displays around the graphic Figure box that contains the graphic image. Small black handles (boxes) at the edges and corners of the graphic Figure box indicate that the graphic Figure box is selected. Also, the Graphics Box Feature Bar displays below the Power Bar. If the mouse pointer is located within the graphic box, it displays as a four-headed arrow.*

5. Move the mouse pointer away from the graphic box and click once to deselect the box.

Finish-Up Instructions

- Use the *new* filename **13drill2.fli** and save the file.

Start-Up Instructions

- The file named **13drill2.fli** should be displayed on the screen.
- The Graphics Box Feature Bar should be displayed. If necessary, select **Graphics**, **Edit Box** to display the Graphics Box Feature Bar.

Steps to Position a Graphic Box

1. Move the mouse pointer anywhere in the graphic box and click once to select the box {Alt, g, e}.

   For example, move the mouse pointer anywhere in the graphic Figure box containing the **hotair.wpg** graphic image and click once.

   Note: *Small black handles display at the edges and corners of the box indicating that the graphic box is selected.*

2. Select the Position button the Graphics Box Feature Bar {Alt and Shift and p}.

   Note: *The Box Position dialog box displays.*

3. In the Vertical area of the Position Box dialog box, move the mouse pointer to the box beside the word "Place" and double-click {Alt and a}.

4. Type the desired vertical position for the graphic box.

   For example, type **2.5** to place the graphic figure box 2.5" below the first line of text in the flier.

   Note: *The graphic figure box moves down the page 2.5 inches below the first line of text.*

5. Select OK {Enter}.

FIGURE 13.4

Flier with a graphic image

FIRST ANNUAL
HOT AIR BALLOON RACE
AND COMPETITION

WHERE: Camelback Inn

WHEN: Saturday and Sunday
April 13 and 14

WHAT: Action in the Air

COST: $100 Entry Fee

PRIZES: $1,000 First Place
$500 Second Place
$250 Third Place

ACTIVITIES

20K Air Race

Balloon Design Contest

Balloon Rides

Ballooning Lessons

PROCEEDS WILL BENEFIT THE SCOTTSDALE YOUTH PROGRAM

Remove the Border from a Graphic Box

6. With the graphic box selected, choose the Border/Fill button on the Graphics Box Feature Bar {Alt and Shift and b}.

   Note: The Box Border/Fill Styles dialog box displays.

7. Move the mouse pointer to the button to the right of the words "Border Style" and click once to display the Border Style palette {Alt and b, Spacebar}.

8. Click once on the <NO BORDER> border style to remove the graphic box border {press the arrow keys until <NO BORDER> is selected; Enter}.

   Note: The words "Spacing Only" display in the box to the right of the Border Style button.

9. Select OK {Enter}.

   Note: If desired, scroll down to view the graphic image. The graphic image displays at the new position, and the graphic Figure box border has been removed. If the mouse has not been clicked in the document screen, the small black handles (boxes) remain around the graphic Figure box. Your document should look similar to Figure 13.4.

Finish-Up Instructions

- Move the mouse pointer away from the graphic Figure box and click once to deselect the graphic Figure box.
- Use the same filename, **13drill2.fli**, and save the file.

Start-Up Instructions

- The file named **13drill2.fli** should be displayed in the document window.

Steps to Create a Page Border

1. With the insertion point located at any position on the page, select Layout, Page, Border/Fill {Alt, L, p, b}.
2. Move the mouse pointer to the button to the right of the words "Border Style" and click once to display the Border Style palette {Alt and b, Spacebar}.
3. Move the mouse pointer to the desired border style and click {press the arrow keys until the desired border style is selected; Enter}.

   For example, click once on the second double-line border style on the third row (i.e., Thick Double).

4. Select OK {Enter}.

   Note: *To view the page border, select the* ***Page Zoom Full*** *button. Select the* ***Page Zoom Full*** *button again to return to the normal view.*

Finish-Up Instructions

- Use the *new* filename **13drill2.fin** and save the file.
- Print one copy and close the document.

Text with Graphic Overlay

A graphic image can be placed over text to create a graphic overlay. WordPerfect provides several graphic images suitable for creating documents with graphic overlays. (See Figure 13.7 and Appendix C.) By default, when a graphic box containing a graphic image is placed in a document, text is moved to make room for the graphic box. However, WordPerfect can be instructed to place the graphic box over the text.

Start-Up Instructions

- Open the file named **13drill3.txt** located on the data disk.

Steps to Create Text with a Graphic Overlay

1. Place the insertion point at the location where the graphic image should be inserted.

   For example, the insertion point should be located at the beginning of the document.

2. Select the **Figure** button on the Button Bar {Alt, g, f}.

3. Scroll through the list of graphic files and double-click on the desired graphic filename {press the Tab key once, press the down arrow key to highlight the desired filename, press Enter}.

   For example, double-click on the file named **bord11L.wpg**.

   Note: The graphic image displays in the document window. A border displays around the graphic box that contains the graphic image. Small black handles (boxes) at the edges and corners of the graphic box indicate that the graphic box is selected. Also, the Graphics Box Feature Bar displays below the Power Bar.

Change the Size of the Graphic Box

4. Select the **Size** button on the Graphics Box Feature Bar {Alt and Shift and s}.

   Note: The Box Size dialog box displays.

5. In the Width box, select the desired option.

   For example, select **Full** {f}.

6. In the Height box, select the desired option.

   For example, select the **Set** option and type 4 in the Set option box {e, type 4}.

7. Select OK {Enter}.

   Note: The graphic box displays the full width of the document window and the text moves to the bottom of the document window.

Flow the Text Through the Graphic Box

8. Select the **Wrap** button on the Graphics Box Feature Bar {Alt and Shift and w}.

   Note: The Wrap Text dialog box displays.

9. Select the **No Wrap (through)** option {o}.

10. Select OK {Enter}.

    *Note: The text displays within the graphic box, because the wrapping type option of flow text **through** was chosen.*

Remove the Border Around the Graphic Box

11. Select the **Border/Fill** button on the Graphics Box Feature Bar to display the Box Border Fill Styles dialog box {Alt and Shift and b}.

12. Move the mouse pointer to the button to the right of the words "Border Style" and click once to display the Border Style palette {Alt and b, Spacebar}.

13. Select the NO BORDER border style to remove the graphic box border {press the arrow keys until NO BORDER is selected; Enter}.

    Note: The words "Spacing Only" display in the box to the right of the Border Style button.

14. Select OK {Enter}.

    Note: The border line is removed. The small black handles continue to display at the edges and corners of the graphic box to indicate that the graphic box is selected.

Finish-Up Instructions

- Move the mouse pointer away from the graphic box and text and click once to deselect the box.
- Use the *new* filename **13drill3.ovr** and save the file.
- Print one copy. Keep the **13drill3.ovr** file in the document window to use with the following Steps to Edit a Graphic Image Using the WP Draw Program.

Use WP Draw

Graphic images can be created and/or edited using the drawing tools available in the WP Draw program that is provided with WordPerfect 6.0 for Windows. The color, size, location, and rotation of an existing graphic image can be changed, and new graphic images can be drawn or created by combining existing graphic images. Text can be typed and formatted in the WP Draw program and placed into a document as a graphic image.

When a graphic image is placed into a document, a link is established between the graphic image and the WP Draw program. This link is established through the Windows Object Linking and Embedding (OLE) feature. The OLE feature permits the changes made to the graphic image in the WP Draw program to be reflected in the graphic image located in the WordPerfect document. The WP Draw program can be accessed by double-clicking on a graphic image in a document, by selecting the **WP Draw** button on the Button Bar, or by choosing **Graphics**, **Draw**. When the WP Draw program is loaded, the graphic image displays in the WP Draw window.

A graphic image may contain many separate pieces. Each piece of a graphic image is referred to as a graphic item. It is often a good idea to group all the graphic items that make up a single graphic image so that the items can all be edited at one time (e.g., moved, sized, copied, or rotated).

Start-Up Instructions

- The file named **13drill3.ovr** should be displayed in the document window.
- The Graphic Box Feature Bar should be displayed. If necessary, select **Graphics**, **Edit Box** to display the Graphics Box Feature Bar.

Steps to Edit a Graphic Image Using the WP Draw Program

Note: *A mouse is required to complete the following steps.*

1. Select the graphic box containing the graphic image to be edited.

   For example, if necessary, select the **Prev** button on the Graphics Box Feature Bar to select the graphic box containing the **bord11L.wpg** graphic image.

2. Move the mouse pointer anywhere in the desired graphic image and double-click.

   Note: *After a few moments, the WP Draw program window displays with only the graphic image contained in the selected graphic box (see Figure 13.5).*

FIGURE 13.5

WP Draw window

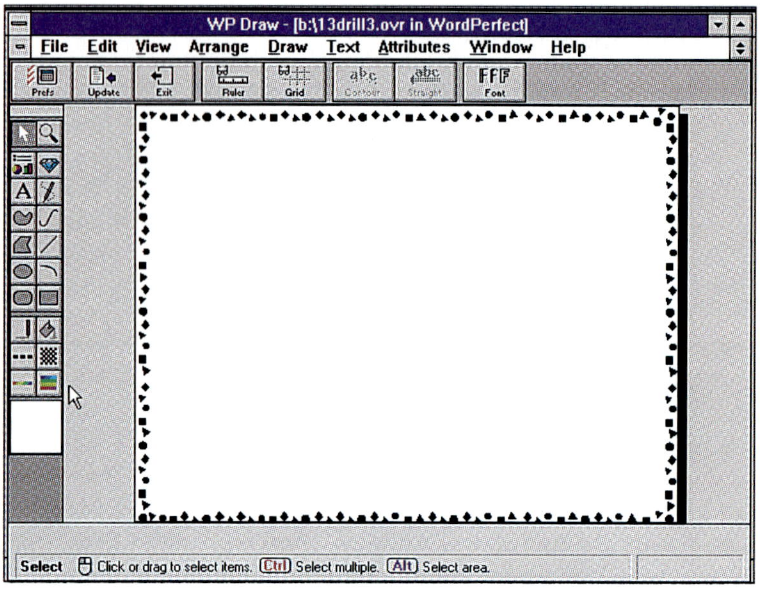

Group Graphic Items

3. Select the graphic items to be affected.

    For example, select **Edit, Select, All** to select all the graphic items that make up the border graphic image.

    Note: A small black handle displays at the left center edge of the graphic image. You will need to look carefully to see the small black handle because the handle is small and looks very similar to the border items. All the graphic items that make up the border graphic image are now considered one item.

4. Select **Arrange, Group**.

Change the Color of the Graphic Image

5. Select the **Set Fill Color** button  located at the left of the WP Draw window. ("Set Fill Color" displays in the Title bar when the mouse pointer is located on the Set Fill Color button.)

    Note: A palette of colors displays.

6. Move the mouse pointer to the desired color and click once.

    For example, move the mouse pointer the to royal blue color square in the center of the first color palette line (row) or make a choice of your own. Click to select the color.

    Note: The fill color for the selected graphic items changes to the selected color.

Insert a Second Graphic Image into an Existing Graphic Image

7. Select **File, Insert File**.

    Note: The Insert File dialog box displays containing a list of available WordPerfect graphic files (.wpg).

8. Scroll through the list of filenames and double-click on the desired filename.

    For example, double-click on the file named **trumpt.wpg**.

    Note: The trumpet graphic image displays within the existing graphic image.

9. Select the desired graphic items.

   For example, to select all the graphic items that make up the trumpet graphic image, move the mouse pointer approximately 1" above the left edge of the trumpet mouthpiece. Press and hold the mouse button and drag down and to the right to encompass the entire trumpet. Release the mouse button.

   Note: Black handles display around the trumpet graphic image. Also, small handles display on each graphic item making up the trumpet graphic image.

10. Select **Arrange, Group**.

   Note: All the graphic items that make up the trumpet graphic image are now considered a single item.

Size a Graphic Item

11. Move the mouse pointer to the black handle at a corner of the graphic image until a double-headed arrow displays.

   For example, move the mouse pointer to the black handle at the lower left corner of the trumpet graphic image until the double-headed arrow displays.

12. Press and hold the mouse button and drag to size the graphic item.

   For example, drag up and to the right to reduce the size of the graphic image to approximately 1.5" x .5".

13. Release the mouse button.

Move a Graphic Item

14. Move the mouse pointer anywhere inside the selected graphic item, press and hold the mouse button, and drag the item to the desired location.

   For example, move the mouse pointer inside the trumpet graphic, press and hold the mouse button, and drag the trumpet down to approximately $\frac{1}{2}$" from the bottom right corner of the border graphic image (see Figure 13.6).

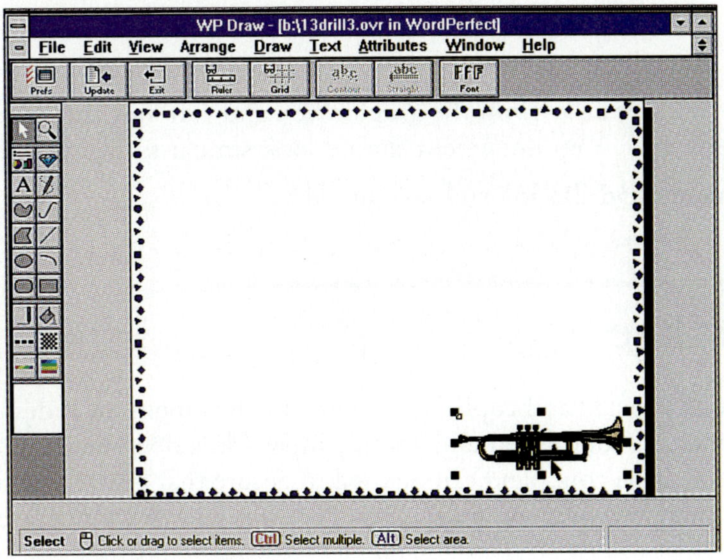

FIGURE 13.6

Move a graphic item in the WP Draw program

FIGURE 13.7

Text with graphic overlay

Join us at the

Blast to the Past Party!

Date: May 15, 199x

Time: 8:30 p.m. - 1:00 a.m.

Location: Tri-City Community Center

Rotate a Graphic Item

15. Select Edit, Rotate.

Note: Small rotation handles are added to the black handles at the edges and corners of the selected graphic item.

16. Move the mouse pointer to a rotation handle until a double-headed arrow displays.

For example, move the mouse pointer to the rotation handle at the bottom left corner of the trumpet graphic.

17. Press and hold the mouse button while dragging to rotate the graphic item. Release the mouse button.

For example, drag down approximately ¼" to rotate the trumpet graphic approximately 30 degrees.

Exit WP Draw and Place the Modified Graphic into the Document Window

18. Select File, Exit and Return to . . .

19. Select Yes to the message "Save changes to. . ."

Finish-Up Instructions

- Move the mouse pointer away from the graphic box and text and click once to deselect the graphic box. Your document should look similar to Figure 13.7.
- Use the *new* filename **13drill3.inv** and save the file.

Copy a Graphic Image

A graphic image can be selected and copied into the same document or, if desired, into a different document. If all the text and graphic images in a document are to be copied, the **Edit**, **Select**, **Page** command can be used to ensure that everything in the document (e.g., text, margins codes, or graphic box codes) is selected. Once selected, the text and graphic images can be copied by using either of the methods of copying text discussed in Chapter 4, pages 77-79.

Start-Up Instructions

- The file named **13drill3.inv** should be displayed in the document window.

Steps to Copy a Graphic Image and Text

1. Select the graphic image and/or text to be copied.

   For example, select **Edit, Select, Page** to select all text and the graphic image.

   Note: *The entire text and graphic image are highlighted.*

2. Select the Copy button {Alt, e, c *or* Ctrl and c}.
3. Move the mouse pointer below the selected graphic image and/or text and click once to deselect.
4. Move the insertion point to the desired location.

   For example, move the insertion point to the bottom of the document and press the **Enter** key six times.

5. Select the Paste {Alt, e, p *or* Ctrl and v}.

   Note: *A copy of the graphic image and text is inserted into the document.*

Finish-Up Instructions

- Select the **Page Zoom Full** button to view both copies of the text and graphic image. Select the **Page Zoom Full** button again to return to the normal view.
- Use the *new* filename **13drill3.cop** and save the file.
- Print one copy and close the document.

Create a Newsletter

A typical newsletter includes text columns, graphics, and borders. Different fonts and point sizes can be used for the newsletter text (see Figure 13.9). A graphic Text box can be used to create the heading portion (nameplate) of the newsletter. The default settings for a graphic Text box include horizontal graphic lines at the top and bottom of the box. If desired, the graphic lines can be changed and a fill (shading) can be created for the Text box.

The **Columns Define** button on the Power Bar can be used to specify the desired number of columns for the newsletter body text. (See Chapter 8, Steps to Create Newspaper Columns on page 175.) Graphic images can be placed in the document to add visual appeal.

Graphic boxes (e.g., Figure boxes, Text boxes, and User boxes) can be *attached* to a paragraph, a page, a fixed position on a page, or a character. A graphic box that is attached to a paragraph remains with the paragraph if the paragraph is relocated. A graphic box that is attached to a page remains at a fixed position on the page relative to the left and top margins/columns. A graphic box that is attached to a fixed page position remains at a specific position on the page relative to the top and left edges of the paper. A graphic box attached to a character remains with the text on a line and is treated as a character. Graphic boxes are usually attached to the page or a paragraph.

Text can be flowed around the edges of a graphic image by using the **Contour Wrap** option. When the **Contour Wrap** option is selected, the graphic box borders are automatically removed.

A mouse can be used to change the position and/or size of a graphic box in the document window. To use the mouse to position or size a graphic box, the graphic box must be selected. To select a graphic box, move the mouse pointer to the graphic image and click once. When selected, a dotted outline with black handles displays around the graphic box. A selected graphic box can be deleted by pressing the **Delete** key.

If desired, a column border can be placed between columns in order to improve the readability of a multi-column document. In order for the column border to begin below the newsletter nameplate, the column border code is placed in the document immediately after the column definition (*Col Def)* code. (See Chapter 8, Steps to Place a Border Line Between Newspaper Columns on page 175.)

Start-Up Instructions

- Open the file named **13drill4.txt** located on the data disk.

Steps to Use a Text Box to Create a Newsletter Nameplate

1. Select the Text Box button on the Button Bar {Alt, g, t}.

   Note: *A Text box with graphic lines above and below displays at the top right corner of the document window. Black handles display at the edges and corners of the Text box. Also, the Graphics Box Feature Bar displays below the Power Bar.*

2. Select the Size button on the Graphics Box Feature Bar {Alt and Shift and s}.

   Note: *The Box Size dialog box displays.*

3. In the Width box, select the desired option.

   For example, select **Full** {f}.

4. Select OK {Enter}.

   Note: *The Text box displays the width of the document window. The insertion point is located at the left side of the Text box.*

5. Type the Text box information.

   For example, type:

   Healthy Living (press **Enter** once)
   Planning for a Healthful Life (press **Enter** twice)
   Spring, 199x (press **Alt** and **F7**) **Sheridan Medical Center**

6. Format the Text box information.

   a. Select the first two lines and choose **Center** justification. Change the font to **EngraversGothic BT, 24-point.**

      Note: *When the EngraversGothic BT font is selected, the text changes to large and small uppercase letters. (Notice that the first letter of each main word is taller than the other letters.)*

b. Select the last line and change the font to **EngraversGothic BT, 14 point.**

Fill (shade) the Text Box

7. Select the Border/Fill button on the Graphics Box Feature Bar {Alt and Shift and b}.
8. Select the button located to the right of the words "Fill Style" {Alt and f, Spacebar}.
9. Select the desired fill style {press the arrow keys until the desired fill style is selecter; Enter}.

   For example select the **Rectangular Grad** fill style (the fifth button on the bottom row).

   Note: *A sample of the selected fill styles displays at the right of the dialog box.*
10. Move the mouse pointer to the box at the right of the word "Foreground" and click once {Alt and r, Spacebar}.

    Note: *A color palette displays.*
11. Move the mouse pointer to the desired color and click once {press the arrow keys to select the desired color; Enter}.

    For example, move the mouse pointer to a very light gray (on the second line on the color palette) and click once.

    Note: *The sample of the rectangular gradient fill style changes to reflect the new color choice.*
12. Select OK {Enter}.

    Note: *If the fill style does not display correctly in the document window, move the mouse pointer away from the text box and click once to deselect the box. The fill for the Text box redraws and displays correctly.*
13. Select the Close button on the Graphics Box Feature Bar to remove the feature bar from the screen {Alt and Shift and c}.

Finish-Up Instructions

- Use the *new* filename **13drill4.box** and save the file.

  Note: *The following steps are for your information only.*

Steps to Edit a Text Box

1. Move the mouse pointer to the Text box and click once to select the box.

   Note: *Black handles display at the edges and corners of the selected Text box.*
2. If necessary, click the *right* mouse button to display the Graphics QuickMenu and select Feature Bar to display the Graphics Box Feature Bar {Alt, g, e}.
3. Use the options on the Graphics Box Feature Bar to change the size, position, border, fill, or wrap for the text box.

Edit the Text in a Text Box

4. With the text box selected (see step 1 above), click the *right* mouse button to display the Graphics QuickMenu and select Edit Text {Alt, g, e, Alt and Shift and o, e}.

5. Make the desired changes to the text using normal text editing techniques.
6. Select Close on the Graphics Box Feature Bar {Alt and Shift and c}.

Start-Up Instructions

- The file named **13drill4.box** should be displayed in the document window.

Steps to Format the Newsletter Body Text

1. With the insertion point located where the columns should begin, move the mouse pointer to the Columns Define button on the Power Bar, press and hold the mouse button, and drag to select the desired number of columns. Release the mouse button {Alt, L, c, d, type the number of columns, Enter}.

   For example, place the insertion point to the left of the E in the sidehead "Exercise" and select **2 Columns.**

2. If desired, place a column border between the columns by selecting Layout, Columns, Border/Fill. Move the mouse pointer to the Border Style button and click once; click on the Column Between border style (second button on the bottom row) and select OK {Alt, l, c b, Tab, press "c" to display "Column Between," Enter}.

Finish-Up Instructions

- Save the file again using the same filename, **13drill4.box**.

Start-Up Instructions

- Place the insertion point at the beginning of the first paragraph in the first column.
- Insert the graphics image named *racebike.wpg*. (See Steps to Retrieve a Graphic Image on page 304.)
- Change the size of the graphic box containing the *racebike.wpg* graphic image. (Select the **Size** button on the Graphics Box Feature Bar. In the Width box, double-click in the box to the right of the word "Set" and type .75. Select **OK**.) If necessary, see Change the Size of a Graphic Box on page 308.
- Change the position of the graphic box containing the *racebike.wpg* graphic image. (Select the **Position** button on the Graphics Box Feature Bar. Move the mouse pointer to the From box below the word "Horizontal," press and hold the mouse button, and drag to select **Left Margin**. Release the mouse button and select **OK**.)

Steps to Contour the Flow of Text Around a Graphic Image

1. Select the Wrap button on the Graphics Box Feature Bar {Alt and Shift and w}.
2. Select the Contour option {c}.
3. Select OK {Enter}.

Note: When the Contour option is selected, WordPerfect automatically removes the graphic box borders. The text flows around the shape of the graphic image with white space between the graphic image and the text.

Steps to Mirror (Flip) a Graphic Image

1. With the mouse pointer located anywhere in the selected graphic image, click the *right* mouse button to display the Graphics QuickMenu.
2. Select Image Tools {Alt and Shift and l}.

   Note: A palette of image tools displays beside the selected graphic box.
3. Select the Mirror Vertical button in the Image Tools palette.

   Note: The graphic image is flipped around the vertical axis.

Finish-Up Instructions

- Move the mouse pointer away from the graphic box and click once to deselect the box.

  Note: The Image Tools palette is removed from the document window when the graphic box is deselected.
- Use the *new* filename **13drill4.new** and save the file.
- Select the **Close** button on the Graphics Box Feature Bar.

Create TextArt

WordPerfect for Windows provides a graphics feature called TextArt that is used to create text in special shapes, such as circles, pennants, flags, and buttons. Font, justification, fill color, outline color, and shadow effects for TextArt can also be specified, and the width and height for the graphic box containing the TextArt can be set. The font size of the text created in TextArt is based on the width and height of the graphic box containing the TextArt.

TextArt is placed in a graphic box. The graphic box is *sized* by moving the mouse pointer to the black handles that display at the edges and corners of the selected graphic box and dragging to resize the box. When the graphic box reaches the desired size, release the mouse button. TextArt is *moved* by placing the mouse pointer anywhere inside the graphic box containing the TextArt, pressing and holding the mouse button, and dragging the graphic box to the desired location. When the graphic box is in the desired location, release the mouse button.

TextArt can be edited by moving the mouse pointer to the graphic box containing the TextArt and double-clicking to display the TextArt in WordPerfect dialog box. Make changes as desired to the text, font, shape, color, or shadow. When the changes are complete, select **File**, **Exit and Return to WordPerfect** and choose **Yes** to place the edited TextArt into the document.

Start-Up Instructions

- The file named **13drill4.new** should be displayed in the document window.

FIGURE 13.8

TextArt in WordPerfect dialog box

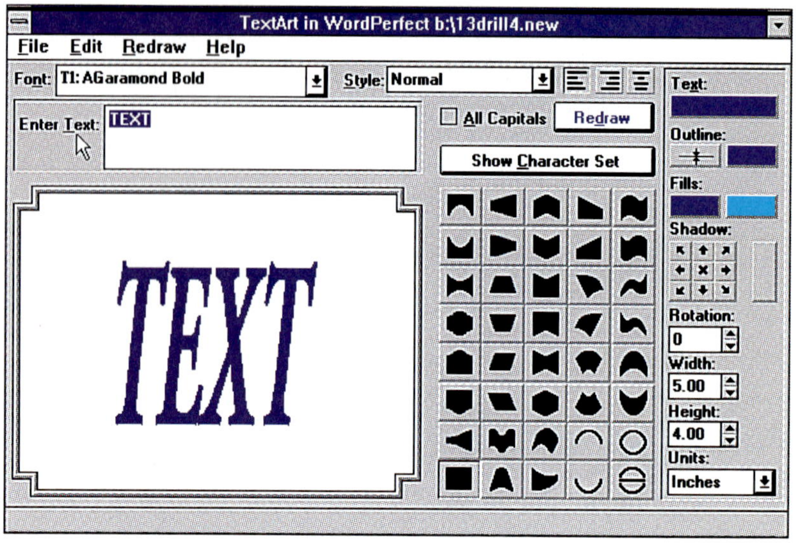

Steps to Create TextArt

1. Move the insertion point to the location where the TextArt is to be inserted.

   For example, move the insertion point below the last line of text in the second column.

2. Select the TextArt button on the Button Bar {Alt and g, x}.

   Note: The TextArt in WordPerfect dialog box displays (see Figure 13.8) and the word "Text" is highlighted in the Enter Text box.

3. Type the desired text in the Enter Text box.

   For example, type the following:

   Eat Healthy (press Enter)
   Exercise (press Enter)
   Be Healthy (do not press Enter)

4. Move the mouse pointer to the Font box and click once {Alt and n}.

5. Scroll through the list of font names and click on the desired font {press the first letter of the font name and repeat until the desired font name displays}.

   For example, click on **EngraversGothic BT**.

6. Move the mouse pointer to the desired shape and click once {press the Tab key until a light gray highlight displays around the first shape, press the arrow keys to move the gray highlight to the desired shape, press the Spacebar}.

   For example, move the mouse pointer to the **Button** shape (last button in the last row) and click once.

7. To create a shadow effect for the TextArt, select the desired shadow arrow button {press the Tab key repeatedly until a light gray highlight displays around the first shadow arrow button, press the arrow keys to move the highlight to the desired shadow button, press the Spacebar}.

   For example, select the down arrow button (↓) in the Shadow box.

8. Move the mouse pointer to the **Width** box and double-click {press the Tab key until the Width box is highlighted}. Type the desired width for the graphic box that will contain the TextArt.

   For example, type **3** in the Width box.

9. Move the mouse pointer to the **Height** box and double-click {press the Tab key until the Height box is highlighted}. Type the desired height for the graphic box that will contain the TextArt.

   For example, type **2.75** in the Height box.

10. When the TextArt is formatted, select **File**, **Exit and Return to WordPerfect** {Alt, f, x}.

11. Select **Yes** to the message "Update embedded object(s) in WordPerfect?" {y}.

    Note: *The TextArt is placed in a graphic box at the location of the insertion point in the document window. Your newsletter should look similar to Figure 13.9.*

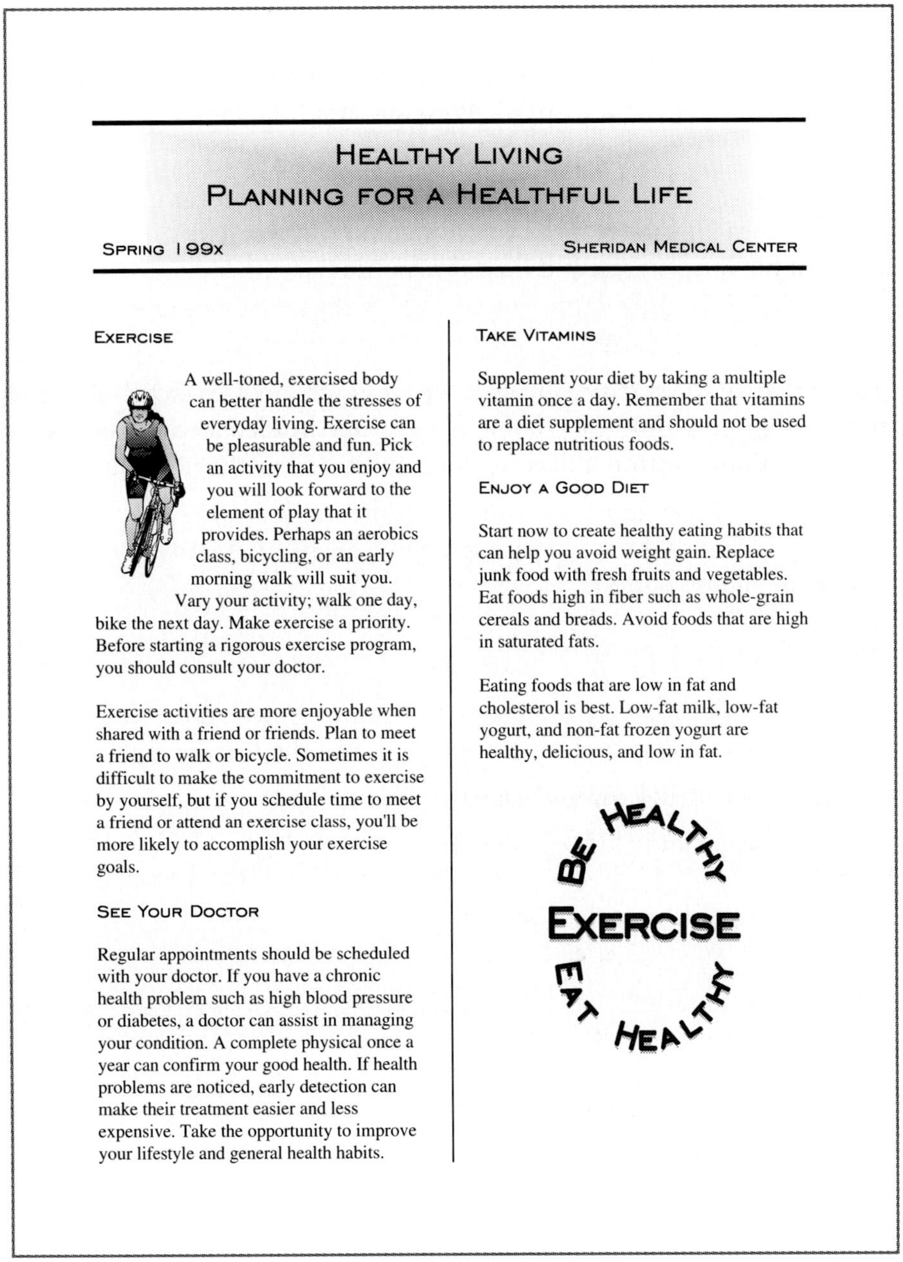

HEALTHY LIVING
PLANNING FOR A HEALTHFUL LIFE

SPRING 199X — SHERIDAN MEDICAL CENTER

EXERCISE

A well-toned, exercised body can better handle the stresses of everyday living. Exercise can be pleasurable and fun. Pick an activity that you enjoy and you will look forward to the element of play that it provides. Perhaps an aerobics class, bicycling, or an early morning walk will suit you. Vary your activity; walk one day, bike the next day. Make exercise a priority. Before starting a rigorous exercise program, you should consult your doctor.

Exercise activities are more enjoyable when shared with a friend or friends. Plan to meet a friend to walk or bicycle. Sometimes it is difficult to make the commitment to exercise by yourself, but if you schedule time to meet a friend or attend an exercise class, you'll be more likely to accomplish your exercise goals.

SEE YOUR DOCTOR

Regular appointments should be scheduled with your doctor. If you have a chronic health problem such as high blood pressure or diabetes, a doctor can assist in managing your condition. A complete physical once a year can confirm your good health. If health problems are noticed, early detection can make their treatment easier and less expensive. Take the opportunity to improve your lifestyle and general health habits.

TAKE VITAMINS

Supplement your diet by taking a multiple vitamin once a day. Remember that vitamins are a diet supplement and should not be used to replace nutritious foods.

ENJOY A GOOD DIET

Start now to create healthy eating habits that can help you avoid weight gain. Replace junk food with fresh fruits and vegetables. Eat foods high in fiber such as whole-grain cereals and breads. Avoid foods that are high in saturated fats.

Eating foods that are low in fat and cholesterol is best. Low-fat milk, low-fat yogurt, and non-fat frozen yogurt are healthy, delicious, and low in fat.

BE HEALTHY
EXERCISE
EAT HEALTHY

FIGURE 13.9

Newsletter with Text box, contour text flow around a graphic image, and TextArt

Finish-Up Instructions

- Use the same filename **13drill4.new** and save the file.
- Print one copy.

Start-Up Instructions

- The file named **13drill4.new** should be displayed in the document window.

Steps to Change the Size and Position of a Graphic Box Using the Mouse

1. Move the mouse pointer to the graphic box and click once to select the graphic box.

   For example, move the mouse pointer to the graphic box containing the *racebike.wpg* graphic image and click once.

   ***Note:** Black handles display along the edges and at the corners of the graphic box containing the graphic image.*

2. *To change the size of the graphic box,* move the mouse pointer to one of the black handles until a two-headed arrow displays. Press and hold the mouse button and drag to size the graphic box and image.

   For example, place the mouse pointer on the black handle at the bottom right corner of the graphic box containing the *racebike.wpg* graphic image, press and hold the mouse button, and drag down and to the right approximately ¼". Release the mouse button.

3. *To change the position of the graphic box,* select the graphic box (see step 1 above); move the mouse pointer within the graphic box. A four-headed arrow displays. Press and hold the mouse button and drag the graphic box to the new location.

   For example, drag the graphic box containing the *racebike.wpg* graphic image down to the second paragraph in the first column and release the mouse button.

Finish-Up Instructions

- Use the mouse to practice moving and sizing the graphic image until the graphic image is positioned attractively on the page and the text is easy to read.
- Use the *new* filename **13drill4.rev** and save the file.
- Optional. Print one copy and close the document.

The Next Step

Chapter Review and Activities

Self-Check Quiz

T F 1. A horizontal graphic line can be created by selecting **Graphics**, **Horizontal Line**.

T F 2. The border that appears around a graphic box cannot be removed or changed.

T F 3. A horizontal graphic line can be placed below or around a paragraph.

T F 4. In order for a graphic box to overlay text, the **No Wrap (through)** option must be selected in the Wrap Text dialog box.

T F 5. The vertical and horizontal positions of a graphic box cannot be changed once a graphic image has been retrieved into a document.

6. After selecting the **Wrap** button on the Graphics Box Feature Bar, the ______ option is chosen to flow text around the edges of a graphic image.
   a. **Square**
   b. **Contour**
   c. **No Wrap (through)**
   d. **Neither Side**

7. The black handles that display on the edges and corners of a graphic box __________.
   a. indicate that the graphic box is selected
   b. can be used to size the graphic box
   c. allow text to flow through a graphic box
   d. both a and b

8. TextArt is used to create text in special shapes such as _____.
   a. pennants
   b. circles
   c. buttons
   d. all of the above

9. Write down the name of the directory where WordPerfect graphics files are stored on your system.

10. When a graphic image is placed in a document, a ______ is established between the graphic image and the WP Draw program.

Enriching Language Arts Skills

Spelling/Vocabulary Words

extensive wide, broad; comprehensive.

HMO Health Maintenance Organization. A term used by insurance companies that provide health care coverage; the client is seen by the HMO's selected doctor(s).

reputation a measure of a person's or organization's character as viewed by others.

Initials Abbreviated

Periods or spaces are not placed after the letters of an acronym such as IRS (Internal Revenue Service) or TWA (Trans World Airlines).

Examples:

Always remember to mail your tax return to the IRS by April 15.

St. Louis is a hub for TWA.

Activities

Activity 13.1—Create a Flier with a Graphic Image

1. Type and center all text of the flier using the information shown in the flier on page 323.
2. Place the insertion point to the left of the first character at the top of the document. Retrieve the graphic file named **hotrod.wpg** (select the **Figure** button on the Button Bar, double-click on **hotrod.wpg**).
3. Make the following changes to the selected graphic box containing the hotrod.wpg graphic image:
   a. Select the **Position** button on the Graphics Box Feature Bar. In the Vertical area of the Position Box dialog box, double-click in the box to the right of the word "Place" and type 5. Select **OK**.
   b. Select the **Size** button on the Graphics Box Feature Bar. In the Width area, double-click in the box to the right of the word "Set" and type 3.75. Select **OK**.
   c. Remove the graphics box border (select the **Border/Fill** button on the Graphics Box Feature Bar, click on the **Border Style** button, select **No Border**, select **OK**).
   d. Move the mouse pointer away from the graphic box and click once to deselect the box.
4. Place a border around the entire page. Select **Layout**, **Page**, **Border/Fill**, click on the **Border Style** button, select the fourth button on the third row (Thick/Thin 2), and select **OK**.
5. If desired, select the **Page Zoom Full** button and view the entire flier. Select the **Page Zoom Full** button again to return to the normal view.

Humanst521 Lt BT, 48 point

2 Enters

Auto Auction

3 Enters

Humanst521 Lt BT, 24 point

May 5-6, 199x
10:00 a.m.

2 Enters

at

Humanst521 Lt BT, 36 point

2 Enters

Auto Liquidators Unlimited

3 Enters

Humanst521 Lt BT, 18 point

1349 East Avenue
Sacramento, California

4 Enters

All makes, models, and years.

2 Enters

You name it, we probably have it!!!

3 Enters

Come and see for yourself.

2 Enters

Preview is May 4 from 10:00 a.m. - 2:00 p.m.

Note: Your flier will look similar to the flier above. However, the lines may not end at exactly the same place.

6. Use the filename **13act1.hot** and save the file.
7. Print one copy and close the document.

Activity 13.2—Create a Letterhead with Horizontal Graphic Lines

1. Create a letterhead using the following information. Use a style similar to the one shown in Figure 13.3 and fonts of your choice. Press the **Enter** key once before you begin typing the letterhead text.

Mountain Technology Services

P.O. Box 3002 Bellevue, WA 98009	Voice: (206) 555-4300 Fax: (206) 555-2364

2. Select the company name and change the font to **EngraversGothic BT, 14-point**. Select the address, city, state, zip, voice, and fax numbers and change the font to **EngraversGothic BT, 10-point.**
3. Place a single horizontal graphic line above the company name (move the insertion point to the blank line above the company name, select **Graphics, Horizontal Line**).
4. Place a Thick/Thin 2 horizontal graphic line below the company name (move the insertion point to the blank line below the company name, select **Graphics, Custom Line**, select the **Line Style** button, click on the desired line style, select **OK**).
5. Use the filename **13act2.lth** and save the file.
6. Print one copy and close the document.

Activity 13.3—Create a Flier with Text and a Graphic Overlay

1. Change the left, right, top, and bottom margins to .25".
2. Type and format the text as shown in the flier shown below.

3. Place the insertion point at the top of the document.
4. Retrieve the graphic image file named **bord17.wpg** (select the **Figure** button on the Button Bar, double-click on **bord17.wpg**).
5. With the graphic box containing the border graphic image selected, make the following changes:
   a. Select the **Size** button on the Graphics Box Feature Bar. In the Width box, select the **Full** option and choose **OK**.
   b. Select the **Wrap** button on the Graphics Box Feature Bar and choose the **No Wrap (through)** option. Select **OK**.
   c. Select the **Border/Fill** button on the Graphics Box Feature Bar. Click on the Border Style button and select **No Border**. Choose **OK**.
   d. Move the mouse pointer away from the graphic box and click once to deselect the box.
   e. Select the **Close** button on the Graphics Box Feature Bar to remove the feature bar.
6. If desired, select the **Page Zoom Full** button to view the entire flier. Select the **Page Zoom Full** button again to return to the normal view.
7. Use the filename **13act3.des** and save the file.
8. Print one copy and close the document.

Activity 13.4—Create a Newsletter with a Graphic Image

1. Open the file named **13act4.txt** located on the data disk. Use the following information and the newsletter style shown in Figure 13.9 to create an employee newsletter for Campanella Systems.
   a. Place the insertion point at the top of the document and create the nameplate using a Text box. (If necessary, see pages 314-315.)
   b. Place the insertion point to the left of the E in "Eastern" and create two newspaper style columns.
   c. Place a column border between the two columns (select **Layout**, **Columns**, **Border/Fill**, select the **Border Style** button, select the **Columns Between** border style, **OK**).
   d. Place the insertion point to the left of the first character in the first paragraph.
   e. Retrieve the graphic file named **group.wpg** (select the **Figure** button on the Button Bar, double-click on **group.wpg**).
   f. With the graphic box containing the *group.wpg* graphic image selected, click on the **Position** button on the Graphics Box Feature Bar. Move the mouse pointer to the From box in the Horizontal area, press and hold the mouse button, and drag to select **Left Margin**. Release the mouse button. Double-click in the Place box below the word "Vertical" and type .75. Select **OK**.

g. Select the **Size** button on the Graphics Box Feature Bar. In the Width area, double-click in the box to the right of the word "Set" and type **1**. Select **OK**.

h. Select the **Wrap** button on the Graphics Box Feature Bar. Select the **Contour** option and choose **OK**.

2. Move the mouse pointer to the end of the document and create the TextArt shown below using the following information:

a. Select the **TextArt** button.

b. Type the following text:

Employee of the Month
Belinda Fields
Congratulations!

c. Change the font to **EngraversGothic BT**.

d. Select the **Button** shape button (last button in the last row).

e. Double-click in the Width box and type **3**.

CAMPANELLA'S
NEWS BULLETIN

FEBRUARY 199X — CAMPANELLA SYSTEMS, INC.

EASTERN REGION

Our flagship account (MCI) has successfully upgraded and has also implemented the Flex program. We have had two teams assisting in these efforts: Monty Gillars and Belinda Fields (upgrade); Glenda King and Elvia Marshall (Flex). June Payton served as Account Manager with liaison responsibilities for both groups. Monty and Glenda are still involved there, integrating a new company into the system and assisting in year end and flex tasks.

We have had two additions to our staff. Tom Burrnell joined us as the Eastern Region Sales Representative and Colleen Duke was hired as a Senior Consultant.

MIDWESTERN REGION

We have been fortunate to have several large projects in place. These have recently been supplemented by the University of Nebraska and Consumers Power of Michigan. Both of these accounts are using our mainframe operating system.

It was conference time again for several of our consultants. Amos Stenson attended the Canadian Human Resources conference in Toronto. Joanna Holt spent a day in Chicago at the Midwest Human Resources conference trying to discover the difference between the HR vendors and the "GUI's." Ted Crutcher traveled to New Orleans to attend the Financial Users Conference. As a direct result of our conference efforts, we are in the process of closing sales with a couple of companies that we met in Toronto and San Francisco.

WESTERN REGION

The Western region has added three new clients during the past month. With the addition of these new clients, the Western region is now serving 15 clients. We are well on our way to meeting our goal for serving 25 new western clients during this fiscal year.

EMPLOYEE OF THE MONTH
BELINDA FIELDS
CONGRATULATIONS!

f. Double-click in the Height box and type **2.5**.

g. Select **File, Exit and Return to WordPerfect**.

h. Select **Yes**.

3. If desired, select the **Page Zoom Full** button to view the entire newsletter. Select the **Page Zoom Full** button again to return to the normal view.
4. Use the filename **13act4.cam** and save the file.
5. Print one copy and close the document.

Challenge Your Skills

Skill 13.1—Create a Flier with Graphics

1. Use the following information and create a flier for the Pelican Beach Club vacation resort.

   a. The resort is located in the Grand Cayman Islands.

   b. A special vacation package including two nights of free lodging, a free glass-bottom boat ride, car rental for two days, and a visit to the Grand Cayman Botanical Garden is available when a seven-day vacation is reserved.

   c. Eugenia McAllister of Global Travel Associates, (919) 555-6288, can assist with scheduling this special vacation package.

   d. Create appropriate TextArt or insert any *two* of the following graphic images:

buterfly.wpg	**golfswgn.wpg**
humbird.wpg	**marsh.wpg**

   e. Make decisions regarding:

   Fonts and point sizes
   Position of graphic box(es)
   Size of graphic box(es)
   Borders around graphic box(es)

2. Use the filename **14skill1.cay** and save the file.
3. Print one copy and close the document.

Skill 13.2—Create a Newsletter with a Graphic Image and Table; Language Arts

1. Create a newsletter using the following information. Use a two-column style similar to the one shown in Figure 13.9 to create the newsletter shown on page 328.

   a. The text for the newsletter is on page 328.

CLIENT RELATIONS NEWSLETTER

Vitacare Health Plan
158 Madison Avenue, Suite 240, New York, NY 10016

Winter 199x
(212) 555-2666

ASU PURCHASES 20% SHARE OF VITACARE

The September 28, 199x, signing of ASU to purchase a 20-percent share of Vitacare represented a significant event in the history of Vitacare and an important step towards retaining large employer accounts.

G.A. Von Stetten, Senior Vice President of ASU's Eastern Region, stated that ASU's investment in Vitacare is based upon "confidence in its strong reputution in the market-place, its very solid and estensive provider network, and a firm commitment from its board and senior management". More than 95% of physicians and thirty-two hospitals have elected to participate.

ASU PRODUCTS

The ASU products to be offered are an EPO (Exclusive Provider Option) and a "point of service" product called CO (Controlled Options). The E P O is a plan that operates just like the Vitacare HMO. It is sold to employers as part of a package called IDO (Integrated Diverse Option) or a "tri-plan option." That means that the employer offers employees a choice of a guarantee pay plan, a physician choice plan, or an exclusive provider option.

The CO is sold to the employer as a "full replacement product." Under CO, an employee can make a choice at any time, i.e, at the "point of service," as to whether to seek care as directed by the primary care physician or to self-refer. All self-referrals result in the patient's paying a larger share of the service cost.

ASU sales representatives and Vitacare report a great deal of excitement in the marketplace about these products, which are aimed at large statewide or national employers. The products allow Vitacare to compete with other national and statewide insurers and will provide physicians with increased membership.

****NEWSFLASH****

You may have heard about a recommendation that Vitacare along with other HOMs be dropped from the panel of HMOs that provide services to New York Employees Retirement System (NYERS). We are pleased to report that the recommendation has been rejected by the NYERS Board. In addition, the organization that prepared the report, H. Keith Wittenberger, an employee benefits consulting firm, acknowledged "a misunderstanding with Vitacare on certain key data included in the study."

b. Insert the graphic image named **medical1.wpg** in the second paragraph. Adjust the size and position of the graphic box and contour the flow of text around the graphic image.

c. Use a Text box to insert the NEWSFLASH information. Change the border around the Text box to a double-line border around all sides of the Text box.

d. Make decisions regarding:

Fonts and point sizes (a 10 to 12 point size is recommended for the newsletter body text)
Justification
Hyphenation
Widow/Orphan protect

2. Correct three spelling and three punctuation/grammatical errors.
3. Use the filename **13skill2.crn** and save the file.
4. Print one copy.
5. If you have completed your work, exit WordPerfect.

CHAPTER 14

Create Documents with Special Features

Features Covered

- Kerning, word spacing, and letterspacing
- Leading adjustment
- Initial font
- Append
- Superscripts and subscripts
- Equation Editor

Objectives and Introduction

After successfully completing this chapter, you will be able to enhance the appearance of documents by using typesetting features such as kerning, word spacing, letterspacing, and leading adjustment. You also will be able to use the Append feature in order to create new documents or to add text to existing files. In addition, you will learn how to create superscript and subscript text and create equations/formulas using the Equation Editor.

After a document is typed, the document can be enhanced to present information in a more attractive way and that is easier to read. For example, the space between letters, words, and paragraph lines can be precisely controlled. Using the Append feature documents can be developed by copying sections from existing documents, thereby eliminating the need to rekey information. Scientific/mathematical documents can be enhanced by the insertion of superscripts and subscripts, and the Equation Editor can be used to create complex formulas and equations.

Use Typesetting Features

WordPerfect provides advanced typesetting features to enhance the appearance of documents. These typesetting features include kerning, letterspacing (tracking), word spacing, and leading adjustment.

Kerning is used to improve the readability of text. After a document is typed, the manual kerning feature is used to adjust the space between two characters. With manual kerning the space between the letters AV can be reduced, for example, AV. In addition, the automatic kerning feature can be used to kern specific pairs of letters. The automatic kerning feature is turned on by selecting **Layout, Typesetting, Word/Letterspacing, Automatic Kerning, OK**. The automatic kerning feature adjusts the spacing for all occurrences of predefined pairs of letters. The WordPerfect program defines which pairs of letters to be kerned depending on the font in use. In other words, kerned pairs of letters will vary when using WordPerfect depending on the font in use.

The letterspacing feature (also known as tracking) is used to increase or decrease the amount of space between *letters* in selected text or an entire document. By tightening the letterspacing, more text can be condensed into the same amount of space. Word spacing is used to increase or decrease the amount of space between *words* in selected text or an entire document. By loosening the letterspacing and/or word spacing, words can be stretched out to create a special effect (see Figure 14.1).

WordPerfect automatically calculates the amount of space to be placed between lines of a paragraph (line height) based on the font and point size selected. For example, if Times New Roman, 12-point is chosen, WordPerfect sets the line height to approximately 0.197"—the size of the text plus 2 points of vertical spacing. If the point size is changed, WordPerfect adjusts the line height accordingly to accommodate the new point size.

WordPerfect adjusts the line height to accommodate the largest point size in each line. At times, however, it is desirable to control the exact amount of spacing between lines of a paragraph, especially if different font sizes are used in the same paragraph. In order to make the line height uniform, the line height can be fixed at a specific amount. Once the line height between lines of a paragraph is uniform, a specific amount of additional space can be added between lines of a paragraph and between paragraphs by using the Leading Adjustment feature.

Start-Up Instructions

- Open the file named **14drill1.ep** located on the data disk.
- The space between the lines of the indented paragraphs is not equal, because two different point sizes have been set. For example, you may notice that in the document on the screen, there is more spacing between the first and second lines than between the second and third lines in the paragraph that begins "Aim the extinguisher..." The sections *Steps to Set the Line Height* and *Steps to Use Line Height (Leading) Adjustment* are used to correct this problem. (Because additional changes will be made to the text, do not be concerned about the spacing and alignment at this time.)
- Use the following Steps to Kern Text before changing the line height.

Steps to Kern Text

1. Place the insertion point between the two letters to be kerned.

   For example, place the insertion point between the R and G in the word EMERGENCY.

2. Select **Layout, Typesetting, Manual Kerning** {Alt, L, t, m}.

Note: The Manual Kerning dialog box displays.

3. *To decrease the amount of space between the letters,* click on the **down triangle** located to the right of the Amount box {press the down arrow key}.

   To increase the amount of space between letters, click on the **up triangle** located to the right of the Amount box {press the up arrow key}.

   For example, click twice on the **down triangle** to decrease the amount of space between the R and G.

   Note: *While clicking on the down arrow key, look in the document window. The two letters will have moved slightly closer to each other. The amount -0.027" displays in the Amount box in the Manual Kerning dialog box.*

4. When the characters are the desired distance apart, select **OK** {Enter}.

Finish-Up Instructions

- Move the insertion point between the letters C and Y in the word EMERGENCY.
- Repeat steps 2–4 and decrease the amount of space between the letters by -0.013".
- Move the insertion point between the letters R and O in the word PROCEDURE.
- Repeat steps 2–4 and decrease the amount of space between the letters by -0.027".
- Use the *new* filename **14drill1.ker** and save the file.
- Optional. Print one copy.

Start-Up Instructions

- The file named **14drill1.ker** should be displayed in the document window.

Steps to Set the Line Height

1. Place the insertion point at the beginning of the text where the line height is to be set.

   For example, place the insertion point to the left of the first character in the first paragraph.

2. Select **Layout, Line, Height** {Alt, L, L, h}.

   Note: *The Line Height dialog box displays.*

3. Select the **Fixed** option. If desired, change the line height {f}.

   For example, the default of approximately 0.197 displays in the Fixed box. No change needs to be made.

4. Select **OK** {Enter}.

   Note: *The spacing between some of the lines of text on the screen is too small. This will be corrected using the following steps. If desired, use Reveal Codes and place the red/shaded block to the left of the* ***[Ln Height]*** *code to view the expanded line height code.*

FIGURE 14.1

The Word Spacing and Letterspacing dialog box

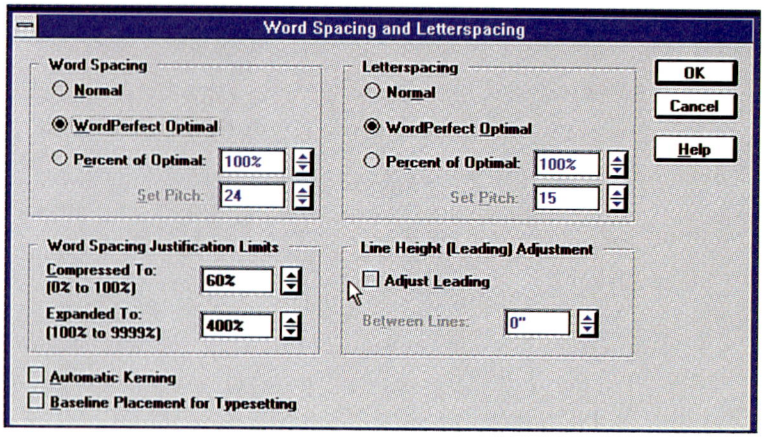

Steps to Use Line Height (Leading) Adjustment

1. Place the insertion point at the beginning of the text where the leading will be adjusted.

   For example, place the insertion point to the left of the first character in the first paragraph.

2. Select Layout, Typesetting, Word/Letterspacing {Alt, L, t, w}.

   Note: The Word Spacing and Letterspacing dialog box displays (see Figure 14.1).

3. Select Adjust Leading {L}.

   Note: An X should display in the Adjust Leading box.

4. Double-click in the Between Lines box and type the desired adjustment amount {t}.

   For example, type **.1**. (Do not type the final period.)

5. Select OK {Enter}.

   Note: Additional spacing has been placed between the lines of text that follow the insertion point. Notice that the spacing between lines of a paragraph are the same even if there are different font sizes within a paragraph. For example, the space between the lines is now the same in the paragraph that begins "Aim the extinguisher . . ."

Finish-Up Instructions

- Use the *new* filename **14drill1.lea** and save the file.

Start-Up Instructions

- The file named **14drill1.lea** should be displayed in the document window.

Steps to Change Letterspacing

1. Select the desired word(s) where letterspacing is to be changed.

   For example, select the first lead word **Pull**. (Only the top portion of the letters in the word Pull may highlight—that's OK.)

2. Select Layout, Typesetting, Word/Letterspacing {Alt, L, t, w}.
3. Select the Percent of Optimal option in the Letterspacing box {r}.

4. Double-click in the Percent of Optimal box {Tab}.
5. Type the desired percentage of letterspacing.

   For example, to increase the amount of space between letters, type **150**. (Do not type the period.)

6. Select **OK** {Enter}.

   Note: Additional space has been placed between each letter in the selected word. (The paragraphs will align after completing the following instructions.)

Finish-Up Instructions

- Repeat steps 1–6 of the Steps to Change Letterspacing and change the optimal letterspacing for the words *Aim*, *Squeeze*, and *Sweep* to 150%.
- Check the alignment of the indented paragraphs. If necessary, add or delete indents in order to align all the paragraphs.
- Save the file again using the same filename, **14drill1.lea**.

Start-Up Instructions

- The file named **14drill1.lea** should be displayed in the document window.

Steps to Change Word Spacing

1. Select the desired words where word spacing is to be changed.

   For example, select the title **Emergency Procedures**.

2. Select **Layout, Typesetting, Word/Letterspacing** {Alt, L, t, w}.
3. Select the **Percent of Optimal** option in the Word Spacing box {e}.
4. Double-click in the Percent of Optimal box {Tab}.
5. Type the desired percentage of word spacing.

   For example, to increase the amount of space between words, type **250**. (Do not type the period.)

6. If desired, change the amount of letterspacing by selecting the **Percent of Optimal** option in the Letterspacing box and typing the desired percentage of letterspacing {Alt and r, Tab, type percentage}.

   For example, change the letterspacing to **110%** of optimal.

7. Select **OK** {Enter}.

   Note: Additional space has been placed between the words in the title and between each letter. Your document should look similar to Figure 14.2.

Finish-Up Instructions

- Use the *new* filename **14drill1.fin** and save the file.
- Print one copy.
- Close the document.

FIGURE 14.2

Document created using leading adjustment, letterspacing, and word spacing

EMERGENCY PROCEDURES

Most fire extinguishers at Wabash Laboratories are type ABC all-purpose and can be operated using these instructions. However, it is important to read the label on the extinguisher used in your work area to be certain of its type and operation. Only fight fires if it is safe to do so and only after alerting the fire department to the situation. To operate a fire extinguisher, remember the following simple steps.

Pull	Pull the pin or plastic loop.
Aim	Aim the extinguisher so that it discharges at the base of the fire. Grip the handle and neck area for better control. Some units have a hose or horn.
Squeeze	Squeeze the handles together.
Sweep	Sweep the base of the fire using a side-to-side motion. The sweeping motion pushes the flames away from you.

Change the Document Initial Font

When WordPerfect is installed, a printer is chosen and a printer initial font (default font) is automatically set. If desired, the initial (default) font for a document can be changed. The initial font can be changed for the current document only, or the **Set as Printer Initial Font** option can be chosen to change the initial font for the current document and all new documents.

The advantage of changing the initial font is saving time. Because changing the initial font affects all document text, including headers, footnotes, equations, page numbers, and text typed in graphics boxes, less time is spent formatting a document (i.e., reducing the number of times the font must be set).

Start-Up Instructions

- Open the file named **14drill2.unf** located on the data disk.

Steps to Change the Document Initial Font

1. Select **Layout, Document, Initial Font** {Alt, L, d, f}.
   Note: *The Document Initial Font dialog box displays.*

2. Select the desired font face and font size {Alt and f, highlight desired font; Alt and s, highlight or type desired size}.

   For example, select the up (or down) arrow in the Font Face scroll bar, choose the **Arrus BT** font face, and **11** as the font size.

3. Select **OK** to change the initial font for the current document {Enter}.

   *Note: To change the initial font for the current document and all new documents, select the **Set as Printer Initial Font** option before selecting **OK**.*

Finish-Up Instructions

- Create the following footer. (If necessary, see Steps to Create a Footer in Chapter 10, page 236.)

  Design Ideas **Page #**

- Use the *new* filename **14drill2.if** and save the file. Print one copy and close the document.

Use Append

Text or graphics can be accumulated in the Clipboard and then transferred to a new location using the Append feature. The Append feature is useful in creating new documents without having to rekey information. For example, the Append feature can be used to copy the main points from the report document to a new file to make overhead transparencies listing the major points in a report. The first item to be accumulated is selected and copied. The second and following items to be accumulated are selected and appended to the Clipboard. Once all items are placed in the Clipboard, the information is retrieved (pasted) in an existing document or in a new document. The information placed in the Clipboard can be retrieved (pasted) to as many different location as needed. The information remains in the Clipboard until other information is copied or deleted, thereby replacing the information in the Clipboard.

The information placed in the Clipboard can be viewed and/or deleted using Clipboard Viewer window. The Clipboard Viewer window is accessed by switching to the Program Manager and double-clicking on the **Clipboard** icon in the Main window. The contents of the Clipboard display in the Clipboard Viewer window. If an error has been made when selecting and appending text, the contents of the Clipboard can be deleted by selecting **Edit**, **Delete**. Once the Clipboard has been cleared, the append process can be repeated.

Start-Up Instructions

- Open the file named **14drill3.ter** located on the data disk.

Steps to Append Text

1. Select the first text to be accumulated in the Clipboard.

For example, select **COMPUTER TERMINOLOGY** and the following two blank lines.

2. Select the **Copy** button {Alt, e, c *or* Ctrl and c}.
3. Select the next text to be accumulated in the Clipboard.

   For example, select **Access** and the following blank line.

4. Select **Edit, Append** {Alt, e, d}.
5. Repeat steps 3 and 4 and accumulate any other desired text in the Clipboard.

   For example, append the terms **Access Time**, **Back-up Drive**, **Back-up File**, **Buffer**, **Command**, **Execute**, **Kilobyte**, and **Megabyte** to the Clipboard.

6. When all desired text has been selected and appended to the Clipboard, open an existing file or select the **New Document** button to create a new file.

   For example, select the **New Document** button.

7. Select the **Paste** button to insert the text appended to the Clipboard {Alt, e, p *or* Ctrl and v}.

Finish-Up Instructions

- If necessary, center the title **COMPUTER TERMINOLOGY.**
- Change the font for all the text to **Swiss721 BlkEx BT, 24-point.**
- Use the filename **14drill3.app** and save the document.
- Print one copy.
- Close both documents (**14drill3.app** and **14drill3.ter**).

Create Superscripts and Subscripts

Superscripts are characters that are printed a fraction above the text line, and subscripts are characters that are printed a fraction below the text line (see Figure 14.3). Superscripts and subscripts are used, for example, when printing chemical formulas, algebraic equations, or degrees of temperature.

When working with superscripts and subscripts, it is sometimes desirable to enlarge the display of the text on the screen in order to see better the superscripted or subscripted text. With the Zoom feature, text and graphics can be displayed as large as 400% or as small as 25%. WordPerfect also provides Margin Width, Page Width, and Full Page zoom options. The Margin Width option displays a complete line of text in the document window regardless of the font size selected. The Page Width option displays the page including the margins within the document window. The Full Page option displays the entire page. The Zoom feature can be accessed by selecting the **Zoom** button on the Power Bar or by selecting **View, Zoom**.

Start-Up Instructions

- An empty document window should be displayed. (If necessary, select the **New Document** button.)

$(x + 4)^2$	NH_4
$(c - d)^2$	Na_2PO_4

FIGURE 14.3

Superscripts and subscripts

Steps to Create a Superscript

1. Type the desired text.

   For example, type **(x + 4)2**. (Do not type the period.)

2. Select the character to be a superscript.

   For example, highlight the **2**.

3. Select **Layout, Font** {Alt, L, f *or* press F9}.
4. Move the mouse pointer to the **Position** box, press and hold the mouse button, and drag to highlight **Superscript**. Release the mouse button {Alt and p, press the up arrow key to display Superscript}.
5. Select **OK** {Enter}.

   Note: *The highlighted character displays as a superscript on the screen.*

6. Before continuing to type, press the right arrow key once.

   For example, press the right arrow key once and then press the **Tab** key twice.

Steps to Create a Subscript

1. Type the desired text.

   For example, type **NH4**.

2. Select the character to be a subscript.

   For example, highlight the **4**.

3. Select **Layout, Font** {Alt, L, f, *or* press F9}.
4. Move the mouse pointer to the **Position** box, press and hold the mouse button, and drag to highlight **Subscript**. Release the mouse button {Alt and p, press the down arrow key to display Subscript}.
5. Select **OK** {Enter}.

   Note: *The highlighted character displays as a subscript on the screen.*

6. Before continuing to type, press the right arrow key once.

   For example, press the right arrow key once and then press the **Enter** key twice.

Steps to Use the Zoom Feature

1. Move the mouse pointer to the **Zoom** button 100% on the Power Bar. Press and hold the mouse button and drag to highlight the desired Zoom option. Release

the mouse button {Alt, v, z; press the up or down arrow keys to select the desired Zoom option, Enter}.

For example, select **200%**.

Note: *The Zoom button displays 200%, and the text in the document window is enlarged to 200%.*

2. If desired, return to the normal Zoom view by moving the mouse pointer to the **Zoom** button, pressing and holding the mouse button and dragging to highlight **100%**; release the mouse button {Alt, v, z; press the up arrow key to select 100%, Enter}.

Finish-Up Instructions

- Using the Steps to Create a Superscript and Steps to Create a Subscript, type the equation and formula in the second line of Figure 14.3. If desired, select **200% Zoom** view.
- Use the filename **14drill4.sup** and save the file.
- Print one copy and close the document.

Use the Equation Editor

WordPerfect provides an Equation Editor window that can be used to create (but not solve) scientific and mathematical equations/formulas. When an equation/formula is created, the equation/formula is placed in either an Equation or Inline Equation graphic box. Both Equation and Inline Equation graphic boxes are defaulted to display and print without borders or shading. An equation box can be moved, sized, or shaded in the same way as discussed using a Figure box or Text box in Chapter 13 and it can be attached to a paragraph, page, or character. An Inline Equation box is inserted within a line of text and moves with that line of text when a document is edited.

When the Equation Editor is accessed, a separate window displays, which is divided into three main sections: the editing window, the palette, and the display window (see Figure 14.4). The *editing window* is the area in which an equation/formula is displayed as it is being created or edited. Text and/or numbers are typed in the editing window, and commands, functions, or symbols are either selected from the palette or are typed in order to build an equation/formula. The tilde (~) is used to insert space between characters instead of the Spacebar.

The *palette* contains commands, functions, or symbols that are used to create a formula. For example, the SQRT command is selected to insert a square root ($\sqrt{\ }$) symbol. The left and right braces ({ }) are used to create a group that will act as a single unit. For example, to create $(\frac{2y}{4x})^2$, the commands and text { ({2y} OVER {4x}) } SUP 2 would be placed in the editing window. Also, commands, functions, and symbols can be typed directly into the editing window. For example, to superscript text in the Equation Editor window, select the **SUP or ^** command or type **SUP** in the editing window.

The *display window* is the area in which WordPerfect shows the equation/formula as it will appear when printed. The **Redisplay** button is selected to view the format-

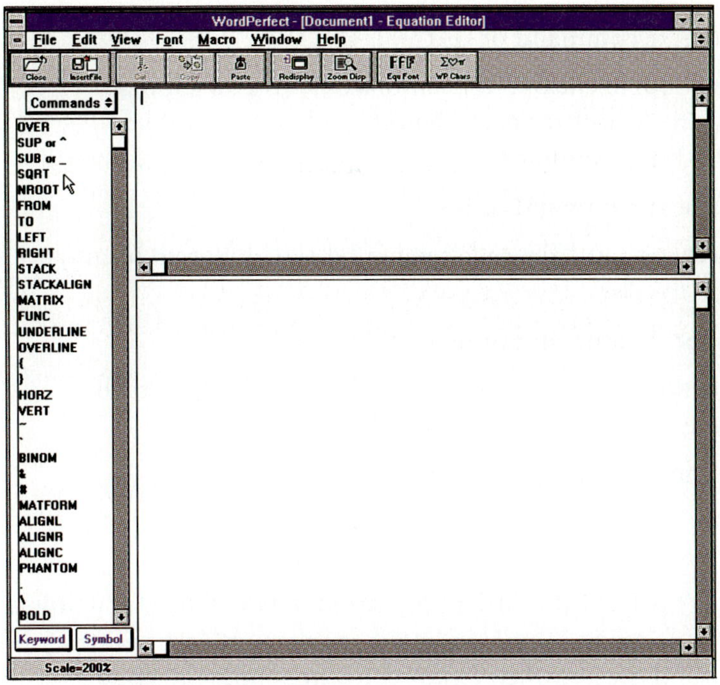

FIGURE 14.4

Equation Editor window

ted equation/formula. An error message, *Incorrect syntax*, displays if an error is made when creating an equation/formula.

After the equation/formula is created, the **Close** button is selected in the Equation Editor window. WordPerfect places the equation/formula in an Equation box or Inline Equation box in the regular document window at the location of the insertion point. (*Note:* A graphic box is inserted even if the editing window is empty when the **Close** button is selected.) To exit the Equation Editor window without inserting the equation and equation graphic box into the document screen, select **File**, **Cancel.** To edit the equation or formula, double-click on the equation/formula and make the desired changes in the Equation Editor window.

Start-Up Instructions

- An empty document window should be displayed. If necessary, select the **New Document** button.
- The following Steps to Create an Equation/Formula will be used to create the formula shown in Figure 14.5.

Steps to Create an Equation/Formula Using the Equation Editor

Note: The insertion point should be located in the document at the place where the equation/formula will be inserted.

1. Select Graphics, Equation {Alt, g, q}.

   Note: The Equation Editor window displays (see Figure 14.4).

2. Select or type the desired command.

   For example, double-click on **SQRT** (square root) {type **SQRT** and press the **Spacebar** once}.

   Note: The command SQRT displays in the editing window.

3. Select or type the next command or text.

   For example, double-click on the left brace ({) {type a left brace ({) and press the Spacebar once}. Repeat to place a second left brace in the editing window.

4. Select or type the next command or text.

   For example, type an **x**. Type a left parenthesis [(] followed by another **x**.

5. Select or type the next command or text.

   For example, double-click on the **SUP or ^** command {press the Spacebar, type SUP, and press the Spacebar again}.

6. Select or type the next command or text.

   For example:

   a. Type a **2**. (Do not type the period.)
   b. Select the ~ (Tilde) command or type a tilde (~) to insert a space.
   c. Type a hyphen (-) to represent a minus symbol.
   d. Select the ~ (Tilde) command or type a tilde (~) to insert a space.
   e. Type a **y**.

7. Select or type the next command or text.

   For example, double-click on the **SUP or ^** command {press the Spacebar once, type SUP, and press the Spacebar again}.

   Type a **2** followed by a right parenthesis [)].

8. Select or type the next command or text.

   For example, double-click on the right brace (}) {type a right brace (})}.

9. Select or type the next command or text.

   For example, double-click on the **OVER** command {press the Spacebar once, type OVER, and press the Spacebar again}.

10. Select or type the next command or text.

    For example, double-click on the left brace ({) {type a left brace ({) and press the Spacebar once}.

    Type **4x**.

11. Select or type the next command or text.

    For example, scroll down the list of commands and double-click on the right brace (}) {press the Spacebar once and type a right brace (})}. Repeat to insert a second right brace.

    Note: *The equation displays on one line and should look similar to the equation shown in the editing window in Figure 14.5.*

12. Select the **Redisplay** button {Alt, v, r *or* Ctrl and F3}.

    Note: *The formatted equation displays in the display window. However, if the equation command or text was entered incorrectly, an equation error message displays in the*

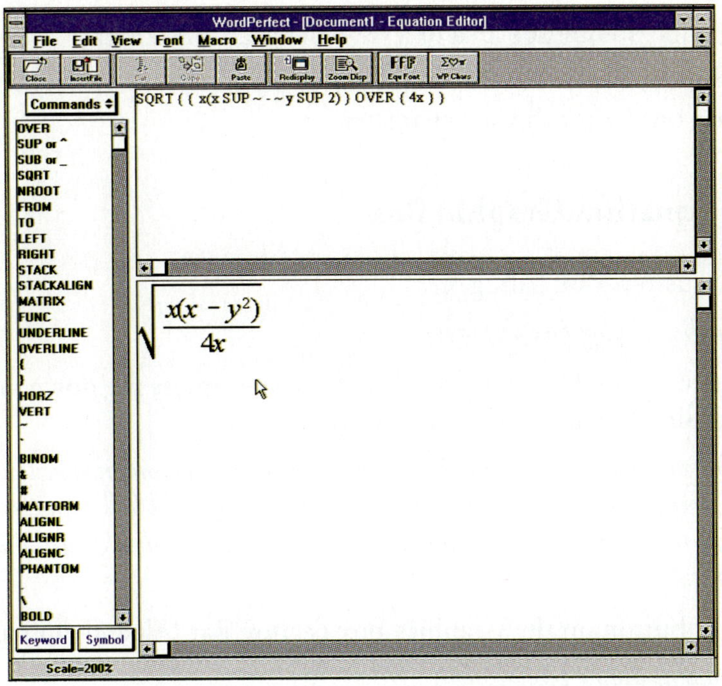

FIGURE 14.5

Equation Editor with completed equation

Status bar. If the commands were typed (and not selected from the palette), a blank space should both precede and follow the commands.

13. Select the Close button to exit the Equation Editor window and place the equation in the regular document window {Alt, f, c *or* Ctrl and F4}.

    Note: The equation displays in the middle of the document window.

Finish-Up Instructions

- Use the filename **14drill5.equ** and save the file.
- Print one copy and close the document.

  Note: The following Steps to Edit an Equation/Formula are for your information.

Steps to Edit an Equation/Formula

1. Move the mouse pointer to the equation in the document window and double-click {Alt, g, e; Alt and Shift and o, e}.

   Note: The Equation Editor window and equation/formula display.

2. Make the desired changes.
3. Select the Redisplay button {Alt, v, r *or* Ctrl and F3}.
4. Select the Close button to exit the Equation Editor window {Alt, f, c *or* Ctrl and F4}.

   Note: The corrected equation/formula displays in the document window.

Start-Up Instructions

- On a clear screen, type the following text that will precede the Inline Equation box:

The formula for finding the area of a triangle when the lengths of the three sides are known is

- Press the **Spacebar** once after the last character.

Steps to Create an Inline Equation Graphic Box

1. Select Graphics, Custom Box {Alt, g, c}.

   Note: The Custom Box dialog box displays.

2. In the Style Name box, double-click on Inline Equation {press the down arrow key to highlight Inline Equation Box, press Enter}.

   Note: An empty Inline Equation graphic box is inserted in the document window and the Graphics Box Feature Bar displays below the Power Bar. Small black handles display indicating that the Inline Equation box is selected; no borders display around the Inline Equation box.

3. Select the Content button on the Graphics Box Feature Bar {Alt and Shift and o}.

   Note: The Box Content dialog box displays.

4. Select the Edit button {e}.

5. Select or type the desired commands and text needed to create the equation.

   For example, create the equation $A=\sqrt{s(s-a)(s-b)(s-c)}$ by typing and selecting the following text and commands: A= SQRT {s(s-a)(s-b)(s-c)}. (A space should follow the SQRT command and the right brace.)

6. Select Redisplay {Alt, v, r *or* Ctrl and F3}.

7. Select Close to display the equation in the document window {Alt, f, c *or* Ctrl and F4}.

8. Continue typing any text that follows the Inline Equation box.

   For example, type a period (.) to complete the sentence.

Finish-Up Instructions

- Use the filename **14drill6.inl** and save the file.
- Print one copy and close the document.

The Next Step

Chapter Review and Activities

Self-Check Quiz

T F 1. To set the line height, select **Layout**, **Line**, **Height**, choose **Fixed**, and, if desired, change the line height and select **OK**.

T F 2. Information placed in the Clipboard can be viewed and/or deleted in the Clipboard Viewer window.

T F 3. Once an equation has been created in the Equation Editor window, select the **Close** button to place the formula/equation in the regular document window.

T F 4. Letterspacing is used to increase or decrease the amount of space between letters in selected text.

T F 5. The **Zoom** button can be used to enlarge the display of text up to 1000%.

6. Letterspacing is also referred to as __________.
   a. tracking
   b. kerning
   c. word spacing
   d. none of these

7. A superscript is a character that prints a fraction ____ the text line.
   a. above
   b. below
   c. on
   d. both b and c

8. List two advantages for changing the initial font in a document.

9. Explain the difference between word spacing and letterspacing.

10. Write an example in which you personally might use the Append feature.

Enriching Language Arts Skills

Spelling/Vocabulary Words

derogatory tending to belittle; negative.
inclusion the act of containing, encompassing, consisting of.
propaganda information spread to help or harm a group, institution, or nation.
rendered to have performed, to have done, supplied.
surreptitious obtained or performed in a secretive or devious manner.

Independent Adjectives

Two adjectives that modify the same noun are separated by a comma.

Example:

The small, blue chair will be used for guests when they visit the president.

Activities

Activity 14.1—Set Initial Font and Use Leading Adjustment

1. Set the initial font for the current document to **Arrus BT**, **12-point**, or choose a font of your own (select **Layout**, **Document**, **Initial Font**, choose desired font, **OK**).
2. Use the following information and type the document shown.
   a. Press the **F7** key three times after typing the lead words **Medical Care**, **Rehabilitation**, and **Disability Income**.
   b. Bold and center the title and bold the lead words.
   c. Press **Enter** twice after the title and after each paragraph as shown.

NOTICE TO EMPLOYEES

If a work injury occurs, you are automatically entitled to workers' compensation. Texas law provides certain benefits to employees who are injured or become ill because of a job-related activity.

Medical Care	All medical treatment required to cure the injury or illness will be performed without cost to the employee. The employee chooses the physician and facility. The facility must be located within a reasonable geographical area. The employee should never see a bill because all costs are paid directly by the employer or its agents.
Rehabilitation	If the injury or illness prevents return to the employee's usual job, the employee may receive vocational rehabilitation. All costs are paid by the employer.
Disability Income	Employees disabled by job injury or job illness receive disability income while unable to work. The payments are two-thirds of the employee's average weekly pay, up to a maximum set by state law.

---

3. Use the filename **14act1.emp** and save the file.
4. Change the font size to **24-point** for the title.
5. Change the word spacing for the title to 200% and letterspacing for the title to 150% of optimal (block the title, select **Layout**, **Typesetting**,

Word/ Letterspacing, choose **Percent of Optimal** in the Word Spacing box, double-click in the Percent of Optimal box and type **200**, choose **Percent of Optimal** in the Letterspacing box, double-click in the Percent of Optimal box and type **150**, **OK**).

6. Select each lead word and change the font size to **18-point**.
7. Check the alignment of paragraphs and make adjustments as needed.

   Hint: Delete or insert indent code(s) between the lead words and indented paragraphs, as needed.
8. Locate the insertion point at the beginning of the first paragraph and set the line height to **Fixed** (select **Layout**, **Line**, **Height**, **Fixed**, select **OK**).
9. Select **Layout**, **Typesetting**, **Word/Letterspacing**, **Adjust Leading**, double-click in the Between Lines box and type **.15**, select **OK**.
10. Use the filename **14act1.fin** and save the file.
11. Print one copy and close the document.

Activity 14.2—Use Append to Create an Overhead Transparency

1. Open the file named **14act2.pd** located on the data disk.
2. Select the title **PAID LEAVES** and the following two blank lines.
3. Select the **Copy** button.
4. Select the first heading **VACATION** and the following blank line.
5. Select **Edit**, **Append**.
6. Select the next heading and the following blank line.
7. Select **Edit**, **Append**.
8. Repeat steps 6 and 7 to append the remaining headings to the Clipboard.
9. When all of the remaining headings have been appended to the Clipboard, select the **New Document** button.
10. Select the **Paste** button to insert the appended text into the new document.
11. Center the title and format the text for use as an overhead transparency (use a large font size).
12. Use the filename **14act2.ovr** and save the file.
13. Print one copy and close both documents.

Activity 14.3—Use the Equation Editor

1. Use the Equation Editor (select **Graphics**, **Equation**) to create the following equations. Select the **Redisplay** button to view the typed equation. Make any corrections necessary. Select the **Close** button after completing each equation/formula to transfer the equation/formula to the document window. (Each equation will display on a separate line.)

$\frac{3y}{5}$ $\frac{3}{7}m = -21m$ $\sqrt{25p^8} = 5p^4$

Note: Below are the equations as displayed in the Equation Editor editing window:

{3y} OVER 5 3 OVER 7 m~=~-21m SQRT {25p SUP 8}~=~5p SUP 4

2. Use the filename **14act3.equ** and save the file.
3. Print one copy and close the document.

Activity 14.4—Use Subscripts

1. Type and center the following text using subscripts as shown.

CHEMICAL FORMULAS--Aluminum

Aluminum Acetate: $Al(C_2H_3O_2)_3$
Aluminum Borohydride: $Al(BH_4)_3$
Aluminum Carbide: $Al_4(C_3)$

2. Use the filename **14act4.sub** and save the file.
3. Print one copy and close the document.

Activity 14.5—Use Superscripts

1. Type and center the following text using superscripts as shown. A lowercase letter *o* is used to represent the degree symbol.

DEGREES OF TEMPERATURE

Celsius vs. Fahrenheit

$20^oC = 68^oF$
$30^oC = 86^oF$
$40^oC = 104^oF$

2. Use the filename **14act5.sup** and save the file.
3. Print one copy and close the document.

Challenge Your Skills

Skill 14.1—Format a Report and Use Append to Create an Overhead Transparency

1. Open the file named **14skill1.txt** located on the data disk.
2. Enhance the document to make it attractive and easy to read. Make decisions regarding:

   Margins
   Fonts
   Bold for title and sideheads
   Justification
   Footer text and placement
3. Save the file as **14skill1.fin** and print one copy.
4. Use the Append feature to create an overhead transparency using the title and sideheads contained in the file named **14skill1.fin**.
5. When the title and headings have been appended to the Clipboard, create a new document and paste the appended text in the new document. Format the overhead transparencies. Make decisions regarding:

   Fonts
   Justification
   Spacing between items
6. Use the filename **14skill1.ovr** and save the overhead transparency file.
7. Print one copy and close the documents.

Skill 14.2—Use Superscripts and Subscripts

1. Create the following table. Make decisions regarding:

   Margins
   Fonts
   Table format (cell width, text justification, etc.)

OPERATING CONDITIONS			
Conditions	Soap Cleaner	Acid Etch	Nitric Acid Wash (HNO3)
Concentration	6 oz./gal.	10% by volume	50% by volume
Temperature	55°-60°C	60°-65°C	Room temperature (20°C)
Time	5-7 minutes	2-4 minutes	45 seconds

2. Use the filename **14skill2.con** and save the file.

3. Print one copy and close the document.

Skill 14.3—Use the Equation Editor

1. Create the following equations.

   Note: Each equation will display on a separate line.

(a) $\sqrt{x^4 y^{12}} = x^2 y^6$ (b) $\sqrt{\frac{25k^6}{36}} = \frac{5k^3}{6}$ (c) $\left(\frac{5x^3 y^5}{7mn}\right)^2$

Note: Below are the equations as displayed in the Equation Editor editing window:

(a) SQRT {x SUP 4y SUP 12}~=~x SUP 2 y SUP 6
(b) SQRT {{25k SUP 6} OVER 36}~=~{5k SUP 3} OVER 6
(c) {({5x SUP 3y SUP 5} OVER {7mn})} SUP 2

---

2. Use the filename **14skill3.equ** and save the file.
3. Print one copy and close the document.

Skill 14.4—Use Document Initial Font, Letterspacing, Word Spacing, and Leading Adjustment; Language Arts

1. Open the file named **14skill4.txt** located on the data disk. Make decisions regarding:

   Margins (left and right margins of .75 or less are recommended)
   Fonts (set an initial document font)
   Justification
   Widow/Orphan protect
   Bold, underline, capitalization for the title and sideheads
   Word spacing and letterspacing for the title and sideheads
   Alignment of paragraphs
   Header or footer text and placement

2. Correct five spelling errors and three punctuation errors.
3. Use the filename **14skill4.tal** and save the file.
4. Print one copy.
5. If you have completed your work, exit WordPerfect.

CHAPTER 15

Create Documents Using Special Functions

Features Covered

- Sort table rows, paragraphs, and lines
- Record and play macros
- Use QuickFormat to copy font and text attributes
- Edit, create, and apply styles
- Use ExpressDoc templates

Objectives and Introduction

After successfully completing this chapter, you will know how to use the Sort feature to sort table rows, paragraphs, and lines numerically and alphabetically. You will also be able to edit, create, and apply styles to quickly format documents. You will learn how to create documents using ExpressDoc templates and to copy the format of text using the QuickFormat feature. In addition, you will learn to record and play macros to expedite your work.

WordPerfect provides many special functions to expedite the production of documents and to eliminate repetitious tasks. The Sort function makes alphabetical and numerical sorting easy and quick. Macros can be created to perform quickly and efficiently tasks that must be repeated on a regular basis. Styles, templates, and the QuickFormat functions make it easy to develop a custom look and apply it to your document(s).

Create Alphabetically and Numerically Sorted Text

The Sort function is used to arrange lines, paragraphs, table rows, merge records, and parallel columns in alphabetical or numerical order. A list of names can be sorted alphabetically and a list of numbers can be sorted numerically.

Text can be selected to sort in *alpha* (alphabetical) or *numeric* (numerical) order. Text can also be sorted either in descending or ascending order. Ascending order begins with letter A through Z or the lowest number to the highest number; descending order begins with letter Z through A or the highest number to the lowest number.

For the purpose of sorting, a line is defined as any text that ends with a single hard return and a paragraph is defined as any text that ends with two or more hard returns. When sorting words that begin with the same character, WordPerfect uses the character(s) that follow to determine the correct order. For example, if there are two last names that begin with the same letter, the second (then the third, fourth, etc.) character in the names are used to determine the alphabetical order.

Before sorting a document, all text to be sorted is selected. The Sort dialog box is used to choose the Sort by option (Line, Paragraph, Table, Merge Record, or Parallel Columns) and to define a key(s). A key identifies the type of sort (alpha or numeric), the order of the sort (ascending or descending), and the portion of text to sort (word, cell, field, or line). Up to nine keys can be defined in the Key Definition area of the Sort dialog box. Key 1 is used for the primary sort criteria; keys 2–9 are used to specify secondary sort criteria.

When a sort is performed, WordPerfect reorders the text in accordance with the Key 1 sort criteria and then uses any additional keys to refine the sort. For example, if a list of names is to be sorted by last name and several individuals have the same last name, Key 1 would specify that the last name is the "primary" sort criteria and Key 2 would specify that the first name is the "secondary" sort criteria.

Before performing a sort, check that the Allow Undo option is selected in the Sort dialog box. This option allows you to undo the sort operation and return the text to the original order if a problem is encountered once the text is sorted.

Start-Up Instructions

- Open the file named **15drill1.tbl** located on the data disk.

Steps to Sort Table Rows Numerically

1. Select the rows of the table to be sorted.

   For example, select all table cells except the table title and column head cells.

2. Select **Tools, Sort** {Alt, t, r *or* Alt and F9}.

   Note: *The Sort dialog box displays (see Figure 15.1). Check that the* ***Allow Undo*** *option is selected. (If necessary, click in the* ***Allow Undo*** *option box to select this option.)*

3. In the Sort By box, check that **Table Row** is selected.

4. In the Key Definitions area, select the desired sort criteria for Key 1.

   For example, to sort the list numerically, edit the Key 1 definition as follows:

   a. Move the mouse pointer to the button under the word **Type**, press and hold the mouse button and drag to select **Numeric**, release the mouse button {Tab until light outline appears around the word in the Type button, press n}.

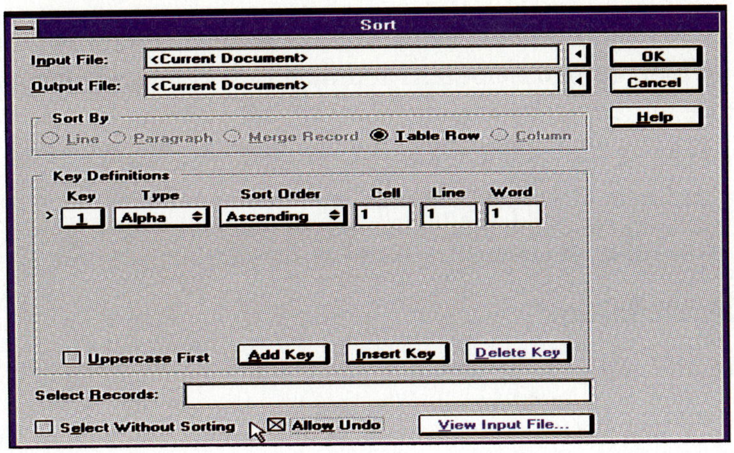

FIGURE 15.1

Sort dialog box

b. Move the mouse pointer to the button under the words **Sort Order**, press and hold the mouse button and drag to select **Descending**, release the mouse button {Tab to select the Sort Order button, press d}.

c. Double-click in the **Cell** box and type **3** (to sort by the third column) {Tab to select the Cell box contents, type 3}.

5. Select **OK** {Enter}.

Note: The Sort Status box displays briefly. After a few short moments, the table (sorted by column 3) displays.

Finish-Up Instructions

- Use the *new* filename **15drill1.num** and save the file.
- Print one copy and close the document.

Start-Up Instructions

- Open the file named **15drill1.tbl** located on the data disk.

Steps to Sort Table Rows Alphabetically

1. Select the rows of the table to be sorted.

   For example, select all table cells except the table title and column head cells.

2. Select **Tools, Sort** {Alt, t, r *or* Alt and F9}.
3. In the Sort By box, check that **Table Row** is selected.
4. In the Key Definitions area, select the desired sort criteria for Key 1.

   For example, to sort the list by last names, edit the Key 1 definition as follows:

   a. Move the mouse pointer to the button under the word **Type**, press and hold the mouse button and drag to select **Alpha**, release the mouse button {Tab until a light outline appears around the word in the Type button, press a}.

b. Move the mouse pointer to the button under the words **Sort Order**, press and hold the mouse button and drag to select **Ascending**, release the mouse button {Tab to select the Sort Order button, press a}.

c. Double-click in the **Cell** box and type **1** (to sort by the first column) {Tab to select the Cell box contents, type 1}.

d. Check that 1 displays in the Line and Word boxes.

Create a Second Key Definition

5. Select the **Add Key** button {Alt and a}.

   Note: Key 2 displays below Key 1.

6. Select the desired sort criteria for the new key.

   For example, check that the following sort criteria display for Key 2:

Type:	Alpha
Sort Order:	Ascending
Cell:	1
Line:	1

   Double-click in the Word box and type 2 to sort by the second word in cell 1 (i.e., the first name).

7. Select **OK** {Enter}.

   Note: The salespeople's names are listed alphabetically. Notice that the first names were used to sort the people with the same last name.

Finish-Up Instructions

- Use the *new* filename **15drill1.alp** and save the file.
- Print one copy and close the document.

Start-Up Instructions

- Open the file named **15drill2.txt** located on the data disk.

Steps to Sort Paragraphs

1. Select all the paragraphs to be sorted.

   For example, select all paragraphs in the document.

2. Select **Tools, Sort** {Alt, t, r *or* Alt and F9}.
3. Check that **Paragraph** displays in the Sort By box.
4. In the Key Definitions area, select the desired sort criteria for Key 1.

   For example, to sort by last names, edit the Key 1 definition as follows:

   a. Check that **Alpha** displays in the Type button. If necessary, move the mouse pointer to the **Type** button, press and hold the mouse button and drag to select **Alpha**, release the mouse button {Tab to select the Type button, press a}.

b. Check that **Ascending** displays in the Sort Order button. If necessary, move the mouse pointer to the **Sort Order** button, press and hold the mouse button and drag to select **Ascending**, release the mouse button {Tab to select the Sort Order button, press a}.

c. Check that 1 displays in the Line, Field, and Word boxes.

Note: *If a second key is displayed, move the mouse pointer to the second key definition and click once on any item in the definition, Then select the* ***Delete Key*** *button {Alt and 2, Alt and d}.*

5. Select **OK** {Enter}.

Note: *The text is sorted by only the first line of each paragraph (section). For the purpose of sorting, a paragraph is defined as any text followed by two hard returns (two Enters).*

Finish-Up Instructions

- Check the spacing between each section. A single blank line should display between each section. If necessary, delete extra blank lines.
- Use the *new* filename **15drill2.par** and save the file.

Start-Up Instructions

- The file named **15drill2.par** should be displayed in the document window.

Chapter **15** Create Documents Using Special Functions

Steps to **Sort Lines**

1. Select the lines of text to be sorted.

   For example, select the four lines under the first line "Delete."

2. Select **Tools, Sort** {Alt, t, r *or* Alt and F9}.
3. Check that **Line** displays in the Sort By box.
4. In the Key Definitions area, select the desired sort criteria.

   For example, check that the following are selected for Key 1:

Type:	Alpha
Sort Order:	Ascending
Field:	1
Line:	1
Word:	1

5. To create additional keys, select the **Add Key** button and select the desired sort criteria for each key.

   For example, create two more keys and check or select the following sort criteria:

   Key 2

Type:	Alpha
Sort Order:	Ascending
Field:	1

Line:	1
Word:	2

Key 3

Type:	Alpha
Sort Order:	Ascending
Field:	1
Line:	1
Word:	3

6. Select OK {Enter}.

Finish-Up Instructions

- Repeat steps 1–6 to sort the lines under each section in the document.
- Use the *new* filename **15drill2.sor** and save the file.
- Print one copy and close the document.

Use Macros

Macros are shortcuts that eliminate repetitious action. Macros are especially useful when your actions involve selecting several menus and submenus or making changes in dialog boxes. For example, to create a horizontal graphic line with the Thick/Thin 2 line style and .1" of space above and below the line, the following steps must be performed: select **Graphics**, **Custom Lines**, click on the **Line Style** button, select the **Thick/Thin 2** line style, double-click in the **Above** box, type **.1**, double-click in the **Below** box, type **.1**, and choose **OK**. Using a macro, the instructions to create the horizontal graphic line could be reduced to only six steps or less. Also, macros can be used to eliminate repetitious typing. For example, creating a standard closing paragraph with a typed signature line, reference initials, and enclosure notation can be reduced to six mouse clicks.

WordPerfect supplies a number of macros, which are stored in the macros subdirectory and are identified by the filename extension *.wcm*. A supplied macro is played (activated) by selecting the desired macro and responding to prompts displayed on the screen. These supplied macros can be used to view the contents of the Clipboard; print a list of available fonts, convert footnotes to endnotes, and many other tasks.

In addition to the macros supplied by WordPerfect, new macros can be created. First, the macro is given a name. Every keystroke and mouse selection is then recorded and finally the recording is stopped and automatically saved.

Because WordPerfect remembers each keystroke and mouse selection made while Record is turned on, plan the macro before selecting **Tools**, **Macro**, **Record**. Write down each step needed to create the macro. Once Record is turned on, Macro Record displays in the Status bar. When all the desired keystrokes and mouse selections have been completed, stop the recording of the macro by selecting **Tools**, **Macro**, **Record** for a second time. The macro is automatically saved.

Once a macro is recorded, the macro can be played as often as needed by selecting **Tools**, **Macro**, **Play**, typing or selecting the desired macro filename, and selecting **OK**. The macro performs each recorded step. When all the recorded steps have been completed, you can edit, save, print, or close the file using normal procedures.

Changes to a document created by a macro do not alter the macro. The macro can be used again and again.

WordPerfect remembers the last macro played and the macro name is displayed on the Macro menu when **Tools**, **Macro** is selected. Macros can be added to the Macro menu by selecting **Tools**, **Macro**, **Menu**, **Insert**, typing or selecting the macro name and choosing **Select**, **OK**. A macro listed on the Macro menu can be played instantly by clicking on the listed macro name.

Start-Up Instructions

❖ A new document window should be displayed. (If necessary, select the **New Document** button.)

Steps to Use a Supplied Macro

1. Select Tools, Macro, Play {Alt, t, m, p *or* Alt and F10}.

   Note: *The Play Macro dialog box displays. The insertion point is located in the Name box.*

2. Click on the List Files button (the small button with a picture of a file folder) to display a list of macros {F4}.

   Note: *The Select File dialog box displays. The macros stored in the default macro directory (e.g., c:\wpwin60\macros) are shown.*

3. Double-click on the desired macro {Tab, press the down arrow key to highlight desired macro name, Enter}.

   For example, double-click on **allfonts.wcm**.

   Note: *The selected filename and the full path displays in the Name box of the Play Macro dialog box.*

4. Select Play {Enter}. Wait a few moments. If necessary, respond to any prompts that display on the screen.

   Note: *In a few moments, the macro creates a document containing a list of available fonts with samples of each font. The macro is now finished.*

Finish-Up Instructions

❖ Use the filename **15drill3.fon** and save the list of available fonts.

❖ Print one copy and close the document.

Start-Up Instructions

❖ A new document window should be displayed. (If necessary, select the **New Document** button.)

Steps to Record a Macro

1. In a clear document window, select Tools, Macro, Record {Alt, t, m, r *or* Ctrl and F10}.

   Note: *The Record Macro dialog box displays.*

2. In the Name box, type the name of the macro (if necessary, include the drive letter and/or directory where the macro is to be stored).

   For example, type **a:closing**. (Do not type the period.)

3. Select Record {Enter}.

   Note: *The insertion point returns to the document window and the words **Macro Record** display (in light gray letters) in the center of the Status bar at the bottom of the screen. Also, the mouse pointer displays as a circle with a line across it when located in the text area of the document window.*

4. Perform the actions to be recorded.

   For example, type the following information:

   I appreciate your interest in our new Trak-Power Lighting systems. A catalog describing our complete product line is enclosed. If you have any questions, please do not hesitate to contact me via E-mail at kunke_st@webhall.com or by calling my office at 207-555-0551, extension 4256.

   Sincerely,

   Stephanie Kunkemueller
   Regional Sales Representative

   SK/xxx

   Enc.

5. Select Tools, Macro, Record {Alt, t, m, r *or* Ctrl and F10}.

   Note: *The macro was automatically saved when **Tools, Macro, Record** was selected for the second time.*

Finish-Up Instructions

- Close the document (do not save the file) or select **File**, **New**.

Start-Up Instructions

- Open the file named **15drill4.ltr** located on the data disk.
- Locate the insertion point at the second blank line below the last paragraph.

Steps to Play the Recorded Macro

1. Select Tools, Macro, Play {Alt, t, m, p *or* Alt and F10}.
2. Type the desired macro name.

   For example, type **a:closing**. (Do not type the period.)

3. Select Play {Enter}.

Note: In a few moments, the closing paragraph, typed signature, reference initials and enclosure notation display in the document window. The document can now be edited, saved, printed, etc., as any other document.

Finish-Up Instructions

- Use the *new* filename **15drill4.bon** and save the file.
- Print one copy and close the document.

Use QuickFormat

The QuickFormat feature is used to quickly copy fonts, text attributes, and/or paragraph format (styles) from one piece of text to another. The QuickFormat feature is accessed by selecting the **QuickFormat** button on the Button Bar or by choosing **Layout, QuickFormat.**

Start-Up Instruction

- Open the file named **15drill5.pho** located on the data disk.

Steps to Use QuickFormat

1. Select and format the desired text.

   For example, select the sidehead **800 Direct**, change the font to **Humanst521 Cn BT**, and select the **Bold** text attribute.

2. With the formatted text selected, click on the **QuickFormat** button on the Button Bar.

   Note: When the mouse pointer is moved into the document window, the mouse pointer changes to an I-beam and a paint roller.

3. Select the text to be formatted.

   For example, select the words **800 Direct** in the first sentence of the first paragraph.

   Note: When the mouse button is released, the format of the text selected in step 2 is applied to the text selected in step 3.

4. Continue to apply the format to desired text.

   For example, apply the format to *each* occurrence of the words **800 Direct, Voice Mail, Three-Way Conference Calling,** and **Call Return.**

5. When the format has been applied to all desired text, select the **QuickFormat** button again to turn off the QuickFormat feature.

Finish-Up Instructions

- Use the *new* filename **15drill5.new** and save the file.
- Print one copy and close the document.

Use Styles to Format Documents

A style is a *group* of formatting instructions that can be applied to related sections of text and can be saved and used in other documents. For example, a style can be used to format the sideheads of a report to print in 18-point EngraversGothic BT. The purpose of using styles is to save time and maintain a consistent format throughout a document. Time is saved by applying the same style repeatedly to related sections. Also, if the format of a style is changed, it automatically changes all text in the current document where the style has been previously applied.

There are three types of styles: *Document*, *Paragraph (paired)*, and *Character (paired)*. A Document style usually affects an entire document. For example, a Document style might change the margins and font for the entire document. Paragraph and Character styles usually affect a portion of the document. For example, a Paragraph style could change the font and point size, set center justification, and bold the title of a report. A Character style might apply the bold and italic text attributes to text.

To apply a Paragraph style, locate the insertion point anywhere in the paragraph to be affected. To apply a Character style, however, select the text to be affected. When a Paragraph or Character style is applied to text, a code is placed at the beginning of the affected text to turn the style on and a second code is placed at the end of the affected text to turn the style off. These are referred to as "paired" codes.

WordPerfect has several predefined styles that can be used to format outline levels, footnotes/endnotes, table of contents entries, etc. These predefined styles are referred to as *System Styles*. The *Open Style: Initial Style* code that displays as the first item in the Reveal Codes screen of each WordPerfect 6.0 document is a System Style. System Styles can be edited but not deleted. When the **Styles** button is selected, a list of styles available to format the document displays. If no new styles have been created, the Style List dialog box will contain only System Styles, e.g., *Initial Style, Heading 1,* and *Heading 2.*

There are two methods for creating new styles: QuickCreate and "normal." The QuickCreate method is used to create styles based on previously formatted text. The "normal" method of creating styles is to select the **Styles** button, choose **Create**, and specify the format for the style using the options available in the Styles Editor dialog box.

Styles are edited by selecting the **Styles** button, highlighting the desired style name, and selecting **Edit**. The menu options in the Styles Editor dialog box are then used to change the existing style contents (format). When a style is edited, any text in the current document that was previously formatted with the edited style is changed to reflect the new format specifications.

When a document containing styles is saved, the edited/new styles are also saved. The edited/new styles can be used to format other documents by retrieving the style information from the existing document into the new document. If any System Styles are modified, the user must tell WordPerfect to retrieve *both* the User Styles and the System Styles.

Start-Up Instructions

- Open the file named **15drill6.unf** located on the data disk.

Steps to Edit a Style

1. Select the **Styles** button on the Button Bar {Alt, L, s *or* Alt and F8}.

   Note: *The Style List dialog box displays containing a list of existing styles. The styles listed are System Styles, which are available for formatting documents.*

2. Highlight the style to be edited {press the up or down arrow keys to highlight desired style}.

   For example, highlight the style named **InitialStyles**.

3. Select **Edit** {Alt and e}.

   Note: *The Styles Editor dialog box displays. A flashing red or shaded block displays in the Contents box and a Menu bar displays at the top of the dialog box.*

4. Use the menu options in the Styles Editor dialog box to make the desired changes to the style.

   a. Select **Layout, Font** and change the font to **Arrus BT, 11-point**. Select **OK** {Alt, l, f, use the arrow keys and Tab to highlight desired font and size, Enter}.

   Note: *As formatting options are selected, codes display in the Contents dialog box (see Figure 15.2).*

   b. To insert page numbers, select **Layout, Page, Numbering, Position, Bottom Center, Font, Arrus BT, 11-point**, select **OK** twice {Alt, L, p, n, down arrow key to display Bottom Center; Alt and f, use arrow keys and Tab to select font and size, Enter twice}.

   c. To turn on widow/orphan control, select **Layout, Page, Keep Text Together, Prevent the first and last lines of paragraphs from being separated across pages, OK** {Alt, L, k, p, Enter}.

   d. Change the left and right margins to 1.25" by selecting **Layout, Margins**, type 1.25 in the Left and Right boxes, select **OK** {Alt, L, m, type

Chapter 15 Create Documents Using Special Functions

FIGURE 15.2

Styles Editor dialog box with formatting codes

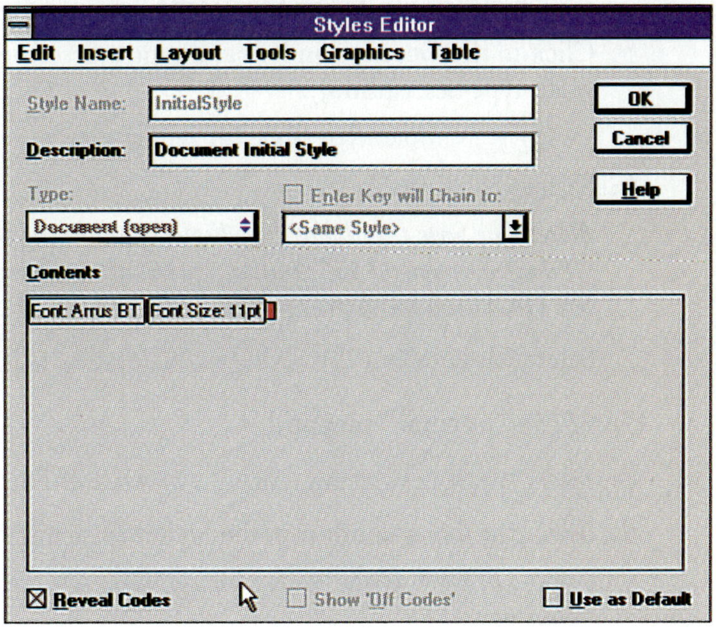

left margin, Tab, type right margins; Alt and f, use arrow keys and Tab to select font and size, Enter twice}.

5. Select **OK** to exit the Styles Editor dialog box {Tab, Enter}
6. Select **Close** to exit to the Style List dialog box {Alt and c}.

   *Note: The font for the document text will have been changed. If desired, select the **Page Zoom Full** button to observe the page number at the bottom center of the page and the changed margins. Select the **Page Zoom Full** button again to return to the normal view.*

Finish-Up Instructions

- Use the *new* filename **15drill6.sty** and save the file.

Start-Up Instructions

- The file named **15drill6.sty** should be displayed in the document window.

Steps to Create a New Paragraph Style

Using the QuickCreate Method

1. Place the insertion point anywhere in the paragraph that contains the desired formatting instructions.

   For example, place the insertion point in the report title "Laboratory Test Program."

2. Select the **Styles** button {Alt, L, s or Alt and F8}.

   Note: The Styles List dialog box displays.

3. Select **QuickCreate** in the Style List dialog box {Alt and q}.

   Note: The Styles QuickCreate dialog box displays.

4. Type the desired style name in the Style Name box.

   For example, type **Report Title**.

5. Click in the Description box and type a description of the purpose of the style {Tab, type description}.

   For example, type **Style for report title.**

6. Select **OK** {Enter }.

   *Note: The Style List dialog box displays containing the new style name "Report Title." (If desired, select the **Edit** button to view the contents of the style in the Styles Editor. Select **OK** to exit the Styles Editor.)*

7. Select **Close** to exit the Style List dialog box {Alt and c}.

Using the "normal" method

8. Select the **Styles** button (Alt, L, s *or* Alt and F8}.
9. Select the **Create** option in the Style List dialog box {Alt and r}.

   Note: The Styles Editor dialog box displays. The insertion point is located in the Style Name box.

10. Type the desired style name in the Style Name box.

For example, type **Sidehead.**

11. Click in the Description box and type a brief description of the purpose of the style {Tab, type description}.

For example, type **Style for report sideheads.**

12. Select Type and choose the desired style type option {Alt and y, Alt and Shift and down arrow key, press the down arrow key to highlight desired type, Enter}.

For example, check that **Paragraph (paired)** displays in the Type box.

13. Click in the Contents box {Tab, Alt and c}

Note: *A flashing red or shaded block displays in the Contents box. Menu options at the top of the Styles Editor dialog box are used to specify the format for the style.*

14. Use the menu options in the Styles Editor dialog box to create the desired style format.

For example, create the following styles:

a. Select **Layout, Font** and change the font to **EngraversGothic BT, 16-point, OK.**

b. Select **Layout, Paragraph, Format, Spacing Between Paragraphs, 1.5, OK.**

15. When all the formatting instructions have been chosen, select OK to exit the Style Editor dialog box.

16. Repeat steps 7–14 to create any additional styles desired.

For example, create the following style:

Style name:	**Company name**
Description:	**Changes font for company name**
Style type:	**Character (paired)**
Font:	**EngraversGothic BT, 14-point**

17. When all needed styles have been created, select Close to exit the Style List dialog box {Alt and c}.

Finish-Up Instructions

- Use the same filename **15drill6.sty** and save the document. (The newly created styles will also be saved.)
- Continue with the Steps to Apply Styles.

Start-Up Instructions

- The file named **15drill6.sty** should be displayed in the document window.

Steps to Apply Styles

1. *To apply a Document style to the entire document,* place the insertion point at the top of the document, select the **Styles** button, and double-click on the desired Document style name {Alt, L, s *or* Alt and F8; highlight desired style name, Enter}.

   For example, when *InitialStyle* was edited earlier in the chapter, the *InitialStyle* Document style went into effect immediately; therefore, continue with step 2.

2. *To apply a Paragraph style,* place the insertion point between any two characters in the paragraph. Select the **Style** button. Double-click on the desired Paragraph style name {Alt, L, s *or* Alt and F8; highlight desired style name, Enter}.

   For example, place the insertion point between any two characters in the report title. Select the **Style** button and double-click on the **Report Title** style name.

3. *To apply a Character style,* select the text to be affected, select the **Styles** button, and double-click on the desired Character style name {Alt, L, s *or* Alt and F8; highlight desired style name, Enter}.

   For example, select the company name, Hanford Consultants West, in the first paragraph of the report, select the **Styles** button, and double-click on the **Company name** style.

4. Use steps 1, 2, or 3 and apply styles as needed to the document.

   For example, apply the Paragraph style named **Sidehead** to each of the sidehead paragraphs, i.e., *In-Situ Moisture Content and Dry Density, Percent Fines, Atterberg Limits, Shear Tests, Consolidation Tests,* and *R-Value.*

Finish-Up Instructions

- Use the same filename, **15drill6.sty**, and save the document.
- Print one copy and close the document.

Start-Up Instructions

- = Open the file named **15rept2.unf** located on the data disk.

Steps to Retrieve Styles to Format Another Document

1. Select the **Styles** button {Alt, L, s *or* Alt and F8}.

2. Select **Options, Retrieve** {Alt and o, Alt and Shift and down arrow, e}.

   Note: *The Retrieve Styles From dialog box displays.*

3. In the Filename box, type the name of the document that contains the desired styles or select the **List Files** button (the small button with a picture of a file folder) and double-click on the desired file.

   For example, type **a:15drill6.sty**. (Do not type the final period.)

4. Check that the Both option is selected in the Style Type area to retrieve both System Styles and User Styles.
5. Select OK {Enter}.

   Note: A message displays, "Overwrite current styles?".
6. Select Yes {Enter}.

   Note: The styles created earlier—Report Title, Sidehead, and Company name—now display in the Style List dialog box and are available to format the document. The edited Initial Style Document style is already in effect.
7. Select Close {Alt and c}.

Finish-Up Instructions

- Place the insertion point in the report title and apply the **Report Title** Paragraph style. (If necessary, see Steps to Apply the Styles, step 2.)
- Select the company name in the first paragraph and apply the **Company name** Character style. (If necessary, see Steps to Apply the Styles, step 3.)
- Place the insertion point in the sidehead, *Selection Committe Responsibilities,* and apply the **Sidehead** Paragraph style. (If necessary, see Steps to Apply Styles, step 2.) Repeat for each sidehead, i.e., *Screening Applicants, Interviews, Confidentiality.*
- Use the *new* filename **15rept2.sty** and save the file.
- Print one copy and close the document.

Use ExpressDoc Templates

WordPerfect supplies over 65 different templates called ExpressDocs. ExpressDoc templates are model documents containing text, formatting instructions, styles, special dialog boxes, Button Bars, graphic lines, text boxes, etc. Each ExpressDoc template is designed to create a specific document style. For example, the *fax3* ExpressDoc template is used to create a traditional style fax cover sheet. Each document created using the same ExpressDoc template will have the same format. Unless another template is selected, the *Standard* template is automatically attached to a document each time a new document is created.

The very first time the Template feature is used, a Personalize Your Template dialog box displays. The information typed into this dialog box is used each time an ExpressDoc template is selected. The personal information can be changed by selecting the **Personal Info** option in the Template Information dialog box.

The **Template** button on the Button Bar is selected to display the Templates dialog box containing a list of ExpressDoc templates. New templates can be created or existing templates can be edited by selecting the **Options** button in the Templates dialog box.

When an ExpressDoc template is selected, the Template Information dialog box displays. Information that will be used to fill in the template document is typed into the boxes that display in the Template Information dialog box (see Figure 15.3). Depending upon the ExpressDoc template selected, the requested information might in-

FIGURE 15.3

Template Information dialog box

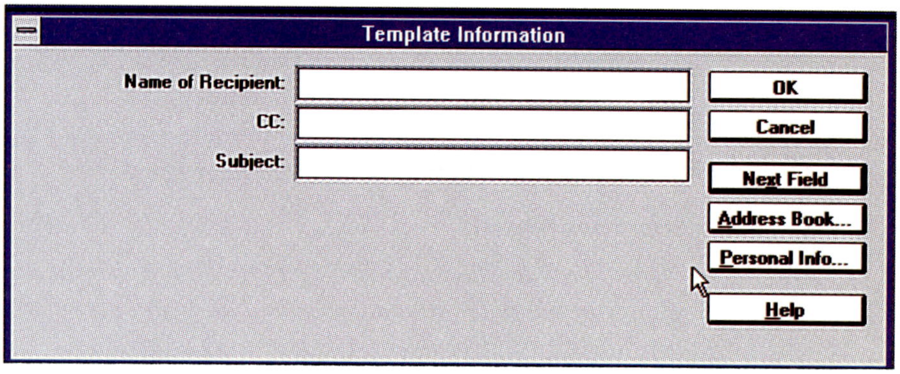

clude a recipient's name, address, phone number, fax number, subject, or copy notation.

Steps to Use an ExpressDoc Template

1. Select the **Template** button on the Button Bar {Alt, f, t *or* Ctrl and t}.

   Note: The Templates dialog box displays containing a list of available templates.

2. Double-click on the desired template name {press the up or down arrow key to highlight the desired template name, press Enter}.

   For example, scroll up the list of templates and double-click on **memo5**.

   Note: After a few moments, the Template Information dialog box displays (see Figure 15.3). In the document window, a portion of the template with formatted text and codes is visible.

   *Note: If personal information has not been entered for your WordPerfect program, a message displays requesting information. Select **OK**, then skip to step 4 and fill in the personal information as shown. Return to step 3 and continue with the steps.*

3. Type the requested information into the appropriate boxes.

   For example, type the following information into the boxes:

Name of Recipient:	**Alice Boyd** (press **Tab**)
CC:	**Vivian Raley** (press **Tab**)
Subject:	**Software Updates**

4. To change the personal information that was created the first time the Template feature was used, select the **Personal Info** button and make the appropriate changes {Alt and p}.

   For example:

   a. In the Name box, type your name and press **Tab**.

   b. In the Title box, type **Software Coordinator** and press **Tab**.

   c. In the Company box, type **Holt & Associates** and press **Tab**.

   d. In the Address box, type **1274 Pennsylvania Ave.** and press **Tab**.

   e. In the City, State Zip box, type **York, PA 17404** and press **Tab**.

   f. In the Telephone box, type **717-555-4800** and press **Tab**.

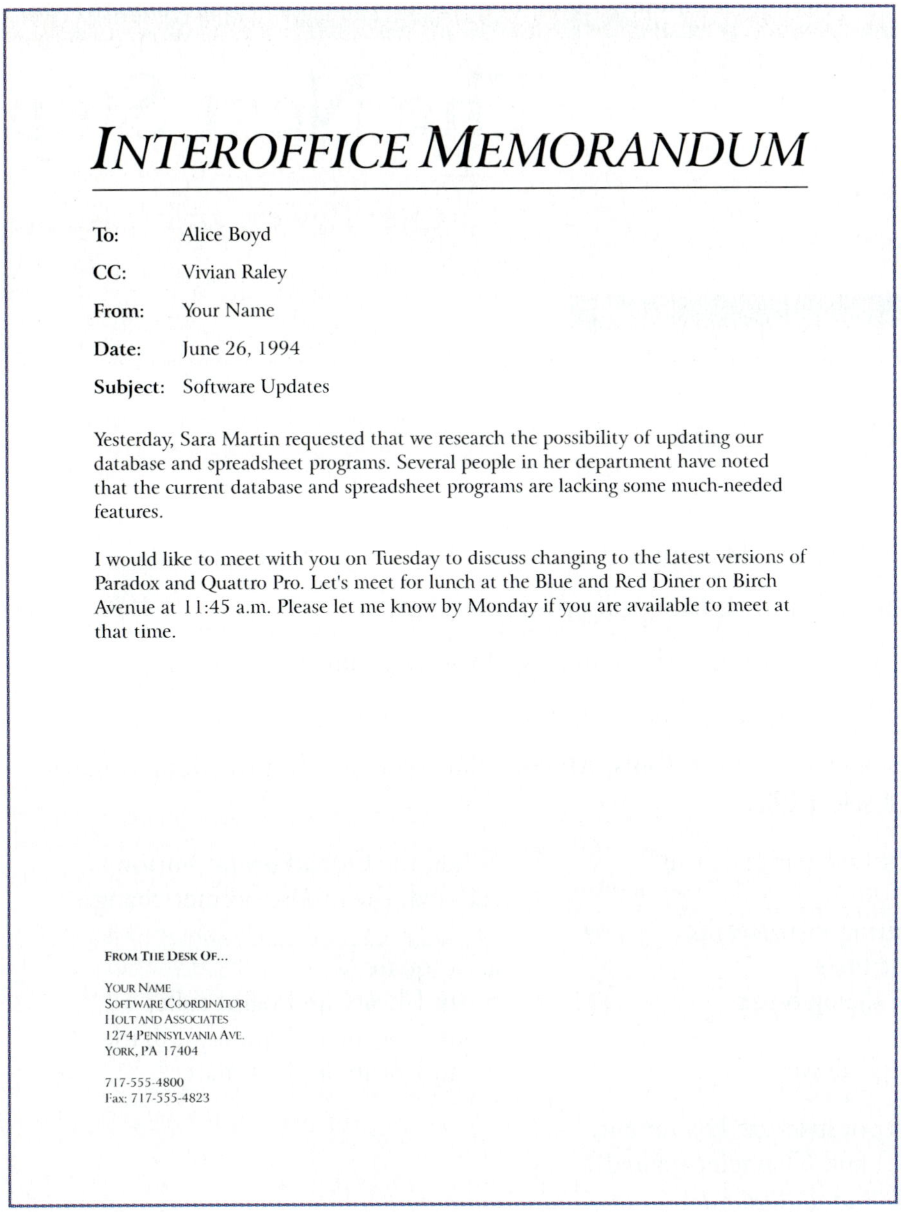

INTEROFFICE MEMORANDUM

To: Alice Boyd

CC: Vivian Raley

From: Your Name

Date: June 26, 1994

Subject: Software Updates

Yesterday, Sara Martin requested that we research the possibility of updating our database and spreadsheet programs. Several people in her department have noted that the current database and spreadsheet programs are lacking some much-needed features.

I would like to meet with you on Tuesday to discuss changing to the latest versions of Paradox and Quattro Pro. Let's meet for lunch at the Blue and Red Diner on Birch Avenue at 11:45 a.m. Please let me know by Monday if you are available to meet at that time.

FROM THE DESK OF...

YOUR NAME
SOFTWARE COORDINATOR
HOLT AND ASSOCIATES
1274 PENNSYLVANIA AVE.
YORK, PA 17404

717-555-4800
Fax: 717-555-4823

FIGURE 15.4

Memorandum created using the *memo5* ExpressDoc template

g. In the Fax box, type 717-555-4823.

5. Select OK to return to the Template Information dialog box {Tab, Enter}.

6. Select OK {Tab, Enter}.

Note: In a few moments, the top portion of a memorandum displays in the document window including the information typed in the Template Information and Personal Information dialog boxes. Notice that the buttons on the Button Bar have changed. The insertion point is located two blank lines below the Subject line. If desired, select the ***Page Zoom Full*** *button to view the entire memorandum. Select the* ***Page Zoom Full*** *button again to return to the normal view.*

Finish-Up Instructions

- Type the body text of the memorandum as shown in Figure 15.4.
- Use the filename **15drill7.tem** and save the document.
- Print one copy and close the document.

The Next Step

Chapter Review and Activities

Self-Check Quiz

T F 1. Before a character style is applied, the desired text must be selected.

T F 2. Text can be sorted in alphabetical or numerical order.

T F 3. Descending sort order is A through Z, or lowest to highest.

T F 4. The Record Macro dialog box is used to play a macro.

T F 5. To activate a macro, select **Tools, Macro, Play,** type or select the desired macro name, and select **Play**.

6. An ExpressDoc template can contain ______________.
   a. formatting instructions
   b. graphic lines
   c. special dialog boxes
   d. text
   e. all of the above

7. When the **QuickFormat** button is selected, the mouse pointer changes to ______________.
   a. a square
   b. an I-beam and paint roller
   c. an I-beam and question mark
   d. an I-beam and a square

8. Three types of styles are Document, ________, and Character (paired).
   a. Table
   b. Paragraph (paired)
   c. Page
   d. Column

9. Describe a style and state two advantages of using styles.

10. Explain why a macro should be planned before selecting **Tools, Macro, Record**.

Enriching Language Arts Skills

Spelling/Vocabulary Words

revenue government income, money.

innovative being creative, having original ideas.

integral necessary for completeness.

acquisition a purchase.

commingle to mix or combine together.

Apostrophe Used to Show Possession

If a noun is singular and used to show possession, add an apostrophe (') and an *s*. If the noun is plural or the final letter in the noun is an s, add only an apostrophe after the *s*.

Examples:

The secretary's table was misplaced.
The brothers' houses and the Lexis' garage are on the corner of Piedmont and High streets.

Activities

Activity 15.1—Retrieve, Apply, and Create Styles

*The file named **15drill6.sty** must have been created in order to accomplish this activity. If this document has not been completed, use the steps shown on pages 359–361 to create the document.*

1. Open the file named **15act1.txt** located on the data disk.
2. Use the following information to format the report.
   a. Select the **Styles** button.
   b. Select **Options**, **Retrieve**.
   c. Type the drive letter where the file disk is located followed by the name of the document that contains the desired style, e.g., **a:15drill6.sty**.
   d. Check that Both is selected in the Style Type box.
   e. Select **OK**.
   f. Select **Yes** to "Overwrite current styles?"
   Note: *The styles created in **15drill6.sty** will now be available for formatting.*
   g. Select **Close**.
   Note: *The **15drill6.sty** InitialStyle format is in effect. The font for the text has been changed to Arrus BT.*
   h. Place the insertion point in the title of the report, **BANKING SERVICES**.
   i. Select the **Style** button and double-click on **Report Title**.
   j. Place the insertion point in the the first sidehead, **Client Banking Services**.
   k. Select the **Style** button and double-click on **Sidehead**.
   l. Place the insertion point in the next sidehead, **Small Business Assistance**.
   m. Select the **Style** button and double-click on **Sidehead**.
3. Place the insertion point in the first third-level heading, **Information about Banking Services**.

4. Create a new third-level heading style.
   a. Select the **Styles** button.
   b. Select **Create**.
   c. In the Name box, type **3rd level**.
   d. In the Description box, type **Style for third-level headings**. Check that **Paragraph** style displays in the Style Type box.
   e. Click in the **Contents** box.
   f. Change the font to **Arrus BT, Bold, 12-point** (select **Layout**, **Font**, choose the desired font, size, and appearance, select **OK**).
   g. Change the spacing between paragraphs to **1.5** (select **Layout**, **Paragraph, Format, Spacing Between Paragraphs, 1.5, OK**).
   h. Select **OK**.
   i. Make sure that the new style, 3rd level, is highlighted. Select **Apply** or double-click on the **3rd level** style name.
   j. Apply the 3rd level style to the remaining third-level paragraphs, i.e., *Client Data Reports, Electronic Banking, Small Business Ledger,* and *SBA-Guaranteed Loans.*
5. Find each occurrence of the company name, Independence Bank, and apply the Company name style. (Place the insertion point at the beginning of the document, select **Edit**, **Find**, type **Independence Bank** in the Find box, select **Find Next**, select the **Styles** button, double-click on the **Company name** style. Select **Find Next** in the Find Text dialog box. Continue until all occurrences of the company name have been found and changed to the Company name style.)
6. Save the formatted report as **15act1.sty**.
7. Print one copy and close the document.

Activity 15.2—Sort Table Columns

Part I

1. Open the file named **15act2.tbl** located on the data disk and use the following instructions to sort the vendors alphabetically.
2. Select all table cells except the table title and column heads.
3. Select **Tools**, **Sort**.
4. Check that the following display in the Key Definition box:

Key:	1
Type:	Alpha
Sort Order	Ascending
Cell:	1
Line:	1
Word:	1

5. Delete any keys displays other than Key 1.

6. Select **OK**.

7. Use the filename **15act2.ven** and save the file. Print one copy.

Part II *Note: use the following instructions to sort the vendors by July purchases from highest to lowest amounts purchased.*

1. Select all table cells except the title and the column heads.

2. Select **Tools, Sort**.

3. Change the Key 1 definition as follows:

Type:	Numeric
Sort Order:	Descending
Cell:	4
Line:	1
Word:	1

4. Select **OK**.

5. Use the filename **15act2.amt** and save the file.

6. Print one copy and close the document.

Activity 15.3—Paragraph Sorting and QuickFormat

1. Type the following information as shown.

BANQUET MENU

Chicken Florentine
$15.95 per person
Boneless Breast of Chicken
Artichoke Pasta Salad
Fresh Fruit

Prime Rib
$19.95 per person
Prime Rib
Fresh Vegetable Sauté
Roasted New Potatoes

Eggplant Parmesan
$12.95 per person
Thinly Sliced Eggplant
Layered with Marinara Sauce,
Ricotta, and Parmesan Cheese
Mixed Green Salad

Pasta with Seafood
$16.95 per person
Shrimp, Scallops, and Clams
over Spinach Spaghetti in a
Light Garlic Sauce
Mixed Green Salad

---

2. Use the filename **15act3.men** and save the file.
3. Select all lines in the menus except for the title.
4. Select **Tools**, **Sort**.
5. To sort the menu selections by the cost per person, define the following key.

Sort by:	Paragraph
Type:	Numeric
Sort Order:	Descending
Line:	2
Field:	1
Word:	1

6. Select **OK**.
7. Place the insertion point at the beginning of the document and change the font to **BernhardMod BT**, **12-point**.
8. Select the words **BANQUET MENU** and change the font to **CaslonOpnFace BT**, **24-point**.
9. Select the words **Prime Rib** and change the font to **CaslonOpnFace BT**, **18-point**.
10. With the words Prime Rib Dinner selected, click on the **QuickFormat** button. Use the QuickFormat feature to format the words, *Pasta with Seafood*, *Chicken Florentine*, and *Eggplant Parmesan*. Select the **QuickFormat** button again to turn off the QuickFormat feature.
11. Optional. Insert a page border (select **Layout**, **Page**, **Border/Fill**, click on the **Border Style** button, click on a border style of your choice, select **OK**).
12. Use the filename **15act3.fin** and save the file.
13. Print one copy and close the document.

Activity 15.4—Use an ExpressDoc Template to Create a Letter; Play a Macro

Note: The macro named ***closing*** *must have been created in order to accomplish this activity. If the macro has not been created, use the steps on pages 355–356 to create the macro.*

1. Create a letter using the following information:

a. The **letter2** ExpressDoc template should be used (select the **Template** button and double-click on **letter2**).

b. Type the following information into the appropriate boxes in the Template Information dialog box.

Recipient:	**Renata Ramanos**
Title:	**Lighting Specialist**
Organization:	**Kosek Research Corporation**
Address:	**P.O. Box 5124**
City, State Zip:	**Portland, ME 04101**
Salutation:	**Ms. Ramanos**

c. The following is the text of the letter:

Thank you for your interest in our Trak-Power Lighting systems. Trak-Power Lighting offers flexibility and versatility at an affordable price.

Because you are in the process of remodeling your office, this is the perfect time to consider the type of lighting that best meets the needs of you and your staff. I am sure that one of the Trak-Power Lighting systems will meet all your requirements.

d. Delete the word **Sincerely** and the typed signature line. Place the insertion point in the second blank line below the last paragraph.

e. Play the *closing* macro to insert a final paragraph, closing, type signature, reference initials, and enclosure notation (select **Tools**, **Macro**, **Play**, type **a:closing**, select **Play**).

2. Use the filename **15act4.ltr** and save the document.
3. Print one copy and close the document.

Challenge Your Skills

Skill 15.1—Paragraph Sorting

1. Open the file named **15skill1.par** located on the data disk.
2. Make decisions regarding margins, justification, and fonts.
3. Select all paragraphs except the report title.
4. Sort the paragraphs numerically in descending order by the first word (i.e., ballot number) of the first line of each paragraph.
5. Use the filename **15skill1.bal** and save the sorted file.
6. Print one copy.
7. Select all paragraphs except the report title.
8. Sort the paragraphs alphabetically in ascending order by the second word of the first line of each paragraph.

9. Use the filename **15skill1.alp** and save the sorted file.
10. Print one copy and close the document.

Skill 15.2—Create and Apply Styles

1. Type the following unformatted presentation text.

WORDPERFECT 6.0 FOR WINDOWS
Features Presentation

1. MENU BAR
a. File
b. Edit
c. View
d. Layout
e. Tools
f. Graphics
g. Table
h. Window
i. Help

2. BUTTON BAR
a. Template
b. Indent
c. Bullet
d. Date Text
e. Envelope
f. Draw
g. Chart
h. TextArt
i. Figure
j. Text Box
k. QuickFormat
l. Styles

---

2. Use the filename **15skill2.txt** and save the unformatted file.
3. Edit the *InitialStyle* as follows:

Margins:	**Left and Right—1.75"; Top—1.25"**
Font:	**Arrus BT, 16-point**

4. Create the following styles.

Name:	**P-Title**
Description:	**Title for presentations**
Type	**Paragraph (paired)**
Justification:	**Center**
Font:	**Humanst521 Cn BT, Bold, 24-point**
Spacing Between Paragraphs:	**2**

Name:	**P-Subtitle**
Description:	**Subtitle for presentations**
Type:	**Paragraph (paired)**
Justification:	**Center**
Font:	**Humanst521 Cn BT, Bold, 20-point**
Spacing Between Paragraphs:	**2**

Name:	**P-Level 1**
Description:	**Topic level 1--presentations**
Type:	**Paragraph (paired)**
Spacing Between Paragraphs:	**1.5**

Name:	**P-Level 2**
Description:	**Topic level 2--presentations**
Type:	**Paragraph (paired)**
Special:	Press **F7** once to indent paragraphs

5. Apply the new styles to the document paragraphs.

   Hint: *A style can be applied to multiple paragraphs by selecting the desired paragraphs before choosing the **Styles** button.*

6. Use the filename **15skill2.for** and save the formatted presentation.
7. Print one copy and close the document.

Skill 15.3—Create a Macro; Use an ExpressDoc Template

1. Create a macro that when played produces the following distribution list. Name the macro **dist_lst** . ***Hint:*** *Type the drive letter where your disk is located followed by the macro name to save the macro to your file disk.*

   Distribution:

   S. F. Acevedo
   V. A. Butler
   J. P. Delaney
   M. T. Epranian
   E. D. Rindfleish
   R. P. Schueler
   C. T. Zornosa

   Hints: *Plan the macro by creating the document before selecting **Tools, Macro, Record.** Write down the steps needed to create the macro.*

2. When the macro is complete, close the document.
3. Use the following information to create a memorandum using an ExpressDoc template.

   a. The *memo1* ExpressDoc template should be used.

   b. The following information should be inserted into the box in the Template Information dialog box.

Recipient:	**See Distribution List**
CC:	**P. S. Perkins**
Subject:	**Company-Funded Retirement Gifts and Luncheons**

c. Change the Personal Information as follows:

Name:	**Pattie Zuecher**
Title:	**Manager, Human Resources**
Organization:	**Digital MicroComputer Products**
Address:	**242 Congress Ave.**
City, State, Zip:	**Austin, TX 78701**
Telephone:	**512-555-6030**
Fax:	**512-555-2846**

d. The following is the text of the memorandum.

This memo is in response to inquiries regarding the Company's policy concerning luncheons and/or gifts to employees who are retiring. Please use the following guidelines to ensure consistent, equitable, and uniform application for such expenditures.

- The equivalent of all luncheon costs for up to 12 individuals may be charged to the Company.
- A reasonable gift may be purchased for the individual. Funds contributed by fellow employees usually cover such expenses; however, a Company contribution towards the cost of a reasonable gift, not to exceed $100, may be charged to the Company.
- All such expenditures are to be charged to individual department accounts.

Please contact me if further clarification is needed.

e. Place the insertion point two lines below the final paragraph and play the **dist_lst** macro to insert the distribution list.

4. Use the filename **15skill3.mem** and save the file.
5. Print one copy and close the document.

Skill 15.4—Sort Table Columns; Language Arts

1. Open the file named **15skill4.mem** located on the data disk.
2. Make decisions regarding:

   Margins
   Justification
   Fonts (the final letter should fit on one page)
   Date of letter
   Table format (including cell widths, alignment of text, table borders)
   Reference initials, document identification, and enclosure notation

3. Correct four spelling errors and two punctuation errors
4. Sort the table cells alphabetically by the Item column.
5. Use the filename **15skill4.fin** and save the file.
6. Print one copy.
7. If you have completed your work, exit WordPerfect.

CHAPTER 16

Managing Document Windows and Files

Features Covered

- Cascade, tile, maximize, minimize, move, restore, and resize document windows
- Create, revise, and print a document summary
- Use File Options to copy, move, rename, and delete files and to create directories
- Use QuickList
- Convert files to and from other word processing formats
- Assign a password
- Use DOS without exiting WordPerfect
- Insert (retrieve) an existing file into a document on the screen
- Use Print Manager to cancel the printing of a document

Objectives and Introduction

After successfully completing this chapter, you will be able to cascade, tile, maximize, minimize, move, restore, and resize document windows as well as create, revise, and print document summary information. You will also learn to use WordPerfect's File Options to open, delete, rename, move, and locate files and to create and delete directories and subdirectories. In addition, you will learn to use WordPerfect's QuickList, QuickMenu, file conversion, and password features. You will learn to access DOS without exiting WordPerfect in order to perform tasks such as checking your hard disk or formatting a new disk. Finally, you will learn to use the Print Manager and to insert an existing file into a document on the screen.

WordPerfect provides tools to manage, organize, access, and secure files. Files can be accessed or managed by using the Windows, Document Summary, and QuickList features. Passwords can be created and used to secure files. Also, files from other word processing programs can be converted to or from the WordPerfect format. If desired, WordPerfect can be temporarily exited in order to accomplish tasks at the DOS prompt or to cancel the printing of a document.

The Windows in WordPerfect

The WordPerfect document window displays after the WordPerfect program is launched. When a new file is created or an existing file is opened, a new window displays. Nine document windows can be open at one time. As each new file is opened, WordPerfect sequentially numbers the document windows, for example, Document1, Document2, etc. The document number displays in the Title bar. If the document has been saved, the filename displays in the Title bar. Any document window can be cascaded, tiled, maximized, minimized, copied/moved, restored, resized, or closed. Manipulating the windows in WordPerfect is called *windowing.*

Start-Up Instructions

- Create five files as follows:

  a. In a new file, type **This is file 1.**; press **Enter** twice.

  b. Use the filename **16file.1** and save the file on your disk.

     Note: *Do not close the file.*

  c. Select the **New Document** button; type **This is file 2.**; press **Enter** twice.

  d. Use the filename **16file.2** and save the file on your disk.

  e. Select the **New Document** button; type **This is file 3.**; press **Enter** twice.

  f. Use the filename **16file.3** and save the file on your disk.

  g. Select the **New Document** button; type **This is file 4.**; press **Enter** twice.

  h. Use the filename **16file.4** and save the file on your disk.

  i. Select the **New Document** button; type **This is file 5.**; press **Enter** twice.

  j. Use the filename **16file.5** and save the file on your disk.

Steps to Cascade Document Windows

1. Select Window, Cascade {Alt, w, c}.

   Note: *When **Cascade** is selected, all open document windows overlap each other so that only the Title bar of each inactive window displays. The active window displays in front of the cascaded windows. In an active window, the Title bar displays in color or is highlighted.*

Steps to Tile Document Windows

1. Select Window, Tile {Alt, w, t}.

   Note: *When **Tile** is selected, all opened document windows are visible. The active window displays at the top or top left of the screen with the Title bar highlighted (see Figure 16.1).*

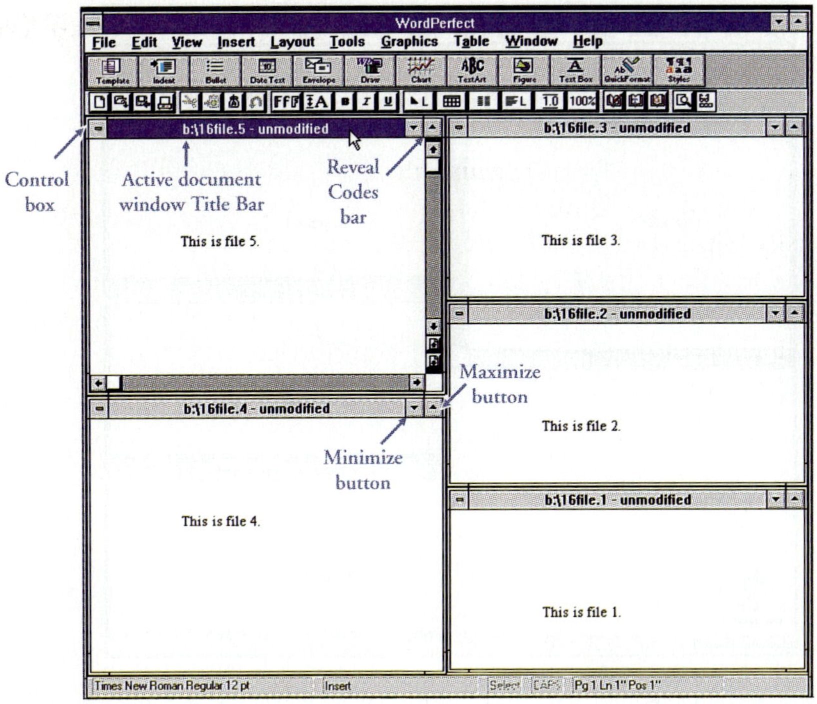

FIGURE 16.1

Tiled document windows with maximize and minimize buttons, control box, and Reveal Codes bar

Steps to Activate/Change the Active Window

1. Place the mouse pointer in the desired window and click once to activate the window {Alt, w, type the number of the desired window *or* Ctrl and F6 until the desired window is activated}.

   For example, move the mouse pointer to the various open windows and click.

Note: Remember, a window is active when the Title bar is highlighted or displayed in a color.

Steps to Maximize a Window

1. If more than one window is displayed on the screen, activate the desired window and select the Maximize button (up triangle) to view the window in full size {activate the desired window; Alt and hyphen, x}.

   For example, maximize the window containing the file named 16file.4.

*Note: The document window containing the file named **16file.4** displays in full size in the document window.*

Steps to Restore a Window

Note: Restoring a document window is the process of returning the document window to its previously determined size.

1. With the document window maximized on the screen, select the Restore button located at the right end of the Menu bar of the desired window to return the window to its previous size {Alt and hyphen, r}.

FIGURE 16.2

Minimized document window

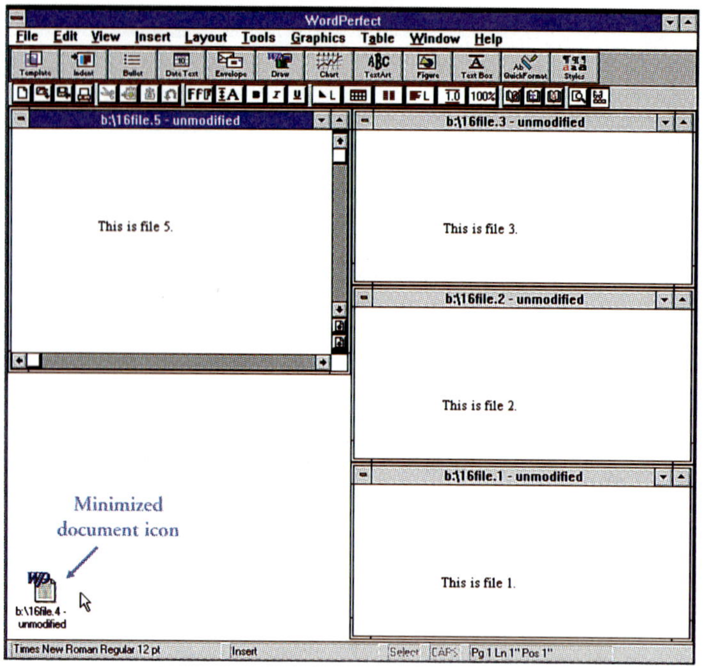

For example, select the **Restore** button in the window containing the file named **16file.4**.

Note: The file is returned to its previous size (before it was maximized).

Steps to Minimize a Window

Note: Minimizing a document window reduces the document window to a small icon (see Figure 16.2).

1. Activate the desired window, select the **Minimize** button located in the Title bar of the document window {Alt and hyphen, n}.

   For example, minimize the window containing the file named **16file.4**.

Note: The document window is changed to a small icon and displays in the bottom left corner of the screen. The document name displays below the icon.

Steps to Restore a Minimized Window

1. Double-click on the icon that contains the desired window {Alt, w, type the number of the windows to be restored}.

   For example, double-click on the icon containing the file named **16file.4**.

Steps to Move a Window

Note: The window to be moved must be smaller than the full, maximized size.

1. Locate the mouse pointer in the desired document window Title bar; press and hold the left mouse button {Alt and hyphen, m}.

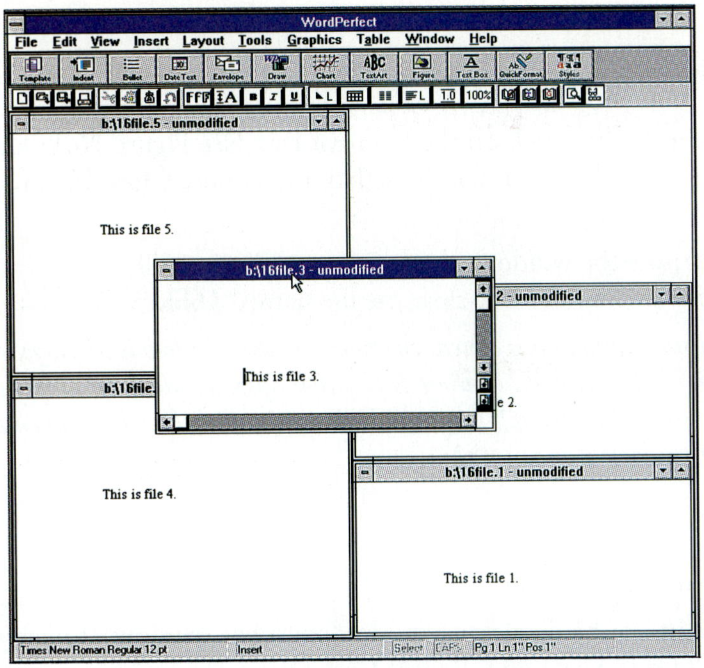

FIGURE 16.3

Moving a document window

For example, move the mouse pointer to the Title bar of the document window containing the file named **16file.3**; press and hold the mouse button.

Note: *A dashed outline appears around the document window.*

2. Drag the dashed window outline to the desired position and release the mouse button {press the up, down, left, or right arrow keys to move the window to the desired location, press Enter}.

For example, drag the dashed outline for the document window containing the file named **16file.3** to approximately the center of the screen and release the mouse button (see Figure 16.3).

Steps to Resize a Window

Note: *The window must be smaller than the full, maximized size.*

1. Locate the mouse pointer on the document window's left, right, or bottom edge until a double-headed arrow displays. Press and hold the left mouse button and drag the dashed outline to the desired size, release the mouse button {Alt and hyphen, s, press the left, right, up, or down arrow keys to obtain the double-headed arrow at the desired document window's edge; press the chosen arrow key again repeatedly until the desired size displays, press Enter. Repeat to change the window size at any edge}.

For example, move the mouse pointer to the bottom edge of the document window containing the file named **16file.2** and enlarge and reduce the window height.

Steps to Close All Windows

1. Select **File, Close** or double-click on the **Control Box** (see Figure 16.1) located at the top, left corner of the document Title bar and choose **Close** {Alt, f, c *or* Ctrl and F4}.

   For example, close the windows that contain **16file.1**, **16file.2**, **16file.3**, and **16file.4**. (Do not close the file named **16file.5**.)

   Note: *When a document window is closed, the next opened window is displayed with the Title bar highlighted. However, if there is no other open window, an empty screen displays with the words "Document1- unmodified" in the Title bar. Each open window must be closed separately one at a time.*

Start-Up Instructions

- Maximize the file named **16file.5**.
- Reveal Codes should not be displaying in the document window. If necessary, turn off Reveal Codes (select **View**, **Reveal Codes**).

Steps to Use the Mouse to Display the Reveal Codes Window

1. Point to the small, dark rectangular bar at the top or bottom of the vertical scroll bar until a double-headed arrow displays (see Figure 16.1).

   For example, point on the small, dark bar at the top of the vertical scroll bar until the double-headed arrow displays.

2. Press and hold the mouse button while dragging the mouse downward; release the mouse when the dividing bar is positioned at the desired location in the document window.

   For example, press and hold the mouse button while dragging the dividing bar below the sentence "This is file 5."

   Note: *When the Reveal Codes window displays, the window size can be changed by pointing to the dividing bar (anywhere along the top edge of the Reveal Codes window) until the double-headed arrow displays and dragging up or down to obtain the desired size.*

Finish-Up Instructions

- Remove the Reveal Codes window from the document window by pointing to the dividing bar until the double-headed arrow displays. Press and hold the mouse button and drag down until the dividing bar touches the vertical scroll bar. Release the mouse button.

Document Summary Information

A document summary can be created to provide specific information about a file, such as a descriptive name, document type, and the name of the document author and typist (see Figure 16.4). The document summary is created by selecting **File,**

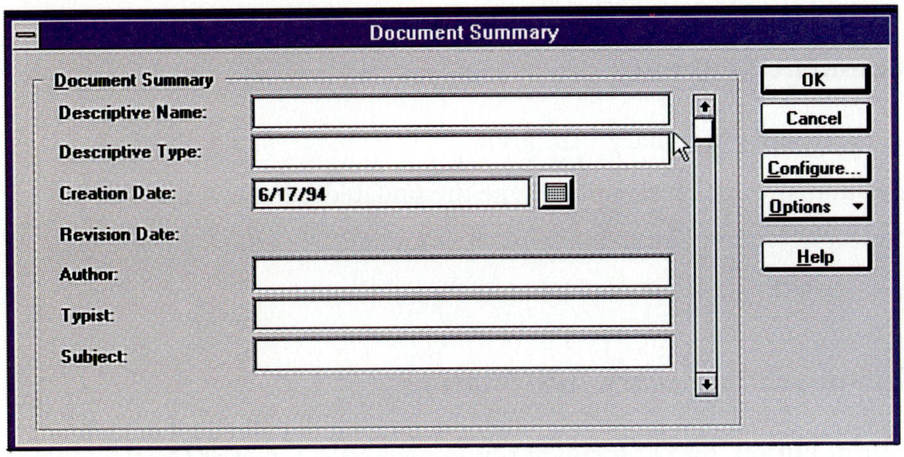

FIGURE 16.4

Document Summary dialog box

Document Summary and typing the desired information into the option boxes in the Document Summary dialog box. If desired, WordPerfect can be instructed to automatically display the Document Summary dialog box the first time a document is saved.

Once the document summary information is typed, the information can be changed and the updated information saved. If desired, the document summary can be printed. The document does not print when the document summary is printed.

Start-Up Instructions

❖ The file named **16file.5** should be displayed in the document window.

Steps to Create a Document Summary After a Document Is Saved

1. Select File, Document Summary {Alt, f, y}.

   Note: The Document Summary dialog box displays. The current date displays in the Creation Date box to indicate the date the Document Summary was/is created. If desired, the Creation Date can be changed to another date. The Revision Date is the date the document was last revised. See Figure 16.4. This date is saved and updated automatically by WordPerfect and cannot be changed by the user.

2. Check that the insertion point is located in the Descriptive Name box and type words that identify the file {press Tab to locate the insertion point in the desired box, type the information}.

   For example, type **This is a sample file.**

3. Click in the Descriptive Type box and type words that identify the document category {see step 2}.

   For example, type **Sample.**

4. Click in the Typist box and type the name of the typist {see step 2}.

   For example, type your name.

5. If desired, type any additional information desired into the option boxes.

6. Select OK {press Enter}.

Steps to Revise a Document Summary

1. Select File, Document Summary {Alt, f, y}.
2. Select the option(s) to be changed and type the updated information.

   For example, in the Author box, type the name of a friend.
3. Select OK to save the updated document summary {Enter}.

Steps to Print the Document Summary Information

1. Select the Print button, select Document Summary {Alt, f, p, a *or* F5, a}.
2. Select Print {p}.

   Note: *The document summary prints; the document does not print.*

Steps to Create a Document Summary When a New Document Is Saved

Note: *The following steps are for your information only. If these steps are followed, the Document Summary dialog box will display* ***every time a new document is saved or exited.***

1. Select File, Preferences {Alt, f, e}.
2. Double-click on the Summary icon {Alt and s}.
3. Select the Create Summary on Save/Exit option {Alt and c}.
4. Select OK {Enter}.
5. Select Close to return to the document window {Alt and c}.

   Note: *If the Create Summary on Save/Exit option is selected, the Document Summary dialog box displays when a new document is saved or exited.*

Steps to Insert (Retrieve) an Existing File Into a Document on the Screen

Note: *The file named* ***16file.5*** *should be displayed in the document window.*

1. Place the insertion point in the document window at the desired location.

   For example, place the insertion point on the second blank line below the sentence "This is file 5."
2. Select Insert, File {Alt, i, i}.

   Note: *The Insert File dialog box displays.*
3. Double-click on the desired file.

   For example, double-click on the file named **16file.1**.

   Note: *The message "Insert file into current document?" displays.*
4. Select Yes {Enter}.

   Note: *The information from the selected file displays on the screen.*

Finish-Up Instructions

- Close the document window. (It is not necessary to save the file.)

Use File Options

The File Options in the Open and Save As dialog boxes are used to perform the usual disk maintenance tasks of copying, moving, renaming, and deleting files. Additional options include changing file attributes, printing files, printing a file list, creating directories/subdirectories, and removing directories.

Changing file attributes are functions that traditionally have been accomplished by using DOS (the disk operating system). In WordPerfect for Windows, the attributes can be changed by selecting **File Options** in the Open or Save As dialog box. One attribute that can be assigned to a file is Read-Only. This attribute allows a file to be read (opened), but the file cannot be overwritten (saved with the same name). When a Read-Only file displays on the screen, the Title bar shows the filename followed by the words "(Read-Only)."

Start-Up Instructions

- The files named **16file.1**, **16file.2**, **16file.3**, **16file.4**, and **16file.5** must be available on your disk.
- A mouse is the most efficient method for performing actions when using File Options. A mouse must be used to perform the File Options functions that follow.

Chapter 16 Managing Document Windows and Files

Steps to Print a List of Files

Note: The drive containing the list of files to be printed should be highlighted in the Directories box. If necessary, select the drive in the file box where your file disk is located.

1. Use the desired Open or Save As dialog box.

   For example, select the **Open** button.

2. Select **File Options**.
3. Select **Print File List**.

   Note: The Print File List dialog box displays.

4. Select **Print Entire List**.

   For example, check that the Print Entire List is selected.

5. Select **Print**.
6. Select **Cancel** to exit the Open dialog box.

Steps to Create a Directory

1. Use the Open or Save As dialog box.

   For example, select **File, Save As**.

2. If necessary, double-click on the desired drive letter in the Drives box.

   For example, check that the drive where your file disk is located displays in the Drives box.

3. If necessary, in the Directories box highlight the drive letter where the new directory is to be located.

   For example, check that the drive letter where your file disk is located (a: or b:) is highlighted in the Directories box. If necessary, click once on the drive letter in the Directories box.

4. Select **File Options**.
5. Select **Create Directory**.

   Note: The Create Directory dialog box displays.

6. Type the new directory name in the New Directory box.

   For example, type your last name (up to eight characters).

7. Select **Create**.

   Note: The directory name displays beneath the disk drive letter shown in the Directories box. Notice the file folder icon displaying next to the directory name.

Create a Subdirectory

8. Repeat steps 4 and 5 under Create a Directory.
9. Type the drive letter followed by a colon, directory name, backslash, and the desired subdirectory name.

   For example, type a: followed by your last name, a backslash, and your first name (a:smith\laura).

10. Select **Create**.

Finish-Up Instructions

- Double-click on your last name directory to display the new first name subdirectory.

Start-Up Instructions

- Double-click on the drive letter in the Directories box to display the list of files on your file disk.

Steps to Copy/Move a File(s)

1. In the Open or Save As dialog box, highlight the name of the file(s) to be copied.

   For example, in the Save As dialog box, select the first file to be copied, i.e., **16file.1**. To select multiple files, point to the last file to be copied, i.e., **16file.5**, press and hold the Shift key while clicking the mouse button once.

   *Note: All files between **16file.1** and **16file.5** are selected.*

2. Select **File Options**.
3. Select **Copy** or **Move**.

For example, select **Copy**.

Note: The Copy/Move Files dialog box displays.

4. In the Copy/Move Selected Files To box, type the drive location where the files are to be copied or moved and, if necessary, type the directory name.

   For example, type a:your lastname (a:smith).

5. Select **Copy** or **Move**.

   Note: The files are copied or moved and the dialog box displays. If files are copied, the filenames remain highlighted. If the files are moved to a different drive location, the filenames no longer display in the current list of filenames.

Finish-Up Instructions

- When the copy process is completed, double-click on your last name directory to display a list of the copied files. If the message "Open marked files?" displays, select **No** {Enter}.
- Select **16file.2**. To select a nonconsecutive file, point to the file name e.g., **16file.4**, press the **Ctrl** key while clicking the left mouse button once.
- Use the steps 2-4 of the Steps to Copy/Move a File(s) and move the files named **16file.2** and **16file.4** to your first name subdirectory. In the Move Selected Files To box, type your subdirectory name, select **Move**.

  Note: The two moved files no longer display in your last name directory. Double-click on your first name. The two copied files display in the Filename list.

Start-Up Instructions

- The files in your first name subdirectory should be displayed in the Save As dialog box.

Chapter **16** Managing Document Windows and Files

Steps to Delete a File(s)

1. In the Open or Save As dialog box, highlight the name of the file(s) to be deleted.

   For example, highlight the files named **16file.2** and **16file.4** located in your first name directory.

2. Select **File Options**.
3. Select **Delete**.

   Note: The Delete File(s) dialog box displays with the message "Do you want to delete selected files?" If only one filename is selected, the Delete File dialog box displays with the name of the file to be deleted highlighted.

4. Select **Delete**.

   Note: The deleted files no longer display in the Filename list.

Steps to Remove a Directory (or Subdirectory)

1. In the Open or Save As dialog box and in the Directories box, highlight the name of the directory or subdirectory to be removed.

For example, highlight your first name subdirectory.

2. Select **File Options**.
3. Select **Remove Directory**.

   Note: *The Remove Directory dialog box displays and the directory name to be removed is highlighted.*

4. Select **Remove**.

   Note: *The directory/subdirectory is removed from the file list. If the directory/subdirectory is not empty (files and/or subdirectories are listed under the directory/subdirectory name) when Delete is selected, a message displays, "WARNING! Directory ... contains files. Remove directory anyway?". Select **Yes**.*

Steps to Rename a File

1. In the Open or Save As dialog box, highlight the name of the file to be renamed.

   For example, highlight the file named **16file.3** in your last name directory.

2. Select **File Options**.
3. Select **Rename**.

   Note: *The Rename File dialog box displays with the file location and filename displayed in the From box.*

4. In the To: box, type the drive location and new filename or edit the name displayed.

   For example, change the filename to **16file3.ren**. (Do not type the final period.)

5. Select **Rename**.

   Note: *The new filename, **16file3.ren**, displays in your last name directory list and the filename **16file.3** no longer displays.*

Start-Up Instructions

- Double-click on the drive letter in the Directories box to display the list of files on your file disk.

Steps to Print a File from the Open or Save As Dialog Box

1. In either the Open or Save As dialog box, highlight the name of the file to be printed.

   For example, highlight a file of your choice.

2. Select **File Options**.
3. Select **Print**.

   Note: *The Print File dialog box displays with the name of the file to be printed highlighted.*

4. Select **Print**.

Note: A message "Preparing Document for Printing" displays briefly. The document prints.

Finish-up Instructions

- Select **Cancel** to close the Open or Save As dialog box.
- Close all open documents.

Steps to Copy Text from the Viewer to the Clipboard

1. Use the Open or Save As dialog box.

   For example, select the **Open** button.

2. Highlight the desired filename.

   For example, highlight the file named **16file.3**.

3. Select the View button.

   Note: The document displays in the Viewer.

4. Select the desired text.

   For example, select the sentence "This is file 3." Point the mouse pointer at the top of the T and drag to the right and/or downward to highlight.

5. Press the *right* mouse button to display the QuickMenu; select Copy to Clipboard.

   Note: The text remains highlighted.

6. Select Cancel in the Open or Save As dialog box to return the insertion point to the document window.
7. Select the Paste button.

   Note: The text copied from the Viewer displays on the screen.

Finish-Up Instructions

- Close the document (do not save).

Steps to Open Multiple Files

1. Select the Open button and choose the first file to be opened.

   For example, highlight the file named **16file.1**.

2. Press and hold the Ctrl key while selecting the next file to be opened.

   For example, select the file named **16file.2**.

3. Repeat step 2 and highlight any additional file(s) to be opened.

   For example, highlight the file named **16file.4**.

   Note: A maximum of nine files can be opened at one time.

4. Select OK.

Note: WordPerfect opens each file into a separate document window. The last file opened displays on the screen.

Finish-Up Instructions

- Select **Window**, **Tile** to display all open document windows.
- Close all document windows.

The QuickList

The QuickList feature provides a fast and easy method to access frequently used directories and subdirectories. Directories and subdirectories can be assigned descriptive names by using the QuickList feature. Instead of typing the full path name for the desired directory/subdirectory when opening or saving files, the descriptive name can be selected from the QuickList box. The QuickList feature can be accessed from either the Open or Save As dialog boxes.

For example, letters authored by B. Smith of the Personnel Department might be saved in the subdirectory c:\persnl\letters\smith. A QuickList entry could be created that identified the subdirectory as B. Smith Letters. To open a file saved in the subdirectory c:\persnl\letters\smith, you would select B. Smith Letters in the QuickList box in the Open File dialog box. A list of all files in the subdirectory would display immediately.

Start-Up Instructions

- The file disk with your last name directory must be available.

Steps to Create a QuickList Directory Entry

Note: The Steps to Create a QuickList Directory Entry can also be accomplished from the Save As dialog box.

1. Select the Open button {Alt, f, o *or* Ctrl and o}.
2. Select QuickList {Alt and L, Alt and Shift and down arrow}.
3. Select Add Item {a}.

   Note: The Add QuickList Item dialog box displays.
4. If necessary, type the name and location of the directory to be added to the QuickList.

   For example, type **a:** or **b:** and your last name directory.
5. To locate the insertion point in the Description box, press the Tab key once or click in the Description box.

   Note: When the insertion point is placed in the Description box, the information in the Directories/Filename box is automatically inserted in the Description box.
6. Delete any information in the Description box and type a descriptive name of the directory (or subdirectory).

For example, type **Sample Files.** (Do not type the period.)

7. Select **OK** {Enter}.

   Note: The Sample Files entry is added to the QuickList box and is highlighted.

8. Select **Cancel** to return to the document window {Esc}.

Steps to Access a Directory Using the QuickList

Note: The Steps to Access a Directory Using the QuickList can also be accomplished from the Save As dialog box.

1. Select the **Open** button {Alt, f, o *or* Ctrl and o}.
2. Double-click on the desired name in the QuickList box {Alt and q, use the up or down arrow key to highlight the desired item, Enter}.

   For example, double-click on **Sample Files.**

   Note: The list of files displays in the Filename list. Your last name directory is highlighted in the Directories box. If desired, open a file.

Finish-Up Instructions

- Select **Cancel** to exit the Open dialog box to return to the document window {press Esc}.

Steps to Delete a QuickList Entry

Note: The Steps to Delete a QuickList Entry can also be accomplished from the Save As dialog box.

1. Select the **Open** button {Alt, f, o *or* Ctrl and o}.
2. In the QuickList box, highlight the name to be deleted {Alt and q, press the up or down arrow key to highlight the desired item name}.

   For example, highlight **Sample Files** in the QuickList box.

3. Select **QuickList** {Alt and L, Alt and Shift and down arrow}.
4. Select **Delete Item** {L}.

   Note: The message displays "Delete item... from the QuickList?".

5. Select **Yes** {Enter}.

   Note: The Sample Files item no longer displays in the QuickList box.

6. Select **Cancel** to return to the document window {press Esc}.

Converting Files

WordPerfect for Windows provides a method to change the file format of a document. A document can be saved to another file format or converted from a different file format. For example, a document originally saved in Microsoft Word for Windows can be converted to a WordPerfect file format. Also, a WordPerfect document can be saved in another format, such as WordStar.

Start-Up Instructions

- Open the file named **16file.1**.

Steps to Save a File in a Different File Format

1. Select File, Save As {Alt, f, a *or* F3}.
2. Type the desired filename in the Filename box.

   For example, type **16conver.fil**. (Do not type the final period.)
3. Select the down arrow button in the Format box {Alt and t; Alt and Shift and down arrow key}.
4. Scroll through the list of file formats and double-click on the desired format {press the up or down arrow keys until the desired file format is highlighted}.

   For example, scroll up the list of file formats and click once on MS Word for Windows 2.0c.{*.doc}.
5. Select OK {press Enter twice}.

   Note: *The message "Conversion in Progress" displays briefly. The file named* ***16conver.fil*** *is now saved in the MS Word for Windows format. The file named* ***16file.1*** *is still available on your file disk and is saved in the WordPerfect 6.0 for Windows file format.*

Finish-Up Instructions

- Close the document.

Steps to Open a File Created in a Different Program

1. Select the Open button and double-click on the desired file.

   For example, double-click on the file named **16conver.fil**.

   Note: *The Convert File Format dialog box displays. MS Word for Windows 2.0c displays in the Convert File Format From box because WordPerfect has attempted to determine the format of the file.*
2. If necessary, select a different file format by selecting the down arrow and clicking on the desired file format.
3. Select OK {Enter}.

   Note: *A "Conversion in Progress" message displays. After a few moments, the converted file displays. The displayed file has been converted to the WordPerfect 6.0 for Windows format. The file must be saved to retain the WordPerfect for Windows format and to record it on the disk.*

Finish-Up Instructions

- Use the *new* filename **16conv.wp** and save the file.
- Close the document.

File Security

Once a file is created, the file can be saved and given a password. Each time the saved file is opened, the password is requested. The password must be remembered by the user because there is no method available for finding a forgotten password. A password can be removed or changed at any time (but only if you remember the current password).

WordPerfect provides two protection options. One option, called Enhanced Password Protection, uses case-sensitive protection but is not compatible with earlier versions of WordPerfect. The second option, called Original Password Protection, is not case-sensitive but is compatible with earlier versions of WordPerfect.

Start-Up Instructions

- Select the **New Document** button.
- Type the following sentence:

  This is a very secret file that no one but me should ever see.

Steps to Create or Change a Password

1. Select File, Save As {Alt, f, a *or* F3}.
2. Type the desired filename.

   For example, type **16secret.fil**. (Do not type the final period.)
3. Select Password Protect located at the bottom right corner of the dialog box {Alt and p}.

   Note: *An X displays in the Password Protect box.*
4. Select OK {Enter}.

   Note: *The Password Protection dialog box displays.*
5. Type the desired password in the Type Password for Document box.

   For example, type **007**. (Do not type the period.)

   Note: *To ensure privacy, the typed characters are displayed as X's on the screen. A password can be 1 to 23 characters and can contain spaces, uppercase and lowercase letters, or any characters found on the keyboard.*
6. Select OK {Enter}.
7. Retype the password to confirm.
8. Select OK to confirm the password and save the file {Enter}.

Finish-Up Instructions

- Close the document.

Steps to Open a File That Has Been Protected with a Password

1. Select the Open button {Alt, f, o *or* Ctrl and o}.

2. Select the desired filename.

   For example, double-click on **16secret.fil.**

   Note: *The Password dialog box displays.*

3. Type the password exactly as typed when the password was created.

   For example, type **007**. (Do not type the period.)

   Note: *As the password is typed, X's display on the screen.*

4. Select OK {Enter}.

Steps to Remove a Password

1. With the password-required document open, select File, Save As {Alt, f, a *or* F3}.
2. Select Password Protect {Alt and p}.

   Note: *An X no longer displays beside the Password Protect option.*

3. Select OK {Enter}.

   Note: *If the file is not saved after the Password is removed, the password will still be needed to open the file.*

4. A message displays "File . . . already exists. Do you want to replace it?"; select Yes {y}.

Finish-Up Instructions

- Close the document window.

Using DOS Without Exiting WordPerfect

DOS commands such as format, chkdsk (check disk), dir (directory), date, erase, and diskcopy can be accessed without exiting the WordPerfect program. Windows allows multiple programs to run at the same time. The names of the programs that are currently running can be viewed by pressing and holding the **Alt** key while tapping the **Tab** key repeatedly to display the program names. When the desired program name displays, release the **Alt** key to switch to the program.

Steps to Use DOS Without Exiting WordPerfect

1. Press and hold the Alt key while tapping the Tab key until the Program Manager option displays. Release the Alt key.
2. Double-click on the MS-DOS prompt icon located in the Main group.

   Note: *After a few moments, the DOS prompt displays.*

3. Type and execute the desired DOS command.

   For example, type **ver** and press **Enter**.

   Note: *After typing* ***ver****, the number of the DOS version in use displays.*

4. If desired, type another DOS command or type exit to return to the Program Manager and close the DOS window.

   For example, type **exit** and press **Enter**.

5. Press and hold the Alt key while tapping the Tab key until the WordPerfect option displays. Release the Alt key.

   Note: *The WordPerfect document window displays.*

Cancel the Printing of a Document

Once a document has been sent to print, the printing may be stopped or canceled. After **Print** is selected in the Print dialog box, the "Preparing Document for Printing" message displays briefly on the screen. As long as the Preparing Document For Printing message displays on the screen, the print job can be canceled if the **Esc** key is pressed immediately. However, once the "Preparing Document for Printing" message disappears from the screen, the print job must be canceled by using the WordPerfect Print Job dialog box or the Windows Print Manager.

The WordPerfect Print Job dialog box monitors the progress of a print job. While a document is being printed, the number of the page that is currently printing, the name of the printer, and the number of the copy (copy one, two, three, etc.) being printed display in the WordPerfect Print Job dialog box. If the job being printed contains multiple pages and/or multiple copies, the printing can be canceled by selecting the **Cancel Print Job** option. However, once the print job has been processed by WordPerfect, the WordPerfect Print Job dialog box immediately leaves the screen and the document prints. Access the WordPerfect Print Job dialog box by selecting the **Print** button and choosing the **Control** button. To cancel the printing of a document, select the **Cancel Print Job** option (in the WordPerfect Print Job dialog box).

To use the Windows Print Manager to cancel the printing of a document, press and hold the **Alt** key while tapping the **Tab** key until the Print Manager box displays; release the **Alt** key. If a document is to be canceled from the print queue (list of filenames), highlight the name of the print job to be canceled, select **Delete**, and select **OK** to the message "Do you want to quit printing the document . . . ?".

If a document does not print, check that the printer is turned on and the printer cables are securely connected. Also, if a printer is shared, check the switch box or Local Area Network (LAN) connection (see your instructor). Before resending a print job, check the Windows Print Manager for any filenames of documents waiting to print. If necessary, delete these filenames.

Chapter 16 Managing Document Windows and Files

Steps to Access Print Manager

Note: *The following steps are for your information only.*

1. After a document has been sent to print, press and hold the Alt key while tapping the Tab key repeatedly until Print Manager displays.

   Note: *The Print Manager dialog box displays.*

2. *To delete a file from the print queue,* highlight the name of the desired document, select the Delete button.

Note: If the document is in the process of printing, a message displays "Do you want to quit printing the document. . .?". Select ***OK****.*

3. *To resume the printing of a document,* select the printer name and select Resume.
4. *To exit Print Manager,* select View, Exit.
5. *To return to WordPerfect without exiting the Print Manager,* press and hold the Alt key while tapping the Tab key until WordPerfect displays. Release the Alt key.

The Next Step

Chapter Review and Activities

Self-Check Quiz

T F 1. When multiple document windows are open, select **Window**, **Tile** to display all the documents on the screen.

T F 2. The **Maximize** button can be selected to reduce the size of a document window.

T F 3. A tiled document window can be moved but not resized.

T F 4. When the document summary is printed, the document does not print.

5. ____ is the maximum number of document windows that can be open at one time.
   a. Nine
   b. Ten
   c. Eleven
   d. Twelve

6. The maximum number of characters that can be used in a password is ___.
   a. 20
   b. 21
   c. 22
   d. 23

7. Text can be ____ from the Viewer and placed in the clipboard.
   a. deleted
   b. copied
   c. moved
   d. none of these

8. The QuickList provides easy access to _________.
   a. directories
   b. subdirectories
   c. a document window
   d. both a and b

9. List five tasks that can be accomplished by using the File Options available in the Open and Save As dialog boxes.

10. List the five steps to access DOS without exiting WordPerfect.

Enriching Language Arts Skills

Proofreading Hints

When proofreading a document, read the document twice: once for content and meaning and once to check grammar, spelling, and punctuation. When proofing your own work, place the original document/draft beside the screen and read across comparing line by line. Read aloud with a second person to compare the printed copy with the original document/draft.

Examples of types of errors to look for when proofreading:

Repeated words	The wedding reception will be held on Sunday *at the at the* Jamestown Country Club.
Misused or missing words	The transaction is *not* legal. The transaction is *now* legal.
Missing punctuation	The cost was *$2516.* (should be *$25.16*)
Misspelled names	Kathryn or Catherine
Transposed letters/ numbers	The *item* is 10:00 a.m. (*time*) The report is due October *21.* (should be October *12*)

Activities

Activity 16.1—Cascade, Tile, and Maximize Document Windows

1. Open four files of your choice from your file disk.
2. Cascade the document windows.
3. Tile the document windows to observe all open windows.
4. Maximize one of the document windows.
5. Close all document windows.

Activity 16.2—Print a List of Files

1. Using File Options, print a list of the files on your file disk (select the **Open** button, select **File Options**, **Print File List**, select **Print Entire List**, **Print.** Choose **Cancel** to exit the menu).

Activity 16.3—Create and Print a Document Summary

1. Open one of the files from your file disk and review the document to determine the document's subject.

2. Create a document summary for your chosen file. Fill in the Descriptive Name, Descriptive Type, and Typist boxes with the appropriate information.
3. Print the document summary.
4. Save and close the document.

Challenge Your Skills

Skill 16.1—Create and Delete Directories, Copy, Move, and Delete Files; Create a QuickList Entry

1. Create two directories on your file disk using the directory names **dir1** and **dir2**.
2. Select and copy four **.wpg** files (WordPerfect graphics files) from the *c:\wpwin60\graphics* subdirectory to **dir1**. (If necessary, check with your instructor or instructional assistant for the drive and/or directory where the WordPerfect graphics files are located.)
3. Move two of the graphics files from dir1 to dir2.
4. Optional. Print the list of files in the dir1 and dir2 directories.
5. Delete the files in the dir2 directory.
6. Delete the dir2 directory.
7. In the dir1 directory, rename one of the graphics files using the filename **graphics2.wpg**.
8. Optional. Print the list of files in the dir1 directory.
9. Create a QuickList entry for the dir1 directory (make a choice of your own for the QuickList entry name).
10. If you have completed your work, exit WordPerfect.

Part 4
Checking Your Step

Production Skill Builder Activities
Chapters 13-16

SCANS

Production Activity 4.1—Newsletter with Table and Graphics; Sorting

1. Use the following information to create the two-page newsletter shown on pages 398 and 399.
   a. Change the top and bottom margins to .75"; change the left and right margins to .5".
   b. Create a footer that includes the newsletter name, issue date, and page number.
   Hint: *When creating the footer, change the left and right margins to .5".*
   c. Use letterspacing and word spacing to adjust the spacing in the title.
   d. Use the ☞ and ➢ characters that are located in the Iconic Symbols character set.
   e. When creating the table, set the table position to Right to place the table in the right column.
   f. The graphics files are named **sun_dsg.wpg** and **medical1.wpg** and are located in the *wpwin60/graphics* directory.
   g. If space is available, create TextArt to call attention to a specific topic in the newsletter. Review the document to determine a topic that should be given more emphasis.
2. Optional. After completing the newsletter, sort the table of upcoming classes by class name or by date.
3. Optional. After completing the newsletter, use paragraph sorting to sort the locations of Bright Medical Center by name.
4. Use the filename **4pact1.new** and save the file.
5. Print one copy and close the document.

COMMUNITY HEALTH BULLETIN

Spring, 199x **Bright Medical Center**

Sunning Health Tips

Summer is almost here and it's time to start thinking about protecting your skin from burns and ultraviolet rays. Take a moment to review the following tips:

☞ Avoid being outside during midday hours (10 a.m. to 2 p.m.) on sunny days.

☞ Wear sunscreen for all outdoor activities year round. Apply sunscreen at least one hour before going out into the sun and again after swimming or perspiring heavily.

☞ If you are taking medication, check with your doctor before going out into the sun. Antihistamines, antibiotics, estrogens, tranquilizers, or birth control pills may cause a photosensitive skin reaction.

☞ Avoid using indoor sunlamps, tanning booths, sun reflectors, tan accelerators, or tanning pills.

Upcoming Health Education Classes

Bright Medical Center offers many health education classes. These classes are held at the Community Center. The fee to attend each class is $15. This fee covers handouts, a community health T-shirt, and refreshments. Your ideas for additional classes are welcome and can be sent to Dr. Deanna Berninger at Rose Valley Hospital. The following table is a listing of upcoming classes.

Cooking for a Healthy Heart	6/19	1:00 p.m.
Anxiety & Phobias	5/15	7:00 p.m.
CPR	4/14	7:30 p.m.
Senior Care Issues	4/20	3:00 p.m.
Food, Fitness & Fun	5/20	9:00 a.m. & 5:30 p.m.
Nutrition	6/11	6:00 p.m.
Stop Smoking	6/10	6:30 p.m.
Sports Injury	4/30	7:30 p.m.

Walking--The Right Exercise

Walking is becoming the exercise of choice for many people, mainly because it's so easy to do. Find a pair of comfortable shoes, a friend, and a park or walking trail and this exercise will lead to a healthier life.

What are the benefits of walking?

➢ Improved cardiovascular fitness

➢ Toned muscles

➢ Reduced stress and tension

➢ Reduced cholesterol

➢ Increased metabolic rate, helping you to keep weight off

Community Health Bulletin **Spring, 199x** **Page 1**

Carpal Tunnel Syndrome

Individuals who keyboard for long periods of time are at risk of developing the painful hand disorder known as "Carpal Tunnel Syndrome." Repetitive motions of the hand such as excessive wrist movement or holding the wrists in a stationary position for long periods of time can irritate nerves, tendons and arteries in the narrow area of the wrist known as the "carpal tunnel." Carpal tunnel syndrome has been very prevalent in careers such as secretarial, word processing, data entry, and cashiering.

Although the actual injury occurs in the wrist area, the pain from the injury is usually felt in the hand. Carpal tunnel syndrome may also cause numbness in the fingers.

Below are a few suggestions for avoiding carpal tunnel syndrome:

☞ Maintain good posture--straight back, shoulders relaxed, elbows alongside the body, wrists straight, and arms parallel to the floor.

☞ Adjust the angle of the keyboard for comfort.

☞ Use a wrist rest to provide support for the wrists and to assist in maintaining the straight wrist position.

☞ Before beginning a job that requires repetitive wrist action, practice a few wrist stretching and strengthening exercises.

☞ Avoid over-reaching with fingers.

☞ Take frequent short breaks, perform other types of activities, or practice wrist stretching exercises.

☞ Avoid pounding on the keys.

☞ Take advantage of computer program features that are designed to reduce repetitive keystrokes. Usually these features allow you to record a set of keystrokes then play them back using only one or two keystrokes. Look for features with such names as "Recorder," "Macro," or "Playback."

Bright Medical Center Locations

For your convenience, Bright Medical Centers are located throughout the city. Please check for the location nearest you.

East Valley Center 555-7800
9900 Jefferson Avenue

Clearlake Center 555-4200
1435 Clearlake Plaza, Suite 1000

Paradise Center 555-5800
4500 Paradise Road, Suite 255

Lakeport Center 555-4425
#525 Lakeport Mall

Production Activity 4.2—Superscripts, Subscripts, and Equations

1. Create the following document using superscripts, subscripts, and equations.

SUPERSCRIPTS, SUBSCRIPTS, AND EQUATIONS

COMPLEMENTARY ANGLES

40° 50°	27° 63°
35° 55°	10° 80°

CHEMICAL FORMULAS

Sodium Hydrosulfite = $Na_2S_2O_4$ Sodium Sulfite = Na_2SO_3

Sodium Phosphate = NaH_2PO_4 Sodium Ethylate = C_2H_5ONa

ALGEBRAIC EQUATIONS

$\frac{1}{y}+\frac{1}{2}=\frac{1}{y-2}$ $\frac{(2a^2c)^2}{5m}$ $\sqrt{\frac{1}{20}}$ $\sqrt{\frac{49a^2}{64b^2}}$

---

2. Use the filename **4pact2.sse** and save the file.
3. Print one copy and close the document.

Production Activity 4.3—Text with Graphic Overlay and Line Sorting; Word Spacing and Letterspacing

1. Use the following information and create a flier similar to the one shown on page 401.
   a. The graphics file is named **marsh.wpg** and is stored in the *wpwin60\graphics* directory.
   b. Use word spacing and letterspacing to adjust the spacing between the words and letters if needed.
   c. Optional. Use line sort to sort the *General Information* items alphabetically.

   Hint: *Perform line sort before formatting (bolding, indenting, etc.) the text.*
2. Use the filename **4pact3.fli** and save the file.
3. Print one copy and close the document.

Join us at the

Blue Heron
Beach
Inn

Where you can enjoy shopping,
tennis, bicycling, biking, or
just relaxing on the beach.

General Information

Full, hearty breakfast included
Afternoon tea and refreshments
Free use of bicycles
Smoking permitted on verandas only
Check-in between 2:00 p.m. and 10:00 p.m.
Check-out time at 12:00 noon
Off-season and mid-week specials
Cocktails available after 5:00 p.m.

Production Activity 4.4—Use Append to Create an Overhead Transparency

1. Open the file named **4pact4.pos** located on the data disk.
2. Use the Append feature and create an overhead transparency consisting of the document title and sideheads contained in the file named **4pact4.pos**.
3. When the title and sideheads have been appended to the Clipboard, create a new document and paste the appended text into the new document.
4. Format the new document as an overhead transparency. Make decisions regarding:

Fonts and point sizes
Justification
Spacing between paragraphs

5. Use the *new* filename **4pact4.ovr** and save the overhead transparency file.
6. Print one copy and close the documents.

Production Activity 4.5—Create and Modify Styles

1. Open the file named **4pact5.doc** located on the data disk.
2. Edit the *InitialStyle* style as follows:

Font:	Arrus BT, 11-point or make a choice of your own
Margins:	Left and Right—1.25"
Page:	Center Current Page

3. Create the following styles:

Style name:	Doc. title
Description:	Style for job description title
Style type:	Paragraph (paired)
Font:	Humanst521 Cn BT, Bold, 14-point or make a choice of your own
Spacing Between Paragraphs:	2
Justification:	Centered

Style name:	Sidehead
Description:	Style for sideheads
Style type:	Paragraph (paired)
Font:	Humanst521 Cn BT, Bold, 13-point or make a choice of your own
Spacing Between Paragraphs:	1.5

Style name:	TV Prog Name
Description:	Changes TV program name font
Style type:	Character
Font:	Use Arrus BT, Bold, Italic, 11-point or make a choice of your own

4. Apply the styles to the document title, sideheads, and TV program name.
5. Correct two spelling errors, two punctuation errors, and one repeated word error.
6. Use the *new* filename **4pact5.for** and save the formatted document.
7. If you have completed your work, exit WordPerfect.

Appendices

- Appendix A—Customizing WordPerfect
- Appendix B—Summary of Enriching Language Arts
- Appendix C—WordPerfect Graphic Images and ExpressDocs
- Appendix D—Answers to Self-Check Quizzes

APPENDIX A

Customizing WordPerfect

WordPerfect Preferences (Setup)

WordPerfect Preferences assist the user in changing options for the WordPerfect program, such as the display, files, keyboard, printer, button bars, and the document summary. WordPerfect creates default options that are suitable for most word processing users. However, by using Preferences, the options are easily changed to accommodate each users' specific needs. Once a Preference is changed, they are in effect each time you load WordPerfect. To obtain specific details for changing any Preference option, use the Help feature.

Preferences is selected from the **File** menu. The different software options that can be changed using Preferences include the Display, Environment, File, Document Summary, Button Bar, Keyboard, Menu Bar, Power Bar, Status Bar, Writing Tools, Print and Import preferences (see Figure A.1).

The *Display* Preference options are used to select choices for displaying various items in the document screen. Following is a list of the Display Preferences Options.

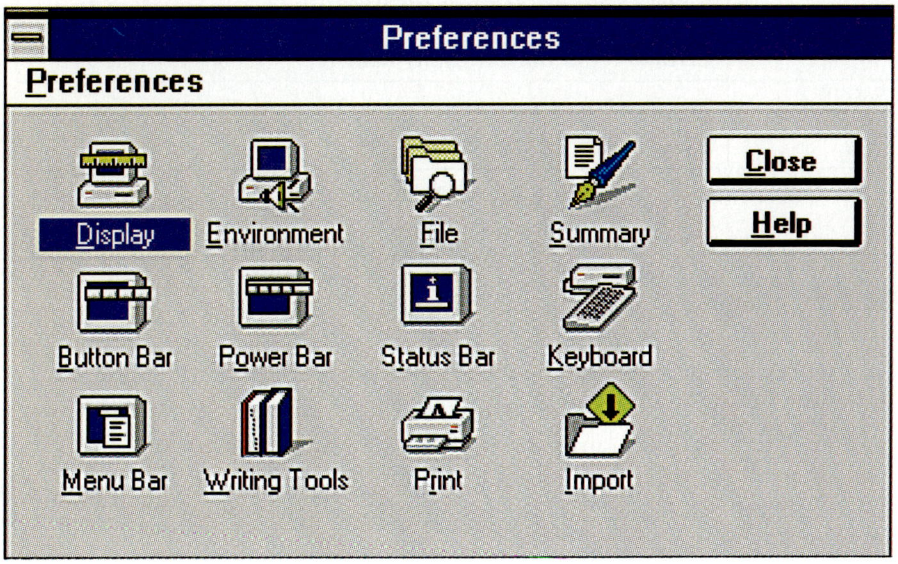

FIGURE A.1

Preferences box

Display Preferences Options	
Document	Show Table Gridlines, Windows System Colors, Comments, Graphics, Hidden Text, Horizontal and Vertical Scroll Bars, Units of Measure (Status and Ruler Bar display) and Sculptured (three-dimensional) dialog boxes
View/Zoom	Default View: Draft, Page or Two Page Default Zoom: standard percentage amounts, Margin Width, Page Width, Full Page or Other
Ruler Bar	Show Ruler Bar on New and Current Document Ruler Bar Options: Tab Snap to Ruler Bar Grid, Show Ruler Bar Guides, Sculptured (three-dimensional) Ruler Bar
Show	Show Symbols on New and Current Document Symbols to display: Space, Hard Return, Tab, Indent, Center, Flush Right, Soft Hyphen, Advance and Center Page
Reveal Codes	Show Reveal Codes on New and Current Document Font and Size options: Wrap Lines at Window, Show Spaces As Bullets, Show Codes In Detail, Show Help Prompts for Codes, Sculptured Codes, and Window Size.
Merge	Merge Codes: Display Merge Codes, Display Merge Codes as Markers, and Hide Merge Codes

The *Environment* Preference options are used to customize settings for various WordPerfect features that are shown in the following table.

Environment Preferences Options	
User Info for Comments and Summary	Name, Initials, User Color
Formatting	Hyphenation Prompt, Confirm Deletion of Codes/Stop Insertion Point at Hidden Codes, Confirm Delete of Table Formulas
Save Workspace	Always, Never, Prompt on Exit
Beep On	Error, Hyphenation, Find Failure
Menu	Display Last Open Filenames, Display Shortcut Keys, Show Help Prompts
Save	Set QuickMark on Save, Reformat Document for Default Printer on Open
Activate Hypertext	

The *Files* Preferences are used to designate the drive and/or directory where files are located for backups, templates, spreadsheets, databases, printers, hyphenation, graphics, and macros. The following table shows each File Preference option.

File Preferences Options	
Documents/Backup	Default Directory, Use Default Extension (wpd) on Open and Save, Backup Directory, Timed Document Backup every (set number of minutes), and Original Document Backup
Templates	Default Directory, Default Template, Additional Directory, Additional Objects Template, and Template File Extension (wpt)
Spreadsheets	Default Directory and Supplemental Directory
Databases	Default Directory and Supplemental Directory
Printers/Labels	Default Directory, Supplemental Directory, Label File, Default Labels to Display: Laser, Tractor Fed or Both
Hyphenation	Default Directory
Graphics	Default Directory and Supplemental Directory
Macros	Default Directory and Supplemental Directory
Update QuickList with Changes	
View All: View File Location Preferences	

The *Document Summary* preferences are used to set Search options for the Default Subject Text and the Descriptive Type. Also, the Use of Descriptive Names and Create Summary on Save/Exit options can be selected.

The *Power Bar* preferences can be changed by adding, moving or deleting items. A list of items, that include attributes such as Superscript and Subscript can be used to select the desired item to be include or deleted from the Power Bar. A separator line can be placed between items to add additional space between desired buttons.

The S*tatus Bar* preferences are similar to the Power Bar preferences. Additionally, boxes on the Status bar can be resized. The Font type and size and appearance can be changed. Also, the Power Bar items can selected to display evenly spaced and/or to display with a Bold Font.

The *Keyboard* preferences include three choices, i.e., the Equation Editor Keyboard, WPDOS Compatible, and/or WPWin 6.0 keyboard. A new keyboard can be created to assign different functions to the keys. Also, the location for storing the new keyboard can be selected.

The *Menu Bar* preferences include three choices, i.e., Equation Editor Menu, WPWin 6.0 Menu and WPWin 6.0a Menu. Similar to the Keyboard preferences, a new menu can be created and the location for the new menu can be selected.

The *Writing Tools* preferences allow you to specify the tools, i.e., Spelling, Grammatik, that you want to display on the Tools Menu. The chosen item can be moved up or down on the list to display in the order you desire.

The *Print* preferences are used to designate default print settings. The following table shows the Print Preferences options.

Print Preferences Options	
Size Attribute Ratio	Specify percentage amount of text for each size attribute: Fine, Small, Large, Very Large, Extra Large, and Super/Subscript
Copies	Specify Number of Copies Select if Generated by Printer or WordPerfect
Document Settings	Select the Print Quality, Print Color and/or Do Not Print Graphics
Define Color Printing Palette	

The *Import* preferences are used to specify how graphics files, ASCII delimited text files, WP4.2, DCA, and DisplayWrite documents are imported into WordPerfect.

Customizing the Button and Power Bars

The WordPerfect Button and Power Bars can be customized to provide for individual preferences. To create a new Button Bar or to edit an existing Button or Power Bar, select the Preferences option in the File menu and choose the Button Bar or Power Bar icon.

A new Button Bar can be created and/or any of the buttons on a Button Bar can be changed. Also, a Button Bar can be rearranged, relocated, and/or displayed differently in the document window. A Button Bar name can be changed, or an entire Button Bar can be deleted. Buttons on a Button Bar can be used to access menu commands, features, macros, and other Button Bars. Power Bar buttons can be added, moved, or deleted.

WordPerfect provides *fifteen* different Button Bars: Design Tools, Equation Editor, Font, Generate, Graphics, Layout, Legal, Macro Tools, Page, Preferences, Tables, Utilities, WordPerfect, WordPerfect 5.1, and Workgroup. Only one Button Bar can display at one time. The list of Button Bars is displayed by pressing the *right* mouse button.

Steps to Add a Button to a Button Bar

1. Point anywhere on the Button Bar and press the *right* mouse button to display the Button Bar list.
2. Select **Edit**.

   Note: *The Button Bar Editor dialog box displays.*
3. Select the desired **Add a Button** to option.
4. Select the desired Feature Category.
5. Select the desired feature.
6. Select **Add button**.

Note: The new button displays at the right of the Button Bar. If a separator (more space) is desired between buttons, point to the Separate button, press, hold and drag the line between buttons, release the mouse.

7. Select OK.

Steps to Delete a Button on a Button Bar

1. Point anywhere on the Button Bar and press the *right* mouse button to display the Button Bar list.
2. Select Edit.
3. Point to the Button Bar button to be deleted.
4. Press the left mouse button to display a "hand," hold and drag the button off the button Bar; release the mouse.
5. Select Cancel to exit the Button Bar Editor.

Steps to Move a Button on a Button Bar

Note: A button can be moved to a new location on the same Button Bar.

1. Point to the Button Bar and press the *right* mouse button to display the Button Bar.
2. Select Edit.
3. Press the left mouse button to display a "hand," hold and drag the button to the desired location; release the mouse.
4. Select Cancel.

Steps to Relocate a Button Bar in the Document Window

1. Point to the Button Bar and press the *right* mouse button to display the Button Bar.
2. Click on Preferences.
3. Select Options.
4. Select the desired location.
5. Select OK.
6. Select Close.

Steps to Change the Text/Picture on a Button Bar Button

1. Point to the Button Bar and press the *right* mouse button to display the Button Bar.
2. Select Preferences.
3. Select Options.

4. Select the desired Appearance.
5. Select **OK**.
6. Select **Close**.

Steps to Create a New Button Bar

1. Point to the Button Bar and press the *right* mouse button to display the Button Bar.
2. Select **Preferences**.
3. Select **Create**.
4. Type a name for the new Button Bar.
5. Select **OK**.
6. Select the desired Feature Category and select the desired Feature.
7. Select **Add button**.
8. Repeat steps 6 and 7 until all the desired options have been chosen, select **OK** to create the new Button Bar.
9. Select **OK**.
10. Choose **Select**.

Steps to Delete a Button Bar

1. Point to the Button Bar and press the *right* mouse button to display the Button Bar.
2. Select **Edit**.
3. Select the name of the Button Bar to be deleted.
4. Select **Delete**.
5. Select **Yes**.
6. Select **Close**.

   Note: To view another Button Bar, select File, Preferences; double-click on the Button Bar icon; highlight the desired Button Bar; choose Select, Close.

Steps to Display a Different Button Bar

Note: A mouse is required to select a different Button Bar.

1. Point to any location on the displayed Button Bar, press the *right* mouse button once to display the list of WordPerfect Button Bars.

   Note: If a Button Bar is not displayed below the Menu Bar, select View, Button Bar.
2. Point to the desired Button Bar and click once with the left mouse button.

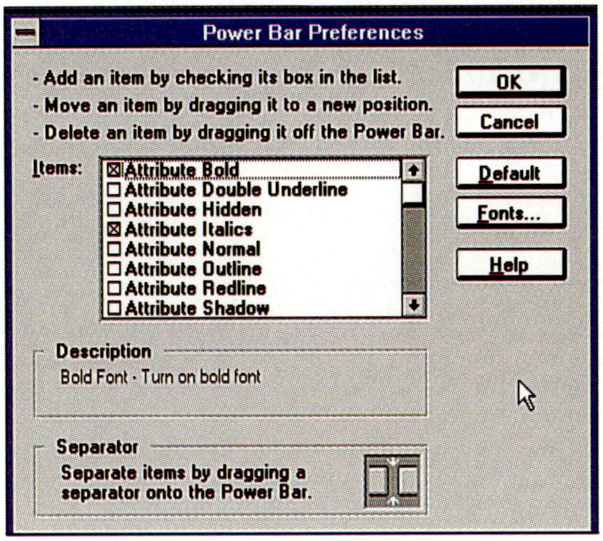

FIGURE A.2

Power Bar Preferences dialog box

Steps to Customize the Power Bar

1. Point to the Power Bar and press the *right* mouse button to display the QuickMenu list.

   Shortcut: *Point to a button separator on the Power Bar, double-click and skip to step 3.*

2. Select **Preferences**.

   Note: *The Power Bar Preferences dialog box displays (see Figure A.2).*

3. *To add an item,* select the desired item.

   Note: *An X displays in the box beside a selected item.*

4. *To move an item,* point to the item on the Power Bar to be moved, click, hold, and drag the item to the desired location; release the mouse.

5. *To delete an item,* point to the item on the Power Bar, click, hold, and drag the item off the Power Bar; release the mouse.

Steps to Add a Power Bar Item Separator

1. Point to the Power Bar and press the *right* mouse button to display the QuickMenu list.
2. Point to the **Separator** button to display a hand.
3. Press and hold the mouse button and drag to the line located between the desired Power Bar items; release the mouse button.

Steps to Change the Power Bar Font/Size Lists

1. Point to the Power Bar and press the *right* mouse button to display the QuickMenu list.
2. Select **Fonts**.
3. Select the desired font and/or size.

Steps to Add TrueType Font Styles to the Font Item on the Power Bar

1. Point to the Power Bar and press the *right* mouse button to display the Quick-Menu list.
2. Select Fonts.

   Note: *The Power Bar Font/Size Lists dialog box displays.*
3. Select the font and/or size to place an X beside the desired choice(s).

   Note: *Choose the Select button to select All Fonts and Sizes, No fonts and Sizes, or to select Default Sizes.*

Steps to Restore the Default Power Bar

1. Point to the Power Bar and press the *right* mouse button to display the Quick-Menu list.
2. Select Preferences.
3. Select Default.
4. Select OK.

Customizing QuickCorrect

The QuickCorrect feature is available starting with the WordPerfect for Windows Interim Release 6.0a. The QuickCorrect feature corrects errors in the document window as text is typed. For example, if "teh" is typed and the Spacebar is pressed, the correct word "the" displays. A list of commonly misspelled words along with the correctly spelled words display in the QuickCorrect dialog box.

Also, abbreviations can be listed for words or phrases that are frequently typed. When the listed abbreviation is typed followed by a space, WordPerfect automatically displays the word or phrase.

An additional misspelled word(s) and/or abbreviation(s) along with the correctly spelled word(s) and/or word(s) that the abbreviation represents can be included in the QuickCorrect list. The QuickCorrect feature can also correct words that are typed with the first two letters capitalized. For example if "THe" is typed and the space bar is pressed, the correct capitalization "The" displays. The SmartQuotes option can be selected to automatically convert the traditional keyboard quotation marks (") to the correct typography symbols (" ").

Steps to Customizing QuickCorrect

1. Select Tools, QuickCorrect.
2. Type the incorrectly spelled word or abbreviation in the Replace box.
3. Click in the With box and type the correctly spelled word or the phrase the abbreviation represents.

4. Select Add Entry.
5. *To delete an entry*, select the desired words in the word list, select Delete Entry, select Yes.
6. *To replace an entry*, select the desired words in the word list, select Replace Entry, type the incorrectly spelled word, select Add Entry.
7. Select Close.

WordPerfect Customer Support

If you encounter difficulties installing, changing preferences, or using any WordPerfect feature, WordPerfect's Customer Support is available to assist you at the following numbers (these customer support numbers are for users within the United States, U.S. territories, or Canada).

In April of 1994, a new WordPerfect policy required that all customers obtain a PIN (personal identification number). Customers will receive 180 days of free support after they receive their PIN number. Various plans for payment are available. Call WordPerfect to select the plan that best suits your needs.

Installation	800-228-7610 801-228-9964 (toll)
Equations, Graphics, Sound, Tables	800-228-8720 801-228-9962 (toll)
Macros, Merge	800-228-2021 801-228-9961 (toll)
All other features	800-228-9907 801-228-9960 (toll)
Laser or PostScript printers	800-228-2803 801-228-9965 (toll)
Dot matrix printers and other printers	800-228-6646 801-228-9966 (toll)
Networks	800-228-8807 801-228-9963 (toll)
Customer support fax number	801-222-4377 (toll)
After-hours customer support number	801-228-9908 (toll)
InfoShare Fax Service number	800-228-9960 801-228-9920 (toll)
BBS (1200 or 2400 baud modems)	801-225-4414 (toll)
BBS (9600 baud V.32 modems)	801-22504444 (toll)

APPENDIX B

Summary of Enriching Language Arts

Chapter	Vocabulary Words	Grammar/Punctuation Rule
1	acquisition, spiraling, enormous, liquidation	Introductory Adverbs and Phrases—A comma often follows an introductory adverb or phrase, because the word or phrase provides a transition from the previous sentence.
2	commendable, nominated, negotiations	Introductory (Dependent) Clauses—A comma should follow a dependent clause. An introductory dependent clause often begins with *if, in, when, since,* or *as.*
3	telecommunications, tailored, existence, description	Appositives—Appositives are words that immediately follow a noun and further identify the noun but usually are not necessary to the meaning of the sentence.
4	dues, affiliation, outweigh, distinguished	Compound Adjectives and Coordinating Conjunctions—Hyphenate two words that precede and describe a noun and function as a single adjective. A comma is placed before a coordinating conjunction (e.g., *and, or, because*) that joins two independent clauses.
5	initiative, strategic, alliances	Dollar Amounts Formats—Use a comma to separate the number digits into groups of thousands. No space is placed between a number and the dollar sign. If even numbers are used in the body of a document or if a column of numbers has even dollar amounts, the zeros are omitted.
6	adversely, per diem, reimbursement	Single and Double Underlines for Dollar Amounts—Place a single underline between the last column amount and the total amount. In a table without lines or borders, a total amount is usually emphasized by placing double underlines beneath the total amount.

Chapter	Vocabulary Words	Grammar/Punctuation Rule
7	implement, incentive, promotional, wholesalers	Commas Used in a Series—Words and/or ideas listed in a series are separated by commas.
8	prompt, unkempt, offensive, antagonistic, attitude	Using the Abbreviations *e.g.* and *i.e.*—The abbreviation *e.g.* is used in place of "for example" and is often used when one or more of many examples are listed. The abbreviation *i.e.* is used in place of "that is" and is used when all potential conditions are listed.
9	partnership, accrual method, maturity, depreciation, liability, amortized	Speller Hint—The Speller approves words that are correctly spelled; however, a correctly spelled word can be incorrectly used in a sentence.
10	phenomenon, biosphere, analysis, profound, euphoria	Quotation Marks with Punctuation—Always place a comma or period inside a closing quotation mark. Place a question mark or exclamation point inside closing quotation marks if the question or exclamation pertains only to the quoted information. Place a question mark or exclamation point outside the closing quotation marks if the question or exclamation pertains to the entire sentence.
11	confirmation, prime rate, virtually	Nonrestrictive Clause—A nonrestrictive clause is a clause that is not essential to the meaning of the sentence and is, therefore, set off by a comma or commas.
12	warranty, components, reliable	Subject-Verb Agreement—Verbs must agree in number with their subject. If a subject is singular, use a singular verb; if a subject is plural, use a plural verb.
13	extensive, HMO, reputation	Initials Abbreviated—Periods or spaces are not placed after the letters of an acronym such as IRS (Internal Revenue Service) or TAW (Trans World Airlines).
14	derogatory, inclusion, propaganda, rendered, surreptitious	Independent Adjectives—Two adjectives that modify the same noun are separated by a comma.
15	revenue, innovative, integral, acquisition, commingle	Apostrophe Used to Show Possession—If a noun is singular and used to show possession, add an apostrophe (') and an s. If the noun is plural or the final letter in the noun is an s, add only an apostrophe after the s.
16	No vocabulary words	Proofreading Hints—When proofreading a document, read the document twice: once for content and meaning and once to check grammar, spelling, and punctuation.

APPENDIX C

WordPerfect Graphic Images and ExpressDocs

approved.wpg

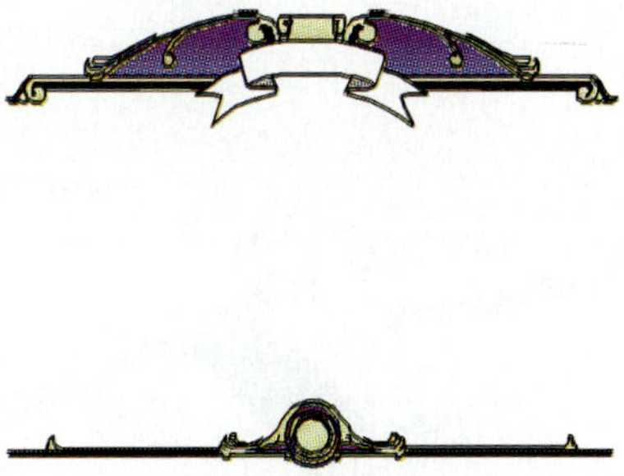

bord01l.wpg

bord04p.wpg

bord05p.wpg

bord08l.wpg

bord10p.wpg

bord11l.wpg

bord12l.wpg

bord13p.wpg

buck.wpg

buterfly.wpg

centerpc.wpg

cheetah.wpg

crane_j.wpg

draft.wpg

drtbord.wpg

ender04.wpg

enger06.wpg

ender11.wpg

estimate.wpg

file_co.wpg

golfswng.wpg

group.wpg

horse_j.wpg

hotair.wpg

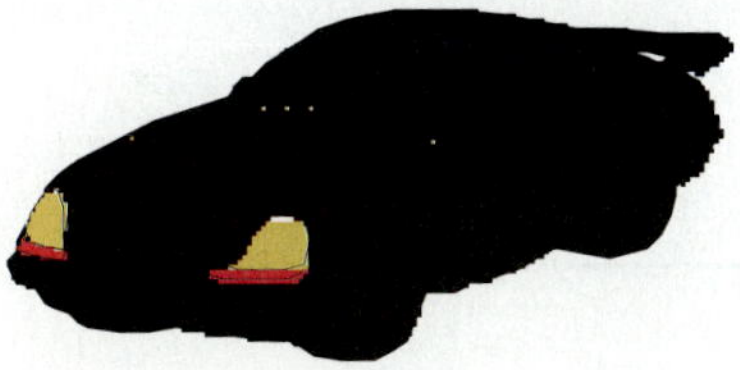

hotrod.wpg

humbird.wpg

importnt.wpg

inkskier.wpg

marsh.wpg

medical1.wpg

overdue.wpg

racebike.wpg

silo2.wpg

skipper.wpg

sun_dsg.wpg

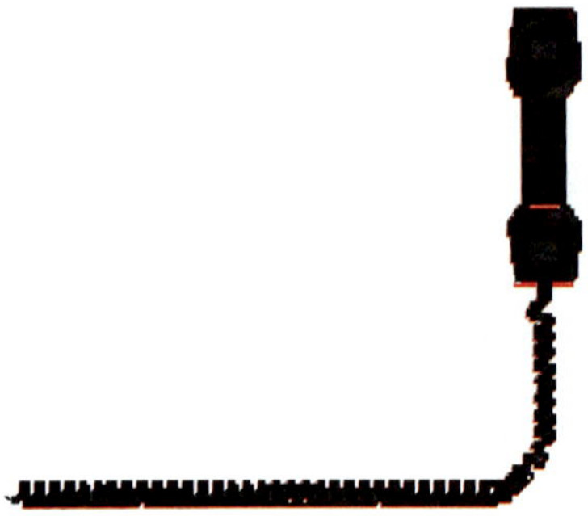
telerec.wpg

thanks.wpg

tiger_j.wpg

trumpt.wpg

windmill.wpg

world.wpg

Sample ExpressDocs

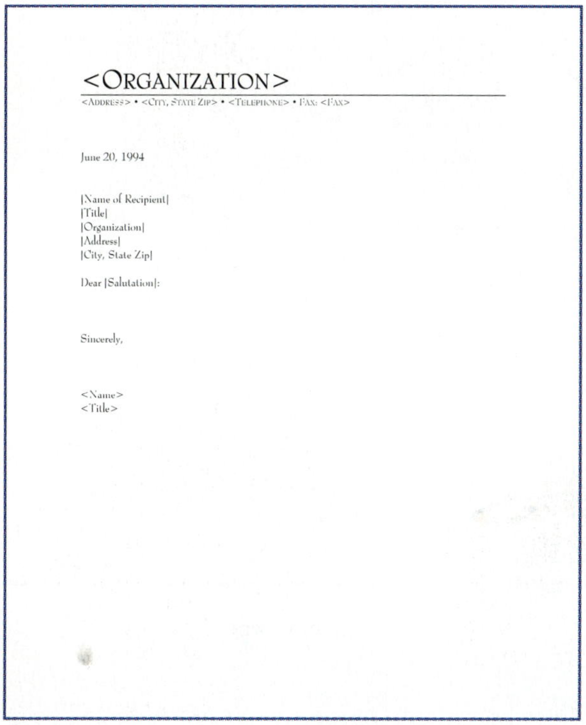
<ORGANIZATION>
<Address> • <City, State Zip> • <Telephone> • Fax: <Fax>

June 20, 1994

[Name of Recipient]
[Title]
[Organization]
[Address]
[City, State Zip]

Dear [Salutation]:

Sincerely,

<Name>
<Title>

letter1.wpt

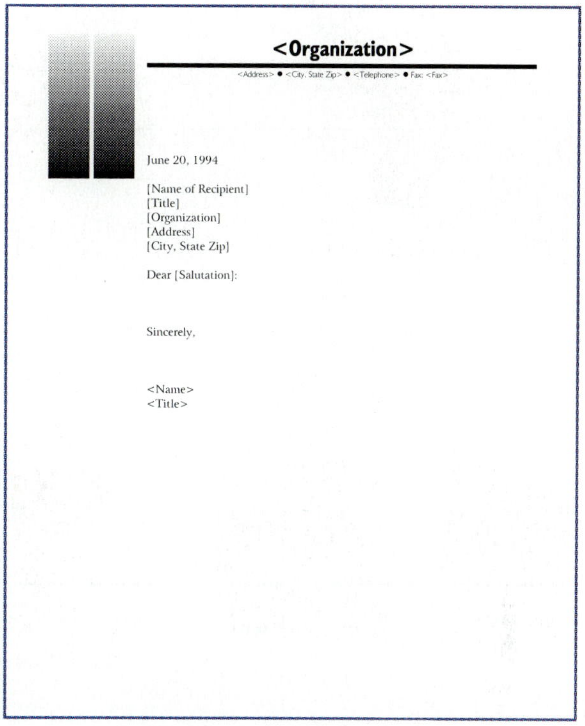
<Organization>
<Address> • <City, State Zip> • <Telephone> • Fax: <Fax>

June 20, 1994

[Name of Recipient]
[Title]
[Organization]
[Address]
[City, State Zip]

Dear [Salutation]:

Sincerely,

<Name>
<Title>

letter2.wpt

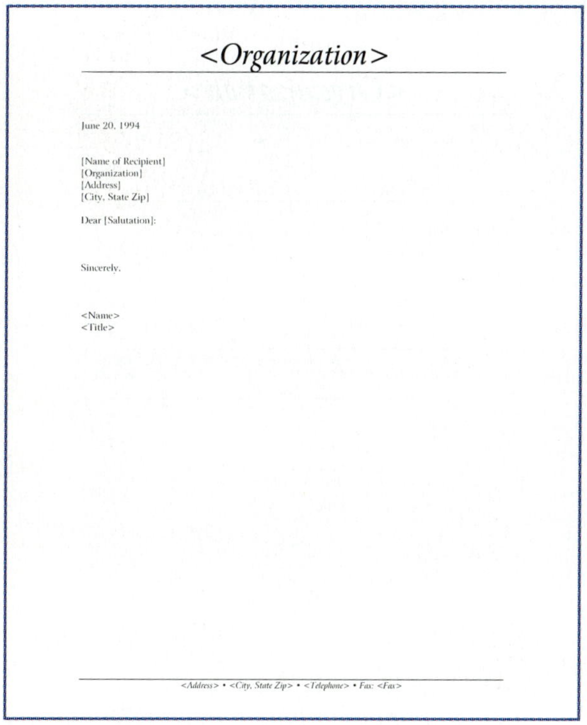
<Organization>

June 20, 1994

[Name of Recipient]
[Organization]
[Address]
[City, State Zip]

Dear [Salutation]:

Sincerely,

<Name>
<Title>

<Address> • <City, State Zip> • <Telephone> • Fax: <Fax>

letter5.wpt

To: [Name of Recipient]
CC: [CC]
From: <Name>
Date: June 20, 1994
Re: [Regarding]

memo

from the desk of...

<Name>
<Title>
<Organization>
<Address>
<City, State Zip>

<Telephone>
Fax: <Fax>

memo1.wpt

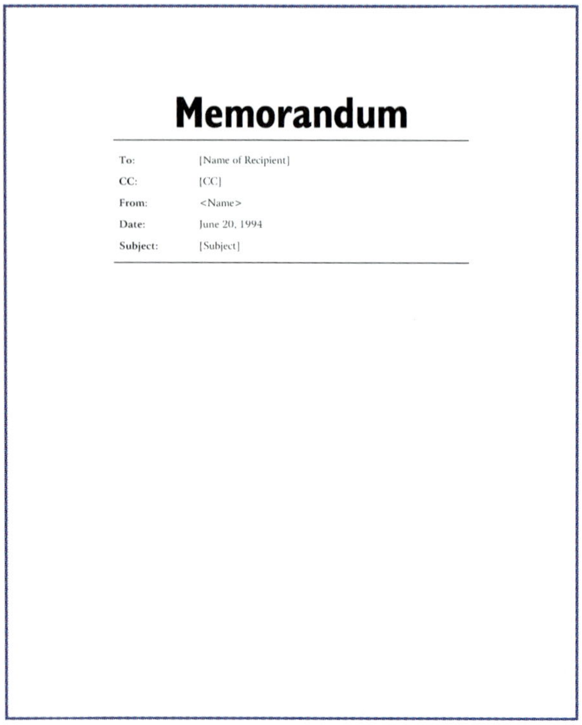

Memorandum

To: [Name of Recipient]
CC: [CC]
From: <Name>
Date: June 20, 1994
Subject: [Subject]

memo3.wpt

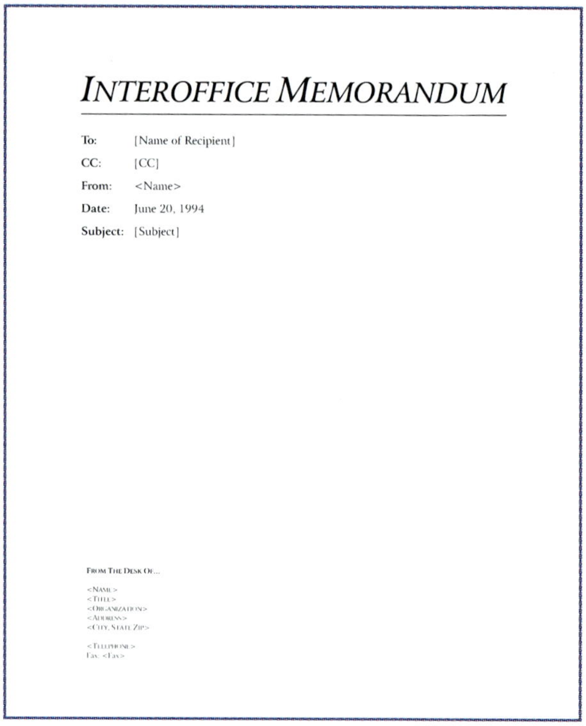

INTEROFFICE MEMORANDUM

To: [Name of Recipient]
CC: [CC]
From: <Name>
Date: June 20, 1994
Subject: [Subject]

FROM THE DESK OF...

<NAME>
<TITLE>
<ORGANIZATION>
<ADDRESS>
<CITY, STATE ZIP>

<TELEPHONE>
FAX: <FAX>

memo5.wpt

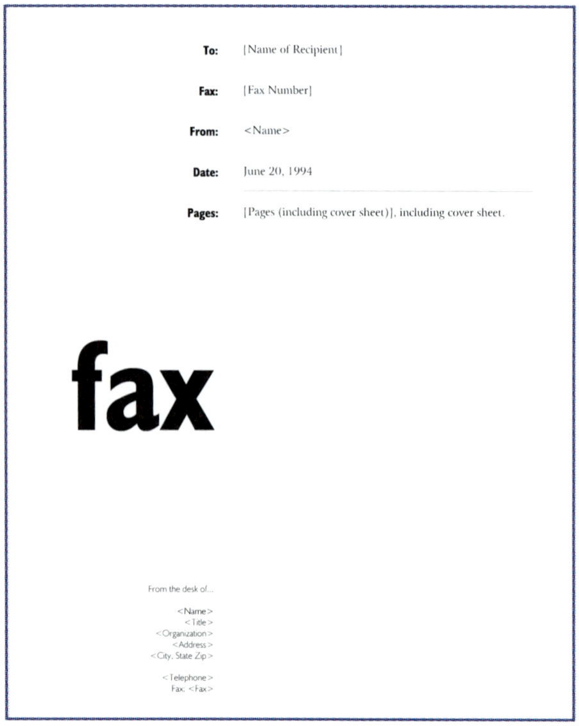

To: [Name of Recipient]

Fax: [Fax Number]

From: <Name>

Date: June 20, 1994

Pages: [Pages (including cover sheet)], including cover sheet.

fax

From the desk of...

<Name>
<Title>
<Organization>
<Address>
<City, State Zip>

<Telephone>
Fax: <Fax>

fax1.wpt

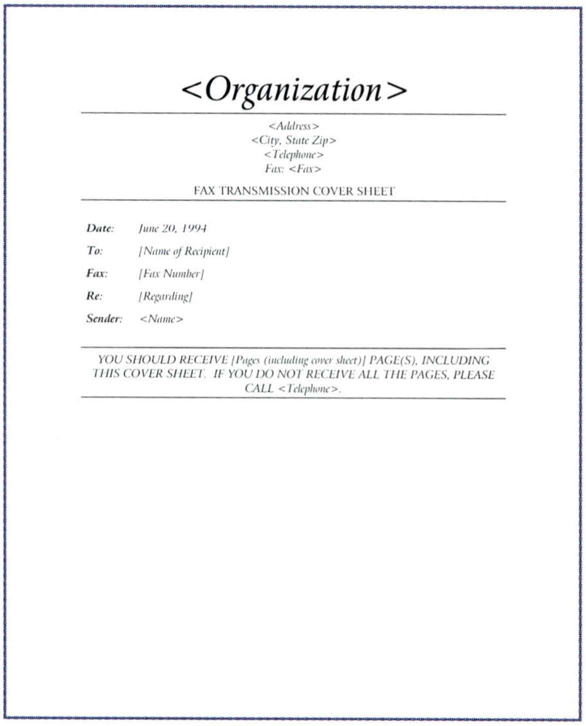

<Organization>

<Address>
<City, State Zip>
<Telephone>
Fax: <Fax>

FAX TRANSMISSION COVER SHEET

Date: *June 20, 1994*
To: *[Name of Recipient]*
Fax: *[Fax Number]*
Re: *[Regarding]*
Sender: *<Name>*

YOU SHOULD RECEIVE [Pages (including cover sheet)] PAGE(S), INCLUDING THIS COVER SHEET. IF YOU DO NOT RECEIVE ALL THE PAGES, PLEASE CALL <Telephone>.

fax3.wpt

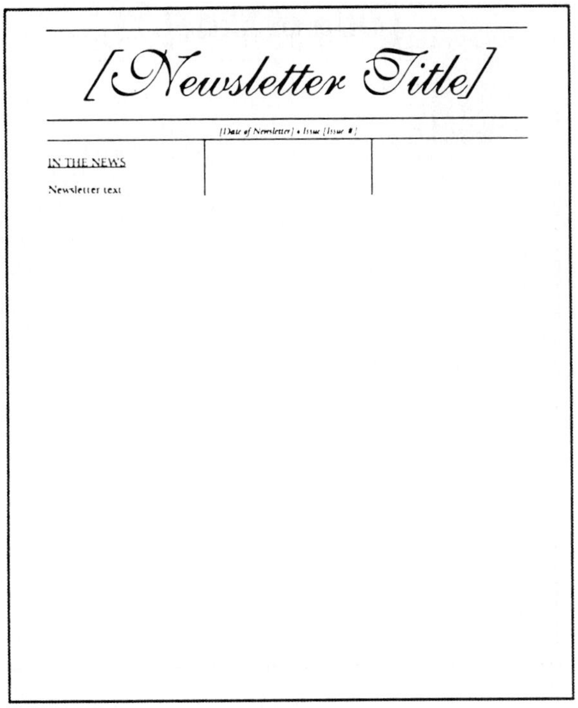

newsltr1.wpt

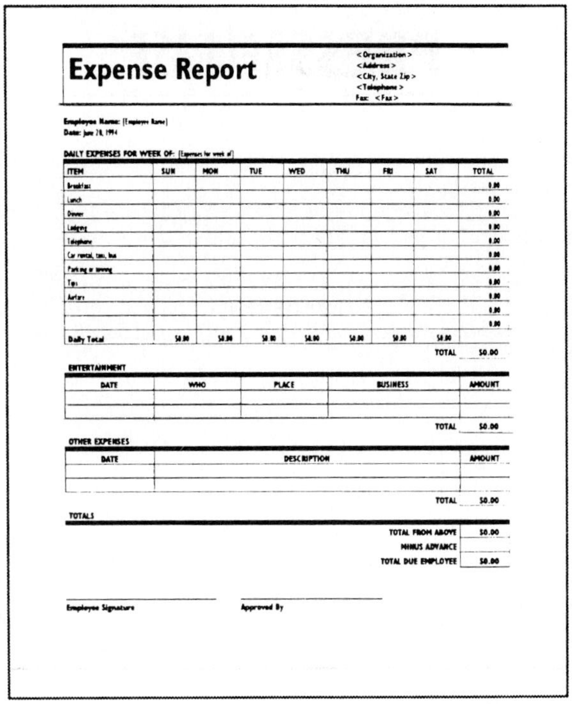

expense.wpt

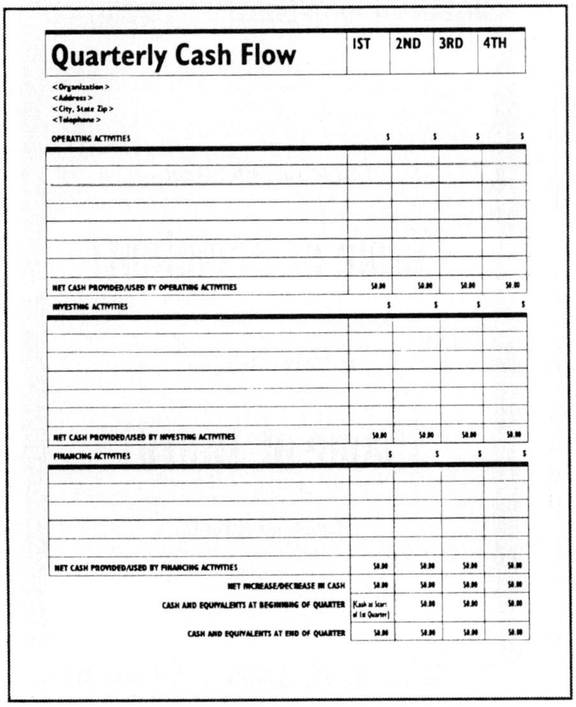

qcashflw.wpt

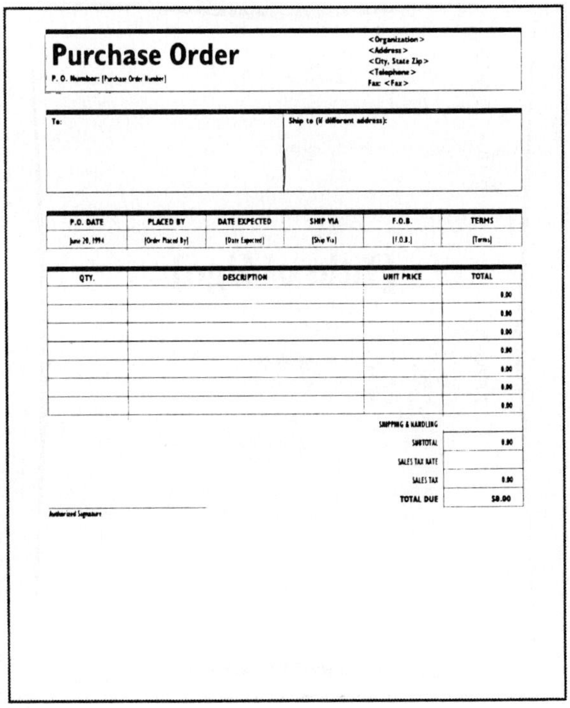

purchase.wpt

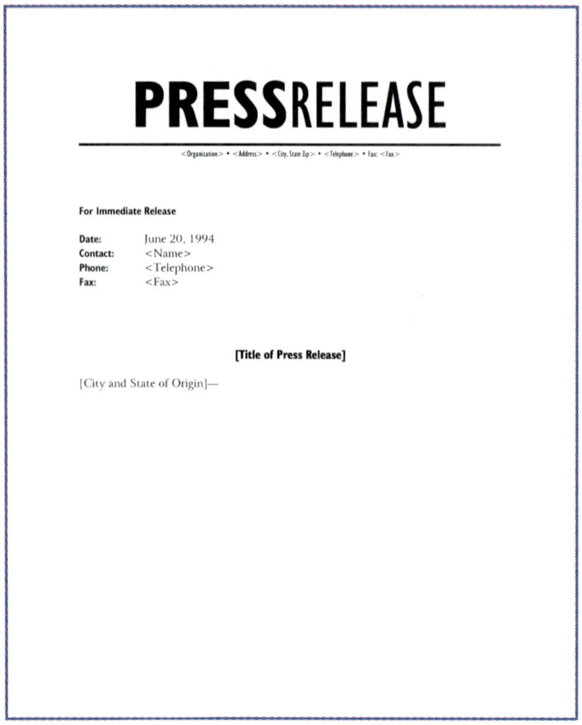
PRESSRELEASE

<Organization> • <Address> • <City, State Zip> • <Telephone> • Fax: <Fax>

For Immediate Release

Date: June 20, 1994
Contact: <Name>
Phone: <Telephone>
Fax: <Fax>

[Title of Press Release]

[City and State of Origin]—

press2.wpt

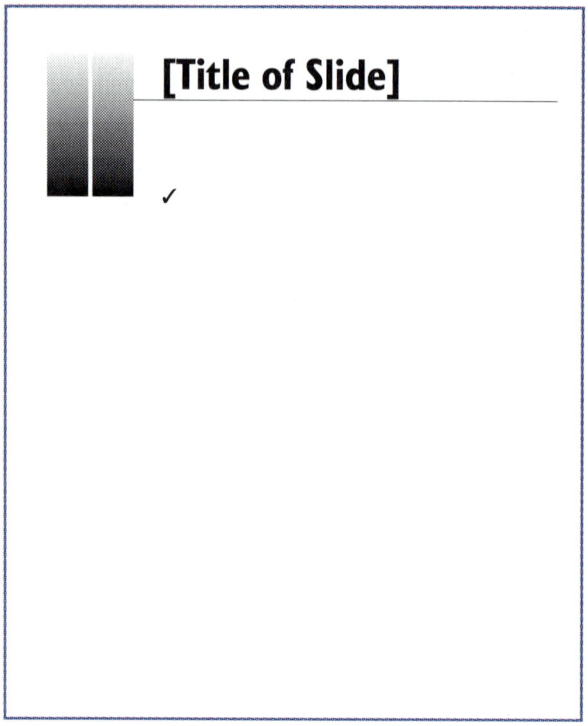

slide1.wpt

sign1.wpt

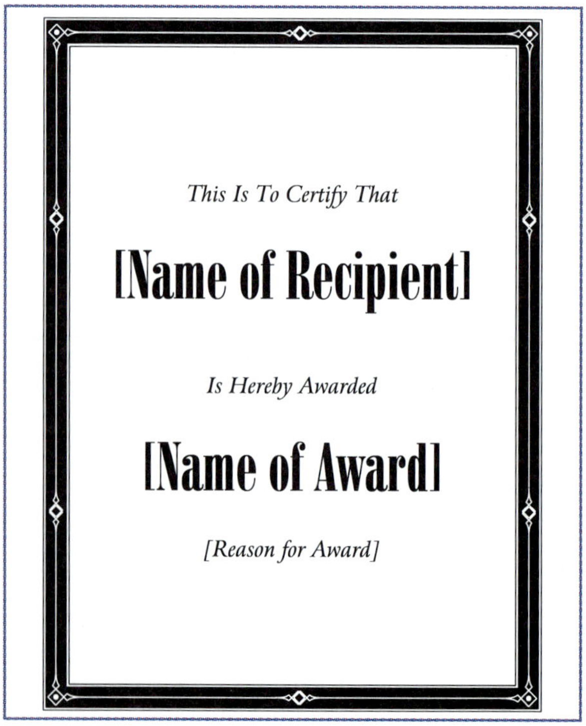

certif1.wpt

APPENDIX D

Answers to Self-Check Quizzes

Chapter 1

1. T
2. T
3. T
4. F
5. F
6. a
7. b
8. c

Chapter 2

1. F
2. T
3. T
4. T
5. T
6. d
7. b
8. d

Chapter 3

1. T
2. T
3. F
4. F
5. b
6. c
7. c

Chapter 4

1. T
2. F
3. T
4. T
5. F
6. a
7. d
8. c

Chapter 5

1. T
2. T
3. F
4. T
5. T
6. d
7. c
8. a

Chapter 6

1. T
2. T
3. T
4. T
5. b
6. b
7. d
8. b

Chapter 7

1. F
2. T
3. T
4. F
5. F
6. d
7. d

Chapter 8

1. T
2. F
3. T
4. F
5. T
6. b
7. d

Chapter 9

1. F
2. T
3. F
4. F
5. d
6. a
7. b
8. a

Chapter 10

1. T
2. T
3. F
4. T
5. a
6. d
7. b
8. d

Chapter 11

1. T
2. T
3. F
4. F
5. T
6. b
7. c
8. d

Chapter 12

1. T
2. T
3. F
4. F
5. F
6. b
7. b
8. c

Chapter 13

1. T
2. F
3. F
4. T
5. F
6. b
7. d
8. d

Chapter 14

1. T
2. T
3. T
4. T
5. F
6. a
7. a

Chapter 15

1. T
2. T
3. F
4. F
5. T
6. e
7. b
8. b

Chapter 16

1. T
2. F
3. F
4. T
5. a
6. d
7. b
8. d

INDEX